From Slavery to Services

‘The new makers of our history profit without guilt and are, in fact, prophets of a policy that will make the island a mall, and the breakers grin like waiters, like taxi drivers, these new plantations by the sea; a slavery without chains, with no blood spilt.’

Derek Walcott, *The Acacia Trees*

From Slavery to Services

The Struggle for Economic Independence in the Caribbean

Victor Bulmer-Thomas

Ian Randle Publishers
Kingston • Miami

First published in Jamaica, 2021 by
Ian Randle Publishers
16 Herb McKenley Drive
Box 686
Kingston 6
www.ianrandlepublishers.com

National Library of Jamaica Cataloguing-in-Publication Data

Names: Bulmer-Thomas, Victor, author.
Title: From slavery to services : the struggle for economic independence in the Caribbean / Victor Bulmer-Thomas. | Revised edition.
Description: Kingston : Ian Randle Publishers, 2021. | Includes bibliographical references.
Identifiers: ISBN 9789766379872 (pbk).
Subjects: LCSH: Caribbean Area – Economic conditions. | Caribbean Area – Economic policy. | Service industries – Caribbean Area.
Classification: DDC 338.47 -- dc23.

Image by Falco (oberhausen/Deutschland/Pixabay.com)

Cover and book design by Ian Randle Publishers

Printed and bound in the United States of America

Contents

List of Figures

List of Tables

Acronyms and Abbreviations

ABC	Aruba, Bonaire and Curaçao
BEC	Belize Estate and Produce Company
BG$	British Guiana Dollar
BH$	British Honduran Dollar
BLS	Bureau of Labor Statistics
BNdH	Banque Nationale d'Haiti
BNRdH	Banque Nationale de la Republique d'Haiti
BVI	British Virgin Islands
BWI$	British West Indian Dollar
CAFTA	Central American Free Trade Agreement
CAP	Common Agricultural Policy
CARICOM	Caribbean Community
CARIFORUM	Caribbean Forum
CBERA	Caribbean Basin Economic Recovery Act
CBI	Caribbean Basin Initiative
CBR	Crude Birth Rate
CD&W	Colonial Development & Welfare
CDR	Crude Death Rate
CEPAL	Comisión Económica para América Latina y el Caribe
CMCF	CARICOM Multilateral Clearing Facility
COM	Collectivité d'Outre-Mer
COMECON	Council for Mutual Economic Assistance
CSA	Commonwealth Sugar Agreement
CTO	Caribbean Tourism Organization
CUC	Cuban Convertible Peso
d	Old British penny (240d is one pound sterling)
DLOC	Digital Library of the Caribbean
DOM	Département d'Outre-Mer
DOTS	Direction of Trade Statistics
DR	Dominican Republic
DUA	Domestic Use Agriculture

ECCB	Eastern Caribbean Central Bank
ECCU	Eastern Caribbean Currency Union
ECLAC	Economic Commission for Latin America and the Caribbean
ECU	European Currency Unit
EEC	European Economic Community
EPZ	Export Processing Zone
EU	European Union
FOA	Food and Agriculture Organization
FAOSTAT	Food and Agriculture Organization Statistical Database
GDP	Gross Domestic Product
GNI	Gross National Income
GNP	Gross National Product
HFCS	High-Fructose Corn Syrup
HIPC	Heavily Indebted Poor Countries
IBRD	Internation Bank for Reconstruction and Development
IDB	Inter-American Development Bank
IFS	International Financial Statistics
ILO	International Labour Organization
INIE	Instituto Nacional de Investigación Económica
INSEE	Institut National de la Statistique et des Etudes Economiques
ISI	Import-Substituting Industrialization
lb	Pound weight
LCU	Local Currency Unit
LDC	Less Developed Country
MDG	Millennium Development Goal
MOxLAD	Montevideo-Oxford Latin American Economic Database
MT	Metric Ton
NTB	Nontariff Barrier
OAS	Organization of American States
OECD	Organisation of Economic Cooperation and Development
ONE	Oficina Nacional de Estadísticas
PAU	Pan-American Union
PDVSA	Petróleos de Venezuela, S.A.
PP	Parliamentary Papers
PPP	People's Progressive Party
SALA	Statistical Abstract for Latin America
SITC	Standard International Trade Classification
STABEX	System of Stabilization of Export Earnings
STUSECO	Stichting ter bervordering van de Studie van de Surinaamse Economie

UBPC	Union of Banana Producing Countries
UK	United Kingdom
UN	United Nations
UND	United Nations Database
UNNA	United Nations National Accounts
UNSY	United Nations Statistical Yearbook
UNWTO	United Nations World Tourism Organization
UNYITS	United Nations Yearbook of International Trade Statistics
US	United States
USSR	Union of Soviet Socialist Republics
USVI	United States Virgin Islands
WDI	World Development Indicators
WTO	World Trade Organization

INTRODUCTION

This is a sequel to my previous book on the Caribbean, *The Economic History of the Caribbean Since the Napoleonic Wars*, published in 2012. That book looked at the region, defined as all the islands plus the three Guianas and Belize, through a thematic lens covering the two centuries since the end of the Napoleonic Wars. This book explores the region, defined in the same way, country by country, over the same time period. Each approach has its advantages and disadvantages, but hopefully the two approaches complement each other.

Today, there are 34 countries in the Caribbean consisting of 16 independent countries and 18 territories. Six of the territories are Dutch, of which three (Aruba, Curaçao, and St Maarten) are autonomous units within the Kingdom of the Netherlands and three (Bonaire, Saba and St Eustatius) are public bodies belonging to Holland. Five are French, of which three (la Guyane, Guadeloupe, and Martinique) are Départements d'Outre Mer and two (St Barthélemy and St Martin) are Collectivités d'Outre Mer. Five territories are British Overseas Territories (Anguilla, British Virgin Islands, Cayman Islands, Montserrat, and Turks and Caicos Islands). There are also two US territories (Puerto Rico and the US Virgin Islands).

The 34 countries have a combined population of 45 million, most of whom (88 per cent) live in the independent countries.[1] This figure would be considerably higher were it not for high levels of emigration that have been such a feature of the Caribbean. Net annual outward migration since 2010, for example, has averaged 160,000, and there are only a small number of countries that have not been affected. This was difficult enough when birth rates were high, but it has become more serious as birth rates have fallen. Indeed, in a number of countries the population itself is now falling while becoming older at the same time.

A comparison of these 34 countries today reveals an extraordinary range in terms of average income (see figure Introd. 1).[2] Gross Domestic Product (GDP) per head varies from less than US$1,000 (Haiti) to nearly US$60,000 (Cayman Islands). The richest countries are all territories, as they enjoy significant economic advantages over the independent states. Indeed, only one independent country (Bahamas) is among the top eighteen in terms of GDP per head.[3] However, there is still a huge range even among the sovereign states themselves.

Figure Introd. 1: Caribbean GDP per head (2010 US$), c.2016

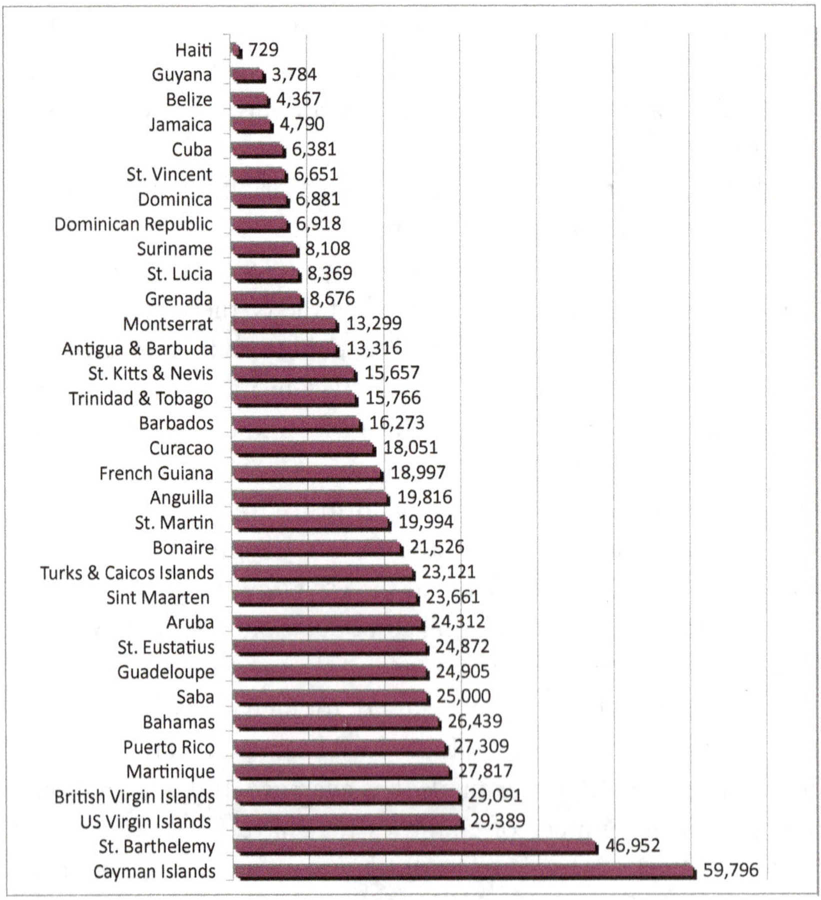

Source: See note 2.

The ranking of countries by GDP per head is closely correlated with their ranking by exports of goods and services per head. This demonstrates the crucial role of foreign trade in the economic development of the Caribbean, and the few exceptions prove the rule since the only countries where the rankings are significantly different are those territories receiving massive transfers and subsidies from a metropolitan state.

Europeans introduced slavery to the Caribbean in order to make commodity exports profitable. Without exports there would have been no slavery and when exports were not profitable, slavery diminished rapidly in importance. Thus, the economic model before slavery was abolished focused on an extreme form of export specialisation in which the productivity of forced labour in the export sector was the crucial variable.

As slavery ended, starting with Haiti in the 1790s and finishing with Cuba in the 1880s, all countries faced the same dilemma: how to maintain the size and profitability of the export sector without forced labour. This led to numerous experiments in coercion, free immigration, and indentured labour – some more successful than others – in order to ensure that the export sector had a sufficient supply of workers to prosper.

An adequate supply of labour may have been a necessary condition for profitability in the export sector, but it was not sufficient. Caribbean countries had to shift resources from one export to another as market conditions changed. Sugar had accounted for 50 per cent of merchandise exports in 1820, but the share had fallen below 40 per cent by the end of the century and below 20 per cent in the 1980s, before withering away subsequently.

At first, countries simply shifted resources from one exportable commodity to another. Haiti, for example, replaced sugar with coffee while French Guiana abandoned annatto and concentrated on gold. The list of commodities in which the Caribbean specialised after the end of slavery was a long one, but none remained permanently profitable.

Manufactured exports became important for a few countries after the Second World War, especially in the assembly industry, but it was the rise in exports of services that transformed the outlook for the

Caribbean. Starting with tourism before spreading to other activities, such as finance, insurance, health, education, and transport, the export of services is now much more important than the export of goods in most Caribbean countries, and this has helped to raise living standards considerably.

The Caribbean has benefited greatly from service exports, but they are not a panacea. Just as in the case of commodity exports, there is still a constant need for diversification as a result of changes in market conditions. As a result, there is no correlation at all between the level of exports per head and the rate of growth of GDP per head. Some countries that were among the first to take advantage of new opportunities to export services now find themselves struggling with falling GDP per head as circumstances have changed.

Adapting to changing external conditions has been a constant feature of the Caribbean since the Napoleonic Wars. The struggle for economic independence is therefore a permanent one, but it has been made more difficult by the emergence of a new challenge in the form of climate change and the greater frequency of extreme weather. This threatens not just the export of the different goods and services, on which Caribbean countries depend, but also the topography of the countries themselves as a result of rising sea levels.

The 15 chapters in this book cover the 34 Caribbean countries. They are grouped in four parts by language, although this entails some simplifications. All but three of the chapters have been written specially for this book. The exceptions are the chapters on Cuba (chapter 1), Haiti (chapter 4), and Belize (chapter 13). These have been taken from my earlier book and are reprinted here in abbreviated form with the permission of Cambridge University Press.

There are frequent references in the chapters to a statistical appendix. This is freely available at the website of Cambridge University Press () by entering the title of my previous book, *The Economic History of the Caribbean Since the Napoleonic Wars*, clicking on 'Resources' and then opening the Tables. A detailed description of the Tables, as well as the methodology used to prepare them, can be found in Bulmer-Thomas (2012, 463–647).

The chapters in this book were written before the spread of coronavirus (COVID-19) to the Caribbean in 2020. While the impact of the virus will be very serious for the region in terms of public health, social conditions and economic performance, I have not attempted to update the chapters to take this into account as there is insufficient evidence at the time of writing to make an informed judgement.

NOTES

1. The figure is for 2016.
2. The data for figure Introd. 1 come from a variety of sources. The World Bank, World Development Indicators has data on GDP per head (2010 US$) on all the independent countries as well as the US territories and some of the British and Dutch territories. The data for the French territories come from INSEE and have been converted from Euros to US dollars. The data for the other British and Dutch territories come from official local sources.
3. The only territory that is not in the top eighteen in terms of GDP per head is Montserrat, which suffered a devastating volcanic eruption in 1995.
4. The rank correlation coefficient is 0.83. When the correlation is done using values, the coefficient is 0.93.
5. Martinique, for example, is ranked fifth in terms of GDP per head, but only 24th in terms of exports of goods and services per head.
6. See V. Bulmer-Thomas, *The Economic History of the Caribbean since the Napoleonic Wars* (Cambridge: Cambridge University Press, 2012), figure 1.3, p.13.
7. Danish, for example, is no longer spoken in the former Danish West Indies.

PART I: The Spanish-speaking Countries

Chapter 1
CUBA

This chapter analyses the Cuban economy since the revolution. The first part of the chapter is devoted to the transition from capitalism to socialism in the years 1959–63. These five years constitute a short period of time, but they were the moments when the foundations of the new Cuba were laid. The tension between the island's government and the US led to a rapid deterioration in the bilateral relationship and the emergence of the Soviet Union (USSR) as a new strategic partner together with China and Eastern Europe in lesser roles. The establishment of socialism was fraught with difficulties and macroeconomic performance was poor, but Cuba was still able to make substantial progress on the social programmes for which it is justly famous. At the same time, the transition introduced a number of structural problems that have still not been overcome today.

The second part covers the quarter century from 1964 to 1989. This is usually broken down by scholars of Cuba into different periods, and it is true that there were sharp swings in performance and policy. Yet, this was a period dominated by state planning in which the price mechanism played only a minor role and in which Cuba could count on solid support from its communist allies in other parts of the world. The Cuban economy performed relatively well in these years – especially in the first half of the 1980s when mainland Latin America and part of the Caribbean were struggling with the aftermath of the 1982 debt crisis. This was also the period when Cuba returned to sugar as the key sector of the economy despite the failure to achieve the target of ten million tons in 1970.

The fall of the Berlin Wall, the collapse of the Soviet Union, and the end of trade privileges with other communist countries caused the economy to go into a tailspin. Even scholars who cast doubt on the reliability of Cuban statistics have no trouble in accepting the official version that GDP per head fell by nearly 40 per cent from peak to trough. As the economy started to decline, Fidel Castro launched the Special Period – a moment of exceptional austerity designed to prevent the complete collapse of the socialist system on the island. A modest recovery in the second half of the 1990s was not enough to reverse the decline, but the years after the millennium brought an improvement in economic performance in which Venezuelan and Chinese assistance would prove to be very helpful.

1.1. From Capitalism to Socialism: 1959–63

Fulgencio Batista seized power in 1952, in defiance of the 1940 Constitution that he himself had introduced, but Cuba continued to receive economic, financial, and military assistance from the US. The Cuban economy performed poorly during his final tenure as a result primarily of the difficulties faced by sugar in world markets. The US sugar quota was reduced, prices drifted downwards, and Batista's government even sold 500,000 tons to the Soviet Union in one year. In an effort to reduce costs, the length of the harvest was cut and unemployment in the sugar industry – already severe – became catastrophic. The decline of the sugar industry led to difficulties for all those rural and urban activities dependent on it. Batista launched a wave of repression against any manifestations of discontent, and the stage was set for the collapse of a regime that was eventually abandoned even by the US.[1]

Fidel Castro was the undisputed leader of the revolution, but he did not become Prime Minister until February 13, 1959 and would not engineer the appointment of a loyal supporter to the presidency until July. The first six months were dedicated to policies that were radical but not exceptional by Latin American standards.[2] These included reducing rent by 50 per cent, intervening in public utilities to reduce tariffs, and adopting the first agrarian reform law. This was aimed at giving title to the smallest farmers and breaking up the largest farms, many of them foreign-owned, and distributing the land to those that previously worked it – in cooperatives or state farms rather than small parcels. Compensation was offered, although in the form of bonds rather than cash, and many large landowners escaped altogether as the maximum size permitted was set generously.[3]

The Eisenhower administration (1953–61) was the first to recognise the new government, but proceeded cautiously. It did not offer to renew military supplies nor did it offer financial assistance. The US was surprised, however, that Castro did not ask for foreign aid on his first trip to Washington, DC, in April, and Vice President Richard Nixon formed the view that Castro was unreliable from the US perspective. This perspective hardened in the second half of the year as the July 26 Movement[4] split into reformists and radicals. Castro sided with the latter and brought known communists into his government despite his previous distrust of their party.[5] Crucially, however, the sugar quota was not changed, and the US contented itself with precautionary measures that included establishing contacts with anti-Castro groups and preparing the Organization of American States (OAS) for a possible rupture in the relationship with Cuba.

The deterioration of the bilateral relationship accelerated rapidly in the following year. This began with the visit of the Soviet Deputy Prime Minister Anastas Mikoyan to Havana leading to a trade agreement including an offer to buy 425,000 tons of sugar in 1960 and supply a limited amount of crude oil.[6] When the Eisenhower administration ordered US refineries on the island not to process the Soviet crude, they were all 'intervened' and immediately supplies were switched from Venezuela to the Soviet Union.[7] This was too much for President Eisenhower, who suspended the remainder of the Cuban sugar quota for 1960 on July 6.[8] Castro responded by nationalising those US companies that had not already been taken over.[9] In turn, Eisenhower imposed, in October, a trade embargo on Cuba, except for essential foods and medical supplies, and broke diplomatic relations in January 1961 just before handing over to President Kennedy.

Any hopes that the new US president might be able to improve the bilateral relationship were ended when Kennedy immediately announced the continued suspension of the Cuban sugar quota and the maintenance of the trade embargo. He also gave covert approval for the Bay of Pigs invasion by anti-Castro groups that took place in April 1961. It was a resounding failure and Castro was left in a stronger position than before. The US was forced to resort to multilateral measures that included suspending Cuba from the OAS in January 1962 and pressuring other countries not to trade with the island.[10] It was only the discovery of Soviet missiles on the island that allowed Kennedy to recover the initiative and force the Soviet Union to withdraw them in October 1962 after promising not to invade Cuba.

Although the Soviet Union had purchased Cuban sugar in the 1950s, this was a purely commercial transaction on both sides. The Cuban Revolution was not seen as heralding a radical new role for the USSR in the Caribbean, since it coincided with Nikita Khrushchev's pursuit of 'peaceful co-existence' with the US. In any case, there was no certainty that the revolution would survive in the face of US hostility. Trade in 1959 remained minimal (see table 1.1) despite a tour of Eastern Europe by Ernesto Guevara,[11] and Cuba bought a mere $10,000 from the Soviet Union in that year.

The Soviet attitude to Cuba started to change early in 1960 and this was reflected in the trade pattern (see table 1.1). Cuban exports to the Soviet Union – mainly sugar, but also minerals – rose sharply and so did imports from the USSR. The US, however, remained by far the most important trade partner despite the suspension of the sugar quota in July and the trade embargo in October. It was not until 1961 that trade with the US collapsed and the Soviet Union became the main market for exports and the principal source of imports. Furthermore, over 70 per cent of Cuban trade in that year was with socialist economies. These included the rest of the Council of Mutual Economic Assistance (COMECON)[12] as well as China, Albania, North Korea, and Yugoslavia.

The architects of the revolution had no doubt that they wanted to diversify the Cuban economy, reduce its dependence on exports (especially sugar) and accelerate import substitution. The agrarian reform was therefore not only intended to transfer ownership of the largest estates, but also to provide the opportunity to grow the products that Cuba had previously imported. The nationalisation of foreign-owned assets in industry, coupled with the introduction of a planned economy, was designed to replace many of the manufactured imports previously obtained from abroad.

Table 1.1: Cuban Trade with US and USSR as Percentage of Merchandise Trade, 1959–63

	Exports		**Imports**	
	To US (%)	**to USSR (%)**	**from US (%)**	**from USSR (%)**
1959	69.9	2.0	68.2	0.001
1960	53.2	16.7	48.6	12.6
1961	5.6	48.6	2.0	37.4
1962	1.3	42.6	1.9	54.2
1963	0.02	30.1	4.6	53.2

Sources: Statistical Appendix, Mesa-Lago (2000, 374), Carter (2006), Vol. 5 and IMF, Direction of Trade Statistics.

Provided the reduction in export dependence was matched by an increase in import substitution, there was no reason for the economy to become unbalanced. However, this was not what happened. The share of exports in GDP fell rapidly after 1958 (see figure 1.1) despite the fact that GDP itself was falling in most years (see below). The import ratio also declined, but at nothing like the same rate as it proved impossible to bring on stream the new industries outlined in the first plan. Thus, the large trade surplus of the 1950s had become a structural deficit by 1963 and required foreign finance to bridge the gap. This was an uncomfortable position for Cuba faced with the difficulties of obtaining credit from Western sources.

Figure 1.1: Cuban Merchandise Trade to GDP Ratio (%), 1950–63

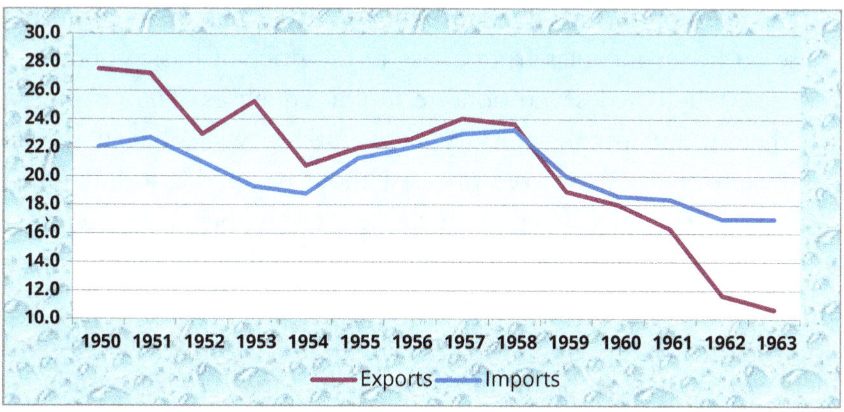

Source: Statistical Appendix.

Income distribution in Cuba before the revolution – between rural and urban areas as well as between deciles – was very unequal and its improvement became another target of the new government. This justified many of the earliest measures such as reducing rents and public utility prices. Land reform, however, had the greatest redistributive consequences since the workers previously employed for only a few months were now given permanent jobs. A second agrarian reform in 1963, lowering the maximum size of landholding to 67 hectares, took this a stage further. New jobs were also being created in education, health, and other public services as the state pushed ahead with its ambitious social goals, including the elimination of illiteracy. A host of new jobs was created as a result of the increase in defence and security expenditure.

All these changes coincided with continued outward migration, although the population continued to grow. The qualitative impact of migration was more important than the quantitative because of the exit of so many professionals with much-needed capital (human and financial). Open unemployment declined in Cuba, although it was still nearly ten per cent in 1963. However, purchasing power ran far ahead of the ability of the economy to supply the goods and services demanded. By 1962, the cumulative monetary surplus (excess of income over expenditure) was estimated at 90 per cent of income and Cuba was suffering from a severe monetary overhang. The Cuban government, therefore, faced a clear choice between inflation and rationing.

The decision to introduce rationing in 1962 may have protected those on lower incomes from a rise in the price of basic goods and services, but it had severe long-term consequences. The peasantry, whether in small-scale plots or cooperatives, was obliged to sell produce to the state at fixed prices without being able to buy much in return. The incentives to increase production were therefore undermined, farm labour productivity fell, and Cuba continued to remain dependent on imported foodstuffs. Urban workers, their jobs now much more secure than before, also had little incentive to increase productivity as the goods available through the ration book declined rather than increased.

GDP per head, already falling before the revolution, continued to decline (see figure 1.2). The drop was not dramatic and there was even an increase in 1962. Furthermore, income distribution improved sharply. However, the model was not sustainable, and the Cuban leadership was forced to engage in a serious debate about future policy in order to ensure that the economy did not shrink any further. The key ingredient in this debate was the role of exports and Castro returned from a visit to the Soviet Union in 1963 to announce that sugar would once again play a pivotal role in the Cuban economy.

By the end of 1963, the Cuban government had gained control of the 'commanding heights' of the economy. One quarter of retail trade was still in the hands of the private sector, but these were small stores. Nearly one-third of agricultural land was outside the state sector, but the farmers were obliged to sell most of their produce to the government at fixed prices. Almost everything else – mining, manufacturing, construction, transport, communications, wholesale trade, and services – were in state hands. Crucially, for an economy as dependent on foreign trade as Cuba, all exports, imports, and banking transactions were controlled by the state.

Figure 1.2: Cuban GDP per head (2000 US$), 1950–63

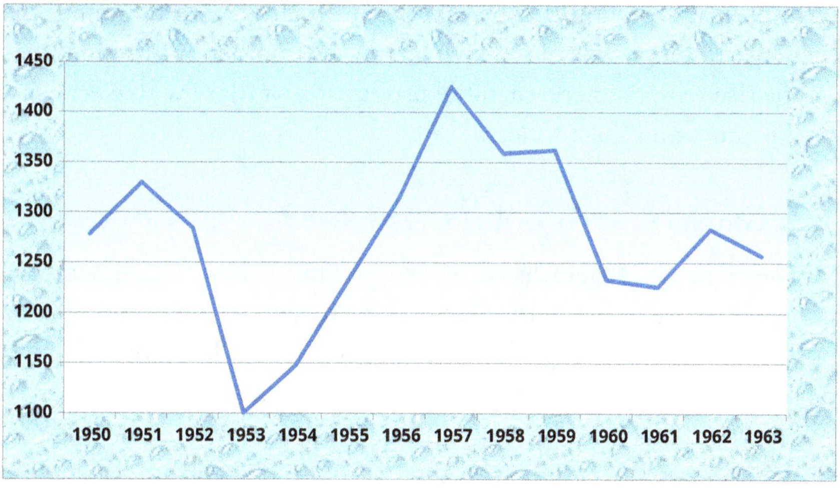

Source: Statistical Appendix from 1960 onwards and Vidal and Fundora (2008) before 1960.

The Cuban economy had, therefore, made the transition from capitalism to socialism in a very short period. Most workers were now employed by the state and wages were regulated. Private profits were negligible and private investment even more so. Thus, investment now depended on capital formation by the state. This, however, was disappointing even by the less than exacting standards of the pre-revolutionary Cuban economy. Gross fixed capital formation, estimated at less than 18 per cent of GDP in the 1950s, had fallen to 13 per cent in 1962/3, and the reasons would become familiar: a shortage of foreign exchange for imports of capital goods and a high level of current spending by the state on social services and defence that left little room for investment.

Yet, there had been solid achievements in these five years despite the hostile external environment, the US trade embargo, the outward migration of those with key skills, the inevitable chaos associated with the transition from the free market to state planning and acts of sabotage by enemies of the revolution. The income of the lower deciles had increased and unemployment fallen without the inflationary pressures that normally accompany massive exercises in redistribution. Economic activity, whether measured by GDP or – as the Cubans were now doing – Global Social Product (GSP),[13] may have been flat or falling, but school enrolments were booming, the literacy campaign was in full swing, and the number of dwellings was on the rise with an increase in the proportion of those with electricity, piped water, and flush toilets.

1.2. Growth with Equity: 1964–89

The return of Fidel Castro in 1963 from his first trip to Moscow not only signalled a return to the primacy of sugar but also a postponement of the push for heavy industry. The Soviet Union promised, over the next few years, to buy increasing quantities of Cuban sugar at a fixed price, and Cuba needed to reallocate resources to the sugar industry to make this possible. Helped by an increase in world sugar prices and a much improved harvest, the value of exports soared in 1964. As a result, the economy grew rapidly from its low level in 1963, helped by a strong performance from nickel as well as sugar exports and impressive growth in the construction and livestock sectors.

The better economic performance in 1964, welcomed though it was to the Cuban leadership, did not mean that the underlying structural problems had been overcome. What followed was a 25-year upswing (1964–89) that broke down into three distinct phases (see figure 1.3). The first was a period of stagnation that lasted until 1970. There were then 15 years of exceptionally rapid growth punctuated only by a brief recession in 1980. This was followed by another period of stagnation in the second half of the 1980s.

The stagnation between 1964 and 1970 had many causes. At the beginning, the OAS had imposed a trade embargo against Cuba[14] that left the island even more dependent on communist countries. The agreements Cuba made with the latter were crucial, but they were not (yet) exceptionally generous. Furthermore, geopolitical disputes led Cuba to be punished from time to time. The Chinese cut rice exports to Cuba in 1966 and the Soviet Union slowed down the supply of oil in 1967. Furthermore, the average price paid for Cuban sugar was slightly below that received by most other countries in the Caribbean (see below).

Figure 1.3: Cuban GDP per head (2000 US$)1964–89

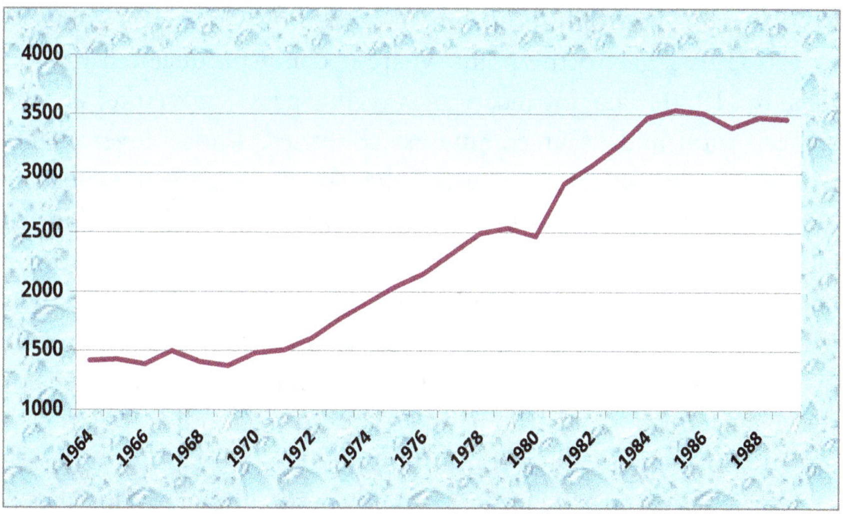

Source: Statistical Appendix.

The period also began with an energetic debate between those, led by Guevara, favouring moral incentives and those, led by Carlos Rafael Rodríguez, who believed that material incentives could not be avoided. This led to a decision by Fidel Castro to allow part (mainly agriculture) to be run under one system (material incentives) and the rest of the economy (including industry) to be an experiment in building Guevara's 'new man'. The operation of the two systems side by side caused considerable confusion, and the budgetary system of accounting favoured by the Guevarists led to a great deal of inefficiency.

A small private sector had survived the first waves of nationalisation, and the shortages of many goods and services allowed a number of businesses to make substantial profits. This led to the Revolutionary Offensive launched by Fidel Castro in March 1968. It eliminated many of the remaining privately owned farms in agriculture, curtailed private sector operations in retailing, and shut down many of the self-employed businesses in services. Henceforth, almost the only legitimate supplier of goods and services was the state and shortages became even more apparent. Many visitors to the island at this time commented on the long queues for even the simplest articles of consumption.[15] Labour productivity suffered both from the time wasted and from the lack of incentives to increase earnings.

On his return from a second visit to Moscow, Fidel Castro made explicit what had only been hinted at before: Cuba was going to specialise in sugar to the point where it could produce ten million tons by 1970. The justification was the growing market in the Soviet Union and other communist countries, whose governments would now be expected to curtail their own – relatively expensive – production of sugar beet. However, to meet this highly ambitious target, the whole Cuban economy had to be subordinated to the needs of the sugar sector. Land previously used for other crops was planted with sugarcane, scarce foreign exchange was used to repair or replace milling equipment, transport was diverted to the needs of the sugar industry, and labour was switched from other activities to prepare for the ten million ton *zafra*.[16]

The 1970 *zafra* produced 8.5 million tons of sugar. This was a record for Cuba and in many ways an astonishing achievement. However, the opportunity cost was enormous. By now Cuba had virtually eliminated unemployment, despite the slow growth of the economy, as labour productivity was stagnant or falling and so many citizens had moved into education or the armed forces. Thus, the sugarcane had to be harvested by many volunteers with no experience or by workers taking time off from their other jobs. Cuba's allies, especially the Soviet Union, were not impressed and called for greater rationality in the allocation of economic resources.

This duly happened and Cuba (re)established conventional Soviet planning methods based on material incentives and, starting in 1976, detailed five-year plans. This would no doubt have led to an improvement in economic performance. However, the new orthodoxy also coincided with a rise in world sugar prices that reached their peak in 1975. Since the price quadrupled, Cuba's communist allies had to adjust the prices they offered for the island's sugar. This assured Cuba an exceptional price for its sugar in whatever market it sold and the volume available was now much greater as a result of the efforts made to achieve a ten million ton *zafra*. Furthermore, the price of nickel and other primary products also increased sharply. Thus, the value of exports soared and the Cuban economy grew rapidly.

The world price of sugar, still far and away the main export, declined rapidly after 1975. If Cuba had been a typical Caribbean country, it would have suffered as a consequence. However, new arrangements with the Soviet Union under the five-year plan allowed Cuba to continue to receive the high price of sugar (and nickel) as well as paying a below market price for oil imports. Furthermore, the Soviet Union agreed that any oil imports saved by Cuba through energy-saving measures would be sold and transferred to the island as hard currency. In addition, the Soviet Union continued to provide loans on concessionary terms.

These arrangements, far more generous than those that prevailed in the first 15 years of the revolution, allowed the Cuban economy to grow very rapidly. GDP per head (at US$2000) reached a peak of US$3,535 in 1985. This implied an annual rate of growth since 1969 of over six per cent. This compared favourably with the performance in the 1960s, with the rest of the Caribbean in the same years and with the rest of the world. Furthermore, the period included the first half of the 1980s when almost all Latin American and many

Caribbean countries experienced a sharp fall in GDP per head as a result of the 1982 debt crisis.

The most generous part of the Soviet package was the price paid for sugar. This implied a large subsidy to the Cuban economy, but the size of the subsidy has been controversial. Many scholars have calculated it by reference to the free market price of sugar. However, the latter is not an appropriate metric as only a small part of world sugar trade passes through the free market. Furthermore, in most years (1973–75 were exceptional) the world price has been artificially low as surpluses have been dumped on it by large exporters such as the European Union (EU).

Most exporters of sugar made from cane sold their surpluses under long-term quota arrangements with importing countries. The most important have been the US, Canadian, and EU sugar quotas allowing exporters to benefit from high domestic prices in importing countries. Thus, the relevant price for comparison is the average price received by other Caribbean countries. We can group these as (a) Dominican Republic, (b) CARICOM, (c) US territories, and (d) all Caribbean countries (excluding Cuba). The results are shown in table 1.2, which shows the annualised premium paid for Cuban sugar as a percentage of GDP. The numbers are calculated as the difference between the sum of the value of Cuban sugar exports in the years stated and the value obtained by multiplying the volume of Cuban sugar exports by the unit value for sugar for each subregion divided by the sum of current GDP for the same years.

Table 1.2: Annual Sugar Subsidy Received by Cuba as Percentage of GDP, 1964–89

	Cuban Subsidy Relative to Sugar Price Received by:			
Year	**Dominican Republic**	**CARICOM**	**US Territories**	**Caribbean (ex Cuba)**
1964–72	-1.3	-0.15	-0.9	-0.8
1973–89	10.0	7.5	6.9	8.6
1964–89	8.2	6.3	5.6	7.1

Source: Statistical Appendix.

The first point to notice about table 1.2 is that the premium received by Cuba up to 1972 was actually negative. In other words, Cuba was paid an average price slightly lower than that received by the other subregions. The Soviet Union and the other communist countries may have paid a price higher than the free market, but it was not as high as the price paid by the EU, US, or Canada under special arrangements. After the new arrangements with the Soviet Union came into force, however, the subsidy was substantial and amounted to between seven and ten per cent of GDP on an annual basis. When the other subsidies are taken into account (see above), it is not unreasonable to suggest that Cuba was receiving a foreign-aid package equivalent to at least ten per cent of GDP per year.[17]

Cuban GDP, therefore, grew rapidly. Indeed, in the second five-year plan (1981–85) recorded growth was faster than planned growth. Furthermore, population growth was steadily declining so that GDP per head grew almost as fast. There was no major diversification of the economy, but there were many small changes. The tourist industry recovered from its nadir in the 1960s, the fishing industry expanded, the foundations were laid for biotechnology exports, and a 1982 law permitted joint ventures with foreign companies in certain areas. There was even a relaxation of the straitjacket in which the private sector operated with farmers' markets being re-established and greater opportunities for self-employment.

The fast growth of the Cuban economy after 1970 allowed the government to make substantial progress towards achieving its social ambitions. Secondary school enrolment jumped from 25 per cent of the age group to 85 per cent in 1985.[18] Tertiary went from five to 21 per cent over the same period. Most urban houses were joined to the main water supply by 1985 and about one-third of rural dwellings. By 1975, the number of doctors per 10,000 inhabitants had surpassed its pre-revolutionary level and would then double in the next ten years. Mortality rates, general and infant, declined sharply and life expectancy reached the standards of the richest countries. And the rate of net outward migration dropped below 10,000 per year after 1972 with the exception of 1979–81.[19]

Despite this economic and social progress, the Cuban Revolution failed to overcome fully the three structural weaknesses that had emerged before 1964: trade deficits, low rates of investment, and the monetary overhang. The increase in the average sugar price had pushed up the ratio of exports to GDP after 1972 (see figure 1.4), but it did not eliminate the trade gap except in the exceptional year of 1975. This trade deficit had to be financed and not all of it could be covered by soft currency loans from communist countries. Thus, Cuba had built up a hard currency debt that may not have been as burdensome as in the rest of Latin America, but which still had to be serviced at a heavy foreign exchange cost. Similarly, the investment/GDP ratio may have risen from its low rate in the 1960s, but it rarely exceeded 20 per cent despite the low level of private consumption as a share of GDP (see figure 1.4).

The low level of *private* consumption was a consequence of the high rate of *public* consumption. Public revenue and expenditure constituted just over 40 per cent of GDP in 1965, but these ratios had risen to 70 per cent by 1980 after which they declined modestly (see table 1.3). By this time, the monetary overhang (the monetary surplus expressed as a percentage of income) had fallen, but it had not disappeared (see table 1.3). This overhang fuelled the black market and allowed the small private sector to make profits much greater than the numbers involved might have implied.

Figure 1.4: Cuban Ratio to GDP (%) of Total Exports and Investment: 1963–89

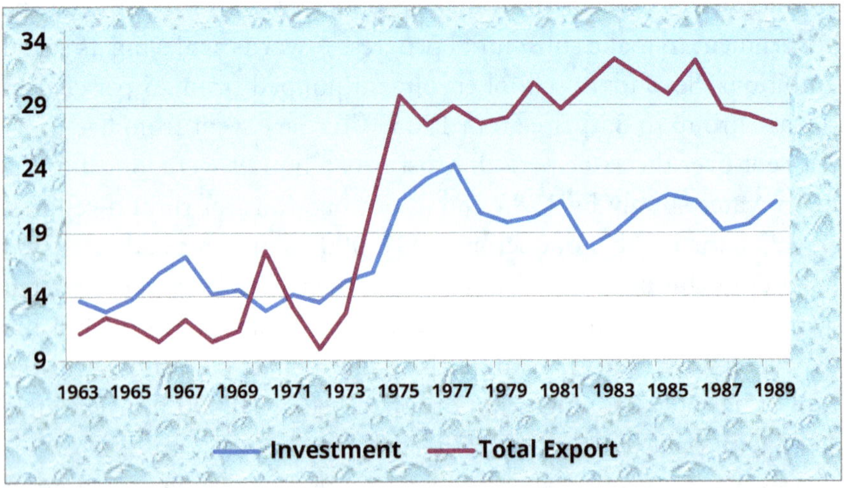

Source: Trade/GDP Ratios from Statistical Appendix; Investment from Mesa-Lago (2000, 355), and Converted to Dollars Using Statistical Appendix.

Table 1.3: Cuban Public Revenue, Public Expenditure, and the Monetary Surplus, 1965–89

Year	Revenue/ GDP (%)	Expenditure/ GDP (%)	Monetary Surplus/ Income (%)
1965	41.5	41.5	72.9
1970	na	na	83.1
1975	71.8 (a)	71.8(a)	36.6
1980	70.4	70.3	30.9
1985	57.9	57.9	30.0
1989	59.3	65.9	35.2

Source: Derived from Mesa-Lago (2000), Table D.4, and Statistical Appendix (a) = 1978.

These were some of the reasons for the Rectification Process launched by Fidel Castro in 1986. This involved a return to many of the policies of the late 1960s including – once again – a major clampdown on the small private sector. Cuban officials explained it as necessary to tackle corruption, crime and waste in the public sector, growing inequality in income distribution, and to revive the revolutionary spirit.

Whatever its causes, the Rectification Process coincided with renewed stagnation of the Cuban economy. The Soviet Union itself was going through a painful process of adjustment and could not maintain the previous level of support for Cuba. The average price received by Cuba for its sugar declined after 1986. The foreign exchange earned from energy savings fell and Cuba defaulted on its hard currency debt leading to a rapid increase in its nominal value as unpaid interest accumulated. These external difficulties were then compounded by the Rectification Process itself, which may have promoted income equality but undermined growth. The only bright spots were the growth of biotechnology exports and an increase in foreign visitors. In time, Cuba would no doubt have overcome its economic difficulties. However, no one had anticipated the possibility that the Soviet Union might collapse.

1.3. THE SPECIAL PERIOD AND ITS AFTERMATH

Mikhail Gorbachev came to power in 1985 and attempted to tackle the economic problems of the Soviet Union, in 1986, with the policies that became known as *perestroika*. Cuba began to feel the shock of these economic reforms almost immediately, but it was not until the collapse of the Berlin Wall on November 9, 1989 that the full implications would become clear. In January 1990, the members of COMECON (including Cuba) agreed that henceforth trade between member states would be conducted at market prices and paid for with hard currency. At the same time, soft loans on concessionary terms disappeared. All that remained was the military assistance and that would soon vanish as well.

The impact on Cuba was dramatic. GDP at constant prices fell drastically after 1989 (see figure 1.5) and did not stop falling until 1993. In this short period, GDP per head fell by 36.6 per cent – one of the biggest declines ever recorded in Latin America or the Caribbean. Thus, Cuba suffered five years of economic stagnation in the second half of the 1980s, followed by five years of collapse. The US Congress, wishing to accelerate the long-anticipated demise of the Castro regime, then chose this moment to pass into law the Cuban Democracy Act[20] that tightened the embargo on Cuba, imposed sanctions on foreign subsidiaries of US companies that traded with Cuba, penalised ships from using Cuban ports on their way to or from the US, and severely limited the amount of remittances that Cuban-Americans could send to their relatives on the island.

In any other Caribbean or Latin American country, an economic collapse of this magnitude would have led to mass unemployment, currency devaluation, imported inflation, and almost certainly a change of government at the next available opportunity. This did not happen in Cuba. This is not only because the electoral route to political change did not exist but also because it was not a market economy. Thus, the collapse took a different form. The crisis years were designated the Special Period in Time of Peace by Fidel Castro, drastic – even radical – measures were taken by the government and the regime survived despite a stream of books and articles predicting the imminent end of communism on the island.

Figure 1.5: Cuban GDP and GDP per head (2000 US$), 1989–2018

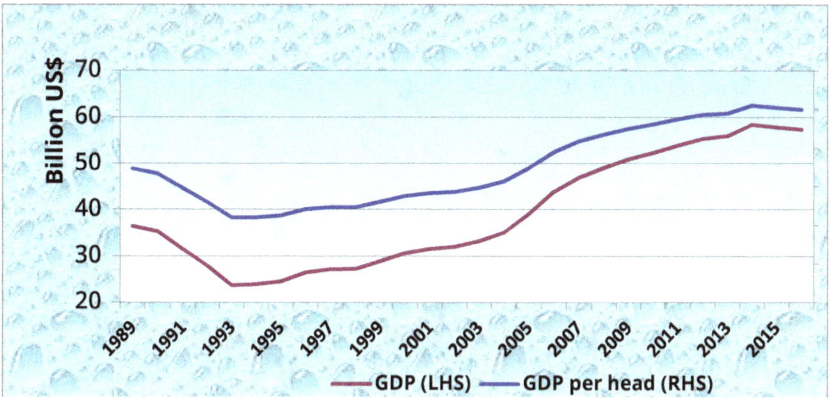

Source: Statistical Appendix and UNNA.

The crisis at first took a familiar form. The sale of commodity exports at world prices pushed the value of merchandise exports down from $5.35 billion in 1989 to a low of $1 billion in 1993. Total imports, valued at $8.1 billion in 1989, then fell even more sharply as there were no more soft loans to finance a balance of payments deficit and loans from Western creditors were unavailable because the hard currency debt had been in default since 1986. The absence of imported spare parts and raw materials crippled the ability of manufacturing to maintain production and output fell in all sectors. Government revenue, heavily dependent on the circulation tax applied to the products of state-owned enterprises, declined as well.

In a capitalist country this would have required a drastic cut in public expenditure. Yet, this did not happen in Cuba. Instead, the state maintained the level of overall public spending (see table 1.4). The unemployment rate, which had been creeping up in the 1980s, then remained virtually unchanged. Inevitably, there was a big increase in the public sector deficit (see table 1.4), but this did not bring inflation as the state controlled the price of almost most goods and services. Instead, there was a huge increase in the monetary overhang, which was reflected in the rise of the liquidity to GDP ratio and the collapse of the unofficial exchange rate (see table 1.4). The investment ratio also fell sharply (see table 1.4) as the state was only able to maintain or increase *current* spending while *capital* spending, more heavily dependent on imports, collapsed.

Table 1.4: The Crisis Years in Cuba: 1989–94

Year	mn pesos Expenditure	mn pesos Deficit	mn pesos Liquidity	Liquidity % of GDP	Unofficial Exchange Rate (per US$)	Investment/ GDP ratio
1989	13,904.2	-1,403.4	4,162.0	19.7	5.0	21.4
1990	15,481.6	-1,958.1	4,986.0	23.1	7.0	20.4
1991	14,713.8	-3,764.8	6,563.0	36.8	20.0	19.5
1992	15,048.3	-4,869.0	8,361.1	51.2	35.0	13.9
1993	14,566.5	-5,050.6	11,044.2	66.7	78.0	11.4
1994	14,178.3	-1,421.4	9,943.8	47.2	95.0	8.0

Sources: Banco Nacional de Cuba (1995) for state expenditure and deficit; Marquetti (1998) for liquidity (money in circulation plus bank deposits), unofficial exchange rate from Barberia (2004) and investment ratio from figure 1.4 for 1989 and CEPAL (2010) for other years.

The Special Period demanded special measures and these were not long in being adopted. The desperate need for foreign exchange led to a revision of the foreign investment law and a more welcoming attitude to new proposals. State farms were converted into co-operatives and renamed *Unidades Básicas de Producción Cooperativa* (UBPC). Farmers and artisans' markets, closed since 1986, were re-established. Prices of goods and services controlled by the state were adjusted upwards. Small businesses and self-employment were permitted in a much wider field of activities. Finally, the US dollar was legalised in 1993 and the black market exchange rate became a parallel rate. When the following year the government introduced the Cuban convertible peso (CUC) at parity with the US dollar, Cuba had three legal currencies circulating side by side.[21]

With one exception, these measures proved to be timely and in different degrees important. The number of joint ventures with foreign companies soared, and the country began to develop a first-class tourist infrastructure as well as expertise in mining. Uncontrolled markets and upward price adjustments in controlled ones helped to soak up liquidity, which fell sharply between 1993 and 1994, while reducing the fiscal deficit (see table 1.4). The parallel market exchange rate peaked at 130. There was a big increase (from a very low base) in those registered as self-employed. The one reform that did not work as planned was the UBPCs. They failed to bring about the much needed reversal of agricultural decline (their ability to do so was crippled by the shortage of foreign exchange and continuing controls on what products they could grow and where they could sell them).

These reforms helped the economy to recover from its low point in 1993. The recovery, however, was desperately slow and neither GDP nor GDP per head (at constant prices) exceeded its 1989 level until 2005 (this meant that the Cuban economy had lost *two* decades since GDP per head had actually peaked in 1985). This was only partly due to the further tightening of the US embargo in 1996, which was aimed, in particular, at discouraging foreign investment in Cuba.[22] It also had much to do with the long-standing inefficiencies in the Cuban economy and the continued shortage of foreign exchange. As a consequence, although there was plenty of scope for import substitution (in both agriculture and industry), this did not contribute much to economic growth after 1993 since firms often could not gain access to foreign exchange for spare parts and raw materials (the one exception was energy, as oil and gas production climbed steadily from their low levels in 1989 and made Cuba less dependent on imports).

The recovery was in fact export-led. This had virtually nothing to do with sugar, which suffered under the weight of low world prices and antiquated mills. Indeed, following the closure of many mills in 2002, sugar exports ceased to be of much importance with the volume dropping to its level before the Second War of Independence (1895–98). Instead, export growth was due to an increase in earnings from mining, other goods and – above all – services (see figure 1.6). Mining benefited both from an increase in output (especially nickel and cobalt where Canadian companies became strategic partners of the Cuban state) and also from much higher world prices. Other goods included biotechnology exports.

Merchandise exports never recovered their value in 1989. Thus, the growth of total exports, as figure 1.6 shows, came to depend on services that were more important than goods by 1997. Cuba joined the growing ranks of Caribbean countries where exports were dominated by services rather than merchandise despite the fact that cruise visitors were for many years blocked by the US trade embargo.

Figure 1.6: Cuban Composition of Total Exports ($mn), 1989–2008

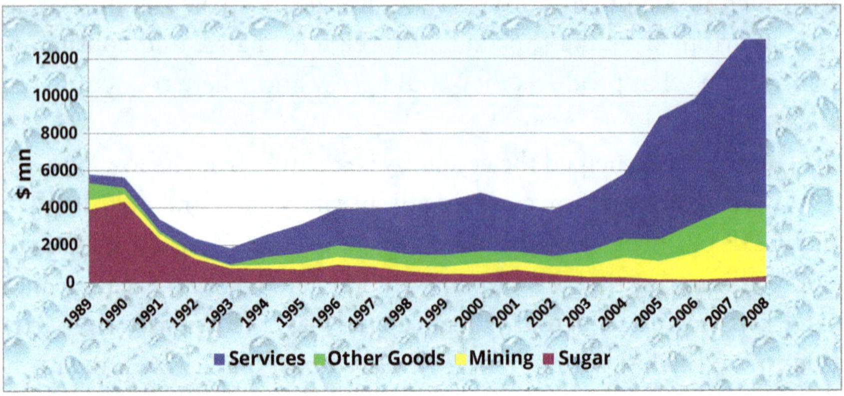

Source: Statistical Appendix.

The number of tourists, a mere 270,000 in 1989, had exceeded one million by 1997 and nearly five million by 2018. In the 30 years after the collapse of the Soviet Union, Cuba had become one of the most important destinations for tourists in the Caribbean with large numbers of visitors from Canada, Europe, and Latin America as well as a rapidly increasing number from China.

Until 2004, service exports were dominated by tourism. The following year, however, the contribution of tourist earnings to service exports dropped to one-third. This was a consequence of the bilateral agreements with Venezuela, the first of which had been signed in October 2000.[23] The cornerstone of the Cuban-Venezuelan accords was the supply of crude oil to Cuban refineries in return for the provision of medical and educational services in Venezuela by Cuban professionals,[24] although there were many other elements as well.[25] Thus, Cuba imported Venezuelan oil – nearly 100,000 barrels per day at its peak – and paid for it through professional services.

Critics of Cuba – and there have always been many – argued that Venezuela had simply replaced the Soviet Union as the provider of subsidies without which the island economy would have collapsed. Yet the size of the subsidy clearly depended on the price of oil. At US$25 a barrel, there was arguably *no* subsidy as Venezuela received a valuable service for which it was paying effectively a market price.[26] As the price of oil rose, there *was* a subsidy that could be roughly valued at US$2 billion when crude oil reached $80 per barrel.[27] With a GDP of around $60 billion at current prices in 2008, this would represent a subsidy of just over three per cent – far lower than the Soviet subsidy for sugar alone (see table 1.2).

Venezuelan support was not limited to the supply of crude oil, and Cuba also received generous assistance from China.[28] At the same time, Cuba did not pay much in debt servicing since loans from the Soviet Union had effectively been written off, hard currency debt was in default, and much of the rest was on very soft terms.[29] Furthermore, remittances to the island from those living abroad also rose rapidly. Most of this was from Cuban-Americans in the US despite the restrictions imposed during the presidency of George W. Bush (2001–09).[30] Thus, the growth rate of the Cuban economy started to accelerate after 2003 (see figure 1.5).

The Cuban economy has therefore not only recovered since 1993, but has also grown with GDP per head at constant (2000) prices exceeding $5,000 by 2015. However, this time it was not growth with equity. The authorities still controlled wage and pension rates for most of the population, but they had lost control of a large part of household income through the impact of remittances, tips paid in hard currency and the earnings of those in self-employment or small businesses. Furthermore, many Cubans had become highly skilled at stealing from their workplace and selling goods in the black market, while the state itself oversaw an expansion in incentive payments to key workers in the form of convertible rather than national pesos.[31]

The result was not only an increase in inequality but also in poverty. Inequality increased not so much because of the variance in wages paid in pesos, which remained very low.[32] It had much more to do with access to hard currency (including convertible pesos). Official estimates suggested that about half of Cuban households received such payments while the rest did not. As a result, the Gini coefficient was estimated to have jumped from 0.24 in mid-1980s to 0.38 15 years later.[33] Those in receipt of hard currency could either use it directly to purchase goods and services not available at subsidised prices or sell it in the parallel market for national currency.

Those without access to hard currency had to survive on their income in national pesos. As the state reduced the amount of goods and services available at subsidised prices, it also increased the minimum wage and average salaries in national pesos duly rose. As the proportion of income spent at subsidised prices fell,[34] those families without access to hard currency struggled to make ends meet in the uncontrolled markets. Indeed, urban poverty – virtually eliminated by 1989 – had risen to between 15 and 20 per cent of the urban population by the early 2000s.[35] Nobody starved in Cuba, but conditions became harsh for some of its citizens and frustration was widespread.[36] The state had also maintained employment beyond what was needed to avoid an increase in open unemployment so that perhaps one million workers were surplus to requirements and suffering from low morale.[37]

The Cuban economy, therefore, survived the Special Period and some of its citizens even prospered. Yet, the revolutionary spirit, so apparent to visitors even in the 1980s, had died somewhere along the road and the island's citizens became increasingly effective in venting their frustrations against the system. The governments of President Raúl Castro (2008–18) and President Miguel Díaz-Canel (2018–) clearly recognised this and were prepared to make a number of concessions both to the liberalisation of markets and to personal freedom. Yet to many the concession seemed too late, while political reform was not included on the agenda at all. By the time Cuba celebrated the 60th anniversary of the revolution, there was no danger of imminent collapse, but the sense of a revolution having run its course was strong.

NOTES

1. The Eisenhower administration suspended military supplies to Batista in March 1958. See R.E. Welch, *Response to Revolution: The United States and the Cuban Revolution, 1959–1961* (Chapel Hill, NC: University of North Carolina Press, 1985), 30.
2. Several of these measures had, in fact, been adopted in Cuba during the short-lived administration of President Grau San Martín (1933–34). See L. Pérez, 'Cuba, c.1930–59,' in *The Cambridge History of Latin America*, vol. vii, ed. L. Bethell (Cambridge, MA: Cambridge University Press, 1990), 459–62.
3. Not only was the maximum set at 30 *caballerías* (403 hectares) but there were also exemptions up to 100 *caballerías* (1,342 hectares) for the most efficient. See L. Huberman and P. Sweezy, *Cuba: Anatomy of a Revolution* (New York, NY: Monthly Review Press), 110–12.

4. This was the name given to the movement formed by Castro in Mexico in 1955 and named after the date of the storming of the Moncada barracks in 1953; at the time Fidel Castro was a member of the Orthodox Party. See T. Szulc, *Fidel: A Critical Portrait* (New York, NY: Morrow, 1986), 147–51.
5. The Partido Socialista Popular (PSP) was the name of the Communist Party in Cuba and it did not support the July 26 Movement until just before the fall of Batista. In particular, it failed to heed Castro's call for a general strike in March 1958 and without PSP support the strike was bound to fail. Relations between Castro and the PSP were therefore tense at first. See J. Sweig, *Inside the Cuban Revolution: Fidel Castro and the Urban Underground* (Cambridge, MA: Harvard University Press, 2002), 154–55.
6. Mikoyan was *en route* to Mexico to open a trade fair, but agreed to include Havana in his tour of the region at Cuba's request.
7. Not all the refineries were US-owned, but they were all intervened anyway. This included the Anglo-Dutch Shell Company.
8. At the time, Cuba had already shipped 2,300,000 tons of its US import quota of 3,120,000 tons, leaving a balance of 700,000 tons, which it was then able to sell to the Soviet Union and its allies at a comparable price. See Welch, *Response to Revolution*, 50. Nonetheless, because of the Cuban economy's dependence on sugar, this was an extremely aggressive act by the Eisenhower administration and it gave Castro little incentive to act with restraint towards US interests in Cuba.
9. It had already taken over some sugar mills, a textile factory, construction firms and the telephone company under an 'ill-gotten gains' law. See E. Boorstein, *The Economic Transformation of Cuba: A First-hand Account* (New York, NY: Modern Reader Paperbacks, 1968), 54.
10. The OAS vote was 14:1 – just enough to force Cuba's suspension – with Argentina, Bolivia, Brazil, Chile, Ecuador, and Mexico abstaining. See Welch, *Response to Revolution*, 97.
11. Ernesto 'Che' Guevara was an Argentine, who met Castro in Mexico in 1955.
12. The Council of Mutual Economic Assistance (COMECON) was the regional integration scheme that embraced the USSR and its Eastern European allies. Cuba joined in 1972.
13. GSP measures the gross value of goods and material services but excludes non-material services, while GDP measures the net value of all goods and services. See A.S. Zimbalist and C. Brundenius, *The Cuban Economy: Measurement and Analysis of Socialist Performance* (Baltimore, MD: Johns Hopkins University Press, 1989).
14. Among the Latin American countries, only Mexico refused to implement it.

15. My own diary, written during a two-month visit in 1968, stated of Havana: 'the queues for restaurants and refreshments were vast, yet the crowds seemed happy to wait patiently.'
16. This is the Cuban name for the sugar harvest.
17. Cuban officials point out that the Soviet subsidy had to be set against the annual cost to the economy from the trade embargo. The latter is hard to quantify, but it has undoubtedly been substantial.
18. These and subsequent numbers are taken from C. Mesa-Lago, *Market, Socialist, and Mixed Economies: Comparative Policy and Performance: Chile, Cuba, and Costa Rica* (Baltimore, MD: Johns Hopkins University Press, 2000).
19. This was due to the Mariel boatlift, when all restrictions were lifted and nearly 150,000 left in one year (1980).
20. Passed into law in 1992, it is usually known as the Torricelli Act after its congressional sponsor. See L. Barberia, 'Remittances to Cuba: An Evaluation of Cuban and U.S. Government Policy Measures,' in *The Cuban Economy at the Start of the Twenty-first Century*, ed. J.I. Domínguez, V.O.E. Pérez, and L. Barberia (Cambridge, MA: David Rockefeller Center for Latin American Studies, Harvard University, 2004), 393.
21. This was at least until 2006 when the US dollar was declared illegal. On the monetary and exchange rate system in Cuba in these years, see A.R.M. Ritter, *The Cuban Economy* (Pittsburgh, PA: University of Pittsburgh Press, 2004).
22. This was the Cuban Liberty and Democratic Solidarity Act, otherwise known as the Helms-Burton Law. For the first time it introduced penalties for trafficking in property allegedly taken from US citizens.
23. These bilateral agreements need to be distinguished from PetroCaribe, in which other countries (not just Cuba) also participated.
24. The Cubans continued to receive their salary in pesos on the island (deposited to their bank accounts), while their expenses in Venezuela were covered by the Venezuelan government. Any savings could be converted into goods or hard currency and repatriated to the island free of tax.
25. Venezuela financed the refurbishment of an oil refinery, guaranteed a regular supply of tourists to the island, provided soft loans and for a time sent tens of thousands of Venezuelans to Cuba for medical operations. See G. Sánchez, *Cuba and Venezuela: An Insight into Two Revolutions* (Melbourne, Victoria: Ocean, 2007).
26. At $25 per barrel, it would cost Cuba around $900 million to replace Venezuelan crude oil with other imports. Assuming the average cost (salaries, overheads, and training) of a health or educational professional

in Venezuela to be $3,000 per month, it would have cost Venezuela the same to replace the 25,000 Cubans working in the country.

27. The cost of replacing Venezuelan crude would rise to $2.9 billion at $80 per barrel (average price between 2005 and 2010), while the cost of replacing Cuban professionals remained the same.
28. Much of this was in the form of soft loans to buy Chinese products. That is why imports from China increased so rapidly after 2000.
29. In 2003, the external debt was valued at $11.3 billion (see CEPAL 2010). The following year it dropped to $5.8 billion as a result of a decision by the Cuban authorities to record only the debt that was being currently serviced. This then rose to $9.9 billion in 2008 (equivalent to 15.8 per cent of GDP). On debt issues more generally, see E. Morris, 'Cuba's New Relationship with Foreign Capital: Economic Policy-Making since 1990,' *Journal of Latin American Studies* 40, no. 4 (2008): 769–92.
30. These were lifted in 2009 by President Obama (2009–16). They were not reversed by President Trump (2017–2020) although other measures were.
31. Before the dollar was outlawed in 2006, some of these payments were made in US dollars. Subsequently, they were all made in convertible pesos or in kind.
32. The range of average monthly salaries in 2009 in state-owned and mixed entities went from 418 in public services to 537 in mining. See Oficina Nacional de Estadísticas (ONE), *Anuario Estadístico de Cuba 2009* (Havana: ONE, 2010), table 7.4.
33. See M. Espina Prieto, 'Social Effects of Economic Adjustment: Equality, Inequality and Trends toward Greater Complexity in Cuban Society,' in *The Cuban Economy at the Start of the Twenty-first Century*, ed. J.I. Domínguez, V.O.E. Pérez, and L. Barberia (Cambridge, MA: Harvard University, David Rockefeller Center for Latin American Studies, 2004).
34. This proportion is difficult to measure accurately, but it had probably dropped to one-third for the average household soon after 2000. For details of the ration book in different years, which excludes subsidised services, see V. Togores and A. García, 'Consumption, Markets and Monetary Duality,' in *The Cuban Economy at the Start of the Twenty-first Century*, ed. J.I. Domínguez, V.O.E. Pérez, and L. Barberia (Cambridge, MA: David Rockefeller Center for Latin American Studies, Harvard University, 2004), 269.
35. This is based on non-fulfilment of basic needs rather than the proportion falling below the poverty line. See Prieto, 'Social Effects of Economic Adjustment.'
36. It is often forgotten that university enrolment plummeted in the 1990s during the Special Period and the number of 'inactive' increased sharply,

so that a whole cohort of the labour force was under-skilled in relation to their older and younger peers. See G.P.M. Monreal, *Development Prospects in Cuba: An Agenda in the Making* (London: Institute of Latin American Studies, 2002).

37. This was the estimate of Raúl Castro shortly after he became president in 2008 and explains the decision in August 2010 to shift 500,000 workers (ten per cent of the labour force) out of state employment.

Chapter 2
Dominican Republic

The economy of the Dominican Republic is today a Caribbean powerhouse, feared and admired in equal respects by its neighbours. An alliance between business and government has forged an economy with close ties not just to the region but to other parts of the world as well. Its Gross National Income (GNI) is the largest in the region after Cuba and its population now exceeds ten million.[1] While the distribution of income and wealth leaves much to be desired, the Dominican economy today exhibits a dynamism that is sadly lacking in many other countries of the region.

Two hundred years ago, it was a different story. Neglected by Spain, the imperial power, for 300 years after the initial conquest and then annexed by neighbouring Haiti in 1822, the eastern part of Hispaniola was a lightly populated territory with minimal trade. Indeed, so unsuccessful was the economy at the time of the Haitian annexation that there were very few slaves that needed to be freed by the new rulers. Even after the Dominicans gained their independence from Haiti in 1844, the new state remained an economic backwater with one of the lowest levels of exports per head (the key metric) in the Caribbean region.

In the two centuries between Haitian annexation and today, the economy of what would come in the 1870s to be called the Dominican Republic underwent an extraordinary transformation. Yet, this was far from being a linear process. As figure 2.1 shows, there was virtually no change in the level of exports per head until the last three decades of the nineteenth century when an export boom occurred for the first time driven by sugar, tobacco, cacao, and coffee. This was made possible by foreign investment and the capital provided by wealthy Cubans fleeing the First War of Independence (1868–78).

This long period, from around c.1820 to c.1900, is the subject of the first part of this chapter.

The trade boom at the end of the nineteenth century may have been a welcome change from the stagnation of earlier years, but it was marred by fiscal and monetary chaos and an unsustainable debt burden leading to major problems with the country's creditors. Concerned that this might be used as an excuse by European powers to intervene in the affairs of the small republic, the US imposed a *de facto* protectorate on the country in 1905 and occupied it militarily as well from 1916 to 1924. The monetary and fiscal chaos ended (US government officials were now in control and American priorities prevailed), but the level of exports per head stagnated throughout the long period of the US protectorate (it ended in 1940 after 35 years).

By this time Rafael Trujillo was firmly in charge, his long dictatorship – it began in 1930 and only ended with his assassination in 1961 – had the same stultifying effect on the dynamism of the economy as had the US protectorate. The upheavals associated with the fall of the dictator brought back US troops in 1965, at which point exports per head were virtually the same as in 1900 (see figure 2.1) – a pitiful performance by any standards. This long period of stagnation is the subject of the second part of the chapter.

Figure 2.1: Dominican Republic: exports per head at constant prices (1900=100), 1820–2016

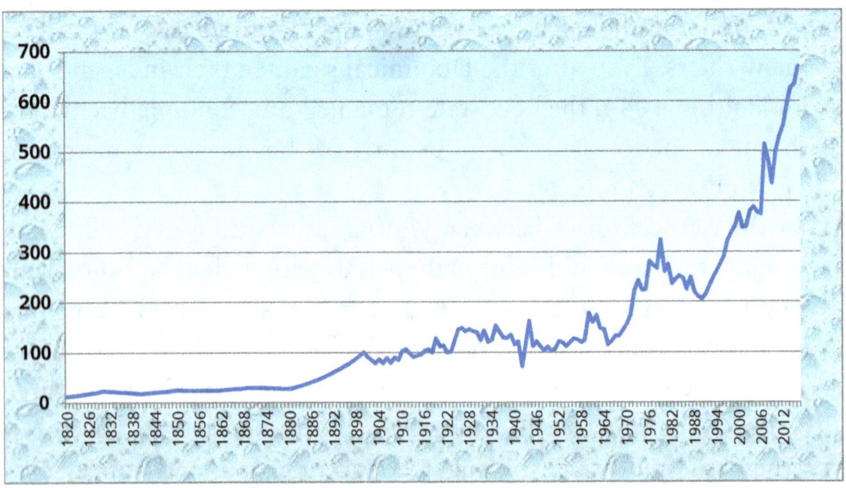

Sources: 1820–1960 from Statistical Appendix. 1960 onwards are from World Bank, World Development Indicators.

It is at this point that the Dominican economy moved up a gear. A beneficiary of foreign investment and the capital provided (again) by Cuban émigrés, the Dominican Republic diversified exports of goods, including assembly operations, and also became a significant exporter of services. It became one of the premier destinations in the region for tourism and took advantage of outsourced manufacturing activity by companies in developed countries, especially the US. Yet this boom, as in the decade before the US protectorate, was eventually undermined by financial chaos that coincided with the Latin American debt crisis. A prolonged economic stagnation followed in the 1980s with high levels of unemployment and outward migration. And the exchange rate, which had been pegged to the US dollar since 1947, collapsed after 1985. This is the subject of the third part of this chapter.

The final part is devoted to the sustained economic boom in the three decades after 1990. Although not without political drama and high levels of corruption, the boom this time has been based on much more solid macroeconomic foundations. Net outward migration has continued, but Dominicans have brought back skills and capital from outside (especially the US) to invest in the domestic economy while at the same time the country has attracted high levels of investment from the rest of the world. And four regional free trade agreements have been signed, making the Dominican Republic into a hub from which firms can export to nearly 50 countries.

While income and wealth inequality remain stubbornly high, the growth of the economy in the last few decades has finally given the Dominican political class the resources with which to address the social deficit if they should choose to do so. Yet, politics is not conducted on traditional left/right lines, and political elites have been able to adopt business-friendly policies without too much concern for distributional impacts. How much longer this can continue is uncertain, as the traditional safety valve – emigration to the US – no longer operates in the same way as before.

2.1. The Nineteenth-century Economy

Although Hispaniola had been the first Spanish colony in the Americas, Spain would soon lose interest after discovering precious metals on the mainland. When the indigenous population died out as a result of disease, maltreatment and war, the colony was relegated to a backwater. Indeed, Spain ceded the western part to France in 1697 and a century later in 1795 – in the middle of the Haitian revolutionary war – went so far as to transfer sovereignty to France over the eastern part of Hispaniola as well.

This meant that the territory over which Haitians claimed sovereignty in their declaration of independence in 1804 included the present-day Dominican Republic since they had defeated the imperial power (France). Haiti, however, was soon distracted by more pressing concerns and was unable to exercise permanent sovereignty over its neighbour (now ruled precariously by France). Spain was able to reclaim its former colony in 1809 following a revolt against the French by the Dominicans, a faction of whom then invited the former imperial power to return. Spain held a tenuous grip on the territory until 1821 when José Nuñez de Cáceres proclaimed the birth of the 'Estado Independiente de Haití Español bajo el amparo de la Gran Colombia'.[2]

The republic established by the Dominican patriots was a feeble affair with a small population – around 65,000 – that had fallen by a third in two decades as a result of emigration and war (Haiti had invaded in 1801 and 1805).[3] In 1820, on the eve of the declaration of independence, exports amounted to a mere US$275,000. The most important commodity exported was mahogany, which – in view of the length of time a tree takes to reach maturity – meant that the country was in effect living off its capital. Indeed, in 1820 alone, 2.58 million board feet were being exported (see table 2.1), most going to the United Kingdom (UK), and denuding the forests in the process.

Table 2.1: Exports from Santo Domingo in 1820 (Volume and Value in US$)

Mahogany	2,580,916 million board ft	$180,664
Tobacco	444,826 lb	$55,603
Hides	30,771 units	$24,617
Cacao	32,888 lb	$3,114
Cigars	156,000 units	$702

Source: Statistical Appendix.

The other exports (see table 2.1) were tobacco, hides, and a tiny amount of cacao and cigars. These five products, together with a few other commodities, then paid for imports, the duties on which were almost the only source of income for the Dominican government. As a result, fiscal revenue in 1820 was a mere $140,000, equivalent to roughly US$2 per head. This was insufficient to provide even the most basic public services and not nearly enough to fund a standing army capable of resisting an armed invasion.

That invasion was not long in coming. Haiti, reunited by President Jean-Pierre Boyer in 1820 after its division into a Kingdom in the north ruled by Henri Christophe and a Republic in the south under Alexandre Pétion, had a population almost eight times larger than its neighbour, a much bigger economy, and an army that was battle-hardened. Dominicans were unable to resist, and Haiti occupied the eastern part of the island in 1822, abolishing slavery and imposing its own fiscal system to the deep resentment of the Dominican elites.

Haitian rule lasted until 1844 when Santo Domingo, as it would now be called, declared its independence for the second time. The 22 years of Haitian rule brought some positive changes, including population recovery thanks to a high birth and low death rate. The value of exports also doubled, reaching $530,000 in 1840. This was partly due to a welcome increase in tobacco exports, but was mainly the result of a large and unsustainable rise in mahogany cutting. This reached 4.8 million board feet in 1840, after which the volume exported steadily declined.

Any hope that independence would mark the birth of a more dynamic and successful economy was thwarted by the fragile nature of the Dominican state. Haiti continued to claim its eastern neighbour, and Dominicans were understandably nervous about their ability to survive given the disparity in population and size of the two armies. Dominican leaders, therefore, sought a protector, approaching France, Spain, the UK, and the US in turn.

The first two decades after independence were, therefore, challenging for the economy. Tobacco exports from the Cibao region in the north did expand and helped to compensate for the sharp fall in mahogany exports. By 1860, the value of Dominican exports had surpassed $1 million, but 85 per cent now came from tobacco, making Santo Domingo dependent on the fortunes of one crop. And as the population had reached nearly 170,000 by 1860, it meant that exports per head were little changed from what they had been 40 years earlier.

All this would start to change in the last three decades of the nineteenth century. However, the prospects for the economy were still so uncertain when the US Civil War started in 1861 that the Dominican elite came to support annexation by Spain. This duly happened and the Spanish flag once again flew from the tops of government buildings. Yet Spanish rule this time around proved no more beneficial than before; armed revolt soon broke out, and the Spanish withdrew in 1865.

The Spanish retreat was not only due to Dominican resistance but also recognition that the end of the American Civil War would render their presence a source of conflict with the US. In recognition of growing US power, the Dominican elite now sought annexation as a US territory, and a treaty was duly signed by both governments in 1869. However, it failed to be ratified by the US Senate despite enormous pressure from President Ulysses Grant (1869–77).

The failure of annexation did not mean the end of US ambitions, and the US commercial and financial presence would steadily increase. Of more immediate importance, however, was the First War of Independence in Cuba (1868–78) and recognition of the Dominican Republic by all interested parties (including Haiti). From now on, the Dominican Republic would start to become of interest – almost for the first time – to foreign investors.[4]

The most significant of these were Cuban exiles, bringing with them skills and capital from the island's sugar industry. In 1870, shortly after the Cuban War of Independence started, sugar exports still only had a value of $90,000 (see table 2.2). In the next few years, however, numerous sugar mills would be constructed in the south of the country, and by 1880 the volume of exports had jumped ten-fold with a value of nearly $850,000. By the end of the century, despite the political turmoil at the time and the fall in sugar prices, the volume of exports had reached 118 million pounds with a value of $2.8 million, making the Dominican Republic a significant contributor to world trade in sugar. So dynamic was the sugar industry that workers needed to be imported from other parts of the Caribbean, including – for the first time – Haiti.

Sugar, largely in the hands of US firms by 1900, was not the only new entrant to the export list. Cacao and coffee expanded rapidly (see table 2.2) as, indeed, did tobacco. All three products benefited from investment in infrastructure, especially in railways, telegraphs, ports, and electrification. By 1890, the value of exports reached $3.25 million, pushing exports per head for the first time above the Haitian level, and by 1900 – now including bananas as well – they exceeded $7 million dollars. With a population estimated at 457,000 at the time, this gave the Dominican Republic a level of exports per head that compared favourably with many European colonies in the Caribbean.[5]

These developments, long overdue, should have put the Dominican Republic on a path towards sustainable growth. Unfortunately, they were accompanied by deterioration in public finances, exchange rate volatility and debt problems. The difficulties had begun immediately after independence in 1844, when political leaders had issued local currency (*peso nacional*) to supplement the hard currency (*peso fuerte*) at par with the US dollar in order to balance the budget. The local currency then fell rapidly in value.

Table 2.2: Dominican Republic: Exports in Volume and Value, 1870–1900

Year	Mahogany (board ft)	Tobacco (lb)	Sugar (lb)	Cacao (lb)	Coffee (lb)	
1870	1,219,000	12,557,988	2,237,292	38,520	59,544	
1880	891,043	6,061,575	21,719,900	312,030	874,107	
1890	754,885	14,151,564	61,020,000	1,729,280	275,616	
1900	444,700	38,500,000	118,720,000	13,118,600	3,938,000	
US$	**Mahogany**	**Tobacco**	**Sugar**	**Cacao**	**Coffee**	**Total (incl other)**
1870	66,669	1,289,705	89,939	2,874	8,932	1,500,000
1880	47,582	480,683	842,732	41,282	118,004	1,562,164
1890	37,065	1,075,519	1,732,968	119,839	44,099	3,255,855
1900	22,235	1,606,490	2,837,742	1,737,917	314,134	7,066,294

Source: Statistical Appendix.

Foreign lenders, therefore, imposed strict conditions for issuing credits. In particular, the Amsterdam-based Westendorp Co. insisted on control of the state's customs duties in return for a loan in 1888 to finance infrastructure development. Since customs duties were virtually the government's only source of funds, this left public finance in the hands of a foreign company. And when Westendorp went bankrupt in 1892, the contract was purchased by the San Domingo Improvement Company, a private US firm.

The Dominican Republic had now moved firmly into the US orbit. Although annexation had been blocked, the US had replaced Great Britain as the main source of exports and imports (over 50 per cent in both cases by 1900) and had secured a bilateral trade treaty with the Dominican Republic in 1892 that reduced tariffs on US imports leading to a big reduction in customs duties.[6] President Ulises ('Lilís') Heureaux, the strongman of Dominican politics, was soon forced to issue unsecured currency (known as *papeletas de Lilís*) that damaged commerce and in 1899 he was overthrown.[7] The following year, the US dollar was adopted as the official currency, placing the Dominican Republic ever more firmly under US tutelage.

2.2. The US Protectorate and the Trujillo Era

As the main bondholders for the Dominican Republic, there was always the danger that the European powers might respond to financial turbulence by intervention. This had happened to Venezuela in 1902, when an Anglo-German-Italian fleet blockaded the main port. President Theodore Roosevelt (1901–09) had even sent the US navy to prevent German troops landing in 1903. The following year in his State of the Union address he, therefore, enunciated his own interpretation of the Monroe Doctrine:[8]

> If a nation shows that it knows how to act with reasonable efficiency and decency in social and political matters, if it keeps order and pays its obligations, it need fear no interference from the United States. Chronic wrongdoing, or an impotence which results in a general loosening of the ties of civilized society, may in America, as elsewhere, ultimately require intervention by some civilized nation, and in the Western Hemisphere the adherence of the United States to the Monroe Doctrine

> may force the United States, however reluctantly, in flagrant cases of such wrongdoing or impotence, to the exercise of an international police power.

The Roosevelt Corollary, as it would come to be known, had far-reaching implications for the US Empire in the Caribbean. Whereas the Monroe Doctrine had warned European powers against attempts at (re)colonisation in the Americas, the Roosevelt Corollary spelt out the likely response to those independent states that threatened US interests in any way. In particular, countries that ran into financial difficulties could expect special attention in order to obviate the need for European intervention.

The first country to feel the full force of the Roosevelt Corollary was the Dominican Republic. A US customs receivership was established in 1905 without waiting for congressional approval, giving American officials control over the duties that accounted for 99 per cent of government revenue.[9] The first call on the receipts was prompt payment of debt servicing costs, ensuring that no foreign power had any reason to intervene. The agreement even allowed up to five per cent of the receipts to be spent to cover the costs of the US receivership itself, including the housing needs of officials. The balance of income was then handed to the Dominican government.

The First World War brought an even greater involvement by the US administration in the affairs of the Dominican Republic. Although the US was at first neutral, it could not rule out the possibility of a German invasion of the Dominican Republic. A Dominican 'revolution' in May 1916 was, therefore, used as the excuse for US military occupation and the Dominican Republic now became *de facto* a US colony. The Dominican presidency was replaced with a military government led by a US naval officer.

By 1922, resistance had been crushed and President Warren Harding (1921–25), who opposed the occupation before becoming president, was ready to look for an exit. In what would become a familiar pattern, a supposedly non-partisan National Guard was established and Dominicans were sent for training. In 1924, the occupation ended and a Dominican assumed the presidency, but not before a second American-Dominican Convention had been ratified. This renewed the customs receivership for a further 18 years.[10] Thus, the Dominican Republic remained firmly inside the US Empire – this time as a protectorate rather than a *de facto* colony.

The new imperial power's priority throughout the long years of the US protectorate was debt repayment. Monetary stability was assured through the use of the US dollar in all financial transactions, while control of the customs houses gave US officials ownership of the main source of public revenue – most of which was used to repay debt. The Dominican government was forced to introduce new taxes, not controlled by US officials, to survive. Yet, as figure 2.2 makes clear, this was no easy task. Public revenue per head at constant prices did rise at first, following the chaotic years before the imposition of the customs receivership, but did not rise again until after the US protectorate had ended. This put a big strain on what could be accomplished by the weak Dominican government.

It was a similar story with exports. Although the absolute value expanded, the growth of population (it rose three-fold during the protectorate to reach 1.75 million at the end) meant that performance on a *per capita* basis was very disappointing (see table 2.3). Sugar, boosted by new investments, continued to expand until the 1930s, when the US government imposed quotas, and coffee exports benefited from new markets in Europe.

Figure 2.2: Dominican Republic: Revenue per head (1930 US$), 1900–60

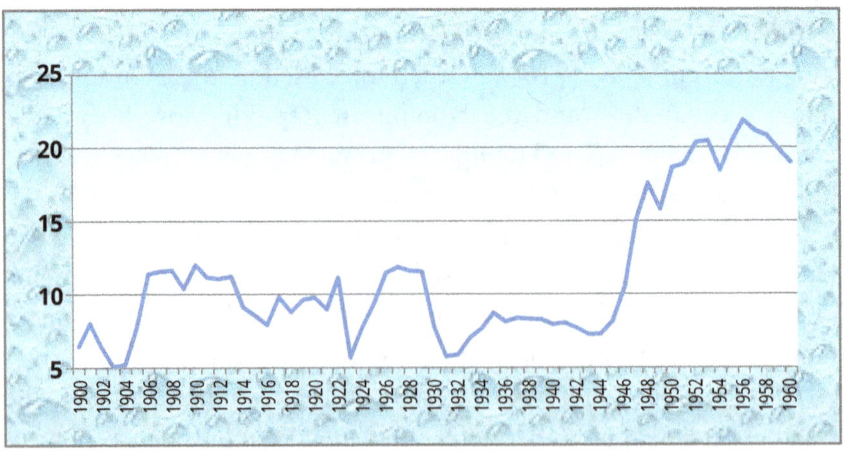

Source: Statistical Appendix.

Table 2.3: Dominican Republic: Volume of Exports per Head, 1905–39

Year	Tobacco (lb)	Sugar (lb)	Cacao (lb)	Coffee (lb)	Bananas (bunches)
1905	20.3	187.1	50.9	3.8	1.7
1910	32.9	302.4	54.0	6.7	1.3
1920	40.4	390.5	57.5	1.5	0.0
1930	22.2	592.6	35.5	8.3	0.1
1939	11.4	533.4	36.6	18.4	0.2

Source: Statistical Appendix.

However, tobacco, cacao, and bananas exports all declined in importance during the years of American tutelage on a *per capita* basis. And the US became a much less important destination for Dominican exports after 1920, since the country did not enjoy the trade preferences given to other US territories in the Caribbean.[11]

Long before the end of the US protectorate, Rafael Trujillo had engineered his way to the top of Dominican politics. Elected for the first time to the presidency in 1930, he immediately had to confront the impact of the Great Depression on the Dominican economy. With falling commodity prices, rising global protectionism and shrinking world demand, the impact of the slump was similar to what was happening elsewhere in the Americas. However, it was made worse for the Dominican Republic by the operations of the US protectorate.

While most countries in Latin America devalued their local currency and defaulted on their external debt, neither option was open to the Dominican Republic. The US customs receivership ensured that debt servicing remained the highest priority even as customs duties shrank, while there was no local currency to devalue. Adjustment to shrinking world demand was therefore brutal (see table 2.4) with the fall in exports and imports between 1927 and 1933 averaging 70 per cent.

This decline was almost entirely due to the drop in prices of the main exports with the unit value also falling by 70 per cent (see table 2.4). The volume of exports remained similar, despite the reduced profitability of production, helped by migrants willing to work for very low wages.

Meanwhile, the sharp contraction in imports created opportunities for import substitution. Trujillo himself was quick to take advantage of this, acquiring an enormous portfolio of companies in sectors where competition could be suppressed.

Table 2.4: Dominican Republic: Exports and Imports (US$), 1927–33

	Current Prices		Domestic Exports	Unit Value of Exports (1930=100)	Merchandise Imports
	Tobacco	Sugar			
1927	2,582,486	16,668,385	31,178,769	183.1	27,784,014
1928	1,274,416	16,911,925	28,754,524	159.1	26,787,940
1929	1,381,482	12,258,831	23,736,497	130.6	22,729,444
1930	1,032,005	9,910,289	18,551,841	100.0	15,229,219
1931	403,676	7,583,908	13,067,162	77.0	10,151,762
1932	224,903	6,859,474	11,164,271	55.6	7,794,343
1933	361,835	4,284,237	9,400,000	53.8	9,322,688
Fall (%)	85.99	74.30	69.85	70.62	66.45

Source: Statistical Appendix.

Trujillo consolidated his political and economic power after the Great Depression, although he risked the ire of his American masters following the infamous massacre of Haitian migrants in 1937.[12] His unswerving loyalty to the US government, however, ensured his survival and he steered the Dominican Republic through the Second World War without further mishap despite the fall in foreign trade. By this time, the US protectorate had ended, and he was therefore able to establish a central bank in 1947 together with the reintroduction of the Dominican peso (fixed at par to the US dollar). The Dominican Republic then joined the International Monetary Fund (IMF) in 1948.

The post-war economy of the Dominican Republic under Trujillo exhibited many of the same features found in other Latin American countries: a large agricultural sector made up of many small farms producing for the home market and a smaller number of large farms focused on exports; a manufacturing sector competing with imports; and a rapidly growing population increasingly unable to find work in the countryside where most of them lived.

During the post-war Trujillo era, however, there were certain distinctive characteristics to the economy. The number of farms less than five acres in size more than doubled between 1950 and 1960, making it increasingly difficult to generate an income that could support a family. The manufacturing sector was dominated by Trujillo family interests with an emphasis on labour-saving technology, while the dictator also invested heavily in the capital-intensive sugar industry. As a result, labour conditions deteriorated dramatically and net migration – positive, if small, before 1950 – turned sharply negative. From this time onwards, large numbers of Dominicans would leave their country in an effort to find work abroad.

2.3. Structural Change and Financial Crisis

The Trujillo era did not end immediately with the dictator's assassination in May 1961. His legacy was too omnipresent to be dismantled quickly, and the politics of the Dominican Republic entered a turbulent period that lasted several years. Nor did the Trujillo era truly end with the US invasion in 1965, since the winner of the presidential election the following year was none other than Joaquín Balaguer – Trujillo's loyal supporter who was serving as the puppet president at the time of the dictator's death.

Balaguer, however, was at least elected freely (if not fairly), and the Dominican Republic now embarked on a period of rapid economic growth and structural change. The year of the US invasion turned out to be the low point of the economic cycle with GDP per head falling by 15 per cent in one year, making the Dominican Republic one of the poorest countries in the Caribbean region (only Haiti had lower *per capita* income). In the next 15 years, however, growth would be rapid, and GDP per head had reached a level that placed the country well above the poorest Caribbean countries by 1980 and above many mainland Latin American countries as well.

This was all the more remarkable given the high rate of growth of population. Even in the nineteenth century, the Dominican Republic had recorded exceptional birth rates with the Crude Birth Rate (CBR) close to 40 in those few years for which data are available.[13] By 1960, however, the CBR had reached 50, placing it among the highest in the world. With a Crude Death Rate (CDR) around 15, this meant the natural growth of the population at the start of the 1960s was 3.5 per cent. This put enormous pressure on the job market, which led to high levels of net outward migration (see figure 2.3) while at the same time leading to a big increase in remittances.

Figure 2.3: Dominican Republic: Net Migration, 1961–90

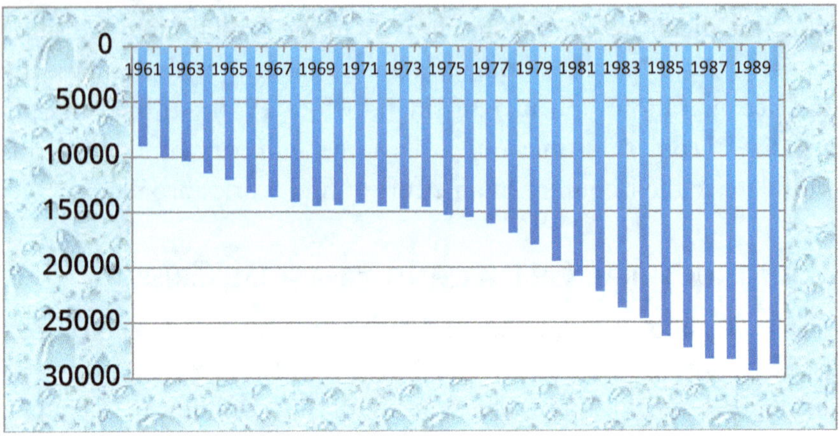

Source: Statistical Appendix.

By the end of the Trujillo era, the Dominican economy was in desperate need of structural change. The biggest obstacle, of course, was the dominant role played by the sugar sector. Trujillo had at first left the industry largely in the hands of US companies, but from the 1940s onwards he himself acquired substantial interests amounting to almost two-thirds of invested capital. These investments were then expropriated by the state after Trujillo's fall, leaving the Dominican government in control of most of the main source of foreign exchange.

Nationalisation of Trujillo's sugar interests also coincided with the reallocation of Cuba's US sugar quota to other Caribbean countries after the rise of Fidel Castro to power. The Dominican Republic, strongly favoured by US administrations after the fall of Trujillo, was the largest beneficiary and soon received nearly 20 per cent of the US quota. And when the world price of sugar quadrupled in the first half of the 1970s, sugar became an even greater asset to the Dominican Republic.

Despite this, structural change did take place and accelerated as the favourable conditions for sugar evaporated from the mid-1970s onwards. Sugar prices soon fell back towards their previous levels, and the US quota was cut in response to increased US production of beet sugar and the replacement of cane and beet sugar by cheaper alternatives in food manufacturing – especially high-fructose corn syrup.[14] The largest private sector companies in the Dominican Republic now looked to sell their interests and the state would eventually privatise its own holdings.

Sugar did not, of course, disappear, and the Dominican Republic remained an exporter of global importance. By the end of the 1980s, however, its once dominant position in the Dominican economy was coming to an end. The reasons for this were numerous and included diversifying exports of goods, developing free trade zones, and increasing the export of services. In addition, the sectors geared to the domestic economy became much more important, especially manufacturing, finance, and real estate.[15]

Throughout the Trujillo era, exports had been dominated by commodities, and these were represented mainly by sugar and its derivatives such as molasses. By the end of the 1950s, however, bananas were once again emerging as an important source of foreign exchange, while chocolate, maize, and meat were becoming more significant commodity exports. Mining, in the form of bauxite, would appear on the list for the first time in 1959 and would become a major export – along with gold, silver, and gypsum – in the next few years. As a result of these developments, the sugar share of commodity exports had fallen to around 30 per cent by the end of the 1980s (it had been close to 60 per cent at the end of the Trujillo era).

Assembly exports, previously unknown, were given a boost by the passage of an industrial incentives law in 1963. Foreign companies, especially from the US, took advantage of the free zones established, at the end of the 1960s, by the government. The contribution of the assembly industry to export diversification was modest initially, but by 1987 the value of free zone exports had exceeded the value of traditional exports for the first time[16] – helped by the passage in the US Congress of the Caribbean Basin Initiative (CBI), giving tariff preferences to companies based in eligible countries.[17] The free zones – being very labour-intensive – were also becoming a major source of employment, although the conditions of work, the absence of trade unions and the low wage rates paid attracted a great deal of negative publicity.[18]

Trujillo had built up a large holding of manufacturing companies, which passed to the state after his death. This gave the Dominican government a strong interest in policies to promote import substituting industrialisation (ISI) since these companies were not expected to be able to export their products. Private sector companies were also quick to take advantage of policies to promote ISI, and manufacturing increased in importance. These developments were then further encouraged by a financial sector that took advantage of the fixed exchange rate and low interest rates to expand rapidly.

The virtuous circle starting with structural change and leading to rapid GDP growth had one fatal flaw that made it eventually unsustainable: the fixed nominal exchange rate of one peso per US dollar. Annual inflation, fuelled by rapid monetary expansion, accelerated in the 1970s, leading to a marked appreciation of the real effective exchange rate as price increases exceeded those in the main trading partners – especially the US. This had the effect of reducing the competitiveness of exports (disguised at first by the rise in world sugar prices) and making imports cheaper. The deficit in the current account of the balance of payments, therefore, jumped from $100 million in 1970 to over $700 million in 1980.

A parallel (legal) market was introduced in 1972 in which the rate steadily diverged from the official rate, but the supply of foreign exchange (mainly from tourism and remittances) was insufficient for the demand. Foreign borrowing soared and the dollar-denominated debt jumped five-fold a few years after 1975. The Dominican Republic was now on the brink of a major financial crisis and was forced into a three-year Standby Agreement with the IMF in 1983.

The IMF targeted price controls and the fixed exchange rate. The government, despite massive social protests, was forced to comply. By 1985, it had accepted the need for the official exchange rate to float. Its decline was dramatic and it had reached 6.34 pesos per US dollar by the end of the decade. The Dominican economy, based on the US dollar from 1900 to 1947 and with a peso at par with the US dollar from then until 1985, was now in uncharted territory.

The first casualty of the crisis was the working population. The rate of unemployment, already 21 per cent in 1981, jumped to 27 per cent by 1985,[19] and the rate of youth unemployment was much higher. Living standards for those still in work fell sharply as wages could not keep up with an inflation rate that averaged 50 per cent a year in the first few years after the exchange rate floated.[20] Not surprisingly, net outward migration (see figure 2.3) accelerated.

The financial crisis meant that the Dominican Republic suffered a lost decade – in common with many other countries in Latin America and the Caribbean. GDP per head at constant prices had grown rapidly after 1965 and had doubled by the early 1980s. This was a better performance than almost any other independent country in the Americas and was a welcome contrast with what had happened during the US protectorate and the Trujillo era. However, GDP per head peaked in 1983 and would not return to this level for a decade. It was a salutary reminder of the need for more sustainable macroeconomic policies even if this meant abandoning the exchange rate anchor on which the Dominican economy had relied for so many years.

2.4. Growth without Equity

The constraints on the Dominican economy in the 1980s were so great that something had to give and in mid-1989 the government announced it could no longer service its external debt. Arrears had built up and even money owed to the IMF had not been paid on time. By April 1991, a new stand-by arrangement had been reached with the Fund and in November of that year the main creditors (all in the so-called Paris Club) agreed to reschedule the debt. After many years of precipitate decline, the exchange rate – and with it inflation – began to stabilise.

It would take a further two years to reach a final agreement with the creditors, but by then the Dominican economy was on its way to a period of rapid growth. Indeed, 1991 would turn out to be the low point in the economic cycle, since the Dominican Republic has subsequently grown faster than almost all countries – large and small – in the Americas. From 1991 to 2016, GDP per head at constant prices rose from $2,555 to $6,909 (see figure 2.4), an average annual increase of 6.85 per cent. This was unprecedented in the history of the country and almost without precedent in Latin America and the Caribbean (LAC). The Dominican Republic was still far from being the richest country in LAC, but it was now firmly established in the middle in both regions to which it belongs.

Figure 2.4: Dominican Republic: GDP per head (2010 US$), 1991–2016

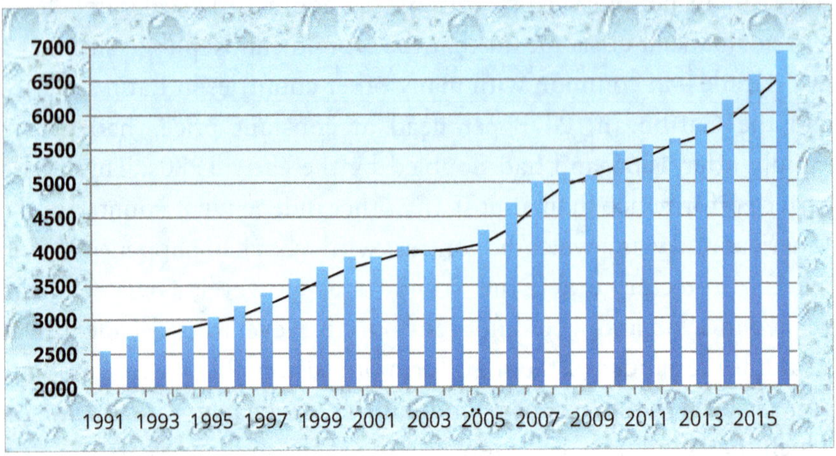

Source: World Bank, World Development Indicators.

This period of rapid growth even included two brief recessions. The first, between 2002 and 2004, was entirely 'home-grown' and was caused by financial institutions lending far in excess of what was prudent. The second, between 2008 and 2010, was entirely 'foreign-grown' since it was caused by the irresponsible lending of financial institutions in developed countries, especially the US. The Dominican economy, however, coped with both recessions relatively well and GDP per head was only mildly affected (see figure 2.4).

There were many reasons the fortunes of the Dominican economy changed, but one was the demographic transition that had begun long before the 1990s. The birth rate had been steadily falling since its peak in 1960 when the CBR reached just over 50. By 1990, it had fallen to 30 and by 2015 it was down to 20. Meanwhile the CDR had gone from 16 to six over the same period. This meant the natural rate of growth of the population was steadily dropping, leading to a fall in the ratio of dependents to those of working age. Dominican demographics were now in a 'sweet' spot that would not last forever, but which gave an opportunity to strengthen public finances, improve labour productivity, and accelerate growth.[21]

Another key contributor has been the role of foreign trade. A founder member of the World Trade Organisation, the Dominican Republic became increasingly 'open' after 1990. Free trade agreements were signed with CARICOM in 1998, with Central America the same year, and with the EU in 2008 as part of CARIFORUM.[22] However, the big prize was a free trade agreement with the US – by far the largest trade partner. This was signed in 2004 after the Dominican Republic was allowed to join the Central America Free Trade Agreement to create CAFTA-DR (it came into force in 2007). The Dominican Republic now had agreements in place with nearly 50 countries, which in combination represented the vast majority of the destination for its exports.

The free trade agreements helped to boost exports of domestic goods. These rose from $600 million in 1993 to nearly $4.5 billion 25 years later. Exports of goods from the free zones also benefited reaching nearly $5.5 billion in 2016, but the rate of growth slowed down sharply after the start of the new millennium. This was partly due to the free trade agreements, since location inside the free zones was now less important, but was mainly due to the shift of assembly production to other countries with lower wage rates and better infrastructure.[23]

The most spectacular export performance was shown by services. These rose from $1.5 billion in 1993 to $8.3 billion in 2016, by which time they accounted for 45 per cent of total exports. Service exports were dominated by tourism with the number of overnight visitors exceeding six million in 2016 and cruise ship passengers reaching nearly one million (other commercial service exports were also important and reached $1.5 billion in 2016). The Dominican Republic had now become the top tourist destination in the Caribbean and was receiving tourists from all over the world.

Despite this rapid growth, the Dominican Republic still found itself with a large gap in the balance of goods and services. This has been filled with remittances from Dominicans living outside the country. By 2011, there were estimated to be 1.5 million people of Dominican origin in the US alone with nearly 60 per cent born in the Dominican Republic itself and nearly two-thirds of these arriving in the US after 1990.[24]

Remittances from Dominicans abroad reached US$1 billion in 1997. They surpassed US$2 billion six years later and US$3 billion by 2007. By 2011, they reached US$4 billion and in 2016 they exceeded US$5 billion dollars. Almost no other country in the world receives such a high share of remittances and none in the Americas. Remittances now represent around seven per cent of GDP, a flow of foreign exchange that has helped to stabilise the exchange rate and reduce the pressure on the balance of payments from which so many Caribbean countries suffer.

However welcome this may be to Dominican governments, it is a terrible indictment of an economic model that until recently prioritised growth over equity. It is not that Dominican growth failed to create jobs, since the numbers employed have grown – albeit at a lower rate than the economy as a whole – and the unemployment rate has fallen.[25] The quality of jobs, however, has been uneven with half of employment still described as 'informal'. And many of those finding work have little education, making it difficult to secure jobs that provide a living wage.

Real wage rates also fell despite increases in labour productivity. A study by the International Labour Organization (ILO), for example, found that real wages in 2010 were 20 per cent below their level in 2000 despite a nearly 40 per cent increase in labour productivity.[26] Minimum wage rates, set by a tripartite commission, also failed to keep up with inflation in many years. As a result, the share of GDP going to wages and salaries dropped during the years of the most recent boom to around 30 per cent. Coincidentally, this was also the share of the population that was still living in poverty in 2015 despite the long period of rapid economic growth.[27]

Dominican governments have recognised the unsatisfactory nature of the growth model and have made important changes to the social security, health, and education systems. As a result, there has been a modest reduction in inequality in recent years. The Gini coefficient, a well-known measure of inequality, fell from 0.5 in 2000 to 0.45 15 years later, while the share of income going to the bottom ten per cent rose from 1.3 to 1.9 per cent over the same period. Given the spectacular growth of the economy over the same years, however, this was a modest change.

Faced with a labour market that was not working as it should, many Dominicans simply emigrated. The Dominican Republic, however, has experienced high levels of immigration as well with the migrants

– notably from Haiti – taking mainly low-paid and unskilled jobs. As resentment increased against the migrants, unfairly blamed for poor labour market conditions, the Dominican government responded by targeting anyone of Haitian origin without documentation (including those born in the Dominican Republic). This act of discrimination put the Dominican government on a collision course with its CARICOM neighbours, not just Haiti, but the constitutional reforms that had made it possible remained in place.

The Dominican economy was transformed during the period of rapid growth that started in the 1990s, but many Dominicans worried about the sustainability of the model. It was not just a concern about the unequal distribution of the benefits from growth but also a concern with the loss of competitiveness. In the space of 30 years, the official exchange rate had fallen from parity with the dollar to nearly 50 to the dollar. And yet the country was losing its comparative advantage in many areas with textile firms in particular moving out of the free zones to other destinations.

Despite these legitimate concerns, the Dominican economy is now much more diversified and, therefore, capable of adjusting to new realities. Politics demands greater attention to equity, especially as the safety valve of emigration to the US appears now to be closing. Globalisation, on the other hand, from which the Dominican Republic has been largely a beneficiary, suggests a need for higher investment in human capital. Both forces may, therefore, combine to promote greater social justice in the Dominican Republic. And all participants in this journey can take some pride in the distance travelled by the Dominican economy since the first declaration of independence two centuries ago.

NOTES

1. Gross Domestic Product (GDP) is higher in Puerto Rico. GNI, however, is smaller as a large share of income in Puerto Rico accrues to non-residents. See chapter 3.
2. As the name implied, the new state hoped to come under the protection of Gran Colombia, the state created by Simón Bolívar out of what would become Colombia, Ecuador, and Venezuela, although the Dominican patriots had not consulted him. See A.M. Tejada, 'Estado, política y gobierno, 1795–2008,' in *Historia de la República Dominicana*, ed. F.

Moya Pons (Madrid: Consejo Superior de Investigaciones Científicas, 2010), 396–405 and R. Marte, *Estadísticas y documentos históricos sobre Santo Domingo, 1805–1890* (Santo Domingo, República Dominicana: Museo Nacional de Historia y Geografía, 1984), 95–99.

3. Both Haitian invasions had been followed by a withdrawal, but the second one led to much bloodshed among the Dominicans as the Haitian troops retreated.
4. Some of these, however, were scoundrels who succeeded in burdening the new republic with external debts that were largely fraudulent but impossible to repudiate. See Tejada, 'Estado, política y gobierno, 1795–2008,' 421–44.
5. The population figures for the Dominican Republic in the nineteenth century are discussed in detail in V. Bulmer-Thomas, *The Economic History of the Caribbean since the Napoleonic Wars* (Cambridge: Cambridge University Press, 2012), 471. See also F. Moya Pons, 'Evolución de la población dominicana,' in *Historia de la República Dominicana*, ed. F. Moya Pons (Madrid: Consejo Superior de Investigaciones Científicas, 2010), 29–54.
6. The Dominican government felt it had no choice in the matter, as the alternative was a rise in US import duties on the Republic's main exports.
7. See J.J. Domínguez, *La dictadura de Heureaux* (Santo Domingo, Dominican Republic: Editora Universitaria, UASD, 1986), 193–206.
8. See Bulmer-Thomas, *The Economic History of the Caribbean since the Napoleonic Wars*, 106.
9. US Congressional approval was finally given in 1907.
10. The Convention should have terminated in 1942, but it was ended two years earlier as the Dominican government was able to persuade the US administration that it was now able to meet all its debt service obligations.
11. The share of exports going to the US reached 87 per cent in 1920. By the end of the protectorate, it had fallen to one-quarter. See Statistical Appendix.
12. See B. Vega, 'La Era de Trujillo, 1930–61,' in *Historia de la República Dominicana*, ed. F. Moya Pons (Madrid: Consejo Superior de Investigaciones Científicas, 2010), 453–55.
13. See Statistical Appendix.
14. From 1978-81, the US quota for the Dominican Republic was 780,000 tons annually. It was cut to 535,000 tons in 1982–83 and 123,000 tons by 1988. See A. Valdés and B. Schaeffer, *Surveillance of Agricultural Prices and Trade: A Handbook for the Dominican Republic* (Washington, DC: World Bank, 1995), 59.

15. See W. Lozano, *Los Trabajadores del Capitalismo Exportador* (Santo Domingo, Dominican Republic: Banco Central de la República Dominicana, 2001), 111–28.
16. See Centro Dominicano de Promoción de Exportaciones, *Boletín Estadístico* 4, (1988): 6.
17. The CBI, formally known as the Caribbean Basin Economic Recovery Act (CBERA), entered into force in 1984.
18. See J. Ferguson, *The Dominican Republic: Beyond the Lighthouse* (London: Latin American Bureau, 1992), 55–74.
19. See C.D. Deere et al., *In the Shadows of the Sun: Caribbean Development Alternatives and US Policy* (Boulder, CO: Westview Press, 1990), 43.
20. The Dominican Republic has no official series on real wages. However, inflation far exceeded increases in the nominal minimum wage rate during the 1980s.
21. This did not bring an end to annual net outward migration, which remained roughly constant at 30,000 throughout the boom years.
22. CARIFORUM consists of CARICOM, the Dominican Republic, and Cuba. It was created in order to facilitate the entry of non-CARICOM countries into the EU Free Trade Agreement (FTA). Cuba, however, remained outside the FTA as finally agreed.
23. The rapid growth of the Dominican economy since 1991 has put particular pressure on electricity supply with frequent blackouts.
24. See Pew Research Center, *Hispanics of Dominican Origin in the United States, 2011* (Chicago, IL: Pew Research Center, 2013).
25. There are many ways in which the unemployment rate has been calculated for the Dominican Republic, but the rate has fallen since 2000 regardless of which rate is used. See International Labour Organization (ILO), *Growth, Employment and Social Cohesion in the Dominican Republic* (Geneva: ILO, 2013), 5–11.
26. Ibid., 12.
27. See World Bank. 'World Development Indicators (WDI),' *World Bank*, n.d. http://data.worldbank.org.

Chapter 3
PUERTO RICO

Puerto Rico, like Cuba, remained loyal to Spain when the rest of Spanish America became independent. Yet, its loyalty did not produce the same results. Very much the junior partner to Cuba, Puerto Rico remained in the shadow of the larger island throughout the nineteenth century. Although exports per head did rise at first after 1820 (see figure 3.1), they had reached a plateau by the middle of the century. Population, however, kept rising and increased six-fold to nearly a million by the end of the century. Much of this was due to net migration, as the island still offered better prospects than many parts of Europe.

What export growth there was in the second half of the nineteenth century came mainly from the expansion of coffee rather than the traditional exports of sugar and tobacco. Indeed, so modest was sugar's progress after 1850 that US domestic interests – unlike in the case of Cuba – had no formal objection to Puerto Rico's colonisation, since they did not think the island's sugar production would represent much of a threat. The Treaty of Paris in 1898, therefore, led to the transfer of sovereignty over Puerto Rico from Spain to the US.

The end of Spanish rule was not as disruptive in Puerto Rico as in Cuba. Yet, the economy did shrink and the island began life as a US colony with exports per head down to the level some 70 years before. Unrestricted access to the American market, however, transformed the island's prospects and exports boomed as never before. US investments in sugar were the main driver of this change.

It could not, and did not, continue (see figure 3.1). Not for the last time, the American colony found itself at the mercy of US trade and fiscal policy. US tariffs on imports from Puerto Rico remained zero, but the Roosevelt administration imposed sugar quotas in

1934 to protect domestic interests. The sugar boom ended and the mass emigration of Puerto Ricans – US citizens since 1917 – began. Even the new opportunities created by the Second World War, when rum exports soared, could not change the fragile state of the island's economy.

Figure 3.1: Puerto Rico: Exports per head at constant prices (1900=100), Log scale, 1820–2016

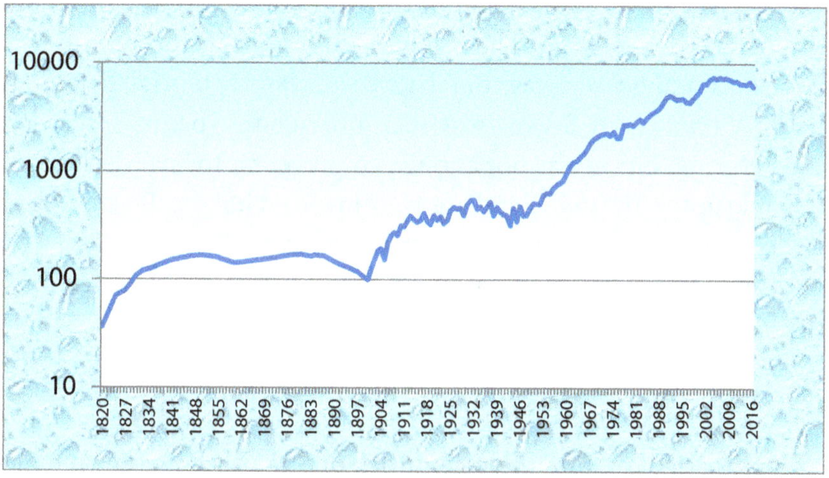

Sources: 1820–2008 from Statistical Appendix. 2008 onwards are from World Bank, World Development Indicators and UNNA.

The war spurred an unprecedented level of intervention in the economy by the colonial administrators. This paved the way after hostilities ended for Operation Bootstrap, when fiscal changes on the island provided US investors with huge incentives. The boom in manufacturing exports that followed had almost no parallel in the economic history of colonial countries, and the sector's share of Gross National Product (GDP) rose to nearly 50 per cent.

Operation Bootstrap was regarded with envy in the Caribbean as it brought in much needed foreign investment. And when US tax law was changed in 1976 to make it easier for US companies to repatriate their insular profits without paying tax, the effect on foreign investment was magnified. A further modification in 1986 to US tax law then allowed Puerto Rican banks to provide cheap finance for projects in most of the Caribbean with the intention of placing Puerto Rico at the centre of a network of supply chains that would eventually export products to the US market. Colonialism, geopolitics, and development were all pushing in the same direction, while exports per head soared (see figure 3.1).

As with the sugar boom in the first decades of the twentieth century, the growth of manufacturing was susceptible to a change in US policy. As their cost became increasingly difficult to justify, the fiscal incentives were phased out starting in the mid-'90s. The impact was savage with only a handful of industrial sectors maintaining a substantial presence. The island's government turned to debt to protect public services, but had to declare a partial default in 2015. A reluctant US Congress then provided a roadmap for debt restructuring, but it was not enough to prevent a formal declaration of bankruptcy by the island's government. With the Puerto Rican model of development now in tatters, the islanders' problems were made even worse by the devastation wrought by Hurricane María in 2017.

3.1. The Spanish Colony

Puerto Rico, despite three centuries of Spanish imperial rule and a magnificent harbour at San Juan, was a colonial backwater when Napoleon invaded the Iberian Peninsula in 1808. Its population, estimated at 163,000 in 1810, was largely dedicated to subsistence farming.[1] The standard of living was, therefore, modest, although rural conditions were not especially unhealthy, and the natural rate of growth of the population was positive.[2]

As the war ended, the restored Spanish crown introduced a number of measures to increase the attraction of its Caribbean colonies. These included in 1815 the *Real Cédula de Gracias*, under which migrants to Puerto Rico from any country would receive land for free subject to a number of conditions, the most important of which was the adoption of Catholicism. The result was a big increase in net migration inwards not just from Spain (including the Balearic and Canary Islands) but also from other parts of Europe. By 1820, the population had jumped to 272,000, and soon the turmoil in the rest of Spanish America persuaded a number of those loyal to Spain to come to the island rather than return home.

The slave population in 1820, estimated at 21,700, was less than ten per cent of the total – one of the lowest ratios in the Caribbean outside of Hispaniola. This was not duc to high levels of manumission but was much more a reflection of the lack of profitable opportunities in the export sector. Held back by the restrictions on trade imposed by Spain under its mercantilist system, the value of exports in 1820 – a mere US$3.5 per person – was still less than $1 million dollars. Revenue per head in the same year was only US$2.1, insufficient to provide more than the most basic government and far too little to attract the best colonial administrators.

The commercial freedoms given by Spain to Cuba in a series of steps also applied to Puerto Rico. Soon after the Napoleonic Wars, therefore, the island was free to export to, and import from, countries other than Spain. Trade was not truly free, since there was still a large tariff preference in favour of goods carried in Spanish ships to and from the Spanish market. However, freedom to trade with other countries was a substantial reform and Puerto Rico took full advantage. By the middle of the nineteenth century, the share of exports going to Spain was barely two per cent and the share of imports was only five per cent.[3]

The big winner resulting from freedom to trade was the US, which was taking half of all Puerto Rican exports by 1850. The US had, therefore, become by far the biggest export market and much more important than the UK, although the latter still provided the largest share of imports until the supply of manufactured goods accelerated from the US after the Civil War (1861–65). Only one Puerto Rican export could account for such a dramatic change and that was sugar. Thus, as in Cuba, the insatiable demand for sugar in the US transformed the island economy.

Sugar had not been the main export in 1820 (see table 3.1). Instead, coffee had provided nearly two-thirds of earnings. The crop was well suited to the rugged terrain and could be grown by small farmers without the need for large investments. And coffee could survive the rough journey from farm to port without serious loss or damage. Indeed, the volume of coffee exports would double by 1850 as it continued to suit the island's topography and social structure.

It was sugar, however, that brought new investment to Puerto Rico. By 1830, the volume and value of sugar exports had risen nearly tenfold (see table 3.1) and it had overtaken coffee as the most important export product. It never rivalled Cuba in scale, but its importance in Puerto Rico continued to rise until the middle of the nineteenth century when it accounted for almost 70 per cent of exports. Puerto Rico was now a sugar island, with sugar eclipsing not just coffee but also tobacco – the other traditional export.

Table 3.1: Puerto Rico: Exports by Volume and Value, 1820–90

Volume	Sugar (lb)	Coffee (lb)	Tobacco (lb)	Molasses (gal)
1820	3,166,300	5,873,000	1,116,500	
1830	29,189,200	12,517,600	3,363,400	631,292
1840	79,328,300	10,468,700	4,607,000	3,033,034
1850	105,243,700	10,699,000	4,021,000	3,060,000
1860	107,568,000	12,980,000	5,065,600	3,089,652
1870	138,325,100	18,672,300	3,463,200	3,029,239
1880	157,066,700	33,124,400	4,453,300	2,968,826
1890	130,000,000	44,000,000	4,000,000	2,908,413
Value (US$)	**Sugar**	**Coffee**	**Tobacco**	**Molasses**
1820	157,365	587,300	139,563	
1830	1,275,568	1,105,304	201,804	64,518
1840	3,157,266	1,778,632	368,560	511,976
1850	4,209,748	1,069,900	281,470	530,910
1860	4,302,700	1,298,000	329,264	552,739
1870	4,149,753	1,867,230	346,320	595,245
1880	4,649,174	4,902,411	612,774	745,769
1890	3,900,000	5,720,000	304,000	747,462
Share (%)	**Sugar**	**Coffee**	**Tobacco**	**Molasses**
1820	16.4	61.4	14.6	0.0
1830	41.6	36.0	6.6	2.1
1840	47.6	26.8	5.6	7.7
1850	69.0	17.5	4.6	8.7
1860	61.5	18.6	4.7	7.9
1870	59.3	26.7	4.9	8.5
1880	41.1	43.4	5.4	6.6
1890	35.5	52.0	2.8	6.8

Source: Statistical Appendix.

The transformation of Puerto Rico's sugar industry required not just capital but also labour. Slave imports, although banned under various Anglo-Spanish treaties, soared and the number of slaves had reached nearly 50,000 by 1840. By this time, the population of the island had reached 435,000 (double the level in 1815) thanks to the high level of voluntary net inward migration. And even if most of the migrants wanted land for owner-occupied farms, many of them still had to find work to supplement their income. Thus, the labour supply at first kept pace with demand.

A new Spanish law in 1845 marked the beginning of the end of the illegal trade in slaves to Puerto Rico (the last would arrive in 1859).[4] The slave population then steadily declined and had fallen below 30,000 on the eve of emancipation in 1873, when it represented just over four per cent of the population. A three-year period of apprenticeship, during which the former slaves were not free to leave their place of work, finally ended slavery in 1876.

The decline in slavery convinced the colonial authorities that other methods of coercion were needed if the export sector, on which so many hopes were pinned, was to be supplied with labour. The principal target was the legion of workers (*agregados*) who had access to land without either clear title or obligations. A *Reglamento Especial de Jornaleros* was therefore passed in 1849 to force such workers to become wage earners unless they could show they were owners or renters of the land.[5]

The colonial state lacked the resources to enforce the law, and it proved less effective than the authorities had hoped. The expansion of the sugar industry, subject in any case to higher export duties by Spain after 1850, was halted and there was very little growth until the First War of Cuban Independence (1868–78). This war led to a drop in Cuban exports and provided a modest boost for the sister island (see table 3.1). However, the value of Puerto Rican sugar exports suffered from the continuing fall in world prices and by 1890 was well below its level in 1850.

Puerto Rico, therefore, returned to what it knew best: small-scale production and export of coffee.[6] By 1890, (see table 3.1) the volume of coffee exports was four times higher than in 1850. And since coffee prices (unlike sugar) were not falling, the value increased nearly five-fold. Coffee now reclaimed its premier status, overtaking sugar in importance by 1880 and accounting for more than 50 per cent of all exports in 1890. And since the coffee beans were sold mainly to Spain, the Spanish share of the island's exports recovered.

Coffee provided a lifeline for colonial Puerto Rico in the late nineteenth century, but it could not generate the same fiscal benefits as sugar. Revenue per head on the island therefore remained little changed, peaking at US$5 in 1870 before falling to US$4 in 1890. And the real value of the revenue collected was undermined by the debased nature of the currency since in 1878 the Mexican dollar, tied to depreciating silver, had become the island's currency (all the gold dollars subsequently disappeared).

Coffee also failed to provide the same stimulus to infrastructure development as had happened with sugar in Cuba.[7] Shortly before the transfer from Spain to the US, there were less than 200 miles of railways in operation, and the Spanish government had been forced to guarantee a return of eight per cent on capital for six years to a company in the hope of expanding the network (the contract was cancelled before it was completed).[8] Modern banking also came late to Puerto Rico in the nineteenth century and borrowing was extremely difficult for those without the right social connections.

A movement in favour of independence now gathered pace. In addition, the availability of domestic foodstuffs had deteriorated with the shift to greater specialisation in exports leading to periods of severe hardship for many. The resentment at Spanish rule, therefore, led to the *Grito de Lares* in 1868 that coincided with the start of the First Cuban War of Independence (the uprising was quickly crushed by the Spanish authorities).

Another opportunity arose with the launch of a concerted attack in 1895 by Cuban nationalists against the colonial power. Before the independence movement could gather strength in Puerto Rico, however, the US had intervened militarily. The island's sovereignty was then transferred from Spain to the US under the terms of the Treaty of Paris in December 1898. A new colonial period in the island's history was about to begin.

3.2. United States Colony

Puerto Rico was under US military rule from October 1898. The Foweraker Act, passed in April 1900, then established civilian rule under a governor appointed by the US President.[9] The act changed the name of the island to Porto Rico to make it easier for the new colonial masters to pronounce.[10] In 1917, the Jones Act declared Puerto Rico to be an 'organized but unincorporated' US territory, thus ruling out any guarantee of statehood, but the act did confer citizenship on all Puerto Ricans. This gave them the right to emigrate freely to the mainland if they wished.

Although the formal transfer of sovereignty did not occur until the end of 1898, Puerto Rico had already fallen into the American sphere of influence. By the middle of the nineteenth century, a quarter of imports came from the US, and in 1884 a bilateral trade treaty with Spain lowered the remaining barriers on US exports to the island. And, following a reciprocal trade treaty with Spain that went into force in 1892 (a treaty that Spain felt powerless to resist), virtually all US imports entered free of duty despite the fact that the island's main export (coffee) was shipped predominantly to Spain.

The transfer of sovereignty, therefore, accelerated a commercial trend that had started long before. After a short period of indecision, Puerto Rico was brought fully inside the US tariff wall and by 1900 the results were already visible. Two-thirds of exports now went to the US and nearly 80 per cent of Puerto Rico's imports came from the same source. Within a few years these ratios would both reach 90 per cent, cutting off Puerto Rico from trade with the rest of the world and leaving it almost wholly dependent on its new colonial master.

One of the first acts of the new rulers was to appoint a US Insular Commission that was tasked with providing a set of recommendations for imperial administration. The Commissioners identified the lack of formal education under Spain as a key obstacle to progress, since as late as 1883 only 24,132 children were enrolled in school. However, their recommendations were drastic in the extreme:[11]

> The teachers in these schools should, in great part, be Americans, who are familiar with the methods, systems, and books of the American schools, and they should instruct the children in the

> English language....Put an American school in every valley and upon every hilltop in Porto Rico, and in these place the well-fitted and accomplished American schoolteachers, and the cloud of ignorance will disappear as the fog flies before the morning sun.

The US administration needed Puerto Rico to provision its navy and supply bases, but US capitalists wanted the island primarily for its sugar acreage. This meant replacing coffee once again with sugar as the main export, a task made easier by the terrible hurricane that ripped through Puerto Rico in 1898 and uprooted many of the coffee trees. In any case, faced with the loss of its preferential access to Spain, Puerto Rican coffee struggled to compete with cheaper supplies from countries such as Brazil.

There was only one obstacle to the expansion of sugar and that was the limitation on the size of land holdings (500 acres) imposed by the Foweraker Act. When it became clear, however, that the expansion of sugar – an industry subject to economies of scale – was being held back by this well-intentioned colonial decree, it was quietly dropped. Sugar would now become the dominant feature of island life with its dreaded 'dead season' when no work was available for thousands of sugarcane cutters.

Figure 3.2: Puerto Rico: Sugar Exports (mn lb), 1900–60

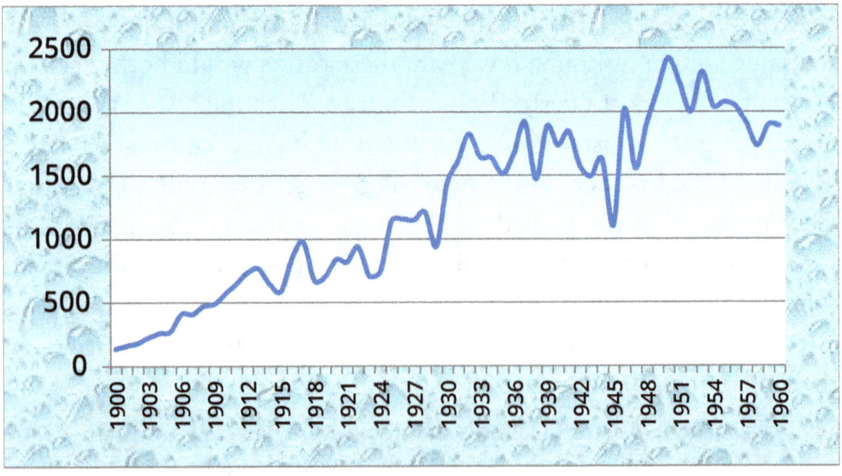

Source: Statistical Appendix.

The relentless expansion of the volume of sugar exports in the first three decades of US rule is shown in figure 3.2. American capitalists purchased existing sugar mills and invested in new ones to take advantage of the privileged access they enjoyed in the mainland market where raw and refined sugar faced neither tariffs nor quotas. Not even Cuba, subject to a preferential tariff, enjoyed such a position.

It could not, and did not, endure. The Great Depression drove down world prices, but the global market failed to clear. Supply exceeded demand, with Puerto Rico even reaching a peak of exports in the worst year of the slump in 1932. The island, despite being a US colony, was not exempt from the sugar quotas imposed by the Federal government in 1934 and the industry ceased to be a source of dynamism until it enjoyed a brief revival at the end of the Second World War. From then onwards, it would decline in importance, until exports disappeared altogether in the 1980s.

The Great Depression hit the island hard. Official figures showed that males with no paid employment and not attending school jumped from 52,343 in 1920 to 97,461 in 1930 and then to 149,006 in 1935, by which time they represented a quarter of all males over ten (the equivalent ratio for females was two-thirds).[12] Inevitably, proposed solutions focused on the all important sugar industry where four US-controlled *centrales* dictated much of what happened to the island's economy.[13]

The result was the Chardón Plan, outlined in 1934 and named after the Chancellor of the University of Puerto Rico. It proposed strict enforcement of the 500 acres limit on landholdings, brazenly flaunted by the sugar companies, and use of the land to create an army of small-scale capitalists in a diversified economy that would reduce the relative importance of the sugar industry. The Plan even proposed a modest set of policies to promote import-substituting industrialisation and manufactured exports, although it also assumed that only a programme to encourage outward migration could bring about equilibrium in the labour market.

Despite the initial support of the Roosevelt administration (1933–45), the plan was undermined by the sugar interests who lobbied hard, and ultimately with success, to maintain their privileged position.[14]

Sugar, therefore, remained the dominant sector, accounting for more than half of all merchandise exports (see table 3.2) even after the Great Depression.

Although the Chardón Plan was never adopted, there were some changes in the economy's structure in the 1930s. The rum industry, destroyed by US Prohibition (1919–33), recovered quickly after sales of alcoholic drinks were again permitted.[15] And the textiles and clothing sector, essentially a cottage industry, started to become an important source of female wage employment and a significant contributor to export earnings (see table 3.2).

One of the biggest problems faced by the island's government was the lack of resources for public spending. While other Caribbean countries relied on customs duties to generate revenue, Puerto Rico received virtually nothing from this source as almost all imports came from the US free of tariffs. As a result, revenue per head at constant prices was virtually the same in 1940 as it had been 30 years before.[16]

Table 3.2: Puerto Rico: Leading Exports by Value and as Share of Total (Percentage), 1900–50

Value (US$)	Sugar & Molasses	Coffee	Tobacco & Cigars	Rum	Textiles & Clothing
1900	5,311,611	1,678,765	681,000	0	8,000
1910	24,145,000	5,670,000	5,738,000	0	37,000
1920	100,202,000	9,034,028	25,030,000	0	807,000
1930	55,148,674	151,550	15,325,226	0	13,204,341
1940	58,042,419	421,910	6,069,040	5,568,476	15,631,035
1950	141,547,298	1,302,163	13,037,422	12,060,764	42,818,101
Share (%)	**Sugar & Molasses**	**Coffee**	**Tobacco & Cigars**	**Rum**	**Textiles & Clothing**
1900	67.8	21.4	8.7	0	0.1
1910	64.9	15.2	15.4	0	0.1
1920	66.8	6.0	16.7	0	0.5
1930	55.8	0.2	15.5	0	13.4
1940	63.4	0.5	6.6	6.1	17.1
1950	61.3	0.6	5.6	5.2	18.5

Source: Statistical Appendix.

The federal government had given emergency relief in the 1930s, but this provided little more than amelioration for the dire circumstances faced by islanders. It was not until rum exports boomed in the Second World War in response to mainland demand that the situation changed. This was due to the decision of the federal government to transfer to the island administration the funds raised by the (federal) excise duty tax on rum sales on the mainland.[17]

Island public revenue soared and it coincided with the electoral victory of the Popular Democratic Party (PDP), whose charismatic leader Luis Muñoz Marín would in 1948 become the first elected governor of Puerto Rico. A government-owned Industrial Development Company was established in 1942 to promote manufacturing through cheap loans and the limit of 500 acres on individual land holdings was now applied strictly in order to diversify agriculture.[18]

Puerto Rico was now on the path towards a different kind of development model to the one that had operated in its first four decades as a US colony. However, it would take many years for the full effects to be felt and in the meantime demographic changes were putting severe pressure on the labour market. While the CBR had risen from 30 in 1900 to 40 some four decades later, the CDR had fallen sharply and was down to ten by the end of the 1940s. This meant the natural rate of increase of the population had reached three per cent with a similar increase in the jobs that the labour market needed to create just to prevent unemployment from rising.

Net migration inwards, which had been such a feature of the island in the first three decades of the twentieth century, turned negative in the 1930s and the trend accelerated in the 1940s. In many years net migration outwards exceeded 40,000 in a population that finally reached two million in 1943. And all classes of Puerto Ricans emigrated from the least to the most skilled. It was a major drain of talent to the mainland and yet it still did not clear the labour market. Even in 1948 unemployment was around ten per cent of the labour force.[19]

3.3. Estado Libre Asociado

The election of Luis Muñoz Marín as governor in 1948 led to a plebiscite two years later, in which Puerto Ricans opted for a new constitutional arrangement giving them more control over their own affairs.[20] An assembly was then elected with responsibility for drafting a new constitution that was put to a popular vote before being adopted. The constitution dealt only with the responsibilities of the insular government and the lawmakers were not permitted to change the relationship with the US.

The Estado Libre Asociado (ELA), as it was called, was formally launched in 1952 and was supposed to end the colonial status of the island.[21] It did no such thing. Just as the Holy Roman Empire was said to be neither holy nor Roman nor an empire, so the ELA was neither a state, nor free nor associated. It could not be a state since it was not independent nor could it become one of the states of the US itself; it could not be free since the federal government continued to control the island's foreign relations, its defence and its currency; and it could not be 'associated' since its relationship with the US was not one of equals. Puerto Rico, therefore, continued to function as an American colony.

Although the new constitution did not fundamentally change the island's colonial status, the structure of the economy would now alter completely. This had little or nothing to do with the ELA, but a lot to do with US and insular fiscal policy. Indeed, not for the first time in the island's history, its economic fortunes would become intimately connected with the tax policy of the 'mother' country.

As a territory, but not a state, Puerto Rico has never been subject to US federal taxes. Subsidiaries of US companies on the island under Section 931 of the US tax code were, therefore, not subject to corporation tax on their insular profits unless they were repatriated.[22] However, they *were* subject to the corporation tax applied by the insular government so that in practice there was no great fiscal incentive for US companies to establish subsidiaries in Puerto Rico as long as the insular rate was similar to the mainland one.

This all changed in 1947 (i.e., before the creation of the ELA) when the insular government passed the Industrial Incentives Act that:[23]

> Not only exempted firms from property, excise, and municipal taxes and license fees, as earlier laws had done, but also provided complete exemption from insular income taxes until

> 1959 and partial exemption until 1962. The law extended this exemption to all firms in an industry...Besides the tax holiday, the government continued to provide subsidized buildings and added work-training programs, 'soft' (i.e., low-interest) loans, and other aid.

This was the launch of Operación Manos a la Obra (Operation Bootstrap), which – as its name in Spanish implied – was designed to create jobs and ease the unemployment problem on the island. Although intended to be temporary, it soon became clear the end year would need to be constantly extended since US subsidiaries were taking advantage of a loophole that allowed them to repatriate all accumulated profits tax-free at the end of the exemption period.

The fiscal cost to the insular government was enormous and not insignificant for the federal government as well. However, the situation was made worse following the passage of the Federal Tax Reform Act in 1976. Section 936 of this legislation replaced the former 931 provisions and allowed US subsidiaries in Puerto Rico to remit their profits to the parent company at any time without paying federal corporation tax in return for a small 'tollgate' tax to the insular government.[24] This change coincided with the moment when the island government shifted from the promotion of labour-intensive firms to those with more advanced technology and much higher capital requirements, making the fiscal incentives even more important.

A few years later the US government launched the Caribbean Basin Initiative (CBI) designed to offer 'friendly' Caribbean countries the chance to replicate Puerto Rico's model of development through duty-free access to the US market for their industrial products. When, therefore, the Caribbean Basin Economic Recovery Act (CBERA) was passed in 1984, it appeared to threaten Puerto Rican inward investment. However, a new tax law in 1986 allowed Puerto Rican banks to use the deposits of so-called 936 companies to finance joint investments in CBERA countries and the threat to Puerto Rico was soon neutralised.

The impact of all this fiscal generosity on inward investment in manufacturing was considerable. Many of the household names in US industry established subsidiaries in Puerto Rico to assemble goods before shipping them to the mainland. Value added in the sector ($120 million in 1950) rose to $1.190 million in 1970 and $5.322 million in 1980. Employment, however, only went from 55,000 in 1950 to 132,000 in 1970 and 143,000 in 1980. In other words, job creation in manufacturing between 1950 and 1970 failed to match expectations despite the incentive of insular wage rates far below the minimum mandated on the mainland by federal legislation.

Despite the disappointing record on job creation, which failed to make much of a dent in the unemployment rate or stop outward migration, the Puerto Rican model of development was much admired in the rest of the Caribbean. As early as 1951, in his book *The Industrial Development of the Caribbean*, the Nobel-laureate Sir Arthur Lewis had used Operation Bootstrap as the appropriate model for a strategy of 'industrialization by invitation'.[25] In the next two decades, thousands of consultants and advisers would follow in Lewis's footsteps to visit the island and learn about the programme.

Yet Operation Bootstrap had plenty of critics and they became more numerous as the impact of the model on the Puerto Rican economy became clearer. A gap between Gross Domestic Product (GDP), which includes income of non-residents, and Gross National Income (GNI), which excludes it, was always to be expected in view of the importance of foreign investment. However, what was not anticipated was that the gap would become bigger and bigger (see figure 3.3) and by 1995 had reached one-third. Thus, the GNI per head of Puerto Rico was only two-thirds the level of GDP per head, and the main reason for this was the exceptionally generous fiscal incentives provided to subsidiaries of US companies both by the federal tax system and the insular authorities.[26]

The growing gap between GDP and GNI meant that the much-vaunted rate of growth of the Puerto Rican economy did not bring the expected benefits to the inhabitants of the island. While the rate of growth of both GDP and GNI per head at constant prices had been high in the 1940s, 1950s, and 1960s, the average annual rate of growth of both in subsequent decades was much lower (see table 3.3). And the growth of GNI per head was far below the growth of GDP per head from 1960 onwards.

Figure 3.3: Puerto Rico: Ratio of GNI to GDP (%), 1960–2010

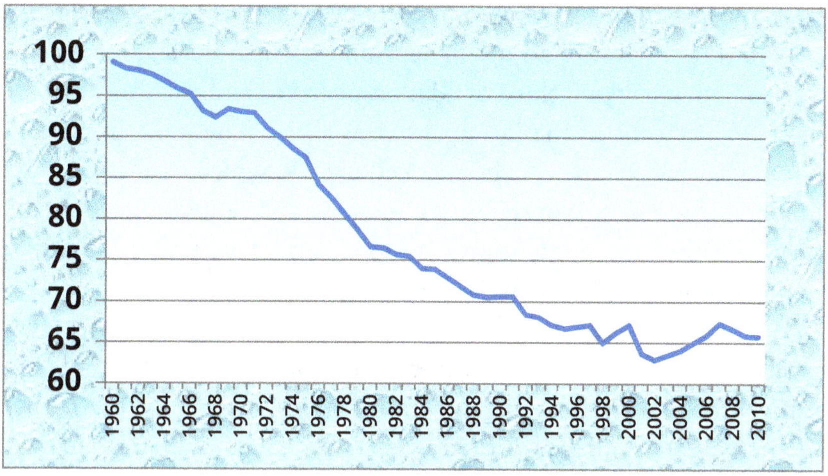

Source: Federal Reserve Bank of St Louis (https://fred.stlouisfed.org/).

Table 3.3: Puerto Rico: Annual Rate of Growth of GDP and GNI per Head (Percentage), 1940–2010

Years	GDP per head (2010 US$)	GNI per head (2010 US$)
1940–50	4.0	4.0
1950–60	4.7	4.7
1960–70	6.2	5.5
1970–80	3.6	1.6
1980–90	1.9	1.1

Source: derived by author from Federal Reserve Bank of St Louis (https://fred.stlouisfed.org/), Dietz (1986) and Perloff (1950), assuming that the ratio of GNI to GDP was the same in 1940 and 1950 as 1960.

Puerto Rican aggregate economic performance, therefore, became much less impressive after the 1960s and the island's model started to lose its shine. The absolute level of GDP per head was high, and higher than almost everywhere in Latin America, but GNI per head was much lower. It is true that the gap between insular and mainland GNI per head had narrowed after the launch of Operation Bootstrap, but it started to widen again after 1970 and had reached 30 per cent by the end of the century.[27]

While aggregate economic performance became a concern after 1970, the distribution of income had been a problem even earlier. In 1940, Puerto Rico had a conventional Latin American economic structure, in which one-third of GDP came from the agricultural sector where 45 per cent of the labour force worked. The most important 'manufacturing' sector was home needlework, which employed large numbers of women. Workers in all sectors represented 52.2 per cent of the working-age population (the so-called participation rate) and the unemployment rate was 15 per cent.[28]

Forty years later, only five per cent of the labour force was in agriculture, and home needlework employment had all but disappeared.[29] Manufacturing employment had increased, but the increases as already noted were not enormous. Instead, the participation rate had fallen, the unemployment rate had risen and most jobs were now in the service sectors where there was a large amount of underemployment. Meanwhile, Puerto Ricans in their thousands were continuing to migrate to the mainland US.

It was the fall in the participation rate that took most observers by surprise. Puerto Ricans were withdrawing from the labour market in large numbers and no one could be sure why this was happening. Neoclassical economists blamed it on the transfer payments from the federal government, especially the food stamp programme (later renamed the nutritional assistance programme) introduced in 1975, on the grounds that these discouraged workers from entering the labour market.[30] And the application of US minimum wage rates to the island in 1981 was also held responsible on the grounds that it might have reduced the number of low-skill jobs created in Puerto Rico.

None of these explanations were satisfactory, as the fall in the participation rate had started in the 1950s, i.e., before the expansion of the transfer programmes and the application of US minimum wage legislation. What was clear, however, was that a smaller and smaller proportion of the working-age population was in full-time jobs after 1950 despite Operation Bootstrap and an increasing share of household income consisted of transfers of one kind or another (including unemployment benefit). Indeed, these transfers had become so important by the end of the century that one-third of household income came from them.

3.4. End of the Illusion

Faced with a growing US budget deficit in the 1980s, Congress had become increasingly concerned about the potential loss of revenue implied by the application of Section 936 of the tax code to US subsidiaries in Puerto Rico. And, in addition to the fiscal damage, Congress was also worried about the way in which companies used transfer pricing to minimise their tax liability on the mainland while failing to create an adequate number of jobs in manufacturing on the island.

The most egregious example of transfer pricing was provided by the pharmaceutical industry. According to the US Government Accounting Office:[31]

> A pharmaceutical company would develop a drug in its U.S. research facilities and transfer the drug patent to its wholly owned subsidiary operating in Puerto Rico. The subsidiary would produce the patented drug and claim the income obtained from the drug sales as tax-free income.

This abuse was so widespread that pharmaceutical companies had come to dominate Puerto Rico's manufacturing sector.[32] And the tax credits they received dwarfed the wage bill they paid, so much so that it would have been cheaper for the US Treasury to pay the workers directly without employing them.

The federal government, lobbied hard by the insular authorities and the island's non-voting representative in Congress, would have preferred to keep the tax credits, but Congress was determined to remove them. President Clinton (1993–2001) therefore signed into law a bill that phased out the federal tax incentives between 1996 and 2005.

The loss of Section 936 would have been a mortal blow to the Puerto Rican economy under any circumstances. However, it was made worse by the series of preferential trade agreements signed by the US government with developing countries that started with Mexico in 1994. By the time all Section 936 incentives ended, many other countries in Latin America and the Caribbean had duty-free access to the US market for goods. Puerto Rico, therefore, lost not only its privileged tax position but also its privileged market access status.[33]

Table 3.4: Puerto Rico: Economic Indicators, 2007–2016

	2007	2016	% change
GNI (US$ mn), 1954 prices	7,261.6	6,233.9	-14.2
GDP (US$ mn), 1954 prices	11,088.4	10,049.1	-9.4
Investment (US$ mn), 1954 prices	1,797.7	1,241.8	-30.9
Participation Rate (%)	48.6	40.2	-17.3
Employment (000)	1,263	1,002	-20.7
Employment in Manufacturing (000)	137	84	-38.7

Source: http://www.jp.gobierno.pr.

The effects on the island's economy were devastating. In the ten years after the incentives were finally ended, Puerto Rico experienced a decline in all the most important economic indicators. GNI, for example, fell by 14.2 per cent between 2007 and 2016 (see table 3.4). Indeed, it fell in every single year except one in this period. GDP also fell, while investment in fixed capital declined by a massive 30.9 per cent.

The most worrying feature after the phasing out of the incentives was the deterioration of the labour market. The participation rate, already below 50 per cent in 2007, had fallen to 40.2 per cent by 2016. Thousands of Puerto Ricans had simply withdrawn from the labour market in the wake of the decline of economic activity. Employment fell by 20.7 per cent, while manufacturing jobs – particularly dependent on the tax incentives – fell by nearly 40 per cent (see table 3.4).

The participation rate declined despite the fact that many Puerto Ricans responded to the crisis by leaving the island. Indeed, the wave of net outward migration since the millennium has been extremely severe (see figure 3.4), rivalling in scale the outflow at the end of the Second World War. This time, however, the impact was even more serious as the birth rate on the island has fallen so sharply that births barely exceed deaths. Thus, large-scale net outward migration now means that the population is falling year on year and by 2016 it had dropped nearly ten per cent in just one decade to reach 3.4 million – the same figure as 30 years earlier.

Figure 3.4: Puerto Rico: Net Migration, 1900–2016

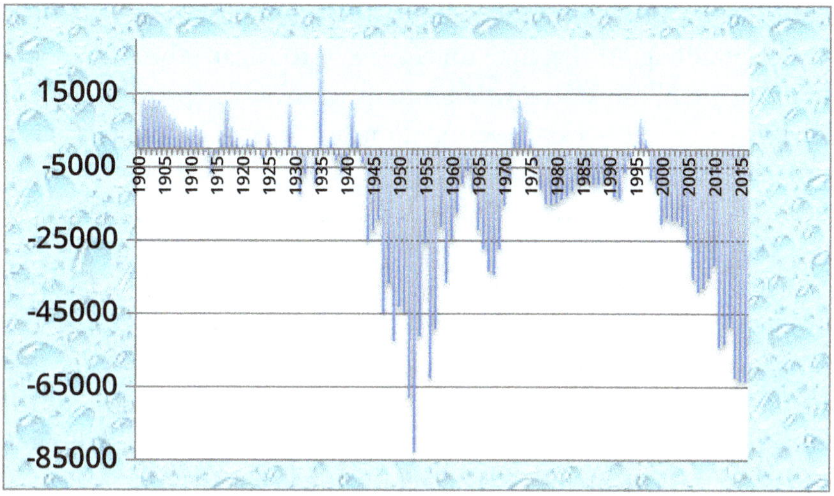

Sources: Statistical Appendix and World Bank, World Development Indicators.

Almost all migrants headed to the mainland, where they are concentrated in a small number of states (especially New Jersey and New York). If those of Puerto Rican descent are included, their numbers – 5.1 million in 2015 – far exceed those living on the island. Yet Puerto Ricans have never enjoyed the political influence in the US wielded by the numerically inferior Cuban-Americans and have not had much success in changing the policy of the federal government towards the island.

The decline of economic activity in Puerto Rico after the phasing out of Section 936 would have produced a huge decline in household income if it were not for the federal transfers to which Puerto Ricans as US citizens are entitled. The value of these transfers rose by more than 60 per cent between 2007 and 2016, at which point they were valued at nearly $17 billion (equivalent to about $5,000 for every man, woman and child on the island). By far the most important payments were social security benefits, followed by Medicare and Nutritional Assistance.

As a result primarily of the federal government's programmes and continued remittances from relatives on the mainland, household income in Puerto Rico did not decline. However, the tax base shrank as a result of the prolonged economic recession. The insular government increased taxes, but this was insufficient to prevent the government's deficit from expanding and tax revenue as a share of GNI kept falling. At the same time, the Puerto Rican government was reluctant to allow state-owned enterprises (SOEs) providing basic services to raise prices above inflation in view of the political cost. Both the government and the SOEs, therefore, issued debt to cover the shortfall with most of the bonds being issued by a small number of SOEs.

Puerto Rican debt was held in high esteem by creditors as the interest was exempt from all kinds of taxes – federal, state, and municipal (the so-called triple lock). As a result, it was easy at first for the government and SOEs to issue bonds – so much so that the value of public debt increased by some $25 billion to $67.2 billion in the seven years before 2014. This represented roughly 100 per cent of GNI, and the markets became concerned that debt would prove too high to be serviced promptly. Inevitably, Puerto Rican debt was then subject to a downgrade by the ratings agencies. Bond prices fell and yields jumped into double figures.

The markets now demanded shorter maturities and higher rates of interest. This made it almost impossible for the Puerto Rican government and SOEs to issue new debt. Debt payments started to be missed from 2015 onwards, and Puerto Rico went into partial default. This was a new and unanticipated situation as Puerto Rico – being a US possession and not a US state or municipality – was not subject to chapter 9 of the US bankruptcy code. Indeed, no US possession (i.e., unincorporated territory) had ever declared bankruptcy so that neither the debtors nor the creditors knew what to expect next.

It was left to a reluctant Congress, pushed by President Obama (2009–17), to formulate a plan. The Puerto Rico Oversight, Management, and Economic Stability Act (PROMESA) was finally passed in mid-2016. It established a Fiscal Control Board, with all members appointed by the US president, which was given extraordinary powers, including the right to veto the island budget. It was also given the authority, in the event of Puerto Rico declaring bankruptcy, to impose a restructuring of the public debt on the island's creditors.

When the island's governor did indeed declare bankruptcy in mid-2017, it was assumed that the Fiscal Control Board would impose a solution to the debt crisis. In September of that year, however, Hurricane María – a Category 4 hurricane – hit the island with devastating effects and killed a large number of people. The electricity distribution system was completely destroyed and the island government, already marginalised by PROMESA, was overwhelmed. The federal government, it was clear, would have to assume greater powers and Puerto Rico would revert once again to its status as an American colony – a status that in truth it had never left behind.

Puerto Rico is not a classic example of a neglected colony, but it has still been a failure under US imperial rule. The federal government prioritised US firms over all other considerations in the provision of fiscal and trade incentives. These, not just those provided under Section 936, massively distorted the economy of the island in favour of US companies starting with the giant sugar companies in the first decades of the American colony. When the incentives were altered or removed, it had major implications that were largely ignored by US lawmakers and government officials.

Instead, mainland authorities were content to adopt palliative solutions, such as the expansion of federal transfers, which sustained household income without increasing labour productivity. The Puerto Rican economy then became increasingly uncompetitive, leading to a big fall in the participation rate and a big increase in outward migration.[34]

Unable to decide its exchange rate or control its monetary regime, the island authorities took refuge in a fiscal policy that replicated the federal government's prioritisation of business interests over everything else. And when PROMESA removed fiscal autonomy from the hands of the elected administration, the threadbare nature of the autonomy proclaimed by the ELA in 1952 was revealed to all.

With independence rejected by most islanders, the option of statehood became increasingly attractive and this was confirmed by a referendum in 2017 (albeit with a low turnout). Yet Puerto Ricans cannot compel the US to make it a state even if that is their wish. Like the proposed annexation of the Dominican Republic in 1869, the decision must be determined by Congress. And since Puerto Ricans – rightly or wrongly – are expected to vote for candidates of the Democratic Party, securing a large enough majority in Congress to support statehood is likely to be well nigh impossible. Thus, Puerto

Rico is caught in limbo and unable to move forward, its population shrinking year by year as islanders vote with their feet and move elsewhere.

NOTES

1. For population figures, see Statistical Appendix. See also J. Duany, 'Población y migración desde 1815 hasta la actualidad,' in *Historia de Puerto Rico*, ed. L. González Vales and M. Luque de Sánchez (Madrid: Consejo Superior de Investigaciones Científicas, 2010), 61–88.
2. The CBR in 1814 was estimated at 43.1 and the CDR at 23.0, implying a natural rate of growth of population of two per cent. See Statistical Appendix.
3. See Statistical Appendix.
4. See J.C. Dorsey, *Slave Traffic in the Age of Abolition: Puerto Rico, West Africa, and the Non-Hispanic Caribbean, 1815–1859* (Gainesville, FL: University Press of Florida, 2003), 5.
5. See J.L. Dietz, *Economic History of Puerto Rico: Institutional Change and Capitalist Development* (Princeton, NJ: Princeton University Press, 1986), 45.
6. See L.W. Bergad, *Coffee and the Growth of Agrarian Capitalism in Nineteenth-century Puerto Rico* (Princeton, NJ: Princeton University Press, 1983), 68 onwards.
7. See A. Santamaría García, 'Economía, 1800–1898,' in *Historia de Puerto Rico*, ed. L. González Vales and M. Luque de Sánchez (Madrid: Consejo Superior de Investigaciones Científicas, 2010), 144–49.
8. See R.T. Hill, *Cuba and Porto Rico, with the Other Islands of the West Indies: Their Topography, Climate, Flora, Products, Industries, Cities, People, Political Conditions, etc.* (New York, NY: The Century Co., 1898), 161.
9. Election of the governor by popular vote was not permitted until 1941.
10. It was changed back to Puerto Rico in 1934.
11. Quoted in J. Navarro, *Creating Tropical Yankees: Social Science Textbooks and U.S. Ideological Control in Puerto Rico, 1898–1908* (New York, NY: Routledge, 2002), 35.
12. See Dietz, *Economic History of Puerto Rico*, 131, table 2.14.
13. See A. Gayer, P. Homan, and E. James, *The Sugar Economy of Puerto Rico* (New York, NY: Columbia University Press, 1938), 62.
14. At least until 1940, when the US Supreme Court ruled that the limit of 500 acres for landholding was legally binding.
15. Especially after Bacardí, a Cuban company, opened a factory in Puerto Rico in 1935. See H. Calvo Ospina, *Bacardí: The Hidden War* (London: Pluto Press, 2002), 10–11.

16. See Statistical Appendix.
17. Puerto Rico, not being a state nor represented in Congress, does not pay federal taxes. Thus, the federal excise duty needed to be returned to the island.
18. See H.S. Perloff, *Puerto Rico's Economic Future: A Study in Planned Development* (Chicago: Chicago University Press, 1950), 39–41.
19. Ibid., appendix B, 401.
20. See C. Ayala and R. Bernabe, *Puerto Rico in the American Century: A History since 1898* (Chapel Hill, NC: University of North Carolina Press, 2007), 162–65.
21. The ELA is referred to in English as the Commonwealth of Puerto Rico.
22. Section 931 took its name from a tax law passed in 1954, but the principle had already been established in 1921 that US subsidiaries were not subject to federal taxes on any profits earned in Puerto Rico.
23. See Dietz (1986), 209–10.
24. The tollgate tax was set at a maximum of ten per cent of remitted profits, but could easily be reduced to less than four per cent by taking advantage of various incentives. See Dietz, *Economic History of Puerto Rico*, 301–02.
25. The phrase was coined by Lloyd Best.
26. In the Puerto Rican national accounts, GNI is referred to as 'Producto Bruto'. This is the equivalent of Gross National Product (GNP).
27. See B. Bosworth and S. Collins, 'Economic Growth,' in *The Economy of Puerto Rico*, ed. S. Collins, B. Bosworth, and M. Soto-Class (Washington, DC: Brookings Institution, 2006), 18, figure 2.1.
28. See T. Weisskoff, *Factories and Food Stamps: The Puerto Rican Model of Development* (Baltimore, MD: Johns Hopkins University Press, 1985), 56, table 7.3.
29. See Dietz, *Economic History of Puerto Rico*, 226.
30. See G. Burtless and O. Sotomayor, 'Labor Supply and Public Transfers,' in *The Economy of Puerto Rico*, ed. S. Collins, B. Bosworth, and M. Soto-Class (Washington, DC: Brookings Institution, 2006), 82–135.
31. See General Accounting Office, *Pharmaceutical Industry: Tax Benefits of Operating in Puerto Rico* (Washington, DC: General Accounting Office, 1992), 2.
32. Roughly two-thirds of manufacturing value added can be attributed to pharmaceutical companies and nearly all of this is profit rather than wages and salaries.
33. Other factors also combined to make a bad situation worse after the end of the fiscal incentives. These included a slump in the housing market, a sharp decline in deposits in the banking system and the US recession from 2007–09. See A. Krueger, R. Teja, and A. Wolfe, *Puerto Rico: A Way Forward* (San Juan: Gobierno de Puerto Rico, 2015), 4–7.

34. On the uncompetitive nature of the Puerto Rican economy, see Federal Reserve Bank of New York, *Report on the Competitiveness of Puerto Rico's Economy* (New York, NY: Federal Reserve Bank, 2014).

PART II: The French-speaking Countries

Chapter 4
HAITI

This chapter focuses primarily on the period before the US invasion of Haiti in 1915. The years immediately preceding the US occupation, which lasted until 1934, were crucial in Haitian economic history. Modern interpretations of Haiti tend to be based on a misunderstanding of its performance before the US invasion, it being often incorrectly assumed that Haiti was the poorest country in the region from independence onwards.

Haiti in the nineteenth century was not the economic failure that it has become today. Its domestic exports were among the most important in the Caribbean, being exceeded only by Cuba, Guyana, and Jamaica in 1820. The subsequent collapse of Jamaican exports left Haiti as the third most important Caribbean exporter for part of the nineteenth century. Its exports exceeded those of the Dominican Republic throughout almost all the century and those of Puerto Rico in parts of it. With exports concentrated on coffee, it was also for most of the nineteenth century the world's third largest exporter of a commodity whose global consumption was steadily rising.[1]

It is true that in *per capita* terms Haiti's performance was much less impressive since it had a large population in comparison with most other Caribbean countries (only Cuba was bigger). However, exports per head were never the lowest in the Caribbean, being either third, fourth, or fifth from bottom in all years after 1820. Furthermore, it was not until after 1890 that Haitian exports dropped sharply in absolute terms. This drop was a consequence primarily of the collapse in coffee prices as a result of the over-production in Brazil after the end of slavery.

Figure 4.1: Ratio of Haitian to Caribbean Merchandise Exports per head (%), 1821–2007

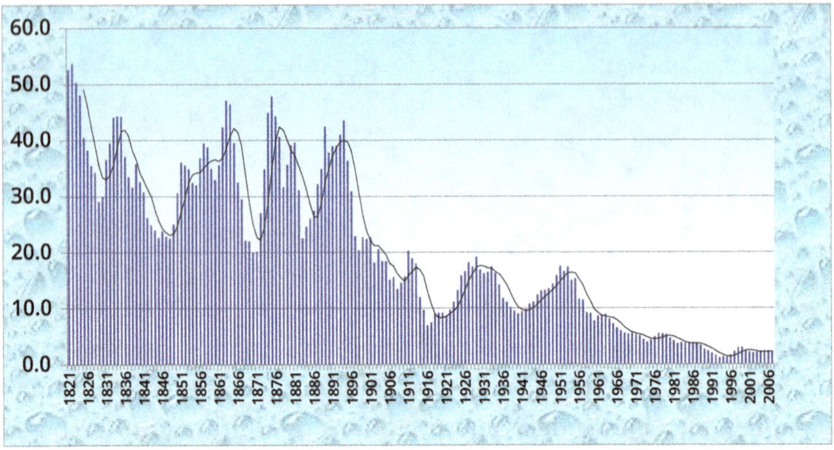

Source: Statistical Appendix.

Until that moment, Haitian exports per head had averaged around 40 per cent of Caribbean exports per head (see figure 4.1). However, following the 1890s collapse in coffee prices the ratio fell below 30 per cent. Furthermore, it continued to fall and had slipped below ten per cent by 1960. Subsequently, it fell to its current level of around two per cent of the Caribbean average. Thus, the Haitian economy entered a downward spiral in the 1890s from which it has never recovered.

The downward spiral, once it started, was not inevitable, but extreme political instability in the years immediately before the First World War and the US occupation thereafter made it difficult to reverse. The US put its own interests far above those of its Haitian protectorate. The inevitable reaction to the occupation then created the ideological movement from which François Duvalier would emerge triumphant in 1957.

This chapter begins with the relations of Haiti with the core, i.e., metropolitan countries. It is not a pretty story, but it needs to be told. There is then a detailed examination of Haitian exports that goes beyond what has previously been possible. This is followed by an analysis of public finance that – far more than foreign trade – was the Achilles heel of the Haitian model.

4.1. Haiti and the Core

The Haitian declaration of independence on January 1, 1804 was greeted with a deafening silence by the rest of the world. Far from being welcomed, it was seen as a threat by all those countries still engaged in the slave trade. Haitian independence also occurred in the middle of the Napoleonic Wars when national interests were even more ruthlessly pursued than usual. The end of the Napoleonic Wars should, therefore, have provided an opportunity for the core to normalise its relations with Haiti. Instead, the Treaty of Paris in 1814 and the Congress of Vienna in 1815 made no mention of Haitian independence, referring instead to the return to France of all its former colonies other than those ceded (e.g., St Lucia and Tobago).

The first French mission was despatched to the Republic of Haiti (the southern part ruled by President Pétion) in 1814 with orders to re-establish French sovereignty but also secret instructions that included the re-imposition of slavery. The mission failed, but not before Pétion had made the potentially fatal admission that Haiti might be prepared to pay an indemnity in return for recognition of its independence. A second French mission in 1816 also ended in failure as France was still determined to regain sovereignty, and neither the Republic governed by Pétion nor the northern Kingdom ruled by Christophe was prepared to consider such a step.

The next opportunity for the core to normalise its relations with Haiti came in the early 1820s following the independence of much of Spanish and Portuguese America from the Iberian colonial powers. The US was the first to recognise their independence closely followed by the UK. The latter, however, still refused to accept an independent Haiti on the specious grounds that it could not do so ahead of France, ignoring that it had recognised the independence of the Latin American republics without waiting for Spain – the former colonial power – to do so. This so enraged President Boyer, under whom Haiti had once again become united in 1820, that he cancelled the trade privileges granted by Pétion to the UK in 1814.

With the US, the issue of Haitian independence was affected above all by slavery. Anxious to include the US in the Pan-American Congress of 1826, where the issue of Haitian recognition by the mainland American republics was on the agenda, Simón Bolívar did not invite Haiti to participate despite the generous support he had received on more than one occasion from Pétion a decade earlier. US recognition of Haitian independence was then delayed until 1862. This was shortly before the abolition of slavery and after the outbreak of the Civil War when the slave states were no longer able to block legislation in Congress. A treaty of commerce duly followed in 1864.

Non-recognition by the core did not rule out trade relations. However, it did pose a potential threat since there was always the possibility of a challenge to Haiti's territorial integrity. The Haitian state from the start was, therefore, highly militarised with a standing army under Boyer in the mid-1820s estimated at 32,000.[2] In comparison with the size of the population this must have been one of the larger armies in the world and it had to be financed.

In addition to requiring a large army, the hostility of the core created the need for a National Guard composed of all adult males. This military reserve, for such it was, could be called upon at short notice to defend the territory of the fledgling state and individuals might be required to move far from their homes. The militarised nature of society then helps us to understand one of the fundamental changes in Haiti after the end of colonisation since estate labour was extremely scarce and peasant labour could be disrupted at any time. Haitian exports, therefore, shifted from sugar and cotton to coffee and timber since the labour requirements of the last two commodities – combined with the absence of capital – were much more compatible with the militarised nature of society.

French recognition in 1825 was grudging and unjust because of the indemnity imposed (see chapter 4.3). Since there was little chance of Haiti being able to comply with the terms of the indemnity, there was the continued risk of French intervention. It was not until 1838 that a renegotiation of the indemnity provided for improved – but still harsh – terms and less risk of intervention. This was also the moment when the UK finally recognised the independence of Haiti as a sovereign state, having sent only a consul in 1826.

Under different circumstances this might have been an opportunity for Haiti to move away from its militaristic society whose armed forces placed such a heavy burden on the public revenue. However, developments in the eastern part of the island precluded this. First, Spain had never renounced its claims to Santo Domingo, annexed by Haiti in 1822, and saw in the French indemnity a possible opportunity to impose similar terms for recognition. A Spanish naval mission arrived in Haiti, in 1842, with hostile purpose, but Boyer was eventually able to diffuse the situation. The incident might even have led to a *rapprochement* with Spain. However, natural disaster struck Haiti the same year. An earthquake caused enormous damage, Cap Haitien was completely destroyed and Boyer was forced into exile in 1843. Within a year the eastern part of the island had declared independence.

The independence of Santo Domingo made it inevitable that Haiti would keep a large standing army for two reasons. First, it felt obliged under its constitution to seek the re-conquest of the eastern part of this island. This was attempted unsuccessfully by President Soulouque (1847–59) on two occasions. Secondly, Haiti anticipated (correctly) that Santo Domingo would be a weak state that might fall prey to outside powers. A foreign power in the eastern part of the island would be a constant threat to the territorial integrity of the western republic and so, once again, the shrinking of the armed forces was postponed.

For their part, the Dominicans had no confidence in their ability to survive as an independent state in the face of the Haitian territorial claim and sought instead the security of annexation by a member of the core. In this respect, the Dominicans were exceedingly promiscuous, seeking the intervention at different times of France, Spain, the UK, and the US. It was Spain, however, that acted first, re-colonising Santo Domingo in 1861 following an invitation from the Dominican president. The Haitians immediately gave military help to the opponents of Spanish annexation and came close to war with Spain herself.

Spain was driven out in 1865 and the first treaty between Haiti and Santo Domingo was signed in 1867, although the Haitian Congress refused to ratify it. However, far from being the prelude to improved security and demilitarisation, it was immediately followed in 1869 by a plan of annexation of the eastern part of the island by the US with the connivance of the Dominican president. Had this plan succeeded (it failed to garner the necessary two-thirds majority in the US Senate), there is no doubt that it would only have been a matter of time before Haiti was engaged in an existential struggle for its own survival as an independent state. Instead, following the collapse of President Grant's dream of annexation, Haiti duly signed a definitive treaty in 1874 with the Dominican Republic, as it would now be called, although the boundaries between the two countries were only finally settled in 1935.

Before its own civil war (1861–65), the US had not shown much interest in controlling Haitian territory. The most serious incident occurred in 1857 when a US citizen claimed Ile de Navase (Navassa Island) under the 1856 Guano Islands Act. The Haitian navy tried to expel the individuals involved, but the US held on to the island and later built a lighthouse. It remains US territory today despite its proximity to Haiti.

After 1865, the US became much more acquisitive. The rise of US naval power and the rivalry between the core states themselves made the control of naval and coaling stations in the Caribbean a geo-strategic necessity. In Môle St Nicholas, Haiti had one of the four finest natural harbours in the region and one that was coveted by the core. Having failed to secure Samaná Bay in the Dominican Republic through annexation or lease, thwarted by the US Senate in its efforts to acquire St Thomas in the Danish West Indies, and unable at this stage to acquire Guantánamo Bay because of Spanish control of Cuba, the US focused on Môle St Nicholas as the most suitable candidate. Haiti refused to cave into US pressure and was punished in 1892 by the application of harsh tariffs on the main US imports from Haiti.

Haiti ended the nineteenth century as an independent country, but it had been a struggle. The need for a large army had drained the public purse while giving serving presidents a means of delaying or blocking the peaceful transfer of power. The core also exploited Haitian relative weakness by pursuing an endless stream of financial claims on behalf of its citizens that were usually grossly inflated and sometimes outrageous. And since the government had to service an enormous debt, Haitian public finances (net of debt service payments) were deeply unsatisfactory and below what was required to support many state responsibilities (see chapter 4.3).

4.2. The Export Sector

The first Haitian leaders understood clearly that the survival of the state depended on the recovery of the export sector after the ravages of the war of independence. In this, as we shall see, they had some success. Subsequent leaders also recognised that the development of Haiti depended in large part on the long-run growth of the export sector and policies were indeed adopted to promote exports. However, these leaders struggled to balance the budget. For reasons that will become clear later, Haitian public finance depended heavily on export taxes. Thus, there was a tension between the short-run needs of public finance and the long-run requirements of export growth.

If there was little alternative to export promotion, Haiti was no different from other countries in the region (including the US before 1860). However, in one respect – the average size of landholdings – Haiti differed greatly. The multitude of small farms made Haiti by the end of the nineteenth century different from most other countries in Latin America and the Caribbean. Exports of agricultural – and to a lesser extent timber[3] – products therefore came to depend on the Haitian peasantry whose access to capital (financial and human) was severely restricted.

It was not always so. Under Toussaint, Dessalines, and Christophe (until just before his death), the large-scale estate was favoured, land grants below a certain size were prohibited and foreigners ('whites' in the 1805 Constitution)[4] were prevented from owning real estate so that the large landowners were Haitians. To ensure an adequate labour supply for these big estates, labour laws made vagrancy a crime. The workers on the estates received a quarter of the produce while the landlord received half. Dessalines went even further than Toussaint and banned the cutting of timber on the grounds that it might prejudice the supply of labour to the large estates. Exports of traditional commodities, including sugar, started to recover – albeit from a very low base.[5]

The state received the remaining quarter of the farm output and, under Christophe, this contribution together with a land tax was sufficient to meet the needs of the government for defence, public works, and even education. However, since the estates were producing commodities destined in many cases for shipment abroad, the land tax under Christophe in effect began the practice of taxing exports. When prices were high and the tax moderate it was not so serious, but when prices were low and the tax high it became a major barrier to export expansion.

In the Republic of Haiti, under Pétion, a different model was followed. A law of 1809 removed the restriction on selling land in small parcels and a large number of small grants were made by the government. Others simply voted with their feet, squatting on land that belonged either to the state or purchasing small plots from the remaining estate owners. The export of sugar collapsed under Pétion, but coffee recovered and logwood – no longer forbidden – prospered. However, Pétion also came to depend heavily on taxes on exports to balance the budget as the state's share of one-quarter was suppressed[6] (instead, workers on large estates were now allowed to keep half the produce).

Boyer, who succeeded Pétion in 1818 and Christophe in 1820, at first allowed both agricultural models to continue.[7] However, following the imposition of the French indemnity in 1825 and the contraction of a loan to pay for the first instalment (see chapter 4.3), he favoured the large estates because they expanded the exports on which debt service would depend. The *Code Rural* of 1826 was as draconian as other measures in the Caribbean to coerce labour to work for the large estates, but it had the opposite effect. By the time Boyer was forced from office in 1843, sugar had ceased to be an export of any importance, and agricultural output had come to depend on the small-scale peasantry combined with sharecropping on the large estates by small gangs of labourers who had control over the product mix.

Boyer had lowered export taxes in 1825, before imposing the French indemnity, in an effort to stimulate exports. He then abolished them altogether in 1827. Unfortunately, the demands of public finance obliged Boyer to reintroduce a specific duty on exports in 1835 and he added an additional burden ('droit de wharfage y pesage') in the same year. Any good this might have done to government revenue was undone by the depreciation of the national currency since the export taxes were paid in paper *gourdes*. By 1843, the paper *gourde* had dropped by one-third in value (see chapter 4.3).

The depreciation of the currency accelerated under the four presidents that succeeded Boyer in quick succession. The export tax was first abolished (1843) and then re-established (1845). When Soulouque became President in 1847, the paper *gourde* had so depreciated that the real value of the export tax had collapsed. Soulouque, therefore, imposed a tax of 20 per cent on coffee payable in kind by growers with the state then selling its share to exporters at a market rate. Hugely unpopular with the peasants and exporters alike, it did at least ensure that government revenue moved more or less in line with the value of coffee exports.

By the time Soulouque was forced from office in January 1859, the *gourde* had fallen to 30 to the dollar, so there was little point in re-imposing an export tax payable in national currency. Instead, President Geffrard (1859–67) in 1860 made the export tax payable in hard currency for the first time. Since the tax was specific, its *ad valorem* equivalent depended on the evolution of the prices of the main commodities (principally coffee and logwood). After a period of confusion during the Haitian civil war (1867–69) when President Salnave re-imposed payment in kind, the export taxes were fixed in August 1870. The duty on coffee was set at US$2.50 per 100 pounds in 1870, that on logwood at US$1.50 per 1,000 pounds and there were also duties imposed on most of the minor commodities such as cacao and cotton.[8] However, the export tax on coffee – by far the most important – was steadily increased and had reached US$3.86 by 1889.

This was a heavy burden for coffee producers, and it was made worse by various other taxes that applied to exports when they left port. When coffee prices were high, the burden was bearable, but it became almost insupportable when prices fell. Furthermore, Haitian coffee was not only taxed heavily in Haiti. It was also taxed heavily in France – its main market – where Haitian coffee received much less favourable treatment than coffee imported from French colonies. It was not until 1904, following the Haitian-French treaty of commerce, that Haitian coffee received any preferential treatment in the French market.

Under these circumstances, it might seem surprising that there was any growth at all in Haitian exports in the century after independence. Yet there was growth, in both volume and value, although neither ultimately was able to keep pace with population growth. Furthermore, exports had come to depend far too heavily on one crop (coffee) whose price declined sharply from the 1890s onwards as a result of Brazilian over-production. Thus, Haiti went into the twentieth century with an export sector that was too small to support the growing needs of public finance and so dependent on one product that it was vulnerable to price movements over which the country had no control.

The four products that collectively determined the value of Haitian exports in the century before the US invasion were coffee, cotton, cacao, and logwood.[9] Raw sugar exports had ceased to be of any importance by the end of Boyer's term. Attempts were made to revive them under different presidents, notably Geffrard and Salomon (1879–1888), and sugar exports were even exempt from taxation for much of the time, but the key constraint was the lack of capital needed to re-establish the industry with modern technology (without which costs would be too high). The export industry only started to recover when the US as the occupying force was able to force through legislation that permitted foreigners to own land, dispossess small farmers, and build the necessary infrastructure. At that point, US capital entered the sugar industry and exports started again (even then they did not prosper).

Haitian coffee (*Arabica*) was considered to be of excellent quality. It was noted in particular for its aroma. After independence, it was sold at first mainly to the UK and US, but consumers in those countries gradually came to prefer the cheaper coffee produced by Brazil, Colombia, Central America, and a handful of European colonies. With the opening once again of the French market in 1825, Haitian coffee came to depend increasingly on the more discerning consumers of continental Europe (especially the Germans to whom Haitian coffee was re-exported from France) who were prepared to pay a premium for quality coffee. Some 60 to 70 per cent of the Haitian coffee crop was normally sold in this way.

Haitian coffee trees flourished above 300 metres in the south, the main growing region, although in the north they could grow at sea level. It was cultivated under shade and was produced organically. The Haitian peasantry did not generally plant the coffee trees, relying instead on natural growth from fallen berries, but occasional weeding and thinning was essential. The coffee was harvested between October and February and was, at first, prepared for export on the farms themselves in the following manner:[10]

> 'After drying on the special patio, or even on the ground, the pulp is generally removed by hand in a wooden pestle, then the beans are deparchmented and more or less sorted before offering for sale.'

This method of preparing coffee for export, although widely disparaged by foreign visitors, was reasonably well suited to the Haitian environment. However, as the market became more specialised, Haitian growers were penalised for their failure to separate the lowest grades of coffee from the highest. Tackling this problem required machinery and a greater division of labour between the grower and the exporter. This process was underway by the early 1880s, helped by measures taken by President Salomon. Thus, the US Consul in 1884 could write as follows:[11]

> To procure for Haytian coffee the very latest improvements in the preparation, thus allowing it to compete advantageously with other sorts, and acquire the rank which from its natural superiority is its due, central mills...are beginning to be established in the principal coffee-growing centers...Thus the grower, who by his very primitive mode of preparation was losing at least one-third of his crop, will now obtain one-half more of money value as the result of his toil.

Coffee preparation, especially before the introduction of central mills, provided only modest scope for an increase in yield. The volume of coffee exports, therefore, depended largely on the ability to expand the supply of labour and land in response to growing demand. As the population in rural areas increased and as there was no shortage of land suitable for coffee growing, the volume of coffee exports rose (see figure 4.2). The annual figures fluctuated greatly because of seasonal conditions and world prices while exports were clearly affected by periods of great political upheaval, such as the second half of the 1860s, but the upward trend is clear from the moving average.

Figure 4.2: Volume of Haitian Coffee Exports (mn lb), 1817–1915

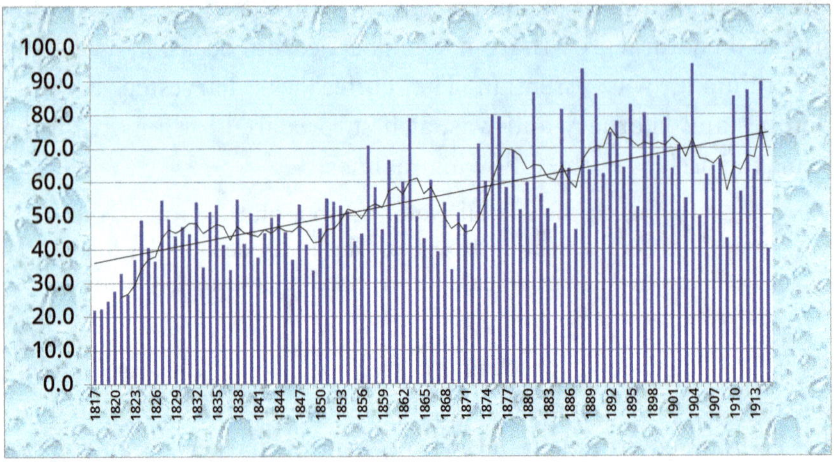

Source: Statistical Appendix. Note: The trend line is a five-period moving average.

Figure 4.3: Volume of Haitian Logwood Exports (mn lb), 1818–1914

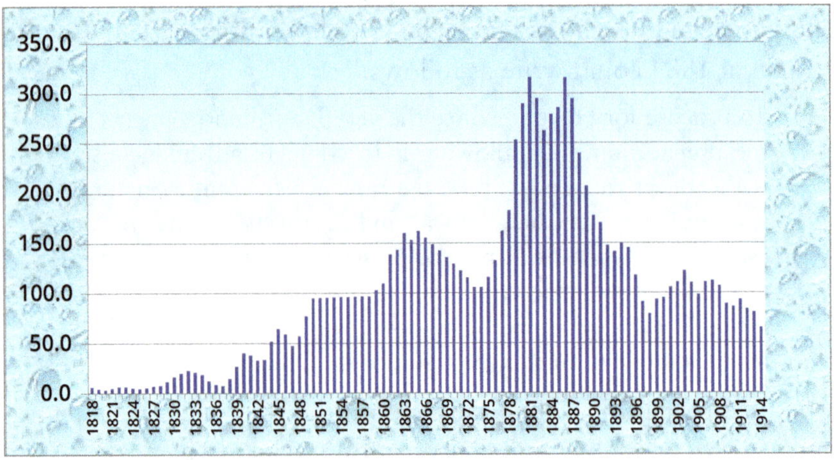

Source: Statistical Appendix.

Logwood, from which a natural dye is obtained, was the second most important Haitian export for most of the nineteenth century.[12] Although the peasantry was at first forbidden to cut it, the volume of exports expanded rapidly after Boyer under whom restrictions had continued. Much of it was sold to the US, although it was also sold to the UK where it was regarded as superior to Jamaican logwood. The volume of exports, however, peaked around 1880 (see figure

4.3). By then the forests had been largely cleared of logwood and contemporaries noted that in subsequent years a large proportion of exports consisted of roots rather than trees.

The sea-island cotton exported from Haiti, as elsewhere in the Caribbean, was not competitive with US cotton. Exports continued at modest levels until the outbreak of the US Civil War. The rise in cotton prices and the promotional measures taken by President Geffrard then stimulated exports. However, Haiti – like so many other countries – was unable to compete when prices returned to more normal levels after the civil war. Exports fluctuated in subsequent decades, but did not return to their level of the mid-1860s.

Haitian cacao, unlike coffee, was not especially valued for its aroma or taste, and exports languished at low levels for most of the nineteenth century. Exports only started to accelerate after 1880 in response both to higher prices and the cacao boom in the Dominican Republic. However, the rise of cacao exports was modest compared with what happened in the neighbouring country for several reasons despite the fact that cacao, like coffee, can be grown successfully on small estates. First, Haitian infrastructure – especially railways – was progressing much less rapidly than in the Dominican Republic and, secondly, cacao exports were much more heavily taxed.

Figure 4.4: Volume per head (lb) of Haitian Coffee and Logwood Exports, 1818–1914

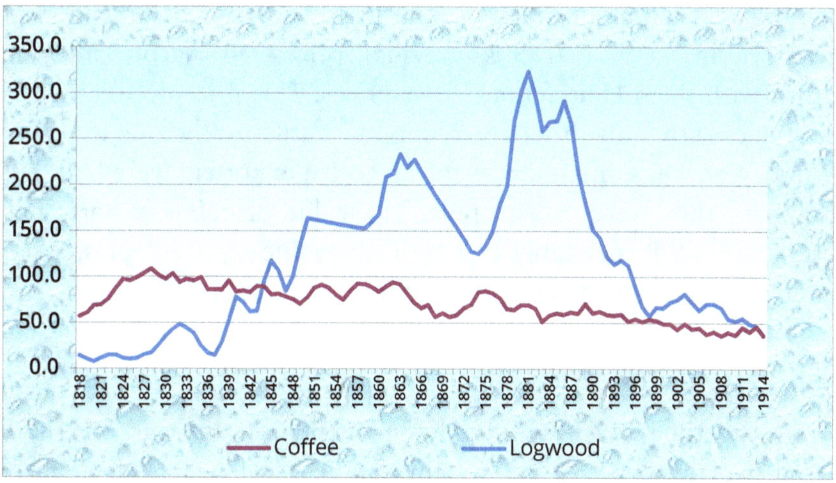

Source: Statistical Appendix.

For economic development to take place, the volume of exports must normally expand by more than the rate of increase of population. This did happen in the case of cacao and cotton, but it did not consistently happen in the case of logwood and coffee (see figure 4.4). Because of its importance to overall exports, the decline in the volume of coffee exports per head after 1890 was particularly serious. Given the dependence of public finance on foreign trade and the dependence of imports on exports, this meant that the Haitian development model was only viable if the terms of trade improved. This depended primarily on the price of exports and, in particular, on the price of coffee.

Haitian coffee may have commanded a premium, but the price still depended on the world market where Brazil was the dominant supplier. What happened in Brazil, therefore, had a large bearing on the price of Haitian coffee. However, the *fob* price of Haitian coffee was also affected by the export taxes applied in Haiti and the import tariffs applied by France. The French (and German) consumer was able to discriminate between Haitian and other coffees, but the demand curve was not vertical. Thus, part of the export and import taxes was born by the Haitian producer through a reduction in the price received by growers. Since the import tariff was largely unchanged, it was the increase in the coffee export tax and Brazilian market conditions that had the most impact.

Coffee prices fluctuated throughout the nineteenth century, but the prices in different markets were highly correlated. After a brief civil war in the early 1890s, Brazilian prices fell sharply dragging down with them Haitian and other prices. This price decline would continue with only brief interruptions until just before the First World War. The consequences for all coffee exporters were bad, but for Haiti they were catastrophic. The value of coffee exports fell, bringing with it inevitably a drop in the value of all exports. What happened then was determined by public finance.

4.3 Public Finance

By the time Boyer re-united the country at the end of 1820, Haiti had developed a tax system that was reasonably diversified. The principal sources of income were taxes on imports, of which the *ad valorem* tariff was by far the most important. This had been introduced by Dessalines in 1806 at ten per cent, raised to 12 per cent by Boyer in 1819 and to 16 per cent in 1827 when it applied to the whole island.[13] The yield had been undermined by the preferences conceded to the British in 1814 and to the French in 1825, but Boyer soon put a stop to both and added an additional ten per cent on the import tariffs applied to US ships in 1829.

The other taxes on trade were export duties, which did not apply to all products and which were in any case suspended from 1827 to 1835. In both cases, imports and exports, there were also various minor taxes based on tonnage and wharfage. The contribution of all these trade taxes to public revenue in Boyer's presidency was around 50 per cent. The other half of public revenue came from the land tax, rent and sale of state lands, sale of patents, stamp duties, and so on.[14] Of these, the land tax, which had been adopted by Christophe as well as Pétion, was the most important.

All taxes at first were paid in the national currency (*gourdes*). Before the introduction of paper money in 1826, the money supply was based on coins (*specie*) so that in theory the *gourde* was equivalent to US or Spanish dollars. In practice, however, a shortage of *specie* had obliged Pétion to debase the coinage by reducing its metallic content and the problem was exacerbated by counterfeit money introduced from outside.[15] By the time Boyer re-united the country, the exchange rate of the *gourde* to the dollar was estimated to be only 3:1.[16] Faced with an acute shortage of currency in 1826 (see below), Boyer then introduced paper money that – not being backed by hard currency – caused a further slide in the currency. Boyer, therefore, decreed in 1835 that import duties must be paid in hard currency, although all other taxes could still be paid in *gourdes*.

At this point, Haiti began its painful experience with two currencies, which did not end until the 1870s. As the fall of the *gourde* continued, the dollar value of those taxes collected in national currency declined further and further. By the end of the 1840s, when the exchange rate was 14:1, the only tax of importance had become import duties since these were collected in hard currency. A change had to be made and in 1850 Soulouque made the export tax on coffee payable in kind at 20 per cent. This rescued public revenue, although the yield from the other taxes – particularly the land tax – generated little income by the end of the 1850s as the exchange rate had fallen to 30:1.

In 1860, Geffrard, who had replaced Soulouque in January 1859, introduced an export tax payable in hard currency. At first, it was applied only to coffee and logwood (the two main commodities). The export tax on coffee payable in kind was then scrapped. Nearly 100 per cent of public revenue now came from customs duties. Other taxes were levied, but – being paid in national currency – the yield was extremely small. By the time the land tax was abolished in 1870, when the exchange rate had fallen to 4,000:1, it had ceased to have any purpose. Soon after, the *gourde* was withdrawn from circulation, and Haiti depended largely on foreign currencies until the introduction of the (new) *gourde* in 1880 at par with the US dollar.

From this point onwards, despite its dependence on customs duties that made the country vulnerable to a fall in coffee prices, public revenue might have been sufficient in Haiti if the state had not faced an increase in expenditure on debt service, claims from foreigners and the need to withdraw paper money. In order to meet these additional expenditures, the Haitian government increased the scale of customs duties (all payable in hard currency) rather than trying to diversify the tax base. These increases were then earmarked for various purposes, principally debt service charges, so that the Haitian people hardly benefited at all.

The increases in export taxes have been described in the previous section.[17] The *ad valorem* import duty remained unchanged at 16 per cent, but a surcharge of ten per cent was applied in 1863. This was followed a few years later by another surcharge of ten per cent to meet the claims arising from the 1867–69 civil war. There was then a surcharge of 25 per cent in 1872 to pay for the withdrawal of paper money. Then in 1876 all these surcharges were replaced with a new one of 50 per cent, which applied to all taxes on imports (not just the *ad valorem* duties). Finally, in 1883 an additional surcharge of 33⅓ per cent was introduced. If we compute the average tariff rate by dividing estimated import duties by imports, we find that it had risen to 35 per cent by the 1880s, and it stayed there until the tariff reform of 1905, when the average rate was temporarily reduced.

Figure 4.5: Haitian public revenue per head (US$), 1820–1914

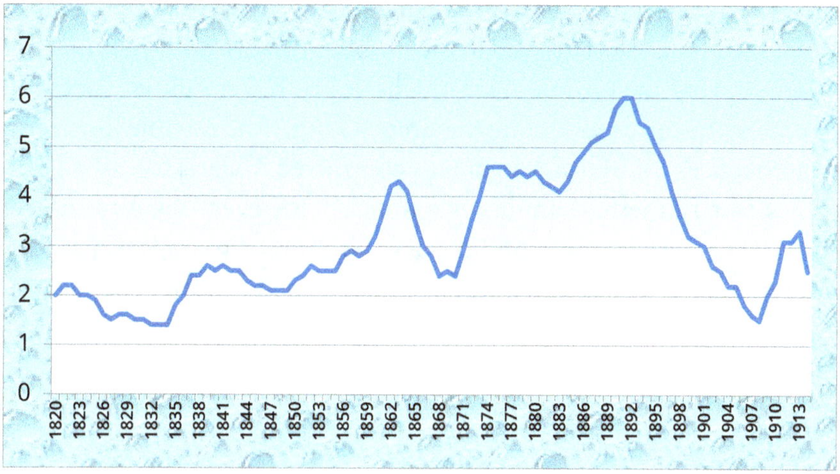

Source: Statistical Appendix.

Haitian governments may have been able to set the rate of taxes on trade, but they could not control world prices. When coffee prices started to fall in the 1890s, public finances in Haiti deteriorated. Customs duties could not be raised further (they were already at – if not beyond – the rates needed to maximise revenues) and exports could not be diversified due to the absence of infrastructure, the shortage of capital and the lack of education among the peasantry. In the two decades before the US invasion, Haitian governments resorted with increasing frequency and desperation to internal debt, including the issue of paper money not backed by reserves. Public revenue itself, still almost entirely dependent on customs duties, declined and the fall was even sharper when expressed in *per capita* terms (see figure 4.5).

Haiti's public expenditure was dominated at first by the need for a large standing army. This absorbed about half the budget in the first decade of Boyer's rule. The size of the armed forces was reduced to around 20,000 under Geffrard in the 1860s and perhaps 16,000 under Salomon in the 1880s.[18] This allowed expenditure on the military to fall below 25 per cent of the budget. However, internal political instability and the ever-present external threat meant that further reductions in the military share of the budget were not possible.

The armed forces may have absorbed 50 per cent of the budget in the early 1820s, but at least Haiti had no debt to service. This changed when the French fleet arrived in the harbour of Port-au-Prince in April 1825 carrying the *Ordonnance* of Charles X. Boyer's unwise decision to accept the terms set out by the French king[19] had terrible long-term consequences for Haiti. A loan was contracted in Paris for 30 million francs to pay the first annual instalment. However, this was subject to a 20 per cent commission, so Boyer was forced to impose a special tax on Haitian citizens to pay the balance due to France for the first year (six million francs).[20] When this proved unsuccessful, he was forced to ransack the Treasury and pay the balance in coins, draining the country of *specie* and forcing him to introduce paper money the following year.

The indemnity and the loan became known as the double debt, although it was not a debt in the usual sense. The money had not been used for productive purposes, thereby creating the resources from which the debt could be serviced, but was instead a subsidy to the French state that then passed it on to the former slave owners and their descendants. The French authorities presented figures suggesting that the indemnity was compensation for expropriation of French property and it was duly itemised, but in practice they had estimated Haiti's annual exports in 1823 (30 million francs), deducted 50 per cent for costs of production and amortised the balance over ten years to reach the magic figure of 150 million francs. Essentially, it was a cynical exercise to extract the maximum subsidy that they thought Haiti could pay.[21]

The double debt was enormously unpopular in Haiti, and there was even an attempted uprising. Wisely, Boyer defaulted on the second and subsequent instalments of the indemnity and made no interest payments on the loan. He also abolished export duties, in effect depriving France of its 50 per cent preference, and also cancelled the reduction of French privileges on import tariffs. However, he did not repudiate the double debt and, after several unsuccessful negotiations, agreed new terms in 1838. It is from this moment, rather than 1825, that Haiti became burdened with external debt service payments since up to that point the only disbursement had been a single off-budget payment for 5.3 million francs ($1 million) in *specie*.

Although payments were occasionally suspended, particularly 1843–48 and 1867–69, Haiti regularly serviced the double debt and finally paid it off in December 1883.[22] However, in 1874, the republic took out its first true foreign loan. The amount received, after the usual enormous commissions, was small, and President Domingue (1874–76) in the following year took out a much bigger loan (again from French bankers). The fraud involved in this so-called Domingue loan was enormous, on both the Haitian and French side, and President Salomon made renegotiation a priority. This he did with some success, but the fact of the matter is that Haiti ended up servicing a large external debt that had brought virtually no benefit to the country. Much the same happened in 1896 and 1910 with two French loans designed in theory to retire the previous debts on more favourable terms.[23]

The third major item of public expenditure was debt service on the internal debt. From an early stage in its independent history, the Haitian government had borrowed from those in the private sector with capital (usually merchants). Some of these were Haitians, while others were foreigners, but in all cases the loans were treated as internal. Haitian governments were not as punctilious in meeting the service charges on the internal debt as they were with the external debt and the terms, therefore, tended to become over time financially more onerous and politically more disadvantageous for the government.[24]

The cost of internal debt servicing was at first manageable. However, following the 1867–69 civil war, it became a major burden. The stock of internal debt, when converted to US dollars, had become as big as the stock of external debt by 1890.[25] In 1900, therefore, an effort was made to consolidate the domestic interest-bearing debt on more favourable terms. This Consolidation Loan, as it became known, was carried out with the participation of the *Banque Nationale d'Haiti* (see below), but it was done in such a fraudulent manner that the Haitian government was left worse off.[26] As coffee prices remained low and the country's external credit was exhausted, the Haitian government resorted to internal debt on more and more onerous terms.[27]

Haitian law restricted ownership of land and retail sales to Haitian citizens. These restrictions, however, were progressively lifted.[28] In any case the ban still allowed plenty of scope for foreigners in wholesale activities, import-export houses, and timber concessions. In addition, a large number of traders had emigrated to Haiti from the Ottoman Empire by the end of the nineteenth century and had successfully, if illegally, circumvented the ban on retailing. Finally, the *Banque Nationale d'Haiti* had even been allowed to participate in the land mortgage market, while several foreign-owned public utilities and infrastructure companies were established under President Florvil Hyppolite (1889–95).

Foreign business interests became more pervasive, and Haitian governments started to face a trickle of financial claims from foreign residents as well as some non-residents arising from alleged damage to property, cancellation of contracts, or false arrest. Gradually this trickle became a stream. These claims were pursued with great vigour by the relevant consuls and their governments with little concern for natural justice.[29] In the face of threats of gunboat diplomacy, Haiti often had no choice but to pay. It has been estimated that in the period up to 1880, Haiti paid $16 million to settle these claims and a further $2.5 million up to 1902.[30] The monetary value of these claims, despite their often frivolous nature, accelerated up to the US invasion and constituted another drain on the public finances.[31]

Figure 4.6: Haitian Public Expenditure by Type as % of Public Revenue, 1840–1914

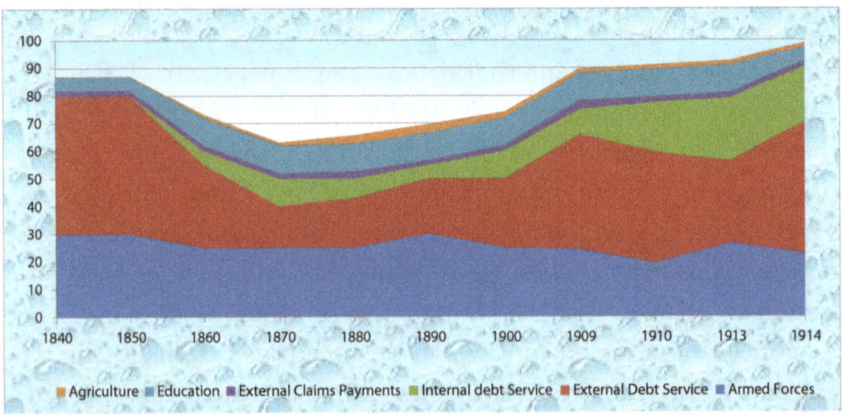

Source: Statistical Appendix.

Expenditure on the military, debt service, and external claims left little room for anything else (see figure 4.6). Indeed, the fact that as much as ten per cent of the budget went on public education from 1860 to 1913 must be regarded as a major achievement. However, it was not enough to make any real inroads into Haitian illiteracy, which remained above 90 per cent of the adult population. The proportion spent on agriculture was even lower, never exceeding three per cent and most of that was absorbed by the salaries of officials. Still, at least agriculture figured in the budget. There was almost nothing for public works, so that Haiti was entirely dependent on private capital for the development of financial institutions, public utilities, and infrastructure projects.

Haitian governments, aware of these constraints, had given priority to establish a national bank since Geffrard's presidency. However, it was not until 1881 that the project was achieved.[32] This French-owned bank, the *Banque Nationale d'Haiti* (BNdH), combined some of the functions of a state treasury with those of a central and commercial bank. However, it did not lend long-term for productive purposes, so its contribution to economic development was minimal. It was restructured in 1910 as the *Banque Nationale de la Republique d'Haiti* (BNRdH) with an infusion of US and German capital giving it some additional powers. In particular, it received the customs duties as they were paid and was only required to remit them to the Haitian government at the end of the fiscal year (September 30). Under an informal arrangement, money needed by the Haitian government was then advanced on a short-term basis until the customs duties were received.

Aware that the Haitian government ran the risk of default on a debt, most of which was owed to foreigners inside or outside the country, the US resolved to gain control of Haitian finances in order to eliminate any risk of European intervention. In collusion with the BNRdH, a plan was hatched under which the bank announced it was withdrawing from its agreement with the government on October 1, 1914, the first day of the new fiscal year. This time, the bank refused to honour the informal arrangements for advancing short-term money, but was not required to pay the customs duties until the end of the fiscal year. The Haitian state was insolvent and the US drew up plans for the invasion.[33] The murder of 168 political prisoners during the uprising against President Guillaume-Sam was the final trigger.[34]

NOTES

1. Haiti was the third most important coffee exporter, behind Brazil and the Dutch East Indies, until it was overtaken by Venezuela in the 1880s. See W.G. Clarence-Smith and S. Topik, *The Global Coffee Economy in Africa, Asia and Latin America, 1500–1989* (Cambridge, UK: Cambridge University Press, 2003), appendix.
2. See D. Nicholls, *From Dessalines to Duvalier: Race Colour, and National Independence in Haiti* (Cambridge, MA: Cambridge University Press, 1979) 68, drawing on figures in C. Mackenzie, *Notes on Haiti: Made during a Residence in That Republic*, vol. 2 (London: H. Colburn and R. Bentley, 1830), 201.
3. Timber was cut and sold for export by the peasantry, but from 1860 large concessions were given to foreigners for timber extraction.
4. The ban on whites became a ban on foreigners in the 1843 Constitution. It did not, however, apply to those blacks who came to Haiti from the US and other parts of the Caribbean.
5. From their high point in 1789 (95.6 million [long] pounds), raw sugar exports fell to virtually zero at the time of independence. They had recovered to 5.4 million pounds in 1818, most of which came from the north. In the case of coffee, exports had reached 76.8 million [long] pounds in 1789 before collapsing in the next 15 years. They had recovered to 26 million pounds in 1818, most of which came from the south. See J. Barros, *Haïti, de 1804 à nos jours*, vol. 1 (Paris: Editions L'Harmattan, 1984), 198 and 341.
6. See P.V. Benoit, *Évolution budgetaire et développement économique d'Haiti* (Port-au-Prince, Haiti: H. Deschamps, 1954), 32 onwards. Pétion raised export taxes no less than four times between 1808 and 1817.
7. Boyer made a number of small grants from state lands at the beginning of his term, but he did not break up the large estates in the north – or, indeed, those that remained in the south – and was keen to preserve them.
8. These are long pounds. They can be converted to the short pounds used in the US and UK by multiplying by 1.083.
9. The combined value of these four products as a share of domestic exports averaged 95 per cent.
10. See 'Two Hundred Years of Coffee in Haiti,' *Tea and Coffee Trade Journal* 68 (1935): 103. New York, NY: F.H.Hobbs & Co.

11. See Department of State, *Commercial Relations of the United States with Foreign Countries*, vol. 2 (Washington, DC: Department of State, 1884), 68.
12. In 1879/80, Haiti was also by far the world's most important exporter of logwood with two-thirds of the market. See A. Turnier, *Les États-Unis et le marché haïtien* (Washington, DC, 1955).
13. See Benoit, *Évolution budgetaire et développement économique d'Haiti*, 55–56. Pétion had maintained the import duties, but Christophe had scrapped them relying principally on the land tax and rents from state lands. See Nicholls, *Economic Dependence and Political Autonomy*, 5.
14. For 1837, each tax is itemised in R. Marte, *Estadísticas y documentos históricos sobre Santo Domingo, 1805–1890* (Santo Domingo, República Dominicana: Museo Nacional de Historia y Geografía, 1984), 108.
15. See Turnier, *Les États-Unis et le marché haïtien*, 278–79. The first debasement in 1811 reduced the value by 18 per cent. Two years later Pétion introduced a new money (*Serpent*) ostensibly at par with the US and Spanish dollar, but with a much lower metallic content so that its intrinsic value was only one-third.
16. See International Bureau of the American Republics, *Haiti: A Handbook*. (Washington, DC: International Bureau of the American Republics, 1893), 96.
17. Nearly all these increases were hypothecated and tied to the payment of debt service or claims by foreigners. This made it very difficult for the state to lower export duties, although they had reached dangerously high levels by the 1880s.
18. See S. St. John, *Hayti: or, The Black Republic* (New York, NY: Scribner & Welford, 1889), 310.
19. These included payment of an indemnity of 150 million French francs ($30 million) payable in five annual instalments and a reduction of 50 per cent in customs duties on both exports and imports. Thus, the French king imposed an enormous burden on Haiti while simultaneously depriving the young republic of the means to pay it.
20. The tax was enforced in Port-au-Prince, but Cap Haitien only paid half and elsewhere nothing at all was raised. See R. Lacerte, 'Xenophobia and Economic Decline: The Haitian Case, 1820–1843,' *The Americas* 37, no. 4 (1981): 505.
21. Although disastrous for Haiti, the indemnity brought almost no benefit to the former slave owners and their descendants. There were 25,838 beneficiaries and the annual payments by Haiti often yielded no more than a few francs for each family. Fairly typical was the case of Jean-Louis Lonchamp whose family of 11 members received in 1841 85 francs ($17) to cover the three years from 1838–40. This works out at

51.5 US cents per year per family member. See F. Blancpain, *Un siècle de relations financières entre Haïti et la France, 1825–1922* (Paris: L'Harmattan, 2001), 77.

22. See J.-F. Brière, 'L'Emprunt de 1825 dans la dette de l'independence haitienne envers la France,' *Journal of Haitian Studies* 12, no. 2 (2006): 132.
23. These four loans – 1874, 1875, 1896, and 1910 – have been analysed at great length by others. See, for example, J.-A. Firmin, *M. Roosevelt, président des États-Unis et la République d'Haïti* (New York, NY: Hamilton Bank Note Engraving and Printing Company, 1905), 438–50; S. Vincent, *Outline of Financial History of the Republic of Haiti.* (Port-au-Prince: Imp. de l'etat, 1939), 12–16; and Blancpain, *Un siècle de relations financières entre Haïti et la France, 1825–1922*, chapters 4 and 5.
24. Rates of interest could be as high as one per cent per month on these loans and repayment was often required in hard currency. Lenders also became involved in the financing of *coups d'état* and normally received commercial advantage if they were successful. See B.G. Plummer, *Haiti and the Great Powers, 1902–1915* (Baton Rouge, LA: Louisiana State University Press, 1988), chapter 2.
25. See International Bureau of the American Republics, 111.
26. President Nord-Alexis (1902–08) was left to clean up the mess. Despite being an octogenarian, he prosecuted the case with such vigour that several of those culpable – including foreigners – were eventually punished. See Blancpain, *Un siècle de relations financières entre Haïti et la France, 1825–1922*, 115–39. However, Haiti's ability to service its internal debt remained fragile.
27. In 1914, the year before the US invasion, an internal loan was raised with a commission of 52 per cent, i.e., the government only received 48 per cent of what it was contracted to pay.
28. The prohibitions on foreigners had been relaxed by two laws in 1860, which allowed those married to Haitians to acquire real estate and also permitted foreigners to gain timber and mineral concessions. Then in 1883 a law was passed giving Haitian nationality to companies formed in Haiti but owned by foreigners provided that they were engaged in exporting agricultural products. See B. Joachim, *Les racines du sous développement en Haïti* (Port-au-Prince: Impr. H. Deschamps, 1979), 176–77. Finally, naturalisation was made easier under President Hyppolite (1889–95).
29. Some of these claims were so outrageous that one can only wonder at the brazenness of foreign governments in pursuing them. The most notorious case involved a slave trader, Antonio Pelletier, who

had become a naturalised US citizen and who was sentenced in 1861 for trying to capture slaves in Haiti for sale in Cuba. The US State Department only dropped the case in 1886. See J.N. Léger, *Haiti: Son histoire et ses détracteurs* (New York, NY: Neale Pub. Co., 1907), 232–35.

30. See Joachim, *Les racines du sous développement en Haïti*, 187.
31. The outstanding claims were examined by a Claims Commission set up by the US after 1915. After careful examination of each claim, with a total value of US$21 million, they recommended settlement of US$2.8 million – a reduction of nearly 90 per cent. See E.G. Balch, *Occupied Haiti: Being the Report of a Committee of Six Disinterested Americans Representing Organizations Exclusively American, Who, Having Personally Studied Conditions in Haiti in 1926, Favor the Restoration of the Independence of the Negro Republic* (New York, NY: The Writers Pub. Co., 1927), 46–48.
32. An offer in 1874 to establish a bank by a US citizen, A.H. Lazare, had been accepted, but he failed to provide the funds. Needless to say, this did not stop him or the US government for pursuing a claim against the Haitian state for breach of contract. See Léger, *Haiti*, 231–32.
33. To ensure that the Haitian government remained insolvent, the US marines embarked in December 1914 and removed $500,000 from the vaults of the BNRdH to New York on the specious grounds that these funds were pledged to the withdrawal of paper money and might be used by the government for other purposes. See Balch, *Occupied Haiti*, 17–18.
34. This gruesome episode in Haitian political history, in which President Guillaume-Sam was dragged out of the French legation and torn limb from limb, as well as the US occupation itself, have been the subject of numerous books and articles. See, for example, H. Schmidt, *The United States Occupation of Haiti, 1915–1934* (New Brunswick, NJ: Rutgers University Press, 1971).

Chapter 5
FRENCH GUIANA

With a rapidly growing population of around 300,000, a GDP per head of some US$20,000, a sophisticated welfare state, and a futuristic space centre, French Guiana [la Guyane] had become the envy of many other countries in the Caribbean by the beginning of the twenty-first century.

This economic success was a relatively recent phenomenon. Two centuries earlier, after the colony was restored to France by the victors in the Napoleonic Wars, it was unclear if the imperial power had either the will or the resources to render la Guyane viable. The labour force, liberated in 1794 and enslaved again in 1802, had no desire to return to the agricultural plantations after the Portuguese occupiers left in 1817 and France had signed a treaty with the UK to end the slave trade.

It was only an illegal trade in slaves, ignored by the state, which made possible the recovery of French Guiana as an agricultural colony. Helped by the restoration of the sugar plantations, exports per head grew rapidly. And when the trade in slaves was finally ended in 1831, la Guyane found a new source of dynamism in exports of annatto (a natural dye). By the 1840s, it looked as if French Guiana had finally re-established itself as an agricultural colony thanks to the rapid growth of exports per head (see figure 5.1).

It would prove to be a false dawn. The end of slavery in 1848 liberated the labour force, and no amount of coercion could drive the former slaves back to the plantations. In despair, la Guyane was chosen by the French imperial state as the site of a new penal colony [le bagne] that would operate for a century. Yet, no sooner was the penal colony established than gold was discovered in commercial quantities. The gold bonanza drove exports per head to the second highest in the Caribbean by the end of the nineteenth century, while at the same time eclipsing almost all agricultural activities except subsistence farming.

The gold boom did not end as suddenly as the previous boom based on agricultural exports, but it ended all the same. During the 50 years from just before the First World War to the 1960s, French Guiana experienced a long period of decline (see figure 5.1) during which gold exports steadily fell, deaths exceeded births, net migration was outwards, and the population fell back to its level in the 1860s.

Although births finally exceeded deaths in the 1950s, nothing, it seemed, could reverse the stagnation despite la Guyane becoming a part of France as a fully-fledged department in 1946. The decision in 1964, however, to place France's space station in French Guiana had an even more dramatic impact than the discovery of gold in 1855. La Guyane would now become a global exporter of transport services of the first rank, which not only transformed exports per head but also had an important multiplier effect on the whole economy. GDP soared, bringing with it a big increase in immigration (much of it undocumented).

***Figure 5.1:** French Guiana: Exports per head at constant prices (1900=100), log scale, 1820–2016*

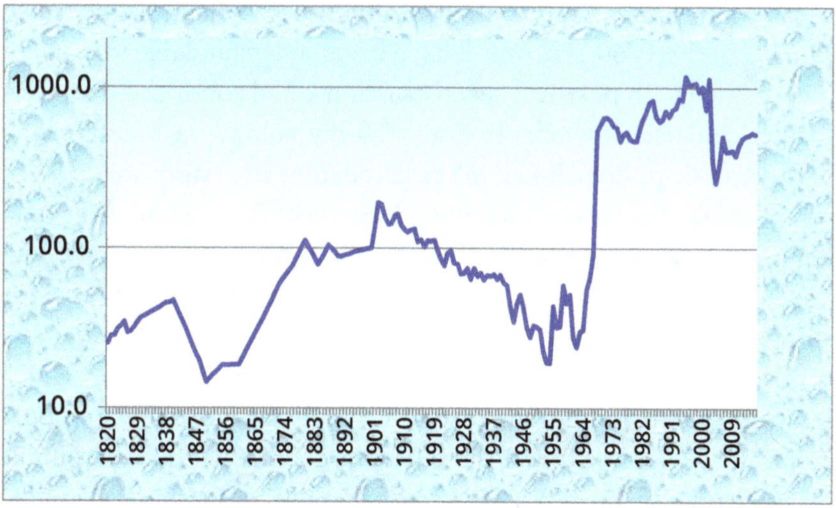

Sources: 1820–2008 from Statistical Appendix. 2008 onwards are from INSEE.

In the last 60 years, French Guiana's population has risen ten-fold. The birth rate is high and – thanks to a young population – the death rate is lower than in metropolitan France [l'Hexagone, as it is known in the French Antilles]. Finding gainful employment, however, for all those of working age has proved impossible and unemployment, inactivity, and informal work are at high rates.

5.1. AGRICULTURAL COLONY

French Guiana, including the capital Cayenne, had been occupied by the British in 1809. However, the British chose not to stay and instead gave responsibility for the occupation to Portugal, allied with Great Britain in the Napoleonic Wars. The Portuguese administered French Guiana from Brazil until the colony was returned to France in 1817, two years after the Napoleonic Wars ended and in accordance with the terms of the Congress of Vienna.

During the long Anglo-French war, slavery and the slave trade had been abolished by France (in 1794) and then restored (in 1802), giving the slaves in French Guiana a few years of freedom that they used to abandon the plantations where they had worked; the colony was then cut off from the mother country from 1809 onwards, and the few agricultural estates that survived the Napoleonic Wars were in ruin.

Given the utter failure of the colonisation scheme launched at Kourou in the 1760s,[1] it would have been understandable if France – preoccupied with post-war reconstruction – had continued to neglect French Guiana. However, as France's only colony on the mainland of the Americas, French Guiana received after its restoration in 1817 considerable attention as the authorities became convinced it could replicate the success of Dutch Guiana, the neighbouring colony.

The products that France hoped the colony would export were all agricultural, although the forests were also expected to make a contribution in due course. The most important was sugar, which – as the French Antilles and the other Guianas had shown – could be produced successfully if there were a guaranteed market. Simple experimentation, however, had shown that the colony was well-suited to exporting a series of other crops as well, including annatto (called roucou in French Guiana), a natural dye that can be added to food to provide colour and flavour or used in the manufacture of textiles, furniture, and leather. There were also high expectations for cotton, coffee, cacao, and cloves.

To convert French Guiana into a successful agricultural colony, several obstacles had to be overcome. The most serious were demographic. At the time that the Congress of Vienna began in 1814, the population had fallen to 14,463. Nearly 85 per cent of the population were slaves, the remainder being either white (881) or free blacks (1,502). This was too small a society to make much of an impact as an agricultural colony, so economic success depended on expanding the workforce and the population.

This was easier said than done. Since the slaves were such a large part of the total and since deaths exceeded births among the slave population, there was no chance of expansion without net inward migration. Yet, attracting free labour before the colony had demonstrated its ability to succeed as an agricultural economy was almost impossible. Thus, French Guiana became dependent on the trade in slaves at a time when it had been declared illegal by the French government.[2]

This required the connivance of the local authorities. Slaves continued to be imported in significant numbers until the trade (but not slavery itself) was finally ended in 1831. In the previous year, the number of slaves had risen to a peak of 19,261 and the population had reached 23,047. In the space of a mere 16 years, therefore, the population had risen by 60 per cent, and most of the increase was due to the rise in the slave population despite that the slave death rate continued to exceed the birth rate by a large margin.

The labour force expansion made possible by the illegal trade in slaves allowed agriculture to flourish. Between 1820 and 1830, just before the end of the trade, the volume of sugar exports increased more than six fold (see table 5.1). Annatto, cacao, coffee, and cloves exports also prospered. The only crop where exports declined in volume was cotton, where prices were falling and which suffered from the intense competition provided by the southern US. This, however, was a common experience for all the countries of the Caribbean – not just French Guiana.

Table 5.1: French Guiana: Volume and Value of Exports, 1820–50

Volume (lb)	Sugar	Annatto	Cotton	Cacao	Coffee	Cloves
1820	548,735	250,000	440,000	100,000	50,000	200,000
1830	3,967,449	422,563	357,150	114,684	71,322	267,727
1840	3,879,446	1,186,678	347,193	68,729	14,533	340,282
1850	794,380	527,630	46,200	78,113	13,000	161,429
Value (US$)	**Sugar**	**Annatto**	**Cotton**	**Cacao**	**Coffee**	**Cloves**
1820	27,272	50,000	86,108	9,470	12,060	6,000
1830	173,378	84,513	51,430	5,344	6,298	8,032
1840	154,402	178,002	49,093	4,955	2,469	10,208
1850	32,887	52,763	4,620	4,601	1,999	4,843

Source: Statistical Appendix.

By 1830, therefore, French Guiana had established itself as an agricultural colony where the labour force was provided almost entirely by slaves, the capital came from French planters, and infrastructure was supplied by the imperial state. Exports per head had risen by 1830 to US$14.50, placing the colony in the top half of the Caribbean rankings and ahead of many other European colonies. The market for exports was overwhelmingly metropolitan France, where imperial preference favoured the colonies and reduced competition from other sources of supply.

So confident now were sections of metropolitan France in the future of the South American colony that a society was formed to promote it. La Société d'Études pour la Colonisation de la Guyane published a series of pamphlets drawing attention to the seemingly limitless agricultural potential of French Guiana:[3]

> On obtient deux récoltes annuelles pour le plus grand nombre des produits. La canne à sucre est entièrement mûre le quatorzième mois. Le sol est traversé par des fleuves magnifiques don't plusieurs sont navigables par les bâtiments à voiles de 250 a 300, et par les bâtiments à vapeur de 4 a 500 tonneaux. Il est couvert de bois et de forêts qui commencent à devenir exploitables a quinze lieues de la côte; dans les terres basses, il n'a pas besoin d'engrais.

The Achilles heel in this model was, of course, its dependence on an illegal trade in slaves. Following the final end of the trade, the slave population – where deaths still exceeded births by a wide margin – declined. From its peak at 19,261 in 1830, the number of slaves had declined to 12,943 on the eve of emancipation in 1848 – a fall of one-third. The colonial state and the French planters tried hard to attract labour on a voluntary basis from other parts of the Caribbean, Africa, Asia (including French India), and the Portuguese Atlantic colonies, but without much success. As a result, the population of French Guiana – not just the number of slaves – also declined from its peak of 23,047 in 1830, falling to a low of 18,927 in 1848 when slavery finally ended.

The decline in the slave population after 1830 changed fundamentally the nature of the economic model. The most labour-intensive activities, especially sugar, were seriously affected. Sugar plantations closed or merged in order to achieve economies of scale with the number dropping from 56 to 28 in one decade.[4] However, the number of slaves employed steadily declined and inevitably the volume of sugar exports started to fall after 1830. Much the same happened with cotton, cacao, and coffee (see table 5.1).

By contrast, the production and export of annatto (and cloves to a lesser extent) prospered in the decade after 1830. Indeed, the number of slaves employed in the production of annatto *increased* in the decade after the end of the illegal trade. Annatto, where the berries are collected from mature trees that did not require annual planting, was so successful that its export had overtaken sugar in value by 1840 (see table 5.1), making French Guiana the only country in the Caribbean where this particular dye was the major source of export earnings. And annatto was spread evenly over 12 of the 13 'quartiers' in French Guiana, helping to integrate the colony much more than other exports where production was highly concentrated.

Annatto was a rare example of agricultural success in French Guiana, helped by its method of production that was ideally suited to local conditions. The spiny fruits were collected from an evergreen shrub [*Bixa orellana*] that is indigenous to South America and the seeds – the size of peas – extracted. These seeds were then prepared for commercial use through a series of simple treatments that resulted in a paste in the shape of a cake or loaf of bread, weighing around five kilos that were wrapped in leaves before being exported in large wooden barrels.

The success of annatto owed a great deal to the demand for it in France. It could be used as a dye in a huge variety of products including textiles, polishes and foods (especially cheese and butter). It could even be used as an antidote to the poison contained in the juice of manioc [cassava]. And with an annual world demand estimated at no more than 400,000 kilos, French Guiana was by far the most important global supplier with the world price largely determined by what happened in the colony.[5] Only later did it face competition from Brazil and the French Antilles.

Thanks to annatto, exports per head in the colony continued to rise, reaching nearly US$20 in 1840. This, however, would be the high point for many years to come. The production and export of all the main exports fell in the decade after 1840, and this time there was nothing to take their place. The number of slaves employed in the production of annatto declined sharply, while the numbers employed in sugar continued to fall as well. Inevitably, the value of exports dropped as well, falling between their peak in 1839 and 1847 by half. Only the subsidies provided by the state kept the colony afloat, allowing imports to exceed exports in every year after 1836.

The sudden abolition of slavery in 1848, following the revolution in the same year, took the planters by surprise. Unable to prevent them from leaving the plantations through an apprenticeship system, as had happened in the British colonies and would be deployed in the Dutch and Spanish ones, the planters were faced with a sudden collapse in their captive labour force. And unlike what happened in the small Caribbean islands, there was no shortage of land for those former slaves willing to move inland and become squatters, some joining the small Amerindian and maroon population that had survived 250 years of European colonisation.[6]

The result was an almost total collapse of the main exports (see table 5.1). By 1850, sugar and annatto yielded little more by value than they had in 1820, although annatto would at least recover in later years. Meanwhile, cotton, cacao, coffee, and clove exports had virtually disappeared. Exports per head were now down to $5, far below their level in 1820, and the colony was increasingly dependent on a small re-export trade from neighbouring countries that created few jobs and added little value. The French imperial state was, therefore, obliged to provide a substantial subsidy to prevent the total collapse of the colony and this helped to sustain the standard of living through the importation of essentials. Indeed, imports per head were US$25 in 1850, some five times higher than exports per head.

The previous optimism regarding French Guiana's vocation as an agricultural colony now vanished.[7] While huge efforts were made in the French Antilles to attract indentured labour to replace the former slaves, la Guyane was considered by the authorities to be a hopeless case. Instead, the French state under the new Emperor Napoleon III chose the country as the site of the first offshore penal colony under a law of 1852.

Much has been written about the fate of these convicts [forçats in French], especially the political prisoners housed on Île du Diable. Yet, the political ones were never more than a small minority of the prison population, which at its height numbered some 7,000. These convicts, nearly all male, might have been expected to play a significant part in improving the infrastructure of the country and reviving its prospects as an agricultural colony, but this never happened. The authorities never saw the prisoners as a strategic asset, preferring instead to emphasise punishment and holding them up as a warning to others. In addition, their life expectancy was very low, with deaths from yellow fever and malaria exceptionally high, and those that survived were often too ill to work.[8]

The convicts soon made up a significant proportion of the population, but – being overwhelmingly male and in prison – could do nothing to reverse the demographic decline of the colony. While other Caribbean colonies, including the French ones, celebrated emancipation with a big rise in births and a fall in deaths, French Guiana continued to have more deaths than births until the last year of the Second World War.

The 'black legend' of la Guyane can be traced to this demographic imbalance, which was widely attributed to deadly conditions in the colony. Yet, French Guiana was not unhealthy, or at least no more so than many Caribbean countries.[9] Instead, the colony suffered for decades from an imbalance between the sexes with a predominance of males. This was due first to slavery and later to the penal colony. However, the imbalance was also exacerbated by the discovery of gold after 1850 that brought thousands of male prospectors to the country.

5.2. The Age of Gold

The Amerindians of French Guiana had long known gold existed. Despite the rumours, however, the colonists had done little to search for it until the 1830s when the first serious attempts were made to organise expeditions into the interior. These early efforts never advanced beyond the planning stage for a variety of reasons.[10] It was not until 1855 that the first successful expedition was organised to the upper Approuague River under the leadership of a local official called Félix Couy and guided by an Amerindian called Paoline.[11]

By good fortune this was also the year in which the Banque Coloniale de la Guyane had started operations. The first bank in the colony, it had been established in 1851 by the French Parliament, along with similar banks in the French Antilles, as a response to emancipation. The new bank, funded in large part by a deduction from the funds voted by Parliament to compensate the former slave owners for the loss of their slaves, was expected to provide loans that would permit economic diversification in French Guiana. The discovery of gold in commercial quantities was, therefore, fortuitous to say the least.

The news that gold had been found reached Cayenne (the colony's capital) in August 1855. The timing could not have been better for the white colonists, who were struggling to maintain their plantations after emancipation and the flight of the former slaves. In no time at all the vast bulk of these plantation owners had formed a society to extract gold. Their company [*Compagnie Aurifère et Agricole de l'Approuague*] then received a royal decree in May 1857 that provided a concession covering 200,000 hectares.

The aim of the shareholders was to establish a monopoly that would generate handsome dividends and operate alongside their agricultural plantations. This could only be done if labour was tightly controlled, which is why they secured a permit to import 463 workers for gold extraction. In this way, they hoped to prevent a mass exodus from Cayenne and their plantations in search of higher incomes.

The first shipments of gold were made in 1857 and nearly all gold extracted was exported (only a tiny part of production stayed in the colony to be used in jewellery). Exports of gold steadily increased for the next few years (see figure 5.2). However, the company was unable to make any dividend payments, as had been forecast in the prospectus, and it had collapsed by 1867. This was the final straw for many of the colony's white elite, who now left French Guiana never to return.

Far from being the end of gold extraction, the company's collapse marked the beginning of a new and more dynamic phase. New companies were created, often formed by investors from metropolitan France, with easy access to finance. Many locals also secured licences to extract gold as self-employed workers or in small groups [bricoleurs]. And, for the first time, there appeared illegal gold miners [maraudeurs], whose activity was conducted in secret and whose output went unregistered.

Figure 5.2: French Guiana: Gold Exports (troy oz), 1857–1913

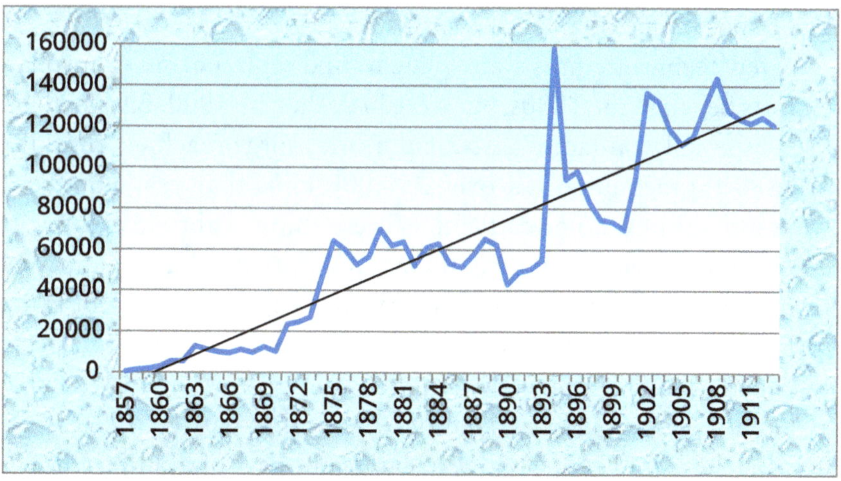

Source: Statistical Appendix and Pétot (1986).

These new entrants to the gold industry transformed the volume of production. By 1875, exports had reached 64,193 troy ounces (nearly two tonnes).[12] New discoveries then led to a further expansion after 1890, including the peak year of 1894 when exports reached nearly five tonnes (see figure 5.2). On the eve of the First World War, French Guiana was exporting around four tonnes each year with a value of US$2 million, and the colony's future as a gold producer seemed assured.

The shareholders in the *Compagnie Aurifère et Agricole de l'Approuague* had expected that gold mining would be complementary to agriculture. This turned out to be a forlorn hope. By 1870, three years after the company collapsed, gold already accounted for nearly 60 per cent of exports. Ten years later, in 1880, the share had risen above 90 per cent, where it would stay until the First World War. In one year (1900), gold as a share of exports reached an astonishing 98.9 per cent, and French Guiana had the second highest level of exports per head in the Caribbean.[13]

French Guiana was now *par excellence* a gold colony, the dream of European imperialists through the ages, importing a wide range of foodstuffs some of which had previously been produced domestically. Other exports had, one by one, been abandoned. Cloves disappeared in the 1850s; cotton collapsed in the 1860s; coffee virtually ceased in the 1870s; sugar ended in the 1890s, by which time annatto exports had almost come to an end along with cacao.

A few feeble attempts were made to find replacements. Phosphate exports began in the 1880s, but were in decline by 1900. Bird feathers, used especially on ladies' hats, had a brief surge reaching 189 kilos in 1888 (France imported over 250,000 kilos that year), but soon went into decline. Some cattle hides were shipped abroad along with animal horns, while fishing and cinnamon provided a small income from exports. Even the famous Cayenne peppers could not make much of an impact. Only rum exports seemed to offer any prospects, but not enough to compete with gold.[14]

Gold at least could be taxed or at least that part recorded in the customs houses. Then, as now, a significant part of gold production was unregistered and smuggled out of the country, although the income was usually spent inside. And the income generated by gold of both kinds (registered and unregistered) led to imports that were subject to tariffs, even if the goods came from France and a much higher tariff if the goods came from outside the French Empire. Indeed, such was the appetite of French Guiana for imported goods that France was 'only' supplying two-thirds of their value in the decade before the First World War.

Figure 5.3: French Guiana: Revenue per head (US$), 1820–1910

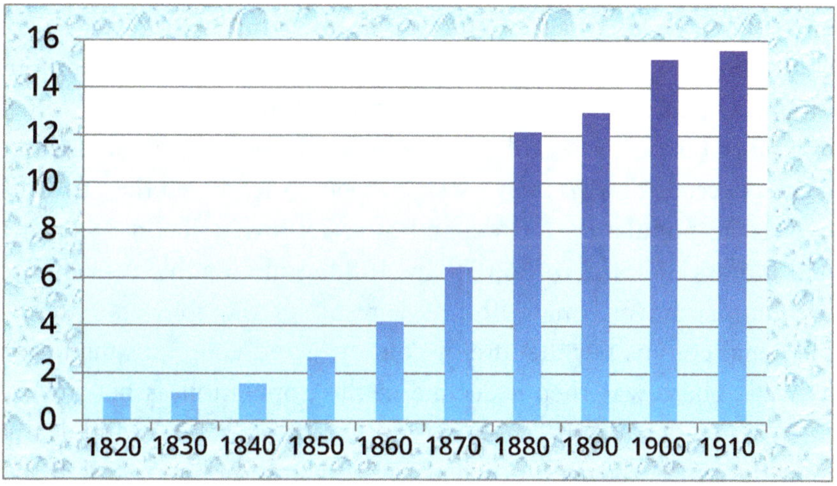

Source: Statistical Appendix.

The age of gold, therefore, led to a big increase in revenue. And since the population was still so small, this meant a large rise in revenue per head (see figure 5.3). From no more than one US dollar in 1820, revenue per head had reached $12 by 1880 and nearly $16 by 1910. This compared very favourably with other parts of the Caribbean (the average for the British colonies was roughly half this amount) and meant that public expenditure could rise on education, health, and infrastructure. Cayenne, with its imposing *Place des Palmistes* and its surrounding private mansions, now became an impressive-looking town that drew praise from visitors and locals alike.

Nowhere was the change in public spending more apparent than in state education. Not being an integral part of France, French Guiana had been subject to rule by decree since 1854 giving exceptional powers to the governor and the local elite. Since the cost of education per pupil in public schools was much higher than in those run by the church, the authorities had spent little on state education and the total school population as late as 1874 was only 1,121. Educational reform was undertaken in the 1890s, however, and by 1910 the school population had jumped to 2,310. Two-thirds of these were now educated in state schools, a much higher figure than before the reforms.[15]

Gold may have displaced other export activities, but this was not an early version of the Dutch-disease as the exchange rate remained unchanged (the colony used the French franc and France was on the gold standard). Instead, gold pulled labour away from the plantations leaving a shortage of workers for agriculture, forestry, and other mining industries. The stubborn demographics of the colony, where deaths exceeded births in every single year, exacerbated the problem.

Yet the population did expand after its low point in 1848 and had almost doubled to 36,079 by 1884. Some of this was due to involuntary inward migration as a result of the convicts entering the penal colony, but the lure of gold attracted voluntary migration as well. There was then a decline in the population as net inward migration failed to compensate for the gap between births and deaths until the end of the century when a new migration boom took place. This was the beginning of the peak decade of the golden age when the population surged to nearly 50,000 on the eve of the First World War (it included, of course, some 7,000 convicts whose numbers fluctuated from year to year).

The migrants to French Guiana would help to define the future social composition of the colony. The first to arrive in large numbers after emancipation were indentured labourers from Africa and India with a few from China and Indochina. In 1861, for example, there were 2,400 such immigrants, nearly all of whom (2,155) were single men. In 1880, there were 3,749 and again nearly all (3,382) were single men. Many deserted their place of work, heading to the gold-panning districts instead. However, the demographic impact of the indentured labourers was limited as so many chose to go home at the end of their contracts.

The second group to arrive in large numbers came from the rest of the Caribbean. Without the burden of contracts, many headed straight for the gold-bearing districts of French Guiana. Their numbers in 1896 were estimated at 12,000, a large proportion of the population at the time. And, of course, many migrants were French officials who had responsibility not only for administering the vast spaces of the colony, but also guarding the convicts in the penal settlements. Indeed, in 1884 there were more than 1,000 police and military officials working in *le bagne*.

Some convicts, overwhelmingly French males, stayed on when their sentences ended (not always by choice). However, their numbers were small. Between 1852 and 1867, for example, 18,069 were transported to the colony (98.4 per cent were male). At the end of this period, 7,173 were still in prison, 7,626 had died, and 1,982 had returned to France. Only 293 stayed in the colony, although 995 had escaped and may have remained as well.[16]

On the eve of the First World War, French Guiana had become a complex society in which the white plantocracy and the social structure it controlled had disappeared. In their place were descendants of slaves, free blacks, indentured labourers, and migrants from the Caribbean. The officials still came from France or other French colonies – as did most of the convicts – but a creole society had taken shape and has survived to this day. It was a relatively prosperous society, thanks to the income generated by gold, but that prosperity was about to be undermined as the First World War erupted.

5.3. Recession

Gold production, at least the part reported to the authorities, had peaked before the First World War. However, no one was unduly concerned as the gold cycle was something to which the colony had become accustomed. What was much more threatening was the outbreak of war in August 1914, which had an immediate impact. France suspended the gold standard, Germany occupied territory where sugar-beet was grown and the French government needed to expand the production of munitions and explosives. Within a few months trade across the Atlantic became much more difficult and dangerous as a result of German submarines and a shortage of shipping.

France now had less of an interest in importing gold. Instead, she wanted sugar to replace the beet fields occupied by the German army and rum to be used in the manufacture of explosives (and to treat the injured soldiers). In addition, France needed the gum from balata trees that could be used as a substitute for natural rubber and which the two other Guianas (British and Dutch) had been exporting successfully for some time.

French Guiana struggled to export sugar, but production increased enough to permit a big increase in rum exports during the war. Only 310 gallons had been exported in 1913, but by 1919 this had soared a thousand-fold to 310,865 gallons. Balata rose from 16 tonnes in 1905 to 1,434 tonnes by the end of the war. And the colony also saw a big increase in rosewood essence, an essential ingredient in perfume, which soared from 3,459 kg in 1905 to 92,990 kg just after the war ended.[17]

Gold exports did not cease, but the decline during the war was significant (see figure 5.4). As a result of the new exports (see above), gold lost its dominance. By the end of the war, gold accounted for 'only' one-third of the value of exports. However, the new exports could not prosper in the post-war environment and gold soon recovered its position. By the 1930s, it was once again responsible for more than 90 per cent of the value of exports, but with a big difference this time as a result of the fall in registered output. French Guiana now found itself in a long period of recession. The value of exports peaked in 1918 and had fallen by half even before the start of the Great Depression.

At least gold could still be exported during the Great Depression, albeit at a lower price. The other commodities withered away leading to a further drop in the value of exports. By 1932, the worst year, they were one-third of their value in 1918. It was a similar story with imports. The only compensation, if it could be called such, was that exports and imports per head did not fall so sharply, as the population was now in decline. Unable to attract many new migrants in the 1920s and with deaths continuing to exceed births, the population had fallen from its peak of 48,810 in 1911 to under 40,000 in 1930.[18]

Figure 5.4: French Guiana: Gold Exports (troy oz), 1914–1965

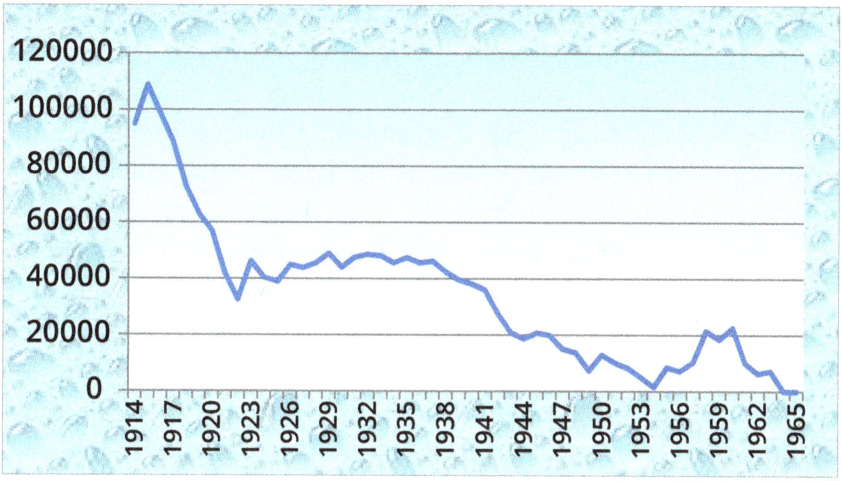

Source: Statistical Appendix and Pétot (1986).

It was a time for bold action, but the colonial authorities had little to offer. Instead, they resorted to administrative changes, creating the new territory of Inini in 1930 out of the colony's hinterland. Designed in part to bring unregistered gold production under the control of the authorities, it did little or nothing to stimulate growth in other activities. And registered gold production itself continued to fall (see figure 5.4) as the most profitable sites became exhausted.

The authorities were still convinced that gold offered a bright future. In 1936, for example, the colonial government mocked the warning given by Henri Coudreau as early as 1887 that the colony would be destined to fail as soon as the gold was exhausted.[19] Writing in the official *Annuaire de la Guyane*, it was said:[20]

> La Guyane vit encore, heureusement; et elle vit bien, toujours et principalement de l'or, – qui n'a point disparu encore, de l'or alluvion; car ses nombreux et riches filons sont encore en reserve, en sommeil. Et l'avenir, loin de s'assombrir, paraît, au contraire, s'éclaircir.

These words, wildly optimistic at the time they were written (see figure 5.4), would soon look ridiculous with the outbreak of the Second World War in 1939. The fall of France in 1940, and the establishment of the Vichy regime the same year, made it impossible for the colony to trade with the 'mother' country.[21] Rum exports ended completely and gold, now in terminal decline, had to be sold elsewhere. And imports, no longer possible from France, had to be purchased from other countries of which by far the most important was the US. Indeed, for the first and only time in its history the US became the principal trading partner for French Guiana, even constructing two military airports in the country during the war.

Supplying French Guiana was hardly a priority for the allies in the Second World War and imports had fallen to one million dollars by 1941. For a colony used to importing most of what it needed to feed and clothe itself, this was an uncomfortable position. Every possible means of increasing domestic food production was tried, although the results were not successful. Rice production, for example, only reached seven per cent of consumption.[22]

As in the French Antilles, the demand for a change in the relationship with metropolitan France in the post-war environment grew in intensity. Few advocated independence, given the fear that gold was now running out and nothing would take its place. Instead, what was wanted was equal status with the mother country. This demand met with a positive response as soon as the war ended, and in 1946 French Guiana, along with Guadeloupe and Martinique, became a *Département d'Outre Mer* (DOM) – no longer a colony but an integral part of France itself.

The change from colony to DOM would have a dramatic effect in the long-term, but it did not happen at once. French Guiana in 1946 was still dependent on gold and still the home of the notorious penal colony. However, change would come soon. The penal colony was finally closed in 1952 (the last convicts had been shipped there in 1937) and gold, increasingly hard to find, was becoming unprofitable at the fixed price established under the gold exchange standard at the end of the war. French Guiana, it was now clear, would have to diversify. And now, as a DOM, it could count on support from the French government.

The need to diversify coincided with a welcome change in the demographics. After the Second World War, births exceeded deaths for the first time and the population started to grow again. Net outward migration, a marked feature of the 1930s, was also reversed with French Guiana receiving net inward migration again in some years during the 1950s. By this time, the CBR (30 per thousand) was almost double the CDR, and the population had reached 30,000 by 1957. This was still far below its peak before the First World War, but a big increase on the interwar period had happened despite the closure of the penal colony.

Diversification proved much harder than expected. Another attempt was made to revive rum exports, but they had little success. Bauxite exports were even more disappointing, while essence of rosewood disappeared from the export list by 1960. Only gold survived and enjoyed a brief resurgence after 1954. Gold, therefore, remained the leading export, but the value of exports was so small that in some years it only reached ten per cent of imports – the difference being largely explained by French Guiana's status as a DOM, allowing it to receive various transfers and subsidies from the French state.

By the early 1960s, therefore, French Guiana had still not ended its long period of stagnation that had begun with the First World War. A modest standard of living was made possible not by productive enterprises but by its status as a DOM. Public administration had become the main employer, and salaries for officials were 40 per cent above those in metropolitan France because of the higher cost of living, but unemployment – especially among the young – was worryingly high.

When gold exports fell to zero in the mid-1960s, it seemed to many as if French Guiana had no economic future. It was as if the warnings of Henri Coudreau had come true. However, this failed to take into account both its geographical location and its status as a DOM. The French government could include la Guyane in its public investment plans and would soon have to make a strategic decision on where to place a planned space station. Its position, so close to the equator, would now usher in a new era in which French Guiana would be catapulted prematurely into the twenty-first century. The space age was about to arrive.

5.4. The Space Age

When the Soviet Union launched the first satellite into orbit in 1957 [Sputnik I], it caused panic among the Western allies. The US response was immediate, and many NATO allies were happy to follow its lead. France, however, desired to maintain its own space capacity and in 1962 founded the Centre National d'Études Spatiales (CNES).

France had already been testing rockets from a site in the Algerian desert. In 1962, however, the terms of French withdrawal from Algeria after the war required closure of the site. Thus, in the same year that CNES was created, France needed to find a new site for its ambitions in space. A shortlist of 14 sites around the world was drawn up and in 1964 French Guiana was chosen as the winner.[23] A few months later, the small village of Kourou (population 659) west of Cayenne was chosen as the site of the space station.

There was little infrastructure in the area at the time. Indeed, Kourou was not even connected with Cayenne by road. Thus, the first impact of the space station was a huge increase in public works, construction, and telecommunications to provide the infrastructure that CNES would need. Work was so swift, however, that the first test rocket (Véronique) was launched on April 9, 1968. Two years later, the first satellite was put into orbit.

The space station resulted in an immediate and dramatic change in French Guiana's balance of payments, as income from the launches was classified as an export of transport services. From dependence on a handful of goods exports, French Guiana overnight had become an exporter of services. And, unlike in the rest of the Caribbean, French Guiana had become dependent on service exports other than tourism and finance – the only regional country of its kind even today to do so.

When the European Space Agency (ESA) was formed in 1975, it was logical that French Guiana would become its base. Following this decision, the ESA formed Arianespace, a semi-private company, which it used for its launches. The three bodies together – CNES, ESA, and Arianespace – then became known as the Centre Spatiale Guyanais (CSG). And the CSG has become a commercial actor in the field of space, reaching agreements with foreign states and private companies to launch satellites. The best known of these agreements is with Russia, which uses the CSG to launch satellites from its Soyuz rockets.

The value of French Guiana's exports now depends more than anything else on the number of launches carried out each year. They are responsible for more than 80 per cent of total exports (goods and services), but the impact of space is much greater than that. In a study on the multiplier effect of space on the economy, it has been found that every euro of value added in the CSG adds 3.1 euros to the value added of the economy as a whole; every euro spent on wages in the CSG adds 3.25 to the total; and every job created in the CSG adds 5.6 to total employment.[24] Altogether, the impact of the CSG on French Guiana's GDP has varied from 15 to 25 per cent in the last 30 years.

GDP per head has risen rapidly in la Guyane since the start of the space station. Official figures on GDP only began in 1975, but it is safe to assume a big increase in the previous ten years. Since 1975, GDP per head has soared (see figure 5.5) with a particularly rapid period of growth after 1986. And growth continued through the global financial crisis of 2007–09 despite the problems that metropolitan France itself faced. The reason, of course, is that the country's GDP is now closely correlated with the number of rocket and satellite launches, a metric that – although volatile – is not dependent on market forces to the same extent as more traditional variables such as oil prices and interest rates.

Figure 5.5: French Guiana: GDP per head (2000 US$), 1975–2016

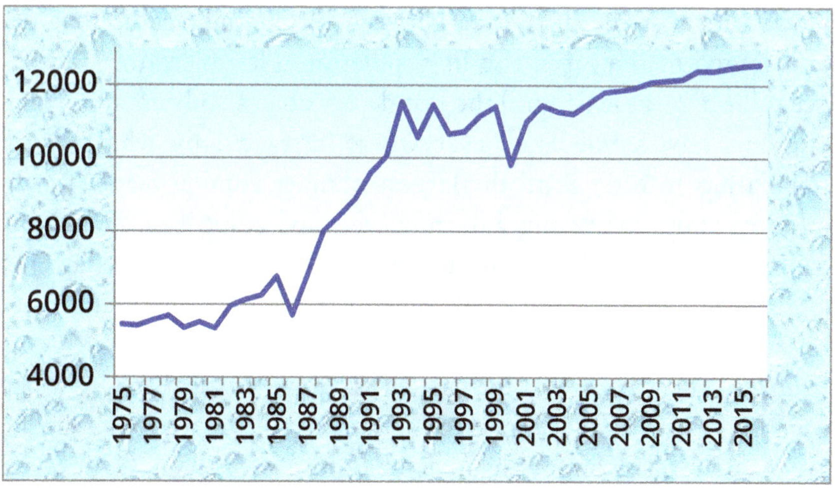

Source: Statistical Appendix and INSEE.

Table 5.2: French Guiana: Demographic Indicators, 1960s–2010s

Period	Population (Start of Period)	Cumulative Births	Cumulative Deaths	Cumulative Net Migration
1960–69	30,900	12,116	4,019	8,164
1970–79	48,147	15,114	4,027	6,786
1980–89	67,386	24,892	4,888	23,650
1990–99	114,678	41,442	5,621	11,552
2000–9	162,018	56,509	6,865	19,065
2010–16	229,040	45,219	5,442	-1,720

Source: Statistical Appendix and INSEE.

French Guiana's take-off into space coincided with a different kind of take-off. Demographic changes, starting even before the choice of Kourou as the location for space activity, have utterly transformed the nature of the country. The CBR, which had risen in the 1950s to 30, has barely changed in the intervening years. The CDR, however, has declined rapidly and today – at just above three – is one of the lowest in the world (not just the Caribbean). The population has risen nearly ten-fold in 60 years (see table 5.2), one of the fastest increases anywhere and the highest in the Caribbean. In a single decade, net births now exceed the size of the whole population just a few decades earlier.

It is not just the difference between births and deaths that has contributed to the rapid rise in population. Net migration inwards (see table 5.2), at least until the last decade, has also been important. Migrants have come from everywhere, attracted by what French Guiana has to offer, with the largest number coming from French-speaking Haiti. Many migrants, however, have come illegally, making it difficult to access the public benefits offered by the French state and forcing them into the informal sector including gold extraction (see below).

Space and the CSG in particular, have transformed French Guiana. However, the impact of space on the economy has begun to lessen as the economy has become more diversified. Agriculture has continued to decline, but fishing has prospered with shrimp exports in particular growing in size. Manufacturing – especially the assembly of sophisticated products for export – has become more important. Services, in common with the rest of the Caribbean, now dominate the economy while French Guiana has joined the rest of the Caribbean by becoming a tourist destination with 90 per cent of visitors being French.

If all this was generally to be welcomed, the same could not be said for gold production. After dropping to zero in the mid-1960s (see figure 5.4), gold extraction experienced a recovery in the 1980s as gold prices soared. Registered exports reached between 2,000 and 4,000 kg in the 1990s, but then started to fall (they were 1,200 kg in 2016). This was due, however, to a sharp rise in unregistered gold extraction. Close to the border with Brazil and far from the eyes of the authorities, between 6,000 and 10,000 'maraudeurs' were working in conditions that were dangerous not just for themselves but also for others whose water supply was contaminated by the poisonous chemicals used.

French Guiana may have differed from the rest of the Caribbean in many ways since the launch of the space age, but in one way it was depressingly familiar: less than half the working-age population was employed. The unemployment rate, even during the years of most rapid growth, has remained stubbornly high and averaged nearly 25 per cent (much higher among the young, women, and the less educated).

The unemployed at least received state benefits as long as they were French citizens. However, they were only 19,000 out of 83,000 classified as 'actifs' in 2016. In that year, there were an additional 73,000 classified as 'inactifs'.[25] And, as the state has clamped down on illegal migration at the same time as GDP per head has virtually stopped growing (see figure 5.5), net migration inwards has been replaced by net outward migration since 2010 (see table 5.2).

The prospects for French Guiana are, therefore, not as promising as when the space station was established. Rockets and satellites will still be launched, but the CSG faces stiff competition from other parts of the world. The ability of space to act as an engine of growth is, therefore, more limited than before. And without growth, it is difficult to see much impact being made on the high unemployment rate – not to mention the large numbers of disillusioned people not even seeking a job.

Net migration outwards will, therefore, not be reversed unless and until the country can find new sources of dynamism. As a DOM, however, French Guiana has enormous advantages over many other countries in the Caribbean. These include the ability to influence key decisions by the French state on investment, lending, and infrastructure. Perhaps one day there will also be a reduction in the barriers the French state has placed on integration with the rest of the Caribbean. That could be a new source of dynamism for French Guiana, one that has been sadly lacking in the 400 years since the first Europeans arrived.

NOTES

1. The colony at Kourou in French Guiana was an ambitious attempt to rescue French imperialism after the loss in 1763 of French Canada to the British and Louisiana to Spain. However, nearly all the colonists died. See M. Godfrey, *Kourou and the Struggle for a French America: War, Culture and Society, 1750–1850* (New York, NY: Palgrave Macmillan, 2015).
2. A domestic law of 1818 was supposed finally to put an end to the French slave trade.
3. See Société d'Etudes pour la Colonisation de la Guyane, *Note sur la Fondation d'Une Nouvelle Colonie dans la Guyane Française* (Paris: Firmin Didot Frères, 1844), 5–6. The English translation is 'The majority of crops can be harvested twice a year. Sugar cane is entirely mature in the 14th month. The land is crisscrossed by magnificent rivers, several of which are navigable by sailing boats of 250 to 300 tonnes and by steam boats from 400 to 500 tonnes. The land is covered in forests that can be worked at 15 leagues [60 kilometres] from the coast. On the lowlands there is no need for manure.'
4. See S. Mam-Lam-Fouck, *La Guyane française au temps de l'esclavage, de l'or et de la francisation (1802–1946)* (Petit-Bourg: Ibis Rouge, 1999), 153.
5. Exports in 1839–41 averaged 540,000 kilos (see table 5.1), greater than estimated world demand for those years. Inevitably, this led to stock piling and a sharp fall in price before the market corrected itself.
6. The largest maroon group were the Boni, who had fled to French Guiana to escape Dutch rule in neighbouring Dutch Guiana. The Amerinidan population, estimated at 30,000 at the time of the French arrival, had been reduced to a few hundred by the time of emancipation.

7. See M.F. Spieler, *Empire and Underworld: Captivity in French Guiana* (Cambridge, MA: Harvard University Press, 2012), 154–59.
8. See S. Toth, *Beyond Papillon: The French Overseas Penal Colonies, 1854–1952* (Lincoln, NE: University of Nebraska Press, 2006), 1–20.
9. See G. Bureau, *La Guyane Méconnue* (Paris: Fasquelle Éditeurs, 1936), 16–17.
10. See Mam-Lam-Fouck, *Histoire de la Société guyanaise. Les annéés cruciales: 1848–1946* (Paris: Editions Caribéennes, 1987), 86–87.
11. See Mam-Lam-Fouck, *Histoire générale de la Guyane française: Des débuts de la colonisation à l'aube de l'an 2000: les grands problèmes guyanais, permanence et évolution* (Cayenne, French Guiana: Ibis rouge éditions, 2002), 95–96.
12. One troy ounce is 31.1035 grams.
13. See V. Bulmer-Thomas, *The Economic History of the Caribbean since the Napoleonic Wars* (Cambridge: Cambridge University Press, 2012), 128, figure 5.8.
14. On these minor exports before the First World War, see Bassières (1900), 200–17.
15. See Y. Farraudière, *École et Société en Guyane Française* (Paris: Sciences Education, 1978), 153.
16. P. See Redfield, *Space in the Tropics: from Convicts to Rockets in French Guiana* (Berkeley, CA: University of California Press, 2000), 102–108.
17. For rum exports, see Statistical Appendix. For other commodities, see Mam-Lam-Fouck, *Histoire générale de la Guyane française*,105, n. 5.
18. It would continue to fall until 1952, when it stood at 25,500. See Statistical Appendix.
19. Henri Coudreau, a well-known French traveller, published his book in 1887 under the title *Voyages à Travers les Guyanes et l'Amazonie.*
20. See *Annuaire de la Guyane* (Paris: 1936), 43. The English translation is: 'French Guiana is still alive, fortunately; and she lives very well, above all because of alluvial gold that has still not disappeared. Its numerous and rich lodes are still there, just waiting to be exploited. The future, far from being gloomy, appears on the contrary to be full of promise.'
21. French Guiana was nominally loyal to Vichy France until 1943, when it allied with the 'free' French led by General de Gaulle.
22. See Mam-Lam-Fouck, *Histoire générale de la Guyane française*, 107.
23. See Redfield, *Space in the Tropics*, 126–27.
24. See Institut National de la Statistique et des Études Économiques (INSEE), *antianEchos*, no. 1 (Paris: INSEE, 2007), 2.
25. See INSEE, *Conjuncture Guyane*, no. 3 (Paris: INSEE, 2017), 13, table 6. With a population of 156,000 for those aged 15 and above in 2016, French Guiana had only 64,000 in work.

Chapter 6
The French Antilles

The French Antilles – Martinique and Guadeloupe together with its dependencies – played a key role in the French imperial project despite their small size. First occupied by France in the 1630s, the islands' economies soon became specialised in the export of sugar and its derivatives while depending on slave labour. Although never as important to metropolitan France as St Domingue (modern Haiti), they were still considered jewels in the imperial crown. Indeed, following France's defeat in the Anglo-French war that ended in 1763, Great Britain seriously considered exchanging the captured provinces in Canada for the island of Guadeloupe.

In the end, Guadeloupe was left in French hands. However, its occupation by British forces in the Napoleonic Wars led to its transfer to Sweden in 1813, a decision that was reversed the following year when Great Britain changed course and returned the island to France at the peace conference to end the war. There would then be no more challenges to French sovereignty. Indeed, Guadeloupe would acquire an additional dependency in 1878, when St Barthélemy – acquired by Sweden from France in 1784 – reverted to France.

Slavery had been abolished in both Guadeloupe and Martinique in 1794, only to be restored in 1802 by Napoleon – a decision sometimes attributed to the Emperor's wife (Joséphine de Beauharnais) who had been born and raised in Martinique. In truth, Joséphine – a much reviled figure whose statue in Fort-de-France is regularly vandalised even today – had little to do with the decision, which was taken by Napoleon in recognition of what he saw as the dependence of colonial exports on slave labour. However, the years of British occupation and the eventual suppression of the trade in slaves in 1831 left the island economies struggling to compete. When slavery was finally abolished in 1848, following the heroic interventions of Victor Schoelcher in the French Assembly, it was widely assumed the French Antilles would face an uphill struggle for economic survival.

Yet, they did survive, and even prospered at first, aided by indentured labour from Asia, establishing a modern banking system, and the support given by the French state to the békés – the white colonials who controlled (and still control) a high proportion of land and other assets in the French Antilles. However, progress was uneven and boom periods were followed by long slumps. This was due to the islands' extreme dependence on sugar and its derivatives that made the French Antilles vulnerable to the vagaries of global commodity prices, colonial tariff policy, world wars, and natural disasters.

Départementalisation in 1946 came at the end of a war that had cut the islands off from their normal commercial arrangements and imposed great hardship. Incorporation into France as *Départements d'Outre Mer* (DOMs) was, therefore, widely welcomed, although a vocal minority still called for independence. From now on, the islands would no longer be dependent on traditional export-led growth for their survival since wage levels, social spending, and budget transfers were all transformed by the new constitutional arrangements.

The results were decidedly mixed. The uncompetitive nature of both economies resulted in high levels of unemployment from which Guadeloupe was particularly affected. The high cost of living in the islands has also been problematic, leading to a wave of strikes and rioting in 2009. Two of the dependencies of Guadeloupe became increasingly disaffected, so much so that in 2003 they opted to withdraw from Guadeloupe's control while staying in France. This required a new status and in 2007 St Barthélemy and St Martin became *Collectivités d'Outre Mer* (COMs).

6.1. Martinique

During their occupation of Martinique in the Napoleonic Wars, the British had left the institution of slavery untouched.[1] However, during their second occupation, starting in 1809, they had not permitted the slave trade (finally ended in British colonies in 1808) and had signed a treaty with France at the end of hostilities committing the French government to suppress the trade.

As deaths often exceeded births among the slave population, this meant the French planters had no intention of observing the law and – with the connivance of the French authorities – an illegal trade was soon under way. By the time it was finally suppressed in 1831, some 25,000 slaves had been brought to Martinique, and the slave population had risen from 80,600 in 1816 to 86,300 15 years later. This meant that slaves continued to be more than 80 per cent of the population and provided virtually all the labour.[2]

The illegal trade in slaves made possible a recovery in exports (see figure 6.1). Based primarily on sugar and its derivatives (molasses and rum), but also including logwood, cotton, coffee, and cacao, exports rose in the years before 1830.[3] Most of the increase, however, came from the export of raw sugar, nearly all of which went to France where it enjoyed heavily protected status.[4]

Export recovery did not last long (see figure 6.1). With the end of the slave trade, the slave population started to fall and had dropped below 73,000 in 1847 – the last year before emancipation. Between 1830 and 1850, the volume of almost all commodity exports fell sharply and cotton disappeared altogether. Only rum defied the trend, a signal of things to come, but the volume exported (350,000 gallons) was still small at the time slaves were freed.

Figure 6.1: Martinique: Exports per head at constant prices (1900=100), 1820–2006

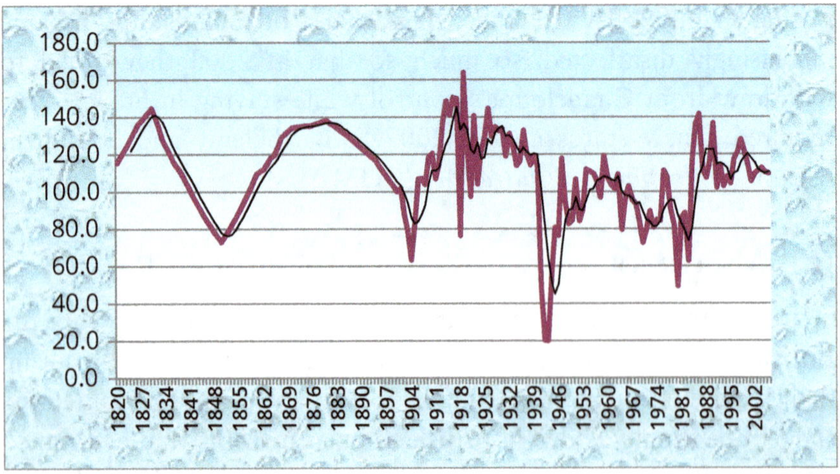

Source: Statistical Appendix.

Emancipation posed an existential threat to the plantation owners on Martinique, almost all of whom were békés. The former slaves were now free not only to leave the plantations but also to leave the island altogether. Indeed, many did so with a significant number emigrating to Haiti as well as other countries in the Caribbean. An immediate response was, therefore, required by the French state, and it took three forms: financial, coercive, and demographic.

The slave owners had been compensated for the loss of their slaves, but the government of Louis Napoleon Bonaparte (President from 1848 and Emperor Napoleon III from 1852 to 1870) held back one-eighth of the funds to establish a state bank that gave Martinique its first real taste of modern finance. Able to borrow on the back of commodity production, the planters now had an instrument to finance the expansion of the export sector provided that the labour force did not continue to shrink.[5]

This meant forcing as far as possible the former slaves to continue to work on the plantations. The French Parliament, therefore, passed laws that allowed the governor to introduce a system of internal controls and poll taxes designed to eliminate 'vagabonds' and compel labourers to work for cash. Draconian though these laws were, the Martinican workers became skilled at evading them, preferring to squat on unoccupied land or work as smallholders producing for the local market only.[6]

The colonial state, therefore, resorted to mass immigration to prevent the labour force from shrinking, through a system of indentured labour, similar to what had been adopted in many British colonies after slavery had ended. As a result, the labour force not only did not shrink but even expanded. Workers came on long contracts (typically ten years) from Africa, French India, and in much smaller numbers from China.[7]

The workers from Africa were not at first hired as free persons. Instead, they were purchased as slaves and then released in Martinique to work as indentured labourers. Their numbers were large, and they helped to make up for the difficulty of recruiting labourers from the small enclaves such as Pondicherry in French India. However, the purchase of Africans as slaves was ended in 1861 following an Anglo-French Convention, in which the British government gave permission to French planters to hire indentured workers directly from British India. African immigration did not end, but they would no longer be purchased as slaves.

Thousands of indentured labourers would come in the years after emancipation from both Africa and Asia. The first Indians, for example, arrived in 1853/4 and the numbers reached a peak in 1867 when 2,220 made the journey to Martinique.[8] Overwhelmingly male, the Indian population had an excess of deaths over births right from the start, and some chose to return to India at the end of their contracts. Thus, the population could only be sustained through high levels of immigration. When these ceased after 1885, the Indian population started to decline.[9] By then, however, births exceeded deaths in Martinique, and the population was starting to increase even without immigration.

In these three decades – 1850s to 1880s – when the labour shortage was addressed through indentured labour, Martinique enjoyed something of a boom (see figure 6.1). The volume of sugar exported doubled, cacao quadrupled, and even logwood, harvested in an unsustainable way, recovered to levels not seen since the 1830s. The star performer, however, was rum where the volume exported jumped from 350,000 gallons in 1850 to 3.4 million 40 years later. Most of this rum was produced directly from sugar cane without the need for molasses, giving it the highly prized *appelation* of 'rhum agricole'.

Despite this, export earnings still depended overwhelmingly on sugar and Martinique could not insulate itself from the collapse of world sugar prices after 1880 nor from the increased production of beet sugar in France itself. A slump in the island's economic fortunes was underway by the end of 1880s and would last for many years. It was made worse by the volcanic eruption in 1902 that destroyed the port of St Pierre and killed thousands of Martinicans. Indeed, the population number in 1900 (215,000) would not be reached again until 1948 – a gap of nearly 50 years.

The volcanic eruption seriously damaged the export of sugar, rum, and cacao – still the three main commodities – and the value of exports halved in a couple of years. The year 1904, however, was the low point. Exports swiftly recovered and soon another boom was underway that relied increasingly on rum rather than sugar. And when the First World War broke out, it gave a new boost to rum because of its use in the production of explosives and for treating injuries. Indeed, rum in these years had greater value than sugar, and the trend continued in the immediate aftermath of the war as Martinican rum was smuggled into the US (via the French islands of Miquelon and St Pierre at the mouth of the St Lawrence river in Canada). In 1919 alone, rum exports (volume and value) trebled from the previous year.[10]

The US authorities took a dim view of rum smuggling and the French authorities agreed to suppress it. Martinique now once again embarked on a long period of stagnation. While some other Caribbean countries boomed in the 1920s, Martinique struggled as a result of the poor state of the French economy to which it was closely tied. The volume of sugar exported did expand after the First World War, but the average price received peaked in 1924 – much earlier than in other sugar-exporting countries. As a result, agricultural diversification became a priority, and bananas were exported for the first time in 1924. However, it would be many years before they would make much of an impression on export earnings.

The difficulties faced by Martinique in the 1920s were soon dwarfed by the Great Depression. Almost wholly dependent on the French market for its exports as a result of the system of imperial preference imposed on its colonies by France, the volume and value of Martinique's principal exports declined sharply. Only bananas bucked the trend, jumping from 27,601 bunches in 1928 to 1.7 million ten years later, but this was still too small to make much of an impact on exports. And exports, which had been valued at nearly $US 11 million in 1929, did not recover even in monetary terms for many years.

Much of this was due to the Second World War. Germany invaded and occupied France in mid-1940, allowing a puppet government to be formed in the south of the country centred on Vichy. The governor of the French Antilles, Admiral Georges Robert, recognised the Vichy government rather than the Free French led by De Gaulle (the switch to the Free French would be made in 1943 as soon as Robert returned to France). The British imposed a naval cordon around Martinique, even before the US entered the war in December 1941, in order to prevent military assets from falling into the hands of Germany. However, it also made trade virtually impossible with Vichy France and its colonies.

Trade, therefore, declined sharply (see table 6.1) and in the case of bananas disappeared completely. What little trade there was had to be conducted almost entirely with the US, which had no particular reason to be generous to Martinique. The trading relation with France, which had survived almost untouched for three centuries, was abruptly terminated. Only after the defeat of Germany on French soil in 1944 did the relationship return to normality.

Table 6.1: Martinique: Exports, 1939–45

Year	Sugar (lbs)	Rum (gallons)	Cacao (lbs)	Bananas (bunches)	Domestic Exports ($)
1939	145,103,200	1,368,479	297,000	1,227,776	8,017,495
1940	127,760,600	2,136,138	466,400	461,736	6,883,378
1941	63,274,200	657,078	292,600	102,608	3,737,592
1942	35,442,000	60,977	19,800	5,412	1,828,796
1943	21,694,200	378,325	55,000	0	1,652,184
1944	74,360,000	712,974	123,200	0	4,995,837
1945	106,119,200	752,173	486,200	0	11,438,301

Source: Statistical Appendix.

Economic disruption since the second half of the 1920s had led to lost job opportunities. This had provoked outward migration, mainly to France, on a large scale. While the population had risen from nearly 200,000 in 1930 to 209,000 in 1946, the Crude Birth Rate (CBR) had jumped from 27.9 to 36.3 over the same period (the Crude Death Rate – CDR – was virtually unchanged at 20). The natural increase of the population was, therefore, accelerating steadily, so an estimated 20,000 – ten per cent of the population left the island during these years.

Départementalisation in 1946 was popular and was overwhelmingly approved when it came to a vote. Not only did it bring the promise of an end to colonial discrimination, but – more important – it held out the prospect of a huge increase in public expenditure. Although France had provided more resources per head to its Caribbean colonies than other European empires, the sums were still modest before 1946. Public expenditure in dollar terms had risen from US$5 in 1900 to US$10, 40 years later. After *départementalisation*, however, it rose sharply and had reached US$60 by 1960. Even after allowing for (dollar) inflation, this was still a huge increase that provided a boost to public sector employment, social services, and infrastructure.

It was not just the public sector that was transformed by *départementalisation*. Private sector workers now enjoyed French wage rates, social security benefits, and pensions. Inevitably, this meant that labour cost increases ran far ahead of labour productivity gains, and those Martinican businesses selling abroad or competing with imports became increasingly uncompetitive. It was only special arrangements in the mainland French market, and from 1958 onwards in the European Economic Community (EEC), that allowed sugar and bananas to compete. Even these protectionist policies would eventually end after the launch of the European Union in 1993. Sugar would now disappear from the export list, with the crop being used primarily in the production of the famous rhum agricole.[11]

The uncompetitive nature of the Martinican economy, an almost inevitable consequence of *départementalisation*, meant that new exports could only be introduced if they were relatively price insensitive. New commodity exports were, therefore, almost impossible, but Martinique did prosper as a destination for tourists from mainland France. Helped by direct flights, good infrastructure, and the absence of a need for foreign currency, French tourists flocked to the island and created many jobs. By 2016, the numbers arriving had reached nearly 900,000 of which 60 per cent were overnight visitors, nearly all of whom had come from metropolitan France.

The other new export activity was oil refining. Since the main cost is the raw material (crude oil), oil refining could be placed almost anywhere and the French government took a decision in 1969 to site a new refinery on Martinique. La Société Anonyme de Raffinage des Antilles, as it would be called, transformed the gross value of Martinican exports, since it supplied other French territories as well. Indeed, by 2015, oil refinery products constituted over half of goods exports. Although its net contribution (i.e., excluding material inputs) was much smaller, it was still large enough to make a difference to the value of exports.

Martinique, therefore, became an oil exporter although it had no oil of its own. However, exports had ceased to be the engine of growth of the economy soon after *départementalisation*. And exports of goods no longer had much relation to imports since they represented less than 20 per cent by the new millennium. GDP was now much more dependent on consumption (private and public) and investment, which in turn depended on a host of decisions taken by the French government.

Figure 6.2: Martinique: GDP per head (2000 US$), 1970–2016

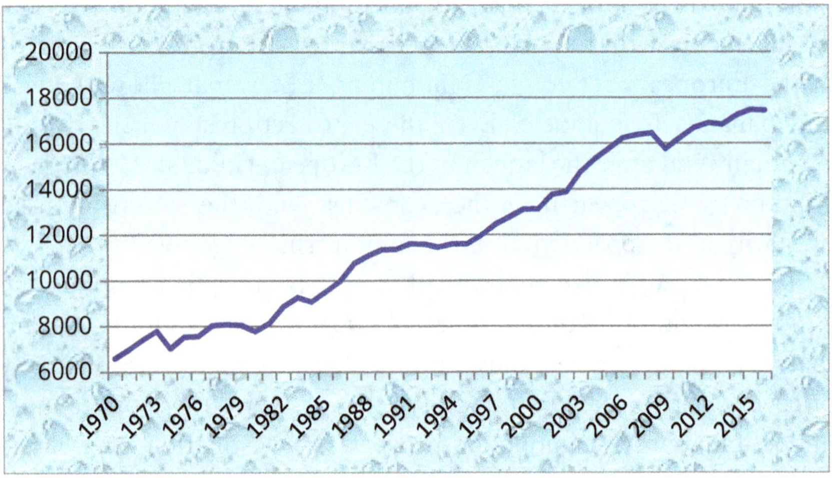

Source: 1970–2008 from Statistical Appendix. Subsequent years are from INSEE.

The growth of GDP per head after 1970, when reliable statistics first became available, was respectable (see figure 6.2). Between 1970 and 2016, GDP rose at an annual average of 1.9 per cent while GDP per head rose at 1.6 per cent (population in these years increased at an annual average of 0.3 per cent). Furthermore, Martinique avoided the 'lost decade' of the 1980s that afflicted so many Latin American and Caribbean countries as a result of its constitutional status as a French DOM.

What the GDP figures concealed, however, was the fact that the labour market could not deliver a sufficient number of jobs, leaving a large proportion of the working-age population dependent on welfare.

The unemployment rate, although not as high as in Guadeloupe or la Guyane, was close to 20 per cent in 2016 where it had remained for many years.[12] In that year, out of a population of 376,847, less than 70,000 were employed. Most of these jobs were in services, including the public sector, since neither agriculture nor industry were able to offer much work.

The chronic failure of the labour market in Martinique had led to persistent outward migration for decades. As the birth rate fell, however, the numbers migrating started to exceed the natural rate of growth of the population. By 2016, the CBR had fallen to ten and the CDR was 8.7, so the number of births only narrowly exceeded deaths. Outward migration now meant that the population itself would start to fall, a trend first observed in 2006. And in the following ten years, the population fell by more than 20,000 (a drop of five per cent in one decade) with no end in sight.

In comparison with many parts of the Caribbean, the standard of living in Martinique is high. However, it remains much lower than in metropolitan France, and the concern of many ever since *départementalisation* is that the island would be unable to remain competitive and would become too dependent on welfare payments. That has clearly happened, but what was not anticipated is that the population itself would start to decline. And since it is the youngest and brightest who leave, Martinican society is becoming prematurely old. This is a new problem for the Caribbean and one for which so far there are no obvious solutions.[13]

6.2. Guadeloupe

Guadeloupe was first occupied by France in the 1630s, and French possession was undisturbed until 1759 when British forces seized it during the Seven Years War (1756–63). The Treaty of Paris in 1763 restored French sovereignty, but British forces would soon return when they tried – and failed – to take the island in 1794 soon after the start of the long Anglo-French War.

British intervention was designed in part to prevent the French authorities from carrying out their promise to end slavery in that year. The British failure to capture the island meant, therefore, that the slaves were freed, unlike in neighbouring Martinique where the British occupation prevented it. Thus, the restoration of slavery in 1802 by Napoleon's forces was bound to be a bloody affair and indeed it was. Those that survived were then enslaved again.

British forces returned again in 1810, one year after capturing Martinique, and this time they succeeded in taking the island. There would be no end to slavery under British rule, although the slave trade was terminated. And Great Britain was at first determined to ensure that France did not recover the island, transferring sovereignty to Sweden in 1813. This decision was reversed the following year at the peace conference, and France was confirmed as the sovereign power at the Congress of Vienna in 1815.

In that year, the French authorities recorded 81,763 slaves out of a population of 102,000.[14] These were almost exactly the same numbers as in Martinique, which is one reason why the two islands are often assumed to be so similar. In the next 15 years, however, Guadeloupe's planters made much more intense use than their counterparts in Martinique of the illegal trade in slaves before it finally came to an end in 1831. Some 38,000 slaves were imported in these years, and the slave population had risen to 99,464 by the time the trade ended.

This would be the peak, since – as in Martinique – the combination of deaths exceeding births and manumission would inevitably lead to a decline in the slave population after the trade in slaves ended. The total population of Guadeloupe, however, continued to grow for a short period despite negative net births in many years. This was a sure sign of, at least, some migration inwards, suggesting that the economic prospects of the island had improved after the end of the Napoleonic Wars.

This turned out to be the case, as figure 6.3 makes clear. Exports in volume and value as well as per head rose after 1820 and, unlike in Martinique, continued to rise in some cases after the end of the trade in slaves. However, although Guadeloupe came out of the Napoleonic Wars exporting sugar, molasses, rum, cacao, coffee, and cotton, it was only sugar that showed real dynamism as the planters chose to focus on the one commodity whose market seemed assured in metropolitan France. By 1840, sugar alone – excluding molasses and rum – accounted for nearly 85 per cent of export earnings.

Figure 6.3: Guadeloupe: Exports per head at constant prices (1900=100), 1820–2016

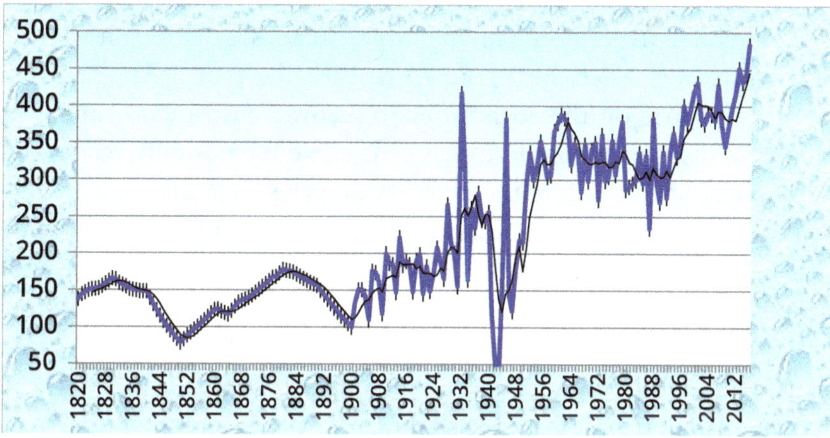

Sources: 1820–2007 from Statistical Appendix. The year 2008 onwards are from INSEE and exclude St Martin and St Barthélemy.

Yet even sugar was not immune to the labour shortage after the slave trade ended. The slave population reached a peak in 1832, and the volume of sugar exported peaked a decade later. In the next few years, sugar exports declined – precipitately after emancipation in 1848. By 1850, sugar had fallen by half in volume and almost as much in value compared with ten years earlier. The decline of other crops was even more dramatic, however, so that sugar was now 90 per cent of export earnings. The only bright spot was the emergence of two (for Guadeloupe) non-traditional exports: annatto and logwood, but their value was still tiny.

As in Martinique, the authorities responded to this crisis in three ways: financial, coercive, and demographic. The financial response was the same as elsewhere. La Banque de la Guadeloupe, funded like its equivalents in Martinique and La Guyane with money held back from the compensation paid to the former slave owners, was up and running by 1853/4 when it lent 616,932 francs (approximately US$120,000) to the planters – almost all of whom were békés – with the crop as security. A decade later, this had risen to some five million francs (nearly $1 million). Two decades later, in 1873/4, the amount loaned was nearly 11 million francs ($2.1 million).[15]

Coercion, as in Martinique, also played a key role in guaranteeing a supply of workers for the plantations. The techniques used were very similar to those employed in the neighbouring island and the former slaves were equally successful at evading them (see chapter 6.1 above). Furthermore, in the four decades after emancipation death rates exceeded birth rates in nearly half the years, putting further pressure on the authorities to secure an adequate supply of labour. Thus, the colonial government came increasingly to depend on immigration to secure the workers that the planters needed.

In this they had some success (see table 6.2). While St Barthélemy (still a Swedish colony until 1878) saw a continuous net outflow of people in the 1850s and 1860s, Guadeloupe enjoyed a steady inflow until the period 1886–90 when economic conditions deteriorated sharply. The population of Guadeloupe rose from 121,041 in 1852 to 145,417 in 1876. However, even after the absorption of St Barthélemy with nearly 3,000 people, the population of Guadeloupe lagged behind Martinique despite the fact that the former had been larger before the end of the trade in slaves. Indeed, even after the demographically disastrous volcanic eruption in Martinique in 1902, Guadeloupe still had the smaller population.

Table 6.2: French Antilles: Net Migration (Percentage of Population), 1850s to 1890s

	Guadeloupe	Martinique	St Barthélemy
1851-55	0.12	0.42	-0.7
1856-60	0.96	2.71	-0.7
1861-65	0.69	0.24	-2.3
1866-70	1.00	0.24	-2.3
1871-75	0.31	0.23	0.1
1876-80	1.21	0.23	0.4
1881-85	0.66	0.22	(a)
1886-90	-0.27	0.21	(a)
1891-95	-0.08	0	(a)

Source: Statistical Appendix. (a) St Barthélemy was part of Guadeloupe in these years.

The reasons are not hard to find. First, Guadeloupe had suffered a severe earthquake in 1843 in which many people had died. Secondly, it had experienced a deadly attack of cholera in 1865. The *New York Times* correspondent wrote on March 2, 1866:

> According to accounts received at Santiago de Cuba from the French West [Indian] ladies, the cholera still continued at Guadeloupe, committing great ravages, the number of deaths up to Dec. 31 was as follows: Pointe-a-Pitre, 1,200; Basse-Terre, 2,000. In thirteen communes of Guadeloupe the number of deaths was 6,500. In Grand-Terre, in twelve communes, included Marie Galante, 12,200.

Even if these numbers would later turn out to be somewhat exaggerated, there is no doubt that Guadeloupe suffered terribly from cholera in the 1860s, pushing the population down and making economic recovery after emancipation harder.

Indeed, economic recovery in Guadeloupe after emancipation took longer than in Martinique. While exports in the neighbouring island had recovered their previous peak around 1860, it would take another decade in Guadeloupe. By 1880, however, the volume of sugar exports had reached nearly 100 million pounds (it had been 70 million in 1840), and Guadeloupe planters were increasingly selling refined sugar from factories rather than the raw sugar on which they had previously relied.

There were also strong export performances from rum (mainly, but not exclusively, produced as in Martinique directly from sugar cane), cacao, coffee, annatto, and logwood. Yet, these products had not grown fast enough to make much of an impact on sugar, whose share of export earnings was still 85 per cent in 1880. Thus, the subsequent fall in the price of sugar hit Guadeloupe hard. Export earnings almost halved between 1880 and 1900, the sugar share dropped to 70 per cent and the previous net inflow of people turned to net migration outwards (see table 6.2).

The start of the new century would mark another turning point in the fortunes of Guadeloupe. Sugar recovered, but much more important was the dynamic performance of the other export commodities. The most spectacular was rum, where Guadeloupe's rhum agricole was – as in Martinique – acquiring an outstanding reputation. Exports rose from 506,804 gallons in 1900 to nearly 3.5 million in the year the First World War started. Almost as impressive, however, were exports of cacao that went from 646,686 pounds in 1900 to nearly 2.5 million in 1914.

All this helped to push the share of sugar in export earnings below 50 per cent even before war commenced. The demand for rum in the war and the need for sugar cane to make the rum then drove the sugar share down to 17 per cent in 1919 – the first year after the war ended. Guadeloupe, it seemed, was finally diversifying away from sugar after nearly 300 years, but it would prove to be a false dawn. As French demand for rum declined in peacetime, sugar once again became the leading export and had reached nearly 50 per cent by the time the Great Depression struck.

Although export performance improved after 1900 (see figure 6.3), it had not been able to provide adequate employment for the labour force. Thus, outmigration continued (see table 6.3) and – with rare exceptions – has continued to this day. Births exceeded deaths in all decades during the first half of the twentieth century (see table 6.3), a welcome change from the nineteenth century, but too many Guadeloupians have felt obliged to leave their country in search of work elsewhere.

Table 6.3: Guadeloupe: Demographic Indicators, 1900–2016

	Population Change	Births	Deaths	Net Births	Net Migration
1900–09	-4,764	37,018	32,530	4,488	-9,252
1910–19	-7,447	31,064	23,306	7,758	-15,205
1920–30	-7,822	29,380	22,019	7,360	-15,182
1931–46	32,190	53,607	32,381	21,226	10,964
1947–56	54,400	75,767	26,117	49,650	4,750
1957–66	62,100	102,505	24,717	77,789	-15,689
1967–76	22,000	93,167	24,110	69,057	-47,057
1977–86	27,500	65,022	22,307	42,715	-15,215
1987–96	53,000	72,922	23,914	49,009	3,991
1997–2006	35,254	70,615	28,044	42,571	-7,317
2007–16	-3,975	58,247	32,609	25,638	-29,613

Source: derived from Statistical Appendix.

One of the rare exceptions to net outward migration was the period 1931–46 (see table 6.3). These were the years that coincided with the Great Depression and the Second World War. Yet, despite this, Guadeloupe appears to have experienced a modest net migration inwards.[16] This was helped in the 1930s by the rapid growth of the banana industry that had begun exporting in 1921 (even before Martinique). By 1938, on the eve of war, the value of banana exports was close to that of sugar and above the value of rum exports.

War in Martinique disrupted trade flows and for several years severed the links with metropolitan France. The worst year was 1943, when Guadeloupe broke with Vichy France and declared for Free France. Recovery thereafter was spectacular and accelerated as soon as Guadeloupe became a *Département d'Outre Mer* in 1946. Net inward migration continued for a few more years (see table 6.3), but exports per head reached a peak in the early 1960s (see figure 6.3). From then onwards, as in Martinique, they would cease to exert much impact on the evolution of economic activity.

With *départementalisation* the economy of Guadeloupe was changed dramatically in many ways. However, some things have stayed the same. The trade and investment ties with metropolitan France (the 'hexagon') are just as strong – if not stronger – and now apply to the export of services as well as goods since tourists come overwhelmingly from France. The békés have preserved their privileged position in the economy, so that tensions and resentment with the remaining 99 per cent of the population have not disappeared. Net outward migration, temporarily reversed in the 1930s and 1940s, has continued and by 2012 exceeded net births leading to a fall in the absolute size of the population. It is now below 400,000 and dropping at approximately 2,000 per year.

The most significant change has been the rise in public spending as Guadeloupe was fully absorbed into the French social security system, and public investment on the island soared. Since the first reliable statistics were produced in 1970, Guadeloupe has enjoyed an impressive rise in GDP per head (see figure 6.4), surviving the oil crises in the 1970s, the 1980s debt crisis in the region, and the loss of St Martin and St Barthélemy in 2007. Strikes and riots in 2009, together with the eurozone crisis from 2008 onwards, may have dented the rate of growth of GDP per head, but the fall in population after 2011 means that even zero growth in GDP now leads to higher income per head.

Figure 6.4: Guadeloupe: GDP per head (2000 US$), 1970–2016

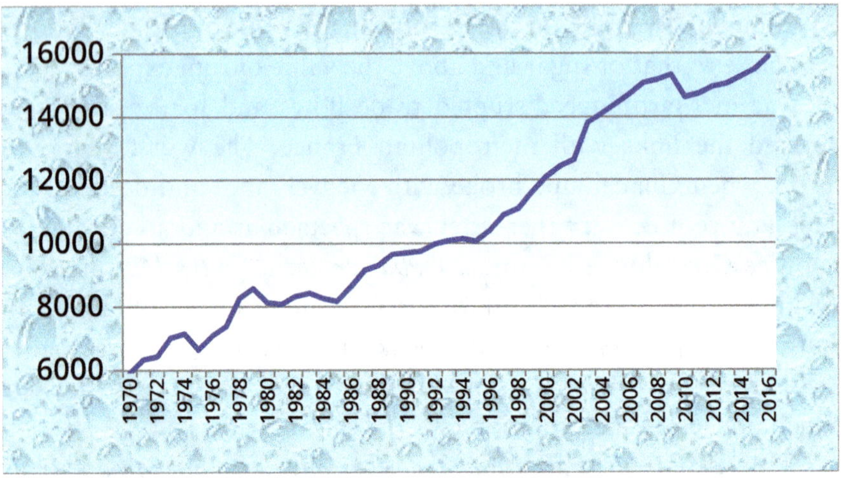

Source: Statistical Appendix for 1970–2007 and INSEE thereafter. The series for 2008 onwards excludes St Martin and St Barthélemy.

The structure of the economy, however, has become very unusual – at least for the Caribbean. Consumption, private and public, now *exceeds* GDP. Furthermore, public expenditure (excluding investment) is almost half the size of GDP and not much smaller than household consumption. Meanwhile, exports of goods and services, including tourism, cover only one-third of total imports.

As in Martinique, *départementalisation* has undermined the competitiveness of the economy and made it difficult for firms in the traded sectors to compete. Out of a population of nearly 400,000, only 69,100 were employed at the end of 2016 and nearly all of these were in non-traded services. In that same year, a mere 1,811 were employed in agriculture as sugar has become increasingly unprofitable (except as an input into rum manufacture), and no other crops have taken its place.

Unemployment has been high. It stood in 2016 at 24 per cent, a figure that has barely changed for many years, and reached nearly 50 per cent for young people under 25 years of age. Outward migration is a natural consequence of this, as is the premature aging of the population. And a fall in the birth rate, coupled with a rise in the death rate, is one of the consequences of an aging population, so that the number of births barely exceeds the number of deaths in modern Guadeloupe.[17] Indeed, the number of births has fallen almost continuously since 2000.

While French Guiana has its space station and Martinique its oil refinery, the French state has failed to find for Guadeloupe a niche sector from which it could prosper. The only significant non-traditional export has been tourism, but that is still quite small compared with most parts of the Caribbean. Less than 300,000 tourists came in 2016 and nearly all of these came from the hexagon or other DOMs. Airline routes tend to reinforce these trends making it difficult for Guadeloupe to diversify. Perhaps that is why the local government has invested so heavily in the detective series *Death in Paradise* that is filmed in Guadeloupe while aimed at an English-speaking market.[18]

6.3. St Barthélemy

Before it became a dependency of Guadeloupe in 1878, the island of St Barthélemy had been a Swedish colony for nearly a century. Acquired by Sweden, in 1784, in return for French trading privileges in the Swedish port of Gothenburg, St Barthélemy was at first the personal property of the Swedish king who was, therefore, entitled to receive any profits the island might generate. And in recognition of the king's role, the name of the capital was changed to Gustavia – the name it still bears today.

Profit, rather than geostrategic considerations, was indeed the motive for the king's interest. However, the terrain was not well suited to growing agricultural crops. Thus, Gustavia became a free port and was soon established as an entrepôt. Merchants from many countries established import-export businesses with the goods imported not just from Sweden but from many other countries as well.

The provenance of the imports was fairly easy to establish. However, the same goods when exported went mainly to European colonies as contraband through smuggling operations. And these clandestine activities became particularly important in times of war. The revolutionary movement in Latin America also took full advantage of St Barthélemy's status to import weapons for use in the struggle against Spain after the end of the Napoleonic Wars.

Table 6.4: St Barthélemy: Exports, 1820–70

	Cotton (lb)	Pineapples (units)	Domestic Exports (US$)	Re-Exports (US$)	Total Exports ($)
1820	154,321	336,474	50,000	124,895	174,895
1830	156,250	254,453	40,000	61,367	101,367
1840	129,969	170,051	33,533	0	33,533
1850	70,000	476,616	17,254	0	17,254
1860	78,740	525,756	19,203	0	19,203
1870	48,000	3,600	13,055	0	13,055

Source: Statistical Appendix.

The island was, therefore, very profitable for the king and the resident merchants as long as it was one of the few free ports in the region. As this began to change after the Napoleonic Wars, the re-export trade went into decline (see table 6.4). The high point was 1820, when re-exports were nearly three times more important than domestic exports (cotton and pineapples). The value of re-exports had halved by 1830 and disappeared by 1840. It would not resurface during the period of Swedish rule.

St Barthélemy's brief existence as an entrepôt had led to a significant increase in population, nearly half of whom were slaves. At its peak in 1812, the population was 5,482 of which 2,406 were enslaved. As the re-export of goods went into decline, so did the population – a demographic reversal made worse by the difficulty for the island's cotton growers of competing with the US (see table 6.4). By 1847, when Sweden ended slavery, the population had fallen to 2,683 of which 514 were slaves.

As the entrepôt trade declined in importance, the island generated less revenue for the king. Indeed, between 1820 and 1840, the income fell from US$46,673 to US$8,377. St Barthélemy not only became less profitable for the king but also started to drain his resources through the need for subsidies. The Swedish Parliament, therefore, agreed with considerable reluctance to take over responsibility. St Barthélemy was now a drain on the public exchequer rather than the king's purse and the Swedish Farmers' Party protested strongly.

Nothing could be done until a purchase could be arranged. However, the other European powers had no interest until 1877 when France, whose geostrategic interest had been stimulated by the plans of Ferdinand de Lesseps for an inter-oceanic canal through Panama, acquired the island. Terms were agreed (France refused to call it a purchase) and St Barthélemy became a dependency of Guadeloupe in 1878 with those Swedish officials who remained generously provided for by the French state. The US, consulted by France in case the transfer ran afoul of the unilateral Monroe Doctrine, raised no objection.

For nearly a century as a dependency of Guadeloupe, the island of St Barthélemy played little part in the economics of the Caribbean. Its population failed to increase – not as a result of a high death rate but through emigration. It played no part in the expansion of Guadeloupe's commodity exports and, lacking an airport, was unable to participate in the expansion of tourism after the Second World War.

All this started to change in the 1950s when the island came to the attention of David Rockefeller and other wealthy celebrities. When an airport was constructed, high-end tourism quickly took off, and the island's population started to expand from its low point of 2,176 in 1961. By 2007, when St Barthélemy ceased to be part of Guadeloupe,[19] the resident population had reached 8,450 and ten years later was close to 10,000. This growth was almost entirely due to inward migration as the birth rate on the island is the lowest in the Caribbean.[20] And this small population caters to some 200,000 visitors a year, including many wealthy people.[21]

6.4. St Martin

A dependency of Guadeloupe until 2007, St Martin has the unusual distinction of sharing the island on which it is located with St Maarten (see chapter 8). The open borders between the two countries have always been a feature of island life, so much so that the Dutch authorities in St Maarten, but in no other Dutch territory, felt obliged immediately to emancipate the slaves when France freed its slaves in 1848.

The end of slavery brought net migration inwards to Guadeloupe, as a whole, but not to St Martin whose population was still only 3,400 in 1885. Sugar was grown and exported from two plantations, but the island struggled to participate in the boom years for Guadeloupe. Indeed, the population had fallen to 3,366 as recently as 1954. From then onwards, however, the population started to grow with a huge increase in the 1980s as a result of the arrival of many Haitians as economic refugees. By 1990, the population had reached 28,518 before peaking at 36,824 in 2009. Unlike St Barthélemy, the subsequent (modest) decline in the population is not due to a low birth rate but to net outward migration. Indeed, since separating from Guadeloupe in 2007, the CBR has averaged 20 and the CDR 3.5.

The referendum to leave Guadeloupe and become a COM, held in 2003, was overwhelmingly supported by those who voted. However, many residents of St Martin did not have a vote, raising questions of how representative the plebiscite was of islanders' wishes. In any case, the change of constitutional status has done little to transform economic activity and income per head remains below that in Guadeloupe.

St Martin, like St Barthélemy, is today overwhelmingly dependent on tourism with a high GDP per head.[22] However, it has neither been able to establish itself as a niche market for high-end tourism like its neighbouring COM nor compete with the brash casino-dominated tourism in St Maarten that depends heavily on cruise ships. And nearly all visitors to St Martin come through the international airport located on the Dutch part of the island. This difficult situation was rendered much worse in 2017 when Hurricane Irma struck the island on September 6. The destruction was so bad that President Macron of France arrived in person a few days later. Money was promised to rebuild the infrastructure, but this will not change St Martin's tourism-dependent economic structure.

NOTES

1. The British first occupied Martinique in 1794 and restored slavery. They returned the island to France after the Treaty of Amiens in 1802. They then reoccupied the island in 1809, only returning it to France at the conclusion of the Napoleonic Wars.
2. A useful source for this period in Martinican economic history is D.W. Tomich, *Slavery in the Circuit of Sugar: Martinique and the World Economy, 1830–1848* (Baltimore, MD: Johns Hopkins University Press, 1990).
3. Martinique also exported cassia (senna) throughout the ninetennth century. A plant endogenous to Mexico, it had – and still has – a wide variety of uses in medicine and gastronomy.
4. The French tariff system was revised in 1860 and again in 1892, but it always gave a high level of preference to colonial products. See A.P. Blérald, *Histoire économique de la Guadeloupe et de la Martinique: Du XVIIe siècle à nos jours* (Paris: Karthala, 1986), 38–52.
5. La Banque de la Martinique was established in 1853 and had a monopoly of note issue until 1944. It merged with la Banque de la Guadeloupe in 1967 to form La Banque des Antilles Françaises.
6. See L. Brown, 'The Three Faces of Post-Emancipation Migration in Martinique, 1848–1865,' *Journal of Caribbean History* 36, no. 2 (2002): 310–35 and R. Renard, 'Labour Relations in Martinique and Guadeloupe, 1848–1870,' in *Caribbean Freedom: Society and Economy from Emancipation to the Present*, ed. H. Beckles and V. Shepherd (Kingston, Jamaica: Ian Randle Publishers, 1993), 161–68.
7. See N. Schmidt, 'Les migrations de main-d'oeuvre dans la politique colonial française aux Caraïbes pendant la seconde moitié du XIXe siècle,' *Le Mouvement Social* 151 (1990): 11–37.
8. See L. Chauleau, *Dans les îles du vent: La Martinique (XVIIe-XIXe siècle)* (Paris: L'Harmattan, 1993), 268–73.
9. The decision to end it was taken by the Conseil Général de la Martinique after a long campaign in which indenture was likened to slavery. In 1889, the UK agreed with France to end Indian emigration to the French colonies. See Chauleau, *Dans les îles du vent*, 273.
10. Prohibition in the US lasted from 1919 to 1933. During these years, no alcoholic drinks could be legally imported.
11. Not all rum in Martinique is rhum agricole. There is also a large production of rum by traditional methods using molasses (rhum sucrerie).
12. The unemployment rate among women is similar to that for men. However, it is much higher among young workers (those aged 15–24). For this group, the unemployment rate in 2016 was 39 per cent for men and 52 per cent for women.

13. Perhaps the best hope lies in education, since the unemployment rate varies inversely with the level of schooling. Those without a high school diploma, for example, face an unemployment rate of nearly 30 per cent regardless of their gender.
14. These figures include St Martin, a dependency of Guadeloupe until 2007, but exclude St Barthélemy as it did not become a dependency until 1878.
15. See A. Buffon, *Monnaie et crédit en économie coloniale: Contribution à l'histoire économique de la Guadeloupe, 1635–1919* (Basse-Terre, Guadeloupe: Société d'histoire de la Guadeloupe, 1979), 344–45.
16. Caution must be used here, as the annual population figures before 1946 are estimates. See Statistical Appendix for a discussion of the methodological problems.
17. In 2016/17, the CBR was 9.6 while the CDR was 8.2. See INSEE.
18. The series is notionally set in a British Overseas Territory, but it is actually filmed in Basse Terre on Guadeloupe using many local actors.
19. The referendum took place in 2003, and the decision to leave Guadeloupe was supported by 75 per cent of voters, although less than half of the electorate bothered to vote.
20. In 2015, the CBR was 0.8 and the CDR was 0.4. The next year, the rates were 1.1 and 1.7 respectively. See INSEE.
21. GDP per head is not officially measured every year, but in 2010 it was calculated as 35,700 euros. See Comptes économiques rapides pour l'Outre-mer, *Estimation du PIB par habitant de Saint-Barthélemy* (Paris: Comptes économiques rapides pour l'Outre-mer, 2014), 1. This made it one of the richest countries in the Caribbean, a position that was put at risk by hurricane damage in 2017.
22. As in St Barthélemy, GDP per head is not officially measured every year. However, in 2014 it was calculated at 16,572 euros. See Comptes économiques rapides pour l'Outre-mer, *Estimation du PIB par habitant de Saint-Martin* (Paris: Comptes économiques rapides pour l'Outre-mer, 2018), 4.

PART III: The Dutch- and Danish-speaking Countries

Chapter 7
SURINAME

Suriname, independent since 1975, had by then been a Dutch colony for over three centuries (it had been exchanged with the British government for Manhattan in New York by the Treaty of Breda in 1667). At that time, Holland already had colonies on the north coast of South America, but three of these – Berbice, Demarara, and Essequibo – were transferred to Great Britain by treaty in 1814 (in due course, the three British colonies would be united to form British Guiana). 'Dutch' Guiana, therefore, referred to all Dutch colonies on the coast before 1814, but only Suriname thereafter. It will be referred to throughout this chapter as Suriname to avoid confusion.

Suriname had been occupied by British forces in 1799 soon after the revolutionary French government established the Batavian Republic in the Netherlands as a client state. Napoleon then put Louis Bonaparte on the Dutch throne in 1806. The defeat of Napoleon in 1814 allowed relations between Great Britain and Holland to return to normal, but Dutch sovereignty over Suriname was not restored until 1816.

The Dutch claim to Suriname would now go unchallenged by other powers, but its borders were disputed as it depended on the course of rivers whose main tributaries were uncharted. It took nearly a century before the southern border with Brazil was agreed in 1906. It took even longer for the Dutch and French governments to agree the eastern border with French Guiana (even now a small part is unresolved) and the maritime boundary was only agreed in 2013. The western border with British Guiana had still not been settled by the time Guyana became independent in 1966 (and is still not settled today), although the maritime border between the two neighbours was resolved by a UN tribunal in 2007.

These border disputes became significant issues when minerals were discovered in the interior in commercial quantities and were also an issue after the discovery of oil deposits offshore. However, they were not a problem at first after the Napoleonic Wars as the Dutch authorities and the Surinamese planters concentrated on the recovery of agricultural exports that were located close to the coast and the capital Paramaribo.

As in many other parts of the Caribbean, the most important export before the Napoleonic Wars had been sugar and its derivatives (molasses and rum) followed by cotton, cacao, and coffee. Thus, the priority for the authorities after the end of hostilities was the rehabilitation of the plantations. In this they at first had some success (see figure 7.1) with exports per head rising sharply between 1820 and 1830.

The recovery did not last long. The end of an illegal trade in slaves in 1826, coupled with an excess of deaths over births among the slave population, steadily reduced the number of slaves. Indentured labour was unable to fill the gap and the export of almost all commodities (cacao was a rare exception) steadily fell. Exports per head reached their lowest point just as slavery was finally abolished in 1863 (see figure 7.1).

Figure 7.1: Suriname: Exports per head at constant prices (1900=100), log scale, 1820–2016

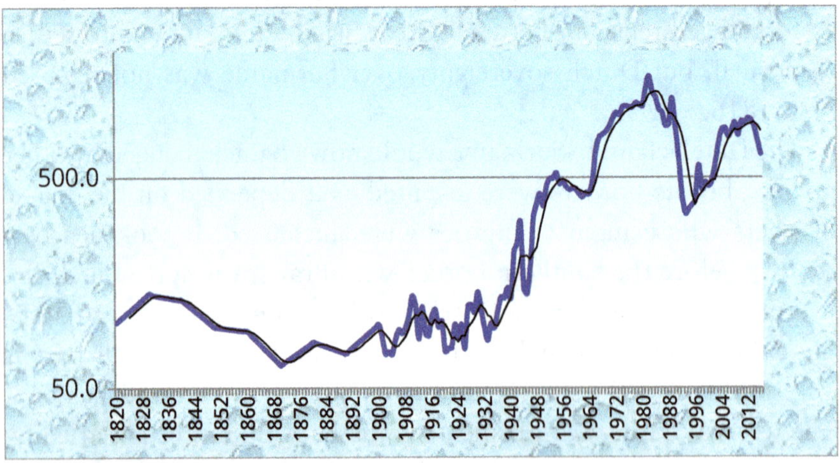

Sources: 1820–2008 from Statistical Appendix. World Bank, World Development Indicators thereafter.

The slaves were required to work for a further ten years as apprentices, giving the planters time to adapt and develop new schemes for indentured labourers. This time it was more successful and net migration inwards rose rapidly as Suriname became a more attractive destination. This was partly due to improved health conditions, but also the development of new exports – notably balata, gold, rice, bananas, and bauxite.

Of all these commodities, it was bauxite that would come to dominate the Surinamese economy giving the country a strategic asset in wartime and a valuable one in peacetime. And when Suriname joined the Kingdom of the Netherlands in 1954, under a new constitutional arrangement that left the Dutch government in control only of foreign affairs and defence, the local authorities used their new powers to reinforce the dependence of the economy on bauxite.

By the time of independence in 1975, Suriname had enjoyed a long and sustained boom in exports per head for almost a century (see figure 7.1). This had started slowly after emancipation and it was many years before exports per head returned to their level in 1830. However, the pace of change accelerated dramatically in the Second World War and continued in the post-war period.

The improved economic performance came swiftly to an end soon after independence. Political change, the suspension of foreign aid, fiscal expansion, currency collapse, and hyperinflation produced a spectacular fall in the economy that led to a big increase in outward migration. The worst moment was reached in 1993, by which time exports per head had fallen by nearly 80 per cent from their peak in 1982 (see figure 7.1).

Currency reform, the restoration of foreign aid, and debt rescheduling slowly put the Surinamese economy back on track. Mineral exports attracted foreign direct investment, and the economy grew significantly after the mid-1990s with a slowdown in net outward migration. The economy then suffered a further decline after 2015 in response to unfavourable external conditions, and recovery has been hampered by disputes between the dominant political forces in Suriname and foreign governments and institutions on which the economy has come to depend. This clash is still unresolved.

7.1. FROM THE NAPOLEONIC WARS TO EMANCIPATION

The restoration of Dutch rule in 1816 over Suriname confirmed that the privileges of the Dutch West India Company in the colony were over (they had been formally terminated in 1792). Suriname was made a Crown Colony (including, for several decades, the six Dutch islands in the Caribbean – see chapter 8), in which the Dutch monarch would rule through the auspices of a governor general. It was not until 1848 that the Dutch Parliament would acquire responsibility for Suriname, a change that was not insignificant since parliament would be more willing to tolerate fiscal subsidies for what was perceived as a failing colony.

In 1810, a few years before the end of the Napoleonic Wars, Suriname had an 'enumerated' population of 60,185 of which 91.1 per cent were slaves.[1] However, there was also an 'unenumerated' population estimated at 9,000.[2] This consisted not only of the survivors of the Amerindian peoples but also of several maroon communities. These had proved so enduring that the Dutch authorities had been forced to reach an accommodation with them in the eighteenth century, signing treaties and appointing commissioners.

The unenumerated population grew steadily during the nineteenth century, becoming a larger part of the total. However, they played little part, at first, in the export economy on which the Dutch authorities placed all their hopes. This sector depended on a slave labour force that by 1815 had shrunk to just under 52,000. With slave deaths exceeding slave births in the colony and an Anglo-Dutch Treaty in 1814 ending the slave trade, the prospects for the planters looked dismal.

The British had ended the slave trade in 1808 during their occupation of Suriname, so no slaves had been imported for nearly ten years when Dutch sovereignty was restored. Inevitably, the planters now carried on an illegal trade in slaves, and the Dutch authorities turned a blind eye. By 1826, when the trade finally came to an end, some 12,000 slaves had been imported and the slave population had not only stopped falling but also started to increase. It had reached 53,000 in the 1831 census, when it still represented more than 85 per cent of the enumerated population.[3]

The end of the slave trade coupled with the high death rate (the CDR for the colony averaged 30 in the years 1839–41), marronage, and manumission meant that the slave population was bound to decline. It had fallen below 40,000 by 1850, but still represented, at that time, more than 75 per cent of the population. By then, a deep sense of gloom hung over the planters and the colonial administrators.

In desperation, the authorities tried various immigration schemes. One scheme involved inviting Dutch settlers from Holland, stipulating that they must be farmers and encouraging them to produce those cash crops that required little capital investment, but the scheme was a total failure.[4] Another scheme launched in 1853 involved immigration by Chinese workers from Java and Portuguese from Madeira, but very few came.[5]

Pressure for emancipation was building in the Dutch Parliament, where the more progressive elements were increasingly concerned that Holland was among the last to retain slavery in its colonies (only Brazil, Portugal, and Spain still allowed it, and the US had taken the first steps to abolish it in 1862). A bill was finally passed in 1862 providing compensation for the slave owners of 300 guilders (US$124) per slave. By 1863, when emancipation went into force, the slave population was down to 33,000, and the enumerated population had fallen below 53,000 – a decline of more than ten per cent from its level in 1810.[6]

This demographic story played a large part in what happened to the economy in the years before emancipation (see table 7.1). The volume of all the main exports, at first, increased after the Napoleonic Wars thanks to the illegal trade in slaves and the restoration of normal trade patterns (an estimated 80 per cent of exports went to Holland up to 1850 while between 60 and 70 per cent of imports came from the 'mother' country).[7] The recovery of sugar – the principal export – was particularly marked, but even the volume of cotton exports increased.

After 1830 it was a different story. The volume of sugar exported increased marginally until 1840, but then declined – slowly at first, but precipitately after emancipation. The ten-year apprenticeship that the former slaves were forced to work (from 1863 to 1873) could not save the sugar sector, and the large state-sponsored schemes for indentured labour (see next section) had not yet taken effect. Molasses exports suffered the same fate, but rum – added to the export list in 1840 (see table 7.1) – did expand, albeit from a very small base.

Cotton and coffee exports, as in many other parts of the Caribbean, declined sharply after 1830. Cotton planters could not compete with the US, and coffee growers could not match the costs in Brazil or Java. Even privileged access to the Dutch market, where they enjoyed imperial preference until the middle of the nineteenth century, could not save them.

Table 7.1: Suriname: Exports by Volume, 1820–70

	Sugar (lb)	Molasses (gal)	Rum (gal)	Cotton (lb)	Cacao (lb)	Coffee (lb)
1820	18,739,395	629,118		1,774,254	16,857	5,001,315
1830	33,079,301	1,000,000		2,033,304	18,455	6,046,102
1840	34,313,897	931,150	65,905	1,993,256	182,984	3,461,902
1850	31,274,955	800,000	50,000	939,774	167,511	723,514
1860	31,014,959	773,043	174,850	577,428	483,691	434,546
1870	21,873,077	393,889	104,191	354,443	1,007,569	13,455

Source: Statistical Appendix.

The only success among the export commodities was cacao, where the volume exported grew from less than 20,000 pounds in 1830 to more than one million in 1870 (see table 7.1). Ideally suited to smallholder agriculture and therefore not dependent on large-scale plantations, cacao was an excellent crop with which to adjust to the decline in the size of the slave labour force. And cacao did not suffer from the lack of banking facilities in the colony, which were still virtually non-existent by the time of emancipation despite several attempts to establish them.[8] Even by 1870, however, cacao was still too small in importance to reverse the decline in merchandise exports that had taken place since 1830.

The fall had been very severe. The value of exports per head had dropped by more than 50 per cent in the four decades after 1830 (see figure 7.1). The enumerated population had also fallen, putting in doubt the future of the Dutch colony. For governments in The Hague, the Dutch colonies in the Caribbean seemed to represent the past when compared with the dynamic colonies in the Dutch East Indies. The end of Crown Colony government in 1848 appeared to have made no difference. Many planters sold or abandoned their estates and returned to Holland.

This was born out by the colony's finances (see table 7.2). Revenue per head rose slowly between 1820 and 1850, but then declined sharply by 1870. By that time, revenue per head in the colony was among the lowest in the Caribbean (it had been well above the average in 1830). The structure of revenue also changed, with tariffs rather than domestic taxes becoming a much more important source of income (80 per cent in 1870 – see table 7.2). Thus, revenue came to depend on the value of imports that, in turn, depended on the value of exports. As these had been falling steadily since 1820 (from US$2.7 million to $1 million in 1870), colonial revenue was bound to be negatively affected.

It was a similar story for expenditure per head. The colony depended on subsidies that the King tried hard to limit during the period of Crown Colony rule. As a result, expenditure per head was not much larger than revenue per head as Crown Colony rule came to an end (see table 7.2). Thereafter, expenditure per head fell rapidly to its low point in 1870, but at least it did not fall as fast as revenue per head. This was because Parliament provided subsidies to Suriname that meant spending was higher than revenue (nearly 50 per cent higher by 1870).[9]

Table 7.2: Suriname: Revenue and Expenditure per Head (US$), 1820–70

	Revenue Per head (1860 prices)	Expenditure Per head (1860 prices)	Tariff Share of Revenue (%)
1820	6.4	8.1	
1830	7.3	9.3	
1840	7.1	9.0	
1850	7.9	8.7	26.6
1860	5.3	6.9	35.0
1870	4.3	6.1	79.6

Source: Statistical Appendix.

Despite this dismal economic panorama, the Dutch authorities had almost imperceptibly succeeded in laying the foundations for a future period of prosperity after emancipation. Immigration schemes may have failed to attract many new workers while slavery was still in force, but they would come to play a vital role later in the century (see next section). And a relaxation of imperial preference in 1849, shortly after Suriname ceased to be a Crown Colony, would pave the way for the diversification of export markets and allow for the purchase of imports from cheaper sources (especially the US). As a result, only one-third of exports went to Holland by 1870, while the share of imports from Holland had fallen to 44 per cent in the same year.[10]

7.2. Emancipation and Net Inward Migration

At the time of emancipation on July 1, 1863, the main ethnic group in Suriname was overwhelmingly Afro-Surinamese. Today, Afro-Surinamese constitute just over one-third of the population, the remainder being of (East) Indian, Javanese, Chinese, Levantine, or European descent. In addition, there is a small group of Amerindians and about 15 per cent of the population is classified as multi-ethnic.

This change in the ethnic composition mainly took place in the half century after emancipation. The Dutch authorities had adopted a ten-year system of apprenticeship (officially called State Supervision) for the former slaves but by no means all signed new contracts by the time the deadline (October 1, 1863) was reached.[11] The planters demanded a scheme for mass immigration, so in 1865 the *Suriname Immigratie Maatschappij* (Suriname Immigration Company) was organised to import labourers, mainly from China, and some 2,000 emigrated to Suriname. However, the British and Portuguese closed their Chinese ports (Hong Kong and Macau respectively) for all emigration except to British colonies, and the company was dissolved in 1869.[12]

The planters pleaded for further action, but the Dutch authorities were divided between those who thought the Afro-Surinamese could provided an adequate labour force if paid properly and encouraged into small-scale activities such as cacao and those who sided with the planters in calling for mass immigration of indentured labourers from other parts of the world.[13]

Figure 7.2: Suriname: Net Migration (% of population), 1871–1930

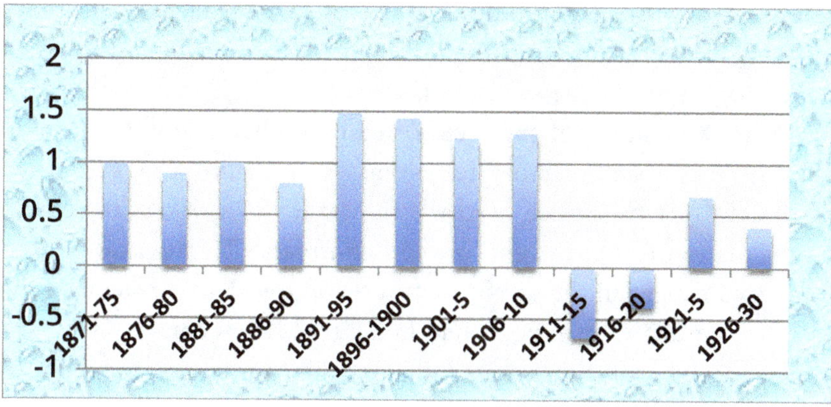

Source: Statistical Appendix.

The second group prevailed in the Dutch Parliament. The British and Dutch government then signed a treaty to permit the import of indentured labourers from British India. The annual entry was large until 1917, when the Indian government finally banned the practice in the light of persistent complaints of ill treatment. By that time, however, the Dutch authorities already had in place a scheme for the large-scale importation of indentured labourers from Java in the Dutch East Indies and immigration continued. This scheme would finally end in 1942 after the Japanese invasion of Holland's Asian colony.

The result was a transformed ethnic mix of the Surinamese population. In the first four decades after emancipation, net inward migration as a share of the population exceeded one per cent per year (see figure 7.2). This was one of the fastest rates of inward migration in the Caribbean. And after a brief period of net outward migration in the second decade of the twentieth century, when immigration from British India was halted, the inward flow resumed again in the 1920s.

Indentured labourers had the right of return at the end of their contracts (the plantation owner paid, but the scheme was subsidised by the Dutch state) to their country of origin. Some chose to do so, but the vast majority did not. Of those that stayed in Suriname, however, most preferred not to sign new contracts with their former employers. Instead, they either moved to Paramaribo or acquired small plots of land. This hastened the transition of Suriname from a colony of large-scale plantations to one of small-scale agriculture.[14]

Mass immigration from Asia, therefore, did not have the effect hoped for either by the plantation owners or the Dutch authorities. By 1890, the volume of sugar exported had fallen below the level in 1820 (it was a similar story for molasses and rum), dragged down by the fall in world prices and the reluctance of workers to remain on the plantations at the end of their contracts. There was a modest recovery in sugar in the 1890s, but by 1900 the share of sugar in the value of merchandise exports had fallen to 23 per cent.

The decline of the sugar industry did not mean the end of agricultural exports as cacao continued its remarkable rise. The attraction of cacao was not just the ability of small-scale farmers to compete internationally due to the absence of significant economies of scale, but also world prices that held up much better than sugar or coffee in the last quarter of the nineteenth century. As a result, cacao accounted for 40 per cent of the value of exports in 1900, almost twice the share of sugar.

Cacao production, however, was not without its problems and would go into decline as soon as the twentieth century started, as the following account makes clear:[15]

> The tiny cocoa estates of Surinam were 'well-tended gardens', but they were not profitable. The coastal strip, naturally under water at high tide, necessitated a complex and expensive system of dykes, sluices, drains and canals, although these also provided cheap and convenient transport. Primary or secondary forest was meticulously cleared to the last stump, and planting was usually on the banks of rivers, to benefit from some drainage...An outbreak of witches' broom in 1895 revealed the weaknesses of this expensive way of growing cocoa. Caused by a fungus epidemic to the Amazon, witches' broom extended throughout the colony by 1903. Heavy pruning and spraying with Bordeaux mixture proved no more than a palliative.

Cacao and sugar together accounted for more than 60 per cent of the value of exports in 1900. The rest came almost entirely from two commodities that had not been exploited during the long years of slavery. The first was gold, which – as in neighbouring French Guiana – was found in the alluvial deposits of the interior, which had become a significant export by 1880. The second was balata, the latex from the bullet tree, which would have a large variety of uses and which was starting to be exported by 1890. The two new commodities, together with cacao, help to explain the recovery in exports per head after emancipation (see figure 7.1).

Gold had inspired generations of Dutch entrepreneurs in Suriname, but nothing of any consequence had been found until 1875. The colonial government then enacted legislation to regulate the gold industry. Exports began in 1876 and increased rapidly. By 1884, there were 306 concessions in the colony, and competition among concessionaries was so intense that the government received little by way of export duties.[16] In addition, the exploitation of gold was held back by the dispute over the boundary between Suriname and French Guiana where gold had been found.

These problems were overcome through arbitration, in 1891, by the Russian Czar, who essentially reconfirmed the border as agreed between France and Holland in 1861 but which had never been ratified by treaty. Large-scale operators were then encouraged, a company was established with foreign investment and the colony's first railway was built. Thousands of workers were recruited, although Asian immigrants were banned. However, the largest company went into liquidation in 1907 and soon production was in the hands of *porcknockers* – small-scale operators – who drove production and exports upwards until their peak in 1910. Gold exports would then steadily decline before new discoveries would lead to a resurgence of the industry after independence.

Balata is produced from the milky juice in the bark of the bullet tree. It had been used for centuries, but exports were insignificant until the manufacturing sector in Europe and North America developed. Balata then found a use in making driving belts, shoe soles, golf balls, and as a substitute for gutta percha and rubber. Dominated by a handful of large companies, the industry employed 5,600 workers at its peak.[17]

Exports rose rapidly after 1890. Indeed, on the eve of the First World War balata alone accounted for 40 per cent of the value of exports with cacao now much less important.[18] And a large part of these exports were destined for the US, which had become the largest market for Surinamese merchandise exports by the beginning of the twentieth century.

Despite this, the recovery of the Surinamese economy was still modest and exports per head had not reached their level in 1830 as the First World War broke out (see figure 7.1). Holland, although neutral, could do little to prevent the disruption of transatlantic shipping during the war years so that the export of many commodities was seriously disrupted. In addition, the gold industry went into decline after 1915 as the volume exported steadily fell in consequence of the previous excess exploitation. Meanwhile, balata exports dropped as a result of a collapse of prices after 1917. Inevitably, imports plummeted imposing great hardship on a population accustomed to consuming many foodstuffs produced abroad.

The war, therefore, convinced the Dutch authorities that a new approach had to be taken to their South American colony, and soon large-scale schemes for growing rice were adopted leading from 1922 onwards to modest exports as well.[19] Ironically, however, it was that year that would mark Suriname's permanent transformation from an agricultural to mineral exporter. This was due to bauxite, the raw material used in the manufacture of aluminium.[20]

7.3. THE AGE OF BAUXITE

Despite vast deposits of bauxite, Suriname did nothing to exploit them before the twentieth century. Instead, the colonial government had used the disintegrated rock that resembles red clay to harden the roads of the colony and the streets of Paramaribo. The colonial government failed to employ Dutch engineers who understood the mineral's potential, and Suriname was expected to remain an agricultural colony. In addition, bauxite could not be exploited by small-scale operators living in the territory because of its heavy capital requirements.

Suriname, therefore, needed major investments before bauxite could be mined. A lack of interest by Dutch companies meant foreign investment and the first company was formed in 1916 just as the gold industry was starting to fade. Surinaamsche Bauxiet Maatschappij, a subsidiary of the Aluminum Company of America (ALCOA), made its first exports in 1922, and 15 years later bauxite accounted for two-thirds of the value of exports. In the following year, the company changed its name to SURALCO, and its success encouraged the Billiton Company, a Dutch enterprise in the Dutch East Indies, to enter Suriname in 1939.

Despite this, Surinamese exports per head were still only back to their level in 1830 (see figure 7.1). However, the eruption of the Second World War changed everything. Holland was occupied by Germany in 1940, putting at risk the supply of bauxite to the US armaments industry where aluminium had become a vital material in the manufacture of aircraft. And German U-boats sank 26 ships on their journey from Suriname to the US.[21]

Although the colonial government in Paramaribo remained loyal to the Dutch government in exile, the US administration of President Franklin Roosevelt (1933–45) took no chances and placed troops in Suriname to protect the bauxite mines. By 1940, Suriname had become the world's most important bauxite producer, and 82 per cent of US bauxite imports came from the Dutch colony in the years between 1935 and 1944.

Exports, driven by SURALCO and Billiton, soared during the war years reaching nearly 1.7 million tonnes in 1943 (they had been 500,000 tonnes in 1939), and bauxite became the only export of significance accounting for nearly 90 per cent of the total value. The demise of sugar accelerated and none would be exported in 1945 – the first time that had happened since Europeans starting growing cane in the seventeenth century.

Production of bauxite temporarily dropped after the end of war, but soon recovered. More than two million tonnes were exported in 1949, more than three million in 1953, and more than four million in 1964. The rapid increase persuaded ALCOA to build a controversial dam south of the capital that created a 1,500 square kilometre lake. The Brokopondo reservoir generated a large amount of hydroelectricity for a new alumina refinery and aluminium smelter, but forced some 6,000 maroons to relocate. By 1973, on the eve of independence, bauxite production reached a peak with almost seven million tonnes exported.

Figure 7.3: Suriname: Birth and Death Rates, 1895–1975

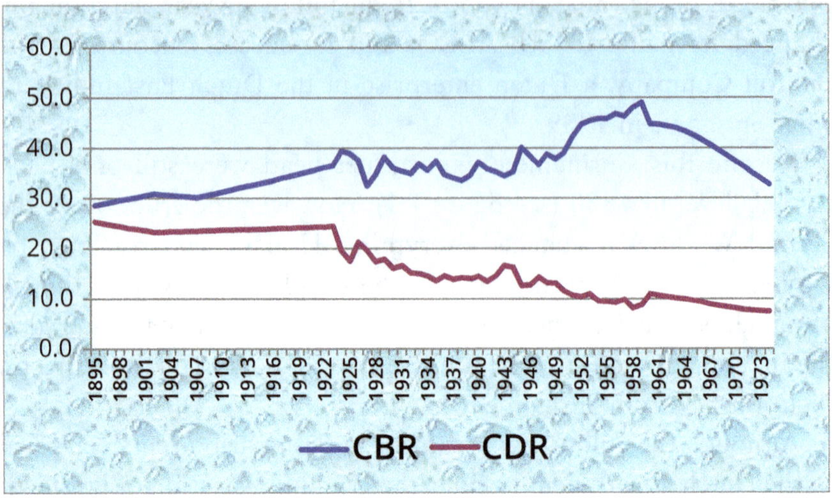

Source: Statistical Appendix.

In 50 years, bauxite had transformed the structure of the Surinamese economy in relation to exports, imports, inward investment, and fiscal revenue. However, as a capital-intensive industry it had done little to create jobs. With the death rate falling and the birth rate steadily rising, the natural rate of increase of the population had gone from 0.5 per cent a year at the beginning of the twentieth century to one per cent in the 1920s, two per cent in the 1930s, three per cent in the 1940s, and an astonishing four per cent in the 1950s (see figure 7.3), after which the birth rate started to decline.

A country accustomed for decades to a labour shortage now found itself with a labour surplus. More and more people entered the labour market, but many were unable to find jobs. From the 1930s onwards, a flow of net outward migration – mainly towards Holland – started to take place. Modest at first, it reached an annual rate of nearly one per cent of the population in the period 1955–70. In the last few years before independence, however, the net outward migration accelerated to three per cent a year. In these years (1971–75), the outward migration was so rapid that the Surinamese population actually fell despite a still high birth and low death rate.

For those that stayed, especially those with secure employment, economic conditions in the years before independence were not unfavourable. In the early 1960s, when the employed labour force was just over 80,000, agricultural workers constituted less than a quarter, and the largest group were classified as 'craftsmen or production-process workers'.[22] Income distribution in 1968/9 was unusually equal with a low Gini coefficient for household income and a share of income for the bottom decile of 5.74 per cent.[23]

A large part of the explanation for the relatively equal distribution of income was the rapid rise in public sector spending. Revenue per head had peaked in 1908 and then drifted downwards (see figure 7.4). Revenue was never sufficient to cover expenditure, and the Dutch Parliament had regularly voted a subsidy for the colony. However, the subsidy was never huge, so spending was largely determined by the revenue collected locally.

After the Second World War, however, revenue rose rapidly. This was made possible by the taxes generated directly and indirectly by the bauxite industry, but also by rising levels of Dutch foreign aid. Incorporated in the revenue stream, foreign aid helped drive public revenue per head at constant prices to exceptional levels and the volume of Dutch aid accelerated in the last years before independence.

Figure 7.4: Suriname: Revenue per head (1930 US$), 1900–1975

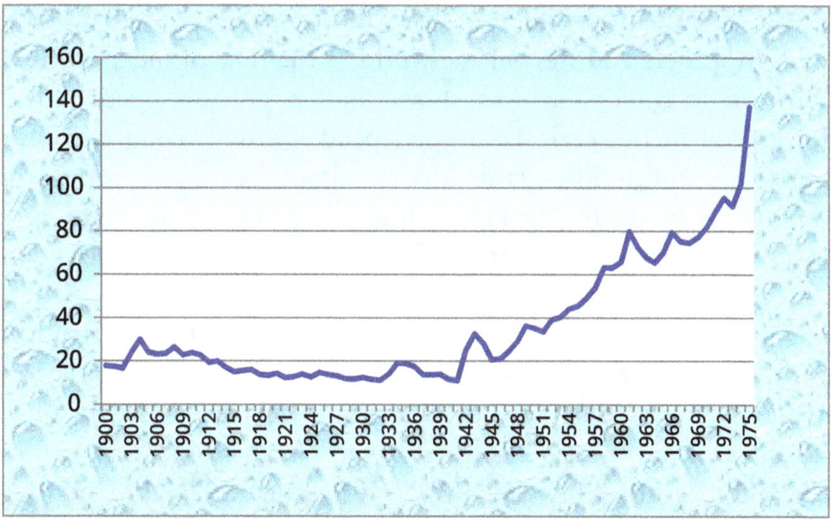

Source: Statistical Appendix from 1900-60; national official sources adjusted for inflation have been used for 1960 to 1975 and spliced to the series before 1960.

The combination of a rapidly expanding export sector, high levels of government spending, and increasing remittances from Surinamese abroad led to a rapid rise in income per head. The first estimates of GDP at constant prices showed that the economy had trebled in size in the 15 years after 1953.[24] Despite the high levels of outward migration, the Surinamese government drew sufficient confidence from the economy's performance to demand independence. The Dutch authorities put up little resistance and promised a generous aid package of 3.5 billion guilders (nearly US$2 billion). Suriname then became independent on November 25, 1975.

7.4. AFTER INDEPENDENCE

Independence took place under what appeared to be favourable economic circumstances. Exports were expanding rapidly and new products, especially bananas and shrimp, had joined bauxite, alumina, and aluminium on the list. GDP and GDP per head were growing, and the former colonial power had promised a generous aid package for the first decade after independence. Inflation was firmly under control, backed by a currency pegged to the US dollar since the collapse of the Bretton Woods system in 1971 and substantial foreign exchange reserves.

Many Surinamese did not share the optimism voiced by their political leaders and the outside world at the time of independence. Outward migration, as was shown in the previous section, had accelerated in the years before independence and would continue almost unbroken afterwards (today almost as many people of Surinamese origin live in Holland as in Suriname itself). The new government was soon embroiled in a series of corruption scandals and was overthrown by a military coup in 1980.

The following decade was among the most traumatic in Suriname's entire history. The leader of the military coup, Desiré Delano ('Dési') Bouterse, murdered many of his critics in December 1982 and, a few years later, the army was engaged in a civil war against the Surinamese Liberation Army (SLA) led by Ronald Brunswijk, with the SLA drawing strong support from the maroon community. Constitutional order was temporarily restored in 1987, but another intervention by Bouterse in 1990 returned the military to power.

Free elections were then held from 1991 onwards at regular intervals with Bouterse himself winning in 2010 and 2015 despite being found guilty by a Dutch court *in absentia* of drug smuggling. As President, Bouterse was then able to close down until 2019 the judicial process against him for the murders in 1982, but was unable to travel outside Suriname (except to a handful of regional meetings and the United Nations) because of the Dutch court's judgement.

It would have been extraordinary if this political turmoil did not do serious damage to the economy, which, of course, is what happened. The first casualty was the Dutch foreign aid programme, which averaged nearly US$100 million per year until 1982 before falling close to zero during the period of military rule (foreign aid from other European Union donors and institutions would follow suit). Net overseas development assistance from all sources fell from US$278 per person in 1982 (equivalent to ten per cent of GDP) to a mere $10 per person the next year.

The military government had now lost a major source of income, but spending – especially on the security forces – continued to grow rapidly. In addition, tax income dropped as the economy went into decline. The result was a surge in the government deficit, which could not be financed other than by borrowing from the Central Bank. Claims on central government, which had been less than one per cent at the time of independence, exceeded 100 per cent by the end of the 1980s.[25]

The loss of the foreign aid programme would eventually have required a major adjustment programme by the government under any circumstances. However, it was made worse by the decline in the value of exports of goods and services. These peaked at $547 million in 1980 – the same year that constitutional rule ended – and would fall sharply in the following ten years. Indeed, they barely exceeded $200 million by the end of the decade.

At this time, exports still depended heavily on bauxite. Services, including tourism, were of minor importance. Production had peaked in 1980, after which world prices had drifted downwards. However, the volume exported was also badly hit by the civil war since much of the fighting took place in the regions where the mines were located. And the plans to modify the dependence on exports through the refining and smelting of bauxite had not achieved as much as had originally been hoped when the first investments had been made.

The squeeze on imports was, therefore, intense as a result of the fall in foreign aid and the drop in the value of exports. The shortage of foreign exchange led to enormous pressure on the exchange rate, fixed since 1972 at 1.79 per US dollar. The fiction of a fixed exchange rate was preserved until 1994, but by then most imports were purchased with foreign exchange acquired in the parallel market. This had reached ten to the dollar by the end of the 1980s before collapsing completely to 442 in 1995, 1,322 in 2000, and 2,601 in 2003.[26] It was then replaced in 2004 with a new currency, the Surinamese dollar, pegged at first to the dollar at 2.73 before it also declined in value after 2010.[27]

Currency collapse in small, open economies dependent on imports normally brings inflation and Suriname was no exception. Indeed, despite the currency peg, Suriname had experienced double-digit inflation occasionally even before independence. After the emergence of a parallel foreign exchange market, however, inflation soared. By 1987, it exceeded 50 per cent a year. More restrictive monetary policy then lowered the rate temporarily, but by 1993 it had reached nearly 150 per cent (it peaked at 368 per cent the following year). Even the introduction of the Surinamese dollar in 2004 failed to eliminate price increases and the fall in the exchange rate, especially after 2015, brought back high levels of inflation.

The economy had grown rapidly in the 15 years before independence and would continue to grow for a few years afterwards (see figure 7.5). GDP per head then reached a peak in 1978, after which it fell precipitately until its lowest point in 1987. It would then take 25 years before the previous peak was reached again in 2012 after which there was a further decline. Suriname, therefore, did not have just a 'lost decade', as happened in most of Latin America, but a 'lost generation'. It has been an exceptional and tragic story.

The human dimension of this tragedy can be found in the high levels of outward migration. It can also be seen in high levels of unemployment, especially among young people where it had reached 25 per cent among men and 50 per cent among women by the 1990s.[28]

And even the flow of remittances back from migrants abroad could not reverse the sharp deterioration in the distribution of income. By the end of the 1990s, for example, the World Bank estimated the Gini coefficient at 57.6[29] – one of the highest in the world – while the share of income of the poorest ten per cent was now down to 1.2 per cent.[30]

Figure 7.5: Suriname: GDP per head (2010 US$),1960–2016

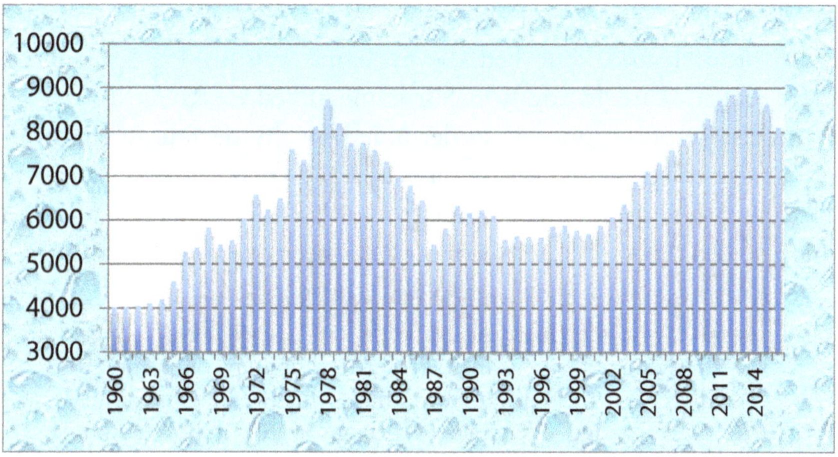

Source: Statistical Appendix and World Bank, World Development Indicators.

The chronic problems of the Surinamese economy from 1980 onwards provoked numerous attempts at macroeconomic stabilisation. The first took place in 1987 after the adoption of a new constitution and the restoration of Dutch aid. Fiscal and monetary measures were taken to lower inflation and the budget deficit, including the amount of excess spending that could be funded (i.e., monetised) by the Central Bank, but it proved impossible to enforce the new policies effectively. In addition, the IMF (Suriname joined in 1978) was not asked to play a role.

A further attempt was made at macroeconomic stabilisation, including a Structural Adjustment Programme (SAP), after the restoration of civilian rule in 1991. According to the Inter-American Development Bank, which Suriname had joined after independence:[31]

> The SAP was drafted with the participation of the Dutch as a condition to restore bilateral aid, following a second suspension in 1991. It included measures to strengthen fiscal

> policy, deregulate the economy, liberalize import/export licensing, and privatize some public enterprises. Ultimately, the National Assembly was unable to achieve consensus on several relevant economic measures and quantifiable targets to offset the impact of external shocks. As a result, the fiscal gap continued throughout the 1990s, except for a brief period (1995–1996) when sound monetary, fiscal, and exchange rate measures coexisted with favorable external conditions.

This second attempt at stabilisation was at least more successful than the first, and it unified the exchange rate in 1994 around a more realistic rate. In addition, Suriname joined CARICOM in 1995. However, stabilisation was undermined by the decline in the price of bauxite that fell from an average of $273 per tonne from 1989 to 1990 and then to $156 per tonne from 1992 to 1994. The impact of this price on the Surinamese economy has been explained as follows:[32]

> A decline in the international price of alumina lowers export revenues and increases the trade deficit. Moreover, it reduces the foreign-exchange transfers of the alumina companies to the CBvS [Central Bank of Suriname], which reduces its ability to supply foreign exchange to private sector importers and tends to put pressure on its stock of international reserves. The decreased supply of foreign exchange causes the exchange rate to depreciate in both nominal and real terms...The decline in the alumina price also lowers alumina company profits and hence government revenues. The decline in government revenues expands the fiscal deficit and pressures the government to rein back expenditures. Second-round effects reinforce the decline in government revenues. Import taxes, the largest source of government revenues, fall as the volume of imports declines, and taxes from non-alumina companies tend to decline in real terms as the rest of the economy goes into recession.

The volatility of the world bauxite price was bound to create cycles in the Surinamese economy, especially as no stabilisation fund was created so that boom years could be used to smooth out expenditure in times of slump. However, the Surinamese economy also suffered from the volatility of foreign aid, mainly from Holland. As figure 7.6 shows, foreign aid after independence was enormous on a *per capita* basis, but it was also volatile as it depended on decisions taken by the donors in response to political events in Suriname. Coping with the cycles in foreign aid was almost as problematic as dealing with the fluctuating price of bauxite.

Figure 7.6: Suriname: Net Oficial Development Assistance per head (US$), 1975–2016

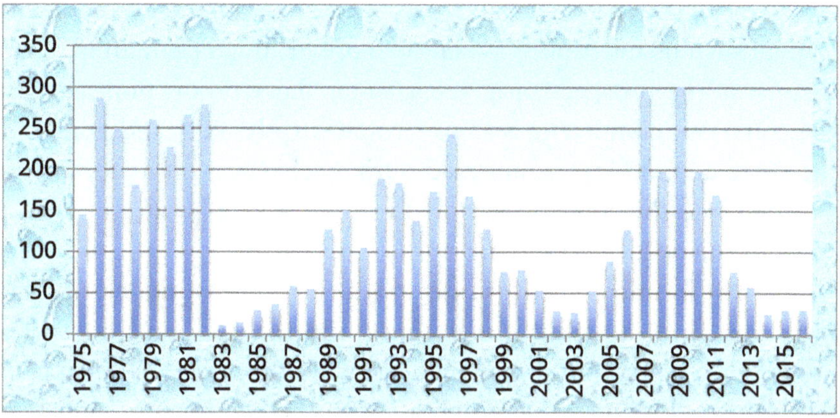

Source: World Bank, World Development Indicators.

A third attempt was made at stabilisation from 2001 onwards when the external environment became more favourable, although banana exports ceased in 2002. And the launch of a new currency in 2004 (the Surinamese dollar) coincided with the entry of a major foreign company (Newmont Mining Corporation) to exploit the gold resources of Suriname. This was a welcome change for an industry that had begun to revive in the 1980s with the entry of *garimpeiros* from Brazil. These miners, perhaps as many as 20,000 at their peak, in most cases operated illegally and caused serious damage to the environment as a result of deforestation and the use of mercury to pollute water supplies.

After the entry of Newmont Mining Corporation, recorded gold exports soared, reaching a peak of 34,213 kg in 2013. Gold now provided an alternative source of export earnings (and government revenue), just as it had before the Second World War. Unrecorded gold exports also boosted the economy, if not the environment, as some of the proceeds were spent within the domestic economy. And when Newmont opened a new mine in 2013, the Surinamese state benefited directly as a public sector company *Staatsolie* took a minority stake.

Staatsolie had been created in 1980 with a monopoly to explore for and extract oil. It pumped its first barrel in 1982, but output was at first small and insufficient to replace all imports. Gradually, however, with the help of production-sharing agreements with foreign companies, daily production increased to 16,000 bpd and there was a small surplus for export. When offshore drilling began after 2015, there was the prospect of a much larger daily production as well. Oil could not compete in terms of value with bauxite and gold, but the three commodities confirmed Suriname's vocation as a mineral exporter and the country benefited from the price boom in the first years of the twenty-first century.

The fall in mineral prices after the 2008/9 global financial crisis was, therefore, an unwelcome shock for the Surinamese people. However, the disruption was made much worse by the decision of ALCOA to close its bauxite operation at the end of 2015 and two years later to leave the country almost completely after a century of continuous operations. A fourth round of stabilisation was needed, this time in cooperation with the IMF, but it soon broke down when the government was unwilling to meet the harsh conditions. Once again, GDP per head fell sharply (see figure 7.5), inflation soared and the currency collapsed.

While most other Caribbean countries after the Second World War had pinned their hopes on the export of services, Suriname had defied the trend and become ever more dependent on mineral extraction. It had brought periods of exceptional economic growth and helped to raise average income. However, the country found itself unable to cope with the volatility associated with the mining industries as a result of price fluctuations and production cycles. Without a mineral stabilisation fund, Suriname had no means of protecting itself from this volatility. Many Surinamese without secure employment, including some of the most highly educated people, emigrated in search of a better life abroad. This export of human capital has been a constant reminder of the dangers of excessive dependence on a handful of minerals.

NOTES

1. See Statistical Appendix.
2. See A. MacDonald, 'Lost and Forgotten? Official Colonial Statistics: Experience in Constructing Historical Statistics for Surinam' *Statistical Journal of the United Nations* 14 (1997): 124–27.
3. See Statistical Appendix.
4. See R.M.N Panday, *Agriculture in Surinam, 1650–1950: An Inquiry into the Causes of Its Decline* (Amsterdam: H.J. Paris, 1959), 48–49.
5. See R. Hoefte, *In Place of Slavery: A Social History of British Indian and Javanese Laborers in Suriname* (Gainesville, FL: University Press of Florida, 1998), 13.
6. See Statistical Appendix.
7. See Statistical Appendix.
8. See C.C. Goslinga, *The Dutch in the Caribbean and in Suriname, 1791/5–1942* (Assen, Netherlands: Van Gorcum, 1990), 442.
9. See J.M. Plante Fébure, *West-Indië in het Parlement, 1897–1917: Bijdrage tot Nederland's koloniaal-politieke geschiedenis* (S Gravenhage: M. Nijhoff, 1918), 49.
10. See Statistical Appendix.
11. The apprenticeship scheme is examined in P.C. Emmer, 'Between Slavery and Freedom: The Period of Apprenticeship in Suriname (Dutch Guiana), 1863–1873,' *Slavery & Abolition* 14 (1993), 87–113.
12. See Hoefte, *In Place of Slavery*, 14.
13. See R.A.J. van Lier, *Frontier Society: A Social Analysis of the History of Surinam* (The Hague: Martinus Nijhoof, 1971), chapter 8.
14. By the 1920s, the contribution of large-scale production units to agricultural output had fallen to 20 per cent. See P. van Dijck, 'Structural Change and Long-Term Growth: The Suriname Experience,' *Integration & Trade* 5, no. 15 (2001): 290, figure 2.
15. See W.G. Clarence-Smith, *Cocoa and Chocolate, 1765–1914* (London: Routledge, 2000), 183.
16. See Goslinga, *The Dutch in the Caribbean and in Suriname*, 481–85.
17. Ibid., 491.
18. See Statistical Appendix.
19. See A. van Traa, *Suriname, 1900–1940* (Deventer: W. van Hoeve, 1946), 107–10.
20. Alumina is extracted from bauxite in a refinery. Alumina is then used to produce primary aluminium. Four to seven metric tons of bauxite make two metric tons of alumina and one metric ton of aluminium.
21. See Goslinga, *The Dutch in the Caribbean and in Suriname*, 703.
22. At this time, the official unemployment rate was ten per cent.

23. See Algemeen Bureau voor de Statistiek, *Armoedegrenzen en armoede in Suriname* (Paramaribo: Algemeen Bureau voor de Statistiek, 2010), 6, table 7.
24. See van Dijck, 'Structural Change and Long-Term Growth,' 295, figure 10.
25. See World Bank, World Development Indicators.
26. See V. Bulmer-Thomas, *The Economic History of the Caribbean since the Napoleonic Wars* (Cambridge: Cambridge University Press, 2012), 606.
27. See International Monetary Fund (IMF), *Suriname: Selected Issues: IMF Country Report, 05/142* (Washington, DC: IMF, 2005), 11–21.
28. See World Bank, 'World Development Indicators (WDI),' *World Bank*, n.d. http://data.worldbank.org.
29. Ibid.
30. See Algemeen Bureau voor de Statistiek, *Armoedegrenzen en armoede in Suriname*, 6.
31. See Inter-American Development Bank (IDB), *Country Program Evaluation: Suriname 1980–2004* (Washington, DC: IDB, 2006), 4–5.
32. See P. van Dijck et al, *The Suriname Economy: Experiences of the 1990s and Challenges Ahead* (Amsterdam: CEDLA, 2000), 11–12, 16, table 2.

Chapter 8
THE DUTCH ANTILLES

The territories of Aruba, Bonaire, and Curaçao (ABC) together with St Maarten, St Eustatius, and Saba (SSS) are the six islands for which Holland still has constitutional responsibilities. The Dutch Antilles no longer exists as a political entity, but for a long period the six islands, of which it was constituted, formed a single Dutch colony despite their geographical and economic diversity.

Following the Napoleonic Wars, the islands were made subordinate to the Dutch authorities in Paramaribo in 1828. However, this unwieldy arrangement changed in 1845, after which the Netherlands Antilles became a separate Dutch colony. The status was changed again in 1954, when the Netherlands Antilles – along with Dutch Guiana – became an autonomous unit within the Kingdom of the Netherlands with its capital at Willemstad in Curaçao.

Autonomy, under which the local authorities were responsible for almost all aspects of policy except defence and foreign affairs, strained the constitutional arrangements established for the Dutch Antilles. The other islands resented control from Curaçao and looked to loosen the ties. The first to insist on leaving was Aruba, which itself became an autonomous unit within the Kingdom of Netherlands in 1986. The remaining five islands then went their separate ways in October 2010, bringing the political history of the Netherlands Antilles to an end.

St Maarten and Curaçao joined Aruba as autonomous units within the Kingdom of the Netherlands, while Bonaire, Saba, and St Eustatius chose to become 'public bodies' (effectively external municipalities) of Holland itself. Political separation had some logic since the islands never had much in common economically. This chapter will, therefore, examine the economic history of the islands one by one, but first a brief sketch will be given for the Dutch Antilles as a whole.

None of the islands are rich in natural resources, so they never formed classical plantation economies as in Suriname or other parts of the Caribbean. Indeed, if their survival had depended only on domestic exports, they would have become a serious burden to Holland. However, right from the beginning of their colonisation in the seventeenth century, some of the islands were important centres of the entrepôt trade. The merchants who controlled this trade came from different countries, not just Holland, and used slaves. Thus, slavery was not limited to agricultural plantations or mining activities but was widespread in commerce as well.

The end of the Napoleonic Wars terminated many of the trade restrictions in the Americas that had allowed the Dutch islands to flourish. In addition, the proximity of the ABC islands to Venezuela led to tensions between the South American state and Holland over trade taxes, shipping rights, and the political activity of exiles. The value of re-exports fluctuated, but was no higher on the eve of the First World War than it had been a century earlier. The Netherlands Antilles, therefore, struggled as a Dutch colony in the nineteenth century and the islands often depended on subsidies from the mother country.

While slavery was in force, the population barely increased. When slavery ended in 1863, followed by a ten-year period of apprenticeship, the population of the Dutch Antilles only increased modestly as net migration outwards now became significant. A few non-traditional domestic exports were exploited, but these merely replaced traditional exports that had begun to decline or even disappear. Indeed, domestic exports per head were stagnant or declining for most of the period before the First World War (see figure 8.1).

All this changed dramatically after the first exports of oil from Venezuela in 1917. Suddenly, the oil companies found themselves in need of oil refineries and the ABC islands being so close to the oil fields created a perfect opportunity. Facilities were built first on Curaçao and later Aruba, transforming the value of domestic exports per head from the Netherlands Antilles (see figure 8.1). Net migration now turned inwards, as the new industries created many jobs directly and indirectly, and the population increased rapidly.

Figure 8.1: Dutch Antilles: Exports per head at constant prices (1900=100), log scale, 1820–2008

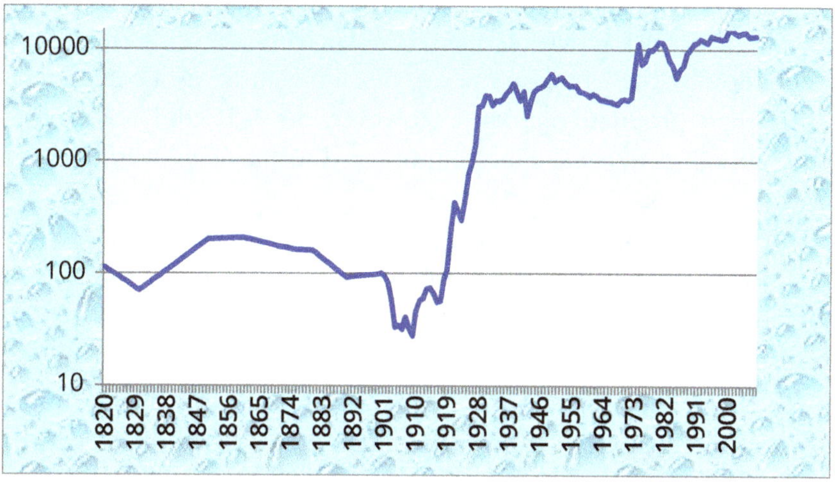

Source: Statistical Appendix. Oil exports are calculated net of oil imports and Aruba is included after 1986 for reasons of consistency.

Petroleum refining turned the Dutch Antilles from a stagnant colony into a prosperous territory. The refineries would face grave difficulties from the 1950s onwards, as a result of conflicts between labour and management over the need for automation as well as shrinking profit margins, but other export activities came to the rescue. The entrepôt trade once again became important, cruise tourism expanded rapidly, and the export of financial services soared. In addition, Holland provided a high level of foreign aid leading to a big improvement in the quality of infrastructure.

The new constitutional arrangements adopted from 2010 onwards have not led to any nostalgia for the former Netherlands Antilles. At the same time, resentment at the dominant role formerly played by Curaçao has been replaced in the other islands by a direct relationship with Holland that has its problems as well. And Curaçao, as well as Aruba to a lesser extent, has struggled to cope with the large number of Venezuelans leaving their country after economic conditions deteriorated. Yet, the movement in favour of independence, even in the larger islands, is small as so many fear the consequences of a final separation from Holland. The Netherlands, it seems, will continue to have a Caribbean dimension for the foreseeable future.

8.1. CURAÇAO

The second most westerly of the ABC islands, Curaçao, had been used by the West India Company (WIC) from the time of its first occupation by the Dutch in the seventeenth century as a commercial rather than productive colony. However, the WIC did not have a monopoly on trade as Adam Smith noted in the *Wealth of Nations* written in 1776:

> Curaçao and Eustatia...are free ports open to the ships of all nations; and this freedom, in the midst of better colonies, whose ports are open to those of one nation only, has been the great cause of the prosperity of those two barren nations.

Curaçao's capacity to produce an agricultural surplus was limited by its arid climate, but it did have large salt deposits that could be used to preserve foodstuffs. The salt deposits were then exploited with slave labour to provision Dutch ships before the long journey back to Holland. Indeed, without the salt from the island, Dutch transatlantic commerce would have been much restricted. US ships would also make intense use of Curaçao's salt after the American War of Independence (1775–83).

Soon after the Dutch crown ended the privileges of the WIC, a treaty was signed between Holland and France in 1795, which created the Batavian Republic as a client state. Since revolutionary France had abolished slavery in its colonies the previous year, this was seen as an opportunity by the slaves of Curaçao to win their freedom. The revolt among the slaves almost succeeded, but the geography of the island and their relatively small number conspired against them.[1] The white population (roughly 4,000) buried their substantial differences and united to defeat the 12,000 slaves while the free black and coloured population (roughly 3,000) remained on the sidelines.

When the British first occupied Curaçao in 1800 during the Anglo-French war, they found an island in economic despair. The merchant class, many of whom were Dutch Jews, had been unable to maintain normal commercial relations with the outside world for many years, the decline of shipping had reduced the demand for salt, and the slave population was more resentful than ever after the brutal measures used to suppress their revolt. The British, however, made no changes during their brief occupation and returned the island to Holland under the terms of the peace treaty in 1802.

When war broke out again the following year between Britain and France, with whom the Batavian Republic was still allied, it was inevitable that the British would try to occupy Curaçao again in order to prevent the island being used to provision enemy ships. This happened in 1807 soon after the Batavian Republic collapsed with Louis Bonaparte becoming king of Holland. The following year, Great Britain ended the trade in slaves in its colonies and applied the policy to all territories it occupied in the Caribbean. The import of slaves into Curaçao now ended.

When the British handed the island back to Holland in 1816, following a treaty that banned the trade in slaves by both countries, it might have been assumed that a clandestine trade in imported slaves would have continued – as took place in Suriname (see chapter 7). This did not happen because the dire state of the economy not only meant that there was no need for more slaves but also encouraged slave owners to sell their slaves abroad.[2]

The number of slaves was, therefore, in decline when Holland took back control. Indeed, the population as a whole – estimated at 12,840 in 1815 – had been falling for some time due to the difficult circumstances the island faced during the war years. The island, now a Crown Colony, was therefore expected to need subsidies. Thus, a priority for the new Dutch governor in his role as the representative of the Dutch monarchy was to find a means for reviving the economy and reducing the need for fiscal transfers.

The solution urged on him by the merchants was to declare the capital Willemstad a free port, as had happened before the Napoleonic Wars in St Eustatius with great success but which had ended in Curaçao before the war started because of the need for trade taxes. Free port status would have allowed the merchants legally to receive goods from all countries free of tax and sell them to the neighbouring countries in South America without paying export duties. And if the Dutch crown were to recognise the Latin American rebels as belligerents in their fight against the Spanish monarchy, it would have allowed the merchants legally to supply arms – as was happening from Danish St Thomas and Swedish St Barthélemy.

King Willem I, to whom the governor reported, was keen to reduce the subsidy required to keep Curaçao afloat. However, he did not expect the rebels to win and was, therefore, not prepared to risk a confrontation with his fellow monarch, the King of Spain. The merchants' hands were now tied, and they resorted to a traditional contraband trade. It was not until 1822 that the Dutch king declared neutrality in the South American conflict, by which time the rebels had won. And it was only in 1827, several years after the Spanish had been defeated, that Willemstad was declared a free port.

The merchants also called for reform of the monetary system. Without its own currency, Curaçao had used a confusing array of coins from different countries that could not easily be exchanged against each other. At the same time, the shortage of currency meant that loans were very expensive, leaving merchants at a severe disadvantage when they purchased goods on credit. The Dutch government, therefore, gave its approval to form a state bank in 1828 with authority to issue notes, stabilise the currency, and make loans to the private sector.

The bank, which at first had no name, but which in 1907 became the Curaçaosche Bank, was one of the first of its kind in the Caribbean and, in time, would play a leading role in re-establishing the island as a centre of the entrepôt trade.[3] However, it would take time before Curaçao could fulfil its ambitions in this respect. The main hope for the merchants was to forge a legal trade with the parts of Latin America that they had supplied clandestinely when they were part of the Spanish Empire.

Unfortunately for the merchants, the neighbouring countries had their own problems when Willemstad became a free port. The newly independent countries of South America – especially Gran Colombia[4] – adopted a policy of freedom to trade from the start, so that the Curaçao merchants had to compete with suppliers from all over the world. And the governor was reluctant to eliminate trade taxes altogether because of fiscal revenue shortage, imposing, instead of tariffs, a 'safety' tax that worked in much the same way. This meant that importers in neighbouring countries risked being burdened with two sets of taxes if they purchased goods via Curaçao.

The breakup of Gran Colombia in 1830 plunged its component parts into political and economic chaos. The most troubled republic was Venezuela, which – as Curaçao's closest neighbour – was also the most important. Although the merchants supplied nearly all goods going to Venezuela through the port of Coro, the republic had little to offer in return. Few ships, therefore, visited Curaçao in these years, and it would not be until the middle of the century that the number of ships landing at Willemstad would return to the level 30 years earlier. By this time, economic conditions in Venezuela had improved, emphasising the vital link that the neighbouring republic had, and continues to have, on the fortunes of Curaçao.

Dutch governors on the island now had little choice other than to emphasise domestic exports. However, the arid climate made it difficult to export much apart from salt. Some 35,000 barrels were exported in 1830, and the number rose in the next decade, but competition – not least from other parts of the Dutch Antilles – was intense so that exports had fallen below 30,000 barrels by 1850 and below 20,000 by 1880. Other exports, such as divi-divi pods, used as a dye in the European textile industry, were of even less importance.

Figure 8.2: Curaçao: Population, 1815–2016

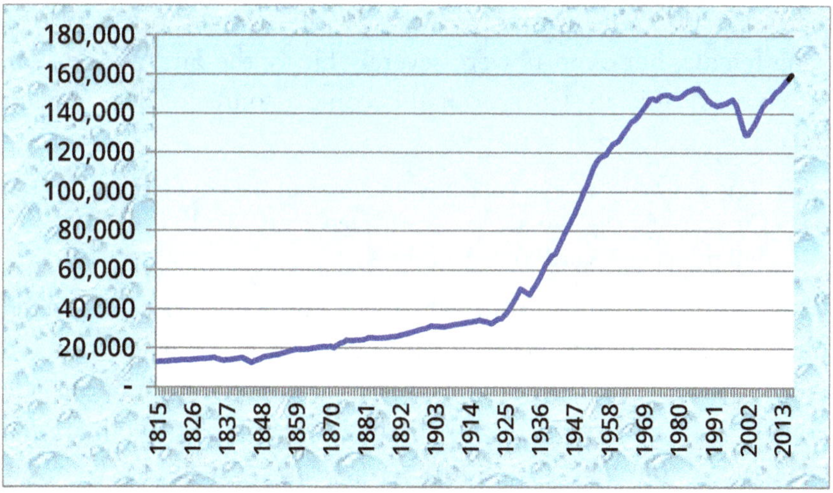

Source: Hartog (1968), 414, for census figures up to 1960 and World Bank, World Development Indicators, annual data subsequently. Gaps have been filled by interpolation.

The population at first failed to increase by much (see figure 8.2). The numbers rose from 12,840 in 1815 to 14,480 in 1840, of which 5,671 – roughly 40 per cent – were slaves. Better economic conditions in Venezuela then led to an increase in trade with the neighbouring republic and a modest increase in population in Curaçao. On the eve of emancipation in 1863, this had reached 19,300, of which 6,751 – roughly 35 per cent – were slaves.

The struggle for emancipation was a long one, finally achieving success with the law of August 8, 1862 setting a date of July 1, 1863 for freeing the slaves. Most of the law was devoted to the compensation payable to the former owners (200 guilders per slave),[5] but three articles were dedicated to the former slaves who were now required to work for their former owners or face severe punishment for vagrancy. Half of the slaves had been employed in rural areas, but the estates – already heavily mortgaged – had little to offer them. Those that could emigrate did so; three hundred left to work on the construction of the Costa Rican railway in 1872.

Some of the surplus labour was employed in the phosphate industry, which began exports in the 1870s, but these had ceased by 1895 (they would start again in 1914). Others found work in the hat industry, which, by 1910, employed one-third of the labour force of nearly 15,000.[6] This was a rare success with most of those employed being female, but exports were severely hit by the First World War. For colonial officials, Curaçao had become a source of despair with one claiming after a visit in 1904:[7]

> 'It is a mystery to everyone how the mass of the population on Curaçao manages to survive....with ten cents' worth of maize and five cents' worth of fish or meat.'

The entrepôt trade, from which so much had been expected following the independence of South American countries, suffered grievously from the poor relationship between Holland and Venezuela in many years. The tradition under which exiles in Curaçao had been left alone by the Dutch authorities was challenged in 1870 by the Venezuelan government. Holland then expelled those considered most at fault, but immediately regretted it when one of the rebels – Antonio Guzmán Blanco – shortly afterwards became president of Venezuela.[8]

Guzmán Blanco was the dominant figure in Venezuelan politics until he was ousted in 1889. He vigorously promoted his country's sovereignty, which meant clamping down on smuggling to and from Curaçao. He also wanted to increase the proportion of the import trade in the hands of Venezuelan merchants, increasing by 30 per cent the duties on goods imported from the Dutch Antilles. The poor relationship with Holland did not end with his death. At the beginning of the twentieth century, many contemporaries held very pessimistic views of Curaçao, as is borne out by one visitor from the US:[9]

> The recent trouble with Venezuela, as has been said, may be traced back to this losing fight with modern conditions. Without Venezuela's trade the island cannot prosper. The Netherlands realizing this, attempts to force Venezuela to permit the transshipment of goods at Curaçao. This she has succeeded in doing, but it is, at best, a temporary relief, and Curaçao will in time be obliged to yield to the inevitable and take the place that her geographic position and climatic conditions have ordained – a lonely island, with little political or commercial importance, and a small and poor population. During the transition from the unstable political and social conditions of a new continent, with its temporary lack of geographic adjustment, to those of social and political stability, Curaçao assumed an importance which will, with the progress of civilization and political integrity on the continent, soon be little more than a memory.

The outbreak of the First World War, in which Holland was neutral, risked a continuation of the dismal economic conditions from which the island suffered. Once again, however, it was developments in Venezuela that had the most profound impact. Royal Dutch Shell had successfully drilled its first oil well in Lake Maracaibo in 1914, but the exit from the lake for large ships was ruled out by its shallowness. Shell therefore needed an alternative location for a refinery, storage facilities and distribution centre. Shell was also anxious to avoid placing facilities in Venezuela in view of the country's recent history of political instability.

For an Anglo-Dutch company with close ties to the government of the Netherlands, Curaçao offered a near perfect location. Close to Lake Maracaibo, the capital Willemstad had deep-water facilities and a supportive administration. In 1915, the Bataafsche Petroleum Maatschappij, a Shell subsidiary, began work and the oil refinery started operations in 1918. In 1925, Shell created a new subsidiary, the N.V. Curacaosche Petroleum Industrie Maatschappij, and production rapidly accelerated.[10] Although output would be affected by the Great Depression, production soon returned to normal and had become vital by the time of the Second World War. Following the invasion of Holland by Germany in 1940, the island was, therefore, occupied by British troops sent from Jamaica to protect the oil facilities. They were joined by US troops in 1942.

The oil industry had a major impact on both the labour and fiscal problems in Curaçao. The island in the space of a few years went from a labour surplus to a labour shortage. Workers, therefore, migrated to Curaçao from elsewhere in the Caribbean, and the population soared (see figure 8.2). At the same time, the tax contribution from the oil industry meant that the island government no longer needed subsidies from Holland and could devote additional resources to infrastructure and public services.

This began to change in the 1950s. Other refineries had been built in the Caribbean, while Venezuela was determined to see at least some of its oil refined locally. Profit margins fell in Curaçao, and Shell responded by cutting costs – including wages and salaries. Relations between labour and capital deteriorated, and a major strike erupted in 1969 that became violent. The problems at the refinery then became so severe that Shell sold its facilities to the government for a symbolic sum of four guilders. The facilities were then leased to the state-owned Venezuelan oil company (PDVSA).

If Venezuela had been the most important influence on the performance of the Curaçao economy before the Second World War, it would be the US after hostilities ended. In fact, the US had been important ever since it declared its independence in 1776, buying salt for its ships in Willemstad, later providing a market for hats and phosphate and being the most significant supplier of imports in most years. And, of course, much of the oil refined in Curaçao went to the US market as well.

The Second World War broke the link between the Antillean and Dutch guilder and led the authorities to peg it to the US dollar instead. The peg has remained unchanged to this day except for a minor readjustment after the collapse of the Bretton Woods system of fixed exchange rates in 1971. The peg, supported by the Bank of the Netherlands Antilles (today, the Central Bank of Curaçao and St Maarten) placed the island firmly in the US economic space and ensured that inflation would be linked to that in the US itself.

One of the first consequences of this was the emergence in Curaçao of offshore financial services. The 1948 tax treaty between Holland and the US was extended to all the Netherlands Antilles in 1955. Curaçao was the island that benefited most from this treaty with many offshore companies formed and designed to reduce tax liability by US legal companies or persons. This was especially useful to US citizens after the interest rate equalisation tax passed in 1963. And foreigners also started to use Curaçao companies from the 1960s onwards to invest in US real estate and securities.

Many of the tax advantages have now been repealed, and offshore financial centres in the Caribbean are under scrutiny as never before. Yet financial services in Curaçao have survived as the sector has met all the conditions placed upon it by the US, European Union (EU), and International Monetary Fund (IMF) and is second only to 'real estate, renting and business activities' in its contribution to GDP. Indeed, together with tourism, financial services helped to raise service exports to the point where they account for the majority of export earnings. However, service exports have not been such a powerful engine of growth in recent years as before, and GDP per head fell by 15 per cent between 2005 and 2016.[11]

Curaçao is still one of the richest countries in the Caribbean with GDP per head in 2018 estimated at nearly US$20,000. Agriculture has virtually disappeared, manufacturing is miniscule, and the economy depends on a combination of service exports, entrepôt trade and Dutch foreign aid. However, it remains vulnerable to external conditions, and its geographical location so close to Venezuela has caused considerable problems following the application against the Bolivarian government of US and EU sanctions. This has led to some tension between the island authorities and the Dutch government.

Yet few inhabitants of Curaçao are keen to push for independence even though Holland would put up little resistance if they chose to do so. In this respect, they are like other citizens of non-independent Caribbean countries who are unwilling to put at risk the advantages of dependent status for the sake of an independent foreign and security policy. This leaves Curaçao outside the decision-making process in the Caribbean and unable to join many regional organisations despite the Caribbean identity that the islanders clearly express on numerous occasions. It is, in many respects, an unsatisfactory situation and one that appears to have no solution.

8.2. Aruba

The small island of Aruba, even closer to Venezuela than Curaçao, had been of little importance to Holland before the Napoleonic Wars. It had served mainly as a source of livestock for supply to other Dutch dependencies. Its lack of commercial importance is one reason why the indigenous population survived in sharp contrast to the other Dutch islands and still numbered around 500 at the commencement of the Anglo-French war at the end of the eighteenth century.

The Dutch could not defend Aruba after the Treaty of Amiens collapsed in 1803, but the British could not hold it without first taking Curaçao. This they did in 1807 leading to nearly a decade of British occupation before the island's return to the Netherlands in 1816. In that year a Dutch census recorded a population of 1,732, of which 562 were 'Indians' and 362 were slaves. Much smaller than Curaçao, this was, in fact, an increase on the 1806 figure when the population was 1,546 with 194 slaves. Since most of the rise in population was in the number of slaves, this suggests that the British authorities had turned a blind-eye to the import of slaves during their occupation.

The Anglo-Dutch Treaty did end the trade in slaves in 1816, and the number of slaves in 1833 was very similar to what it had been at the end of the Napoleonic Wars. However, the population had increased to 2,746. The reasons are not hard to find, as Aruba had found gold in commercial quantities in 1824. The government, at first, monopolised production, but in 1832 the governor general in Paramaribo declared mining open to everyone. This system, in turn, was replaced in 1854 by a private concession to a Dutchman that was withdrawn in 1866 when it no longer proved profitable.

The concession was renewed the next year, but eventually ended up in the hands of the Aruba Island Gold Mining Company Ltd based in London. Production, all of which was exported, was never large with a peak of 34.5 kg in 1896 after which revenue declined and costs rose.[12] The company was then wound up in 1908, and the 'age of gold' came to an end in Aruba. It had never been extensive, but it had provided an alternative to livestock, generated some employment, and brought an increase in public revenue to the government.

The population of Aruba had increased slowly after the Napoleonic Wars (see figure 8.3) reaching 3,258 in 1862 – almost double what it had been in 1816. Not all of this rise was due to the free population, as the number of slaves also increased reaching 480 at the time of emancipation in 1863.[13] Compensation was paid to the slave owners on the same basis as in Curaçao. This was set at 200 florins (US$86) per slave, so that total compensation paid exceeded $40,000.

Fortunately for the Dutch authorities, the decline of the gold industry in Aruba coincided with the rise of phosphate extraction. Substantial deposits had been found in 1874 and a concession was awarded the same year to a British firm with a guaranteed income for the government. Within five years, the concession had been transferred to the newly founded Aruba Phosphate Company, which exported all production to the UK.

Figure 8.3: Aruba: Population, 1806 –2016

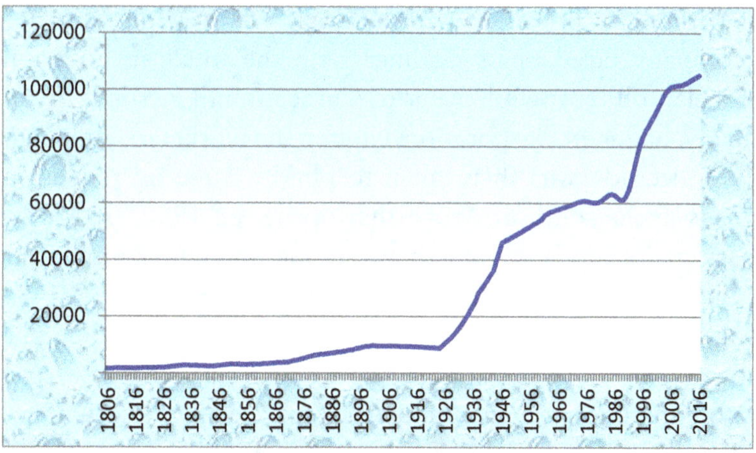

Source: Census data before 1960 from Hiss (1943) and Goslinga (1990). Annual data from 1960 in World Bank, World Development Indicators. Gaps filled by interpolation.

Exports peaked in 1890 at 40,756 cubic metres, but continued at a healthy level to the First World War. By that time, the company had exported phosphate to a value of nine million florins (over US$3.5 million) and had paid four million florins (roughly US$1.6 million) to the government.[14] This transformed the public revenue of Aruba. Revenue per head rose from little more than one US dollar in the 1850s to nearly ten in the 1880s.[15]

Most of the public revenue was transferred to the authorities in Willemstad, temporarily eliminating the need for Dutch subsidies to the other islands. Public expenditure in Aruba, therefore, rose only modestly, but the population increased substantially (see figure 8.3) as migrants arrived in search of work in the new industries. The population, still less than 4,000 before the phosphate boom, had reached 9,591 by the end of the century.

From then onwards, the population would fall for a quarter of a century as exports (gold and phosphates) declined and the First World War disrupted traditional trade links. These were years of outward migration with new employment opportunities emerging in the Cuban sugar industry and the construction of the Panama Canal. By 1924, the population had fallen to 8,785 despite a birth rate that far exceeded the death rate.

It was at this point that the Aruban economy was transformed by oil. A Shell subsidiary built a small refinery at Druif in the north of the island to process oil from Mexico as a result of problems the company faced in its dealings with the Mexican government. Venezuelan oil meanwhile went to Curaçao until a North American company, Lago Oil Corporation, entered the market to compete with Shell. A decision was then taken to build a large oil refinery at St Nicolaas in the south of Aruba that opened in 1930. By 1934, this refinery had a larger output than the one on Curaçao and, indeed, was the largest producer in the world at the time.

Lago would change hands many times, but had become part of Exxon by the time the Second World War started.[16] The refinery, therefore, had geostrategic importance for the allies and Aruba was, like Curaçao, occupied by British and later US troops as soon as Holland was defeated by Germany. Thanks to oil, the demand for workers in Aruba far exceeded the local supply, and immigration for the first time became important. The population had risen to 28,155 by 1938 (more than three times higher than in 1924), 45,907 in 1946, and 56,050 in 1956 (see figure 8.3).

From then onwards the oil industry faced similar problems to what happened in Curaçao (see above). Indeed, the problems were in some respects worse as the large refinery at St Nicolaas closed down in 1985 – the year before Aruba broke away from the Netherlands Antilles. It reopened with a new owner in 1990, but attempts to restore profitability failed and the refinery was sold several times before being purchased by PDVSA (the Venezuelan state oil company). After 2012, PDVSA struggled to supply the refinery with crude oil and production dwindled.

Aruba, therefore, came to depend, like Curaçao and many other Caribbean islands, on the exports of services. These were dominated by tourism before 1986, and Aruba became a favoured destination for cruise ships as well as overnight visitors. However, it was not sufficient to compensate for the difficulties of the oil sector and net migration was outward in every year from 1956 onwards until shortly after Aruba acquired autonomy within the Kingdom of the Netherlands (see figure 8.4).

Figure 8.4: Aruba: Net Migration 1956–2016

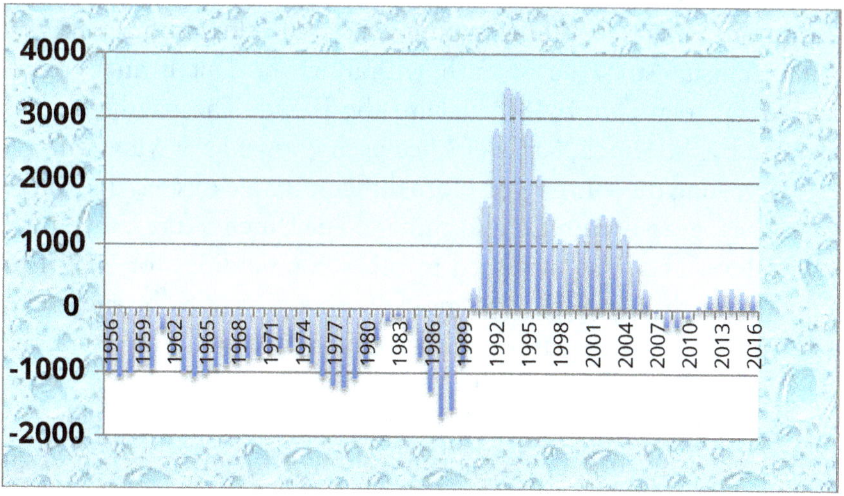

Source: Statistical Appendix and Aruba Centraal Bureau voor de Statistiek (https://cbs.aw/wp.)

GDP per head had been lower in Aruba than in the Netherlands Antilles in 1986, the first year of the island's new status.[17] However, autonomy brought significant benefits, and GDP per head rose rapidly in the next 20 years, overtaking the Dutch Antilles and even Curaçao. Tourism soared with a huge increase in cruise ship visitors, attracted by a large Free Zone, and the establishment of a financial services industry. Net migration turned inwards (see figure 8.4).

The global financial crisis in 2008/9 had a negative impact on Aruba through its impact on tourism and the Free Zone. In addition, Aruba could not escape a negative impact from the political and economic upheavals in Venezuela that brought many Venezuelans to the island despite the difficult economic circumstances.[18] GDP per head fell by 12 per cent (similar to the fall in Curaçao) in the decade after it reached a peak in 2008.[19] Yet Aruba remains a rich island by Caribbean standards with a GDP per head around US$25,000 and no desire to change its constitutional status within the Kingdom of the Netherlands.

8.3. St Maarten

As soon as they entered the Caribbean early in the seventeenth century, Dutch traders sought a secure source of salt for the return journey to Europe. They found one on the island of St Martin, but soon found themselves in a dispute over ownership with the French and Spanish. After the Spanish withdrew, the Dutch and French agreed by treaty, in 1648, to share the island. The southern part, claimed by the Dutch, has ever since been known as St Maarten.

Harvesting the salt proved more difficult than expected due to the island's geography, rainfall, and climate. The Dutch settlers, therefore, using slave labour, soon turned to other commodities for export to supplement their income. The most durable proved to be sugar and cotton. By 1789, the year in which the French revolution started, the population had reached 5,520 of which 4,230 (76.6 per cent) were slaves. St Maarten under Dutch control appeared to have established itself as a conventional European colony with every prospect of moderate growth.

The exact opposite turned out to be the case. It would take nearly 200 years before the population again reached this relatively small level (see figure 8.5). The French effectively controlled the whole island when the Batavian Republic was formed while the British took it by force, in 1810, after several unsuccessful attempts. By the time the British government returned the Dutch part to Holland in 1816, the population was reduced to 3,559, and the number of slaves was down to 2,551. The number of slaves had, therefore, fallen by 40 per cent during the Anglo-French wars with many taking advantage of the chaos in St Maarten to escape.[20]

Figure 8.5: St Maarten: Population, 1790–2017

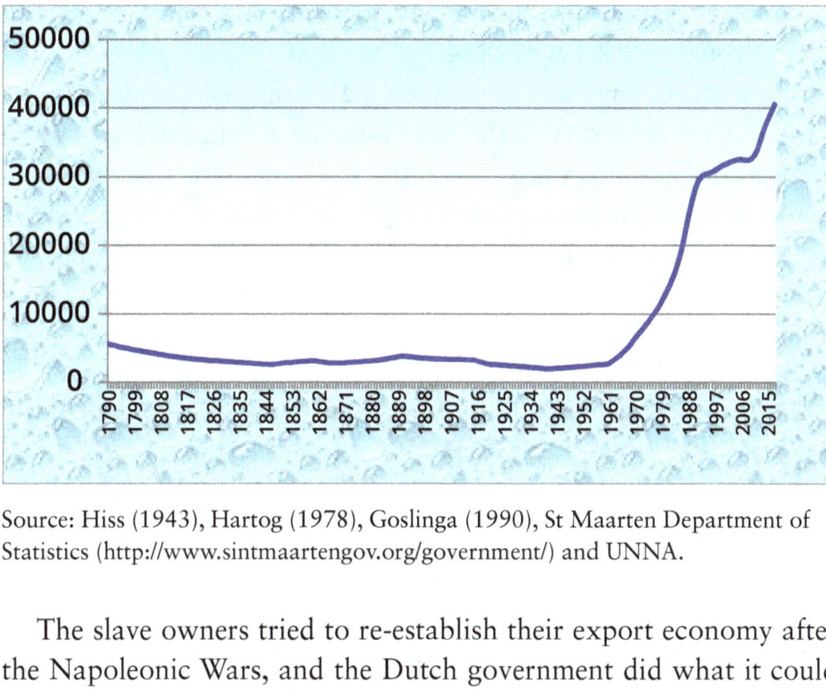

Source: Hiss (1943), Hartog (1978), Goslinga (1990), St Maarten Department of Statistics (http://www.sintmaartengov.org/government/) and UNNA.

The slave owners tried to re-establish their export economy after the Napoleonic Wars, and the Dutch government did what it could to support them. However, the island was never a high priority for officials as it was either subordinate to the administration in Paramaribo or, after 1845, in Willemstad. As a result, there was no recovery and the population continued to fall (see figure 8.5). Sugar production halved between 1817 and 1829, the number of estates also falling, and the cotton farms produced only a meagre yield.

The only bright spot was salt, which had not been harvested at all from 1797 to 1816. In 1837, the harvest climbed to 50,000 barrels and to a peak of 400,000 barrels in 1848.[21] That year, however, the French authorities freed the slaves in St Martin, undermining all attempts by the Dutch slave owners to preserve slavery in St Maarten as slaves on the Dutch side of the island could now simply move to the French part. The slaves, therefore, became free as a result of the local commander abolishing all laws that made a distinction between free and slave.[22]

Slavery was not formally abolished until 1863, the same time as elsewhere in the Netherlands Antilles. There were 1,878 persons registered in St Maarten, for which compensation was paid to the former slave owners. Payment, however, was set at 30 florins per slave rather than 200 as in the other islands. Following protests by the owners, the Dutch government raised its compensation to 100 florins (roughly $US40) in 1864.[23]

The total compensation paid to the former slave owners was, therefore, nearly US$80,000. Given their small number (perhaps no more than 100), this was a substantial sum and twice what was paid to former slave owners in Aruba despite the lower amount per slave. Yet, there is no evidence that the funds were used to invest in the local economy. On the contrary, once the boom in cotton exports caused by the US Civil War was over, the economy continued to stagnate and the population continued to fall. Sugar production ended in 1875; cotton growing and salt harvesting ended in 1923 and 1949, respectively.[24]

Although the birth rate rose and the death rate fell, the population continued to decline after 1920 as many islanders left to seek work in the oil industry in Aruba and Curaçao. The lowest point was reached in 1940, when the population recorded was a mere 2,004 (see figure 8.5). There was then a modest recovery as the automation of the oil refineries in the1950s led to the return of a number of islanders. However, as late as 1960, the population was still only 2,728.

What happened then was extraordinary by any standards and especially by the standards of the Caribbean where net outward migration has become so common. The population jumped more than ten-fold in less than 30 years. This was largely due to the growth of the tourism industry (especially cruise ships), the arrival of jet aircraft to the expanded airport, and the emergence of a small financial services industry. This brought migrants from many countries to St Maarten, especially from the Netherlands.

The population continued to grow and had reached 40,000 by 2017. The new constitutional arrangements in 2010 did not make a big difference to the economy, which by then was already configured on traditional lines with some 500,000 overnight visitors and 1.6 million cruise ship visitors each year. As a result, St Maarten enjoyed a very high GDP per head (over US$27,000) when the Dutch Antilles disintegrated. And, unlike in Aruba and Curaçao, the level of income per head did not fall significantly after the collapse of the Venezuelan economy as St Maarten was much less affected, although it was badly affected by hurricane damage in 2017.

8.4. The Caribbean Netherlands

When the Dutch Antilles was dissolved in October 2010, three islands – Bonaire, Saba and St Eustatius – opted to become public bodies within the Kingdom of the Netherlands and are, therefore, effectively external municipalities of Holland. However, they are not part of the EU as the following explanation by the Dutch government makes clear:[25]

> The Treaties of the European Union (EU) have been signed by the Kingdom of the Netherlands, but are only ratified for the European part of the Kingdom. As a consequence, the EU *acquis* is, in principle, applicable only to the European part of the Kingdom. The Caribbean parts of the Kingdom of the Netherlands are listed as Overseas Countries and Territories (OCTs). This applies to both the autonomous countries Aruba, Curaçao and St Maarten and the public bodies Bonaire, Saba and St Eustatius. This status determines their legal position vis-à-vis the European Union. OCTs are merely associated with the Union. As a result of their OCT status, the autonomous countries and public bodies enjoy a number of benefits, for example, regarding exports to the EU. In addition, they receive funding from various EU sources, for instance the European Development Fund (EDF).

The three islands are collectively known as the Caribbean Netherlands and use the US dollar as their currency rather than the euro. They enjoy a high standard of living, earned by a combination of mass tourism, remittances, and Dutch aid.[26] In this respect, they are similar to other non-independent territories in the Caribbean.

However, each of the three islands followed a different path over the last two centuries to their current relatively privileged status.

Bonaire, the most easterly of the ABC islands and close to Venezuela, was used from its first occupation as a source of salt. The Dutch West India Company had a monopoly until the Anglo-French Wars. The British occupied the island in 1807 and ended the trade in slaves (not slavery), but had little use for production from the extensive saltpans as British colonies in the Caribbean already met their needs. When the island was returned to the Dutch in 1816, it had a population of 1,135 of which 430 were slaves.

The Dutch re-established the monopoly on the output of the saltpans, but this time under state control. Most of the slaves, therefore, became government slaves and their numbers increased, at first, as the Dutch authorities on the other ABC islands sent slaves to work in salt extraction, on Bonaire, in cases of punishment. The revenue from the sale of salt, mainly to the US, was government income, and the costs associated with it were public expenditure.

Table 8.1: Population of Bonaire, St Eustatius and Saba: 1816–2016

Year	Bonaire	St Eustatius	Saba
1816	1,135	2,591	1,145
1850	2,159	1,932	1,661
1860	3,031	1,927	1,700
1880	4,898	2,063	2,149
1900	4,962	1,383	2,189
1930	5,733	955	1,457
1940	5,616	1,130	1,210
1960	5,812	1,014	980
1980	8,753	1,358	965
2000	11,561	2,250	1,367
2010	15,518	3,583	1,781
2016	19,408	3,193	1,947

Source: Hiss (1943) and Goslinga (1990) before 1930. Central Bureau of Statistics (various years) before 2010. From 2010 onwards, https://www.cbs.nl/en-gb/news/2016/29/population-caribbean-netherlands.

In 1860, just before slavery ended, the population of Bonaire was 3,031 (see table 8.1) – almost trebling since 1816. The number of slaves emancipated was 758, roughly a quarter of the population. Slave owners were compensated at the same rate as the other ABC islands (200 florins per slave), but, of course, no payment was made to the biggest slave owner (the state). Compensation was, therefore, only paid for 151 slaves as the vast majority (607) were government slaves.[27]

The Dutch government ended the state monopoly over salt production in 1868, with the sale of five parcels of land to private buyers. Exports, which had averaged around 40,000 barrels per year under state control, rose to a peak of 58,761 in 1876. After this, however, production declined while prices had been falling for longer. Salt, it was clear, was no longer able to sustain the island economy, and experiments were made with alternative export staples, including divi-divi, bricks, and shipbuilding.

Bonaire was occupied by the Allies in the Second World War with the US building a military airport. This was converted to civilian use at the end of the war, opening up Bonaire to mass tourism for the first time. The island did not, at first, become a popular destination and emphasis was instead put on an oil transhipment facility in 1975 that generated substantial public revenue. Tourism, however, had developed substantially by the time the Dutch Antilles was dissolved, bringing with it a big increase in population.

St Eustatius, or 'Statia' as it is often called, became a free port in 1763 and played a key role in eighteenth-century wars by virtue of its entrepôt status and geographic location. It was, therefore, one of the more important Dutch islands, and in 1790 had a population of 7,820 of which 4,944 were slaves. The Anglo-French Wars and British occupation, however, undermined its prosperity. By 1816, (see table 8.1), the population had dropped to 2,591 of which 1,748 were slaves.

Such a large decline in the slave population suggests that Statia had become involved in selling slaves to other islands. Participation by St Eustatius in what now became an illegal slave trade continued after the Napoleonic Wars, but it did not prevent the island's population from falling. Indeed, it continued to fall (see table 8.1) until 1930. An attempt was made to establish the island as a sugar exporter in the nineteenth century using slave labour, but it was not successful. At the time of emancipation in 1863, there were only 1,087 slaves – all of whom were owned privately.

The population recovered slowly after 1930, but had still not reached its level in 1790 by the time the Dutch Antilles was dissolved. Since then, the population has declined again (see table 8.1) although this is probably due to under-recording of earlier emigration.[28] Tourism is limited by the small size of the airport with only 11,000 tourists arriving by air in 2016. There are no cruise ship facilities.

Saba, the smallest of the Dutch islands, has traditionally been the hardest to reach. Its volcanic nature and absence of beaches meant that visitors could only land before 1972 by rowing boat and even that was difficult due to the large swells of the sea. It was never an entrepôt and had no saltpans, but Dutch settlers brought in slaves to establish a small export economy, and the population had reached 1,145 in 1816 of which nearly half (462) were slaves.

Unlike in neighbouring Statia, the population did increase modestly in the nineteenth century, and there were 700 slaves at the time of emancipation. After that, traditional exports (including sugar) declined and islanders mainly found a living either through maritime activities (predominantly male) or through needlework (predominantly female).

The absence of modern means of communication hurt the island in the twentieth century and the population steadily declined from 1900 to 1980 (see table 8.1) as a result of emigration. The opening of a short runway in 1978, however, transformed the prospects for the island. In 2016, there were 9,200 tourist arrivals by air and a further 7,700 (many of whom were tourists) by ferry. In addition, Saba hosts an internationally recognised medical school to train doctors.

The Caribbean Netherlands is a constitutional anomaly, but it appears to have met the desires of the islanders more successfully than any of the previous constitutional arrangements. Since independence is not really an option for such small islands, it can be expected to last a long time. This gives Holland a permanent stake in the Caribbean along with France, the UK, and the US. Holland may not want this role, but it has no choice as it gave the islanders the final say on what they desired.

NOTES

1. See C.C. Goslinga, *The Dutch in the Caribbean and in Suriname, 1791/5–1942* (Assen, Netherlands: Van Gorcum, 1990), 1–20.
2. See J.C. Dorsey, *Slave Traffic in the Age of Abolition: Puerto Rico, West Africa, and the Non-Hispanic Caribbean, 1815–1859* (Gainesville, FL: University Press of Florida, 2003), 199.
3. See J. van Soest, *Trustee of the Netherlands Antilles* (Zutphen: Walburg Pers, 1978), 51–76.
4. Gran Colombia had been declared an independent state by Simón Bolívar in 1821. It survived until 1830, when it broke up into Colombia, Ecuador, and Venezuela.
5. Equivalent to US$82.6 per slave for a total of approximately US$550,000.
6. See R.A. Römer, *Curaçao* (San Juan, Puerto Rico: Association of Caribbean Universities and Research Institutes, UNICA, 1981), 226.
7. Quoted in van Soest, *Trustee of the Netherlands Antilles*, 190.
8. Ibid., 117–19.
9. See H.F. Cleland, 'Curacao, a Losing Colonial Venture,' *Bulletin of the American Geographical Society* 41, no. 3 (1909): 138.
10. See P.H. Hiss, *Netherlands America: The Dutch Territories in the West* (New York, NY: Distributed by Duell, Sloan & Pearce, 1943), 123–25.
11. GDP per head at constant prices fell from US$21,529 in 2005 to US$18,122 in 2016. See UNNA.
12. At the time gold was valued at US$18.10 per troy ounce. With 32.1507 troy ounces in a kilogram, production in 1896 had a value of approximately US$20,000.
13. This increase was probably due to the difference between births and deaths, as in Aruba – unlike in Suriname – births exceeded deaths among the slave population after the Napoleonic Wars. In 1857, for example, the number of slave births was 22 and the number of deaths eight. See *Almanak voor de Nederlandsche West-Indische bezittingen: En de kust van Guinea, voor het jaar 1856, 1859–1861* (Gravenhage: Gebroeders van Cleef: 1860), 209.
14. See Goslinga, *The Dutch in the Caribbean and in Suriname*, 364.
15. The exchange rate for the Dutch guilder/florin to the US dollar is given in Bulmer-Thomas, *The Economic History of the Caribbean since the Napoleonic Wars*, 496.
16. See Hiss, *Netherlands America: The Dutch Territories in the West*, 126.
17. See Statistical Appendix.

18. That is why net migration turned inwards again after 2012 (see figure 8.4).
19. See UNNA.
20. The French had abolished slavery in St Martin between 1794 and 1802, while Haiti had declared its independence in 1804.
21. Each barrel weighed 115 kg and sold for between 25 and 50 US cents per barrel.
22. See Goslinga, *The Dutch in the Caribbean and in Suriname*, 285.
23. See Hiss, *Netherlands America: The Dutch Territories in the West*, 207, Appendix XX.
24. See J. Hartog, *St. Maarten, Saba and St. Eustatius* (Aruba: De Wit, 1978), 53–54.
25. See https://www.government.nl/...netherlands...european...caribbean/the-kingdom-of-the-netherlands.
26. In 2013, the per capita GDP was US$21,600 for Bonaire, $26,400 for St Eustatius, and $23,600 for Saba. See https://www.cbs.nl/en-gb/background/2016/02/all-islands-in-the-caribbean-netherlands-achieved-economic-growth-in-2013.
27. See Hiss, *Netherlands America*, 207, appendix XX.
28. The authorities rely on census data every few years with intervening years estimated from births, deaths, immigration, and emigration. In 2017, they acknowledged that they had seriously underestimated emigration in previous years. Thus, the 'drop' in population between 2010 and 2016 may be a chimera.

Chapter 9

THE DANISH WEST INDIES/ UNITED STATES VIRGIN ISLANDS

The three islands of St Croix, St John, and St Thomas constituted the Danish West Indies (DWI) for nearly two centuries before becoming in 1917 the United States Virgin Islands.[1] The efforts of the colonial power (Denmark) to create a dynamic export economy based on sugar were largely unsuccessful despite the extensive use of slave labour. However, the conversion of St Thomas into a free port in 1764 transformed the fortunes of the DWI and gave the islands a means of survival even after slavery ended in 1848.

The role of St Thomas as an entrepôt started to decline with the advent of steam ships. However, nothing could alter the magnificent character of its protected harbour. This made it a target for the imperialist designs of the US after the Civil War. Denmark was happy to sell, but the plans of President Ulysses Grant (1869–77) were undermined by a US Congress that baulked at the price.

Fifty years later, the price was not an issue. Denmark, neutral in the First World War, was always at risk of a German invasion. This could have put the harbour at St Thomas at the disposal of the German navy, a prospect that the administration of President Woodrow Wilson (1913–21) was not willing to countenance. A sale was hastily agreed in 1916, a few months before the US entered the war, and the formal transfer took place on March 31, 1917.

The DWI would now become known as the United States Virgin Islands (USVI) with responsibility for their administration given to the US navy. The islanders did not become US citizens until 1927, and they had virtually no control over their own affairs. It was only with the Revised Organic Act of the Virgin Islands, passed in 1954, that the islanders acquired some responsibility for their domestic affairs. Relations with other countries, however, were – and are still – controlled by the US government.

The economic history of the islands in the last two centuries divides neatly into four parts. The first corresponds to the period between the abolition of the slave trade (in 1803) and the end of slavery (in 1848). In this period (see figure 9.1), merchandise exports per head at constant prices rose – based less on the expansion of domestic exports and more on the growth of re-exports through St Thomas and, to a lesser extent, St John.

The end of slavery coincided with a long period of decline in merchandise exports per head up to the transfer of the islands to the US (see figure 9.1). Sugar proved unprofitable while increased rum and bay rum exports could not fully compensate for the fall in sugar sales. The re-export trade went into decline with the advent of steam shipping and the opening up of new direct trade routes between pairs of countries. And Denmark was unwilling to provide the level of subsidies that would have given the islands the chance to reinvent themselves on the basis of new activities and non-traditional exports.

US control of the islands, at first, made little difference to economic performance, and exports per head continued to fall, exacerbated by the ban on rum exports during US prohibition (1919–33). It was only after the Second World War, especially after 1960, that the economic fortunes of the USVI began to change with the growth of service exports, including tourism and the installation of an oil refinery.

Figure 9.1: DWI/USVI: Exports per head at constant prices (1900=100), log scale, 1820–2008

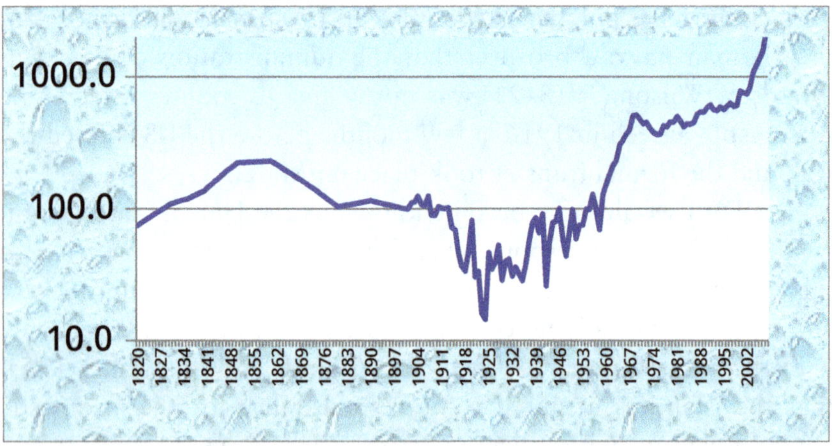

Source: Statistical Appendix.[2]

Exports per head now soared (see figure 9.1), and tax advantages for the rum industry provided by the federal government gave producers a huge boost after the start of the new millennium. However, the boom that had begun in the 1960s turned to bust following the global financial crisis in 2008/9.

Despite the improvement in economic circumstances and a high level of GDP per head, net outward migration has been high in recent years, and the population today is little more than 100,000. Indeed, the population has been falling since the year 2000. As US citizens, Virgin Islanders are free to leave for the mainland without restrictions and many have taken advantage of this opportunity. Yet, in spite of the frustrations associated with their colonial status, few islanders are prepared to demand independence, and the population is too small for the USVI to become a US state.

9.1. From Abolition to Emancipation

Shortly after the French Revolution, the finance minster of Denmark (Ernst Schimmelmann) established the Danish Negro Trade Commission. Completed in 1791, but never published as proceedings were secret, it established beyond doubt that slave deaths exceeded slave births and argued that only the abolition of the slave trade would improve the conditions needed to reduce deaths and increase births. The commission also argued that the aim should be eventually to end slavery itself, although the secret nature of the document meant that this was not discovered until much later.[3]

The government accepted the commission's recommendations, and Denmark was the first European country to abolish the slave trade, doing so in 1792 – 15 years before Great Britain.[4] The preamble to the edict, summarising the commission's report, stated:

> From the results of these enquiries, we are convinced that it is possible, and will be advantageous to our West-India islands, to desist from the farther purchase of new negroes, when once the plantations are stocked with a sufficient number for the propagation and the cultivation of the lands.

Since slave deaths far exceeded slave births on St Croix, where most of the slaves worked, the law allowed all slave owners ten years to adjust so that the date of effective abolition was January 1, 1803.[5] Most took full advantage of permission to import, so that the slave population in 1803 (35,716) was much greater than in 1792 (28,436).

Denmark was allied with Napoleonic France, so the British occupied the islands in 1807 – the same year in which the UK passed a law banning the slave trade with effect from the following year.[6] The return of the islands to Denmark took place in 1815 at the end of the Anglo-French wars. At this point, the number of slaves was 31,632, nearly 80 per cent of the population, most of whom lived on St Croix.[7]

With deaths higher than births, the slave population fell thereafter. In addition, some slaves on St Croix escaped to form maroon communities, while manumission became important on St Thomas.[8] And after 1834, slaves could secure their freedom by fleeing to Tortola in the British Virgin Islands. However, the slave population did not fall quite as fast as might have been expected.[9] This was almost certainly due to a small illegal trade in slaves facilitated by Danish forts on the West African coasts where officials colluded with local chiefs to supply slaves to the Danish West Indies. It was only in 1850, after slavery itself had ended, that Denmark sold its forts to Great Britain and the trade stopped.

Table 9.1: Danish West Indies: Exports (US$), 1820–1900

	Sugar	Rum	Domestic Exports	Re-exports
1820	1,535,658	70,941	1,686,929	1,313,071
1830	1,415,950	65,066	1,555,067	1,944,933
1840	1,053,242	50,545	1,158,976	2,841,024
1850	652,940	59,379	747,935	4,252,065
1860	470,870	85,355	584,037	5,415,963
1870	319,176	80,504	419,663	4,580,337
1880	638,638	49,418	722,458	1,870,964
1890	929,904	19,980	997,378	1,317,222
1900	504,000	13,700	530,000	1,021,112

Source: Statistical Appendix.

Slavery, therefore, remained vital in the three islands, especially St Croix, after Danish sovereignty was restored. The key domestic export was sugar, and a huge effort was made by the Danish authorities to re-establish it as a profitable export. The volume of exports did increase between 1820 and 1830, but the fall in world prices wiped out the gains, and the value declined (see table 9.1). Since sugar exports accounted for more than 90 per cent of domestic exports in these years, this was a severe drain on the islands' economy.

The planters' efforts to maintain the volume and value of sugar exports after 1830 were even less successful. The volume declined, and the value collapsed with sugar in 1850 worth only 40 per cent of what it had earned in 1820 (see table 9.1). The only other domestic export of any significance (rum) also declined in value. Domestic exports in 1850 were, therefore, less than half their value in 1820. Domestic exports per head in 1850 were still valued at nearly US$20, high by Caribbean standards, but this was different from their level in 1820 when they had been one of the highest in the region.[10]

It was fortunate for Denmark, therefore, that the authorities had established St Thomas as a free port even before the Anglo-French wars. The island had proved a magnet for ships from many different countries, and their cargoes attracted buyers from across the Americas and Europe. These included South American revolutionaries buying weapons, smugglers throughout the Americas, legitimate traders in the Caribbean, and European merchants.

The privileges given to St Thomas by the Danish Crown in 1764 were extended to St John in 1815 and St Croix in 1823. All restrictions were lifted by 1833, including the remaining distinctions between Danish and non-Danish vessels. There was a large increase in the value of re-exports after 1820 from the three islands (see table 9.1), although it was St Thomas that benefited most with a doubling in the tonnage of ships visiting the harbour in the decade 1821–30, compared with the previous two decades.

The importance of St Thomas by the 1840s is explained as follows:[11]

> Commercially St. Thomas was a flourishing port in the forties. Its life centred about the harbour and the town on Charlotte Amalia [*sic*]. Of the 14,000 inhabitants of the island only 2,500, of whom more than nine-tenths were slaves, gained

> their living from the plantations. In 1839, there were forty-one large importing houses on the island. Of these, thirteen were English, eleven French, six German, four Italian and Spanish, four American, and only three Danish or Danish West Indian. This situation had not seriously changed by 1850.

Although the status of the three islands as free ports meant that eventually no distinction was made between Danish and non-Danish vessels, it did not mean that trade taxes were zero – even if they were set at a very low level to encourage imports and discourage smuggling.[12] The expansion of the entrepôt trade, therefore, brought a big increase in revenue. On a *per capita* basis, this almost doubled between 1820 and 1850. However, public expenditure rose even more rapidly thanks to subsidies from the Danish government, with spending per head increasing in real terms from US$4.20 to US$10.80 over the same period.[13] This was one of the highest levels in the Caribbean at the time.[14]

The fall in sugar prices before 1850 and the absence of any other significant domestic export meant that the sugar plantation owners faced a squeeze on profitability. They responded by cutting costs. Conditions for the plantation slaves, especially on St Croix, therefore, became even more intolerable. However, it could not, and did not, reverse the decline in the volume and value of sugar exports.

In an effort to ameliorate the conditions of the slaves and in response to domestic pressures, the Danish government in 1847 introduced a law to free the children of slaves and anticipated the end of slavery itself in 1859. It was too little too late. In 1848, a slave revolt began on St Croix, which was so successful and spread so quickly that the Danish governor was forced to declare the end of slavery on all three islands within a matter of days. The governor was then recalled in disgrace,[15] but it was too late to reverse the decision, and his emancipation decree was reluctantly endorsed by the Danish government. The government then paid the slave owners 50 Danish West Indian dollars for each of their slaves.[16] This provided total compensation of roughly US$1 million – a large sum in current terms.

9.2. From Emancipation to Sale

The slaves in the Danish West Indies had secured their own emancipation – a stunning achievement and one matched only by the slaves in Haiti. However, unlike the Haitians, they had not defeated the sovereign European power. This left the former slaves at the mercy of the Danish state once the authorities had re-established control over the three islands. And, not surprisingly, they were in no mood to be gracious in defeat.

The measures taken by the new Danish governor upon his arrival in November 1848 were numerous and included imprisoning and subsequently expelling the leader of the revolt, John Gottliff ('General Buddhoe').[17] Of even greater concern for the former slaves, however, was the introduction, in January 1849, of a draconian labour act that kept the former slaves as far as possible on the plantations. The second and fourth articles stated:[18]

> 2. No labourer engaged...in the cultivation of the soil, shall be discharged or dismissed from, or shall be permitted to dissolve, his or her engagement before the expiration of the same on the first of October of the present, or of any following year....
>
> 4. Notice to quit service shall be given by the employer, as well as by the labourer, at no other period but once a year, in the month of August, not before the first, nor after the last day of the said month...The labourer shall have given, or received, legal notice of removal from the estate where he serves, before any one can engage his services....

Armed with this law, the Danish authorities and the plantation owners then tried to rebuild the domestic export economy. However, they did not have much success. The volume of sugar exported, which had collapsed to 17.9 million pounds in 1850, had fallen to ten million pounds by 1870. The value of sugar exports (see table 9.1) also fell, and by 1870 was worth only US$319,176 – 20 per cent of the value in 1820. Of the principal commodity exports, only rum managed a small increase. However, it was too small to make much of an impact, and the value of domestic exports fell in line with sugar between 1850 and 1870.

After 1870, the planters invested heavily in new technology. This led to labour unrest, including the Fireburn riots in 1878, but the planters continued to modernise their factories, and the sugar yield increased substantially. Indeed, the volume exported in 1890 (32 million pound) was three times higher than in 1870. The value also increased (see table 9.1), but the precipitate decline in sugar prices took a heavy toll in the 1890s when the value slipped back to US$500,000 – still only one-third of the level in 1820.

Once again, it was fortunate for the Danish Crown that St Thomas remained a key port in the entrepôt trade. The value of re-exports increased after 1850, reaching a peak of US$5.4 million in 1860. Even in 1870, re-exports were valued at US$4.6 million. However, the impact of steamships, new trade routes, and other entrepôts led to a steep decline by the end of the century (see table 9.1). By 1900, almost the only commodity of value being traded through St Thomas was coal.

The authorities' hopes of keeping the former slaves on the plantations did not work out as planned. Some of those on St Croix, where most had lived, left for St Thomas or even migrated to other countries in the Caribbean and Central America. Within a decade of emancipation, the Danish authorities were, therefore, actively promoting immigration schemes, and in 1861 they reached an agreement with Great Britain to recruit indentured labour from British India. The first workers arrived in 1863, and most were sent to work on St Croix.[19]

Indian indentured labour did not work well, and the experiment was not repeated. With sugar production in decline, many of the indentured labourers moved with their employers' consent to St Thomas or returned home to India at the end of their contracts. The authorities, therefore, encouraged immigration from the rest of the Caribbean. An estimated 10,000 people migrated to St Croix alone between 1850 and 1917 with a peak of 1,964 in 1863 when the indentured Indians arrived.[20] Most of those who arrived came from the Lesser Antilles, with 77 per cent from Barbados.

Despite this high level of immigration, the population steadily declined after 1850. The fall was barely perceptible at first, but became precipitate after 1870. From nearly 40,000 in 1850, it had fallen to 30,000 in 1900. The decline was partly due to the high death rate (deaths continued to exceed births right up to the transfer of the islands to the US) and partly due to emigration. And net migration outwards accelerated when work on the Panama Canal began in 1904. In 1917, as the Danish flag was replaced by the American one, the population was a mere 26,051.

Domestic exports per head fell after 1850, and re-exports per head after 1860. As a result, merchandise exports per head steadily declined after mid-century (see figure 9.1), and the Danish government reluctantly came to the conclusion that their Caribbean colony was a failure. Unwilling to put in the additional resources that might have improved the islands' prospects, the authorities were open to offers for a transfer of sovereignty to another power.

The first to show interest was the US. Immediately after the Civil War, Secretary of State William Seward raised the prospect of a sale with the Danish minister in Washington, DC. Denmark responded positively, but pointed out that St Croix could only be transferred with French agreement due to the terms of its transfer in 1733. The French government did not agree, but this was not a major concern for the US as the target was St Thomas with its magnificent harbour. A price was agreed (US$7.5 million), Danish parliamentary approval was secured, and there was even a referendum on the islands among the few eligible to vote (only 22 voted against). However, the sale was blocked by the US Senate in 1870.

There would be several other attempts to sell the islands, including to Germany, but in 1902 the US Senate finally gave its approval. This time it was the Danish Upper House (*Landsthing*) that rejected the draft treaty, perhaps acting under German pressure, and the Danish government reluctantly concluded that it would have to take greater responsibility for its neglected Caribbean colony.

There had been no banking facilities on the islands after the only bank on St Thomas had crashed in 1898. To reduce the scarcity of credit, the Danish West-Indian National Bank was, therefore, established in 1904 and given special privileges for 30 years, including a monopoly on note issue. It would take time, however, for the bank to make an impact.

The only encouraging development, from the government's perspective, had been the modernisation of the sugar industry on St Croix from the 1870s onwards. The authorities, therefore, encouraged the creation, in 1902, of the Danish West Indies Plantation Company (not to be confused with the Danish West Indies Company that had ruled the islands up to 1754). A decade later, the Danish West Indian Company was formed with shares sold to the general public. Yet, despite official support, the company was a complete failure and made a loss in most of the years in which it operated.[21]

The greatest problem was the inability of the new corporation to revive the sugar industry despite the investment in mechanisation. The main market (the US was taking over 90 per cent of all DWI exports by the beginning of the twentieth century) was now being increasingly supplied by sugar from Cuba and Puerto Rico. The volume exported fell from 29 million pounds in 1900 to 8.5 million pounds in 1915, the last year before a transfer to the US was finally agreed. The value of the sugar exported during these years (see table 9.2) also fell sharply.

As the volume of sugar exported fell, so did rum. No one doubted the quality of the output from the distilleries on St Croix, but US imperial preference now favoured the territories recently acquired by the American empire. A new use for the alcohol, however, was found through the production of bay rum. This used bay leaves from St John to produce a fragrance for men that was popular in the US and Europe. It appeared on the export list for the first time in 1910 (see table 9.2), but its value was still minuscule at the time of transfer.

The outbreak of the First World War did not affect the DWI as much as other islands. Denmark was neutral and the US (neutral until April 1917) remained the principal market for exports and the source of most imports. Yet, there was no escaping the painful reality for the Danish government that the islands remained a drain on the public purse. In virtually all years since the end of the Napoleonic Wars, public expenditure had exceeded public revenue with the gap filled by the transfer of subsidies from Denmark. And the trends in revenue and expenditure per head had been steadily downwards in the 50 years before the First World War (see figure 9.2).

The renewed offer of purchase by the US administration in 1915 was, therefore, gratefully received. A treaty was agreed in 1916 and approved by a large majority of the Danish population. This time there would be no official referendum in the DWI itself. However, an unofficial poll on St Croix was organised by a labour leader, David Hamilton Jackson, and only seven opposed the transfer. The US flag was then raised on March 31, 1917.

Table 9.2: Danish West Indies: Exports (US$), 1900–15

Year	Sugar	Rum	Bay Rum	Domestic Exports	Re-exports
1900	504,000	13,700	-	530,000	1,021,112
1901	465,618	12,371	-	494,874	973,646
1902	458,165	18,507	-	507,170	916,744
1903	333,637	8,483	-	364,936	1,302,173
1904	393,311	12,423	-	488,278	1,304,662
1905	207,272	6,565	-	219,531	1,453,568
1906	348,870	13,826	-	407,985	1,118,519
1907	422,401	12,703	-	445,833	1,502,273
1908	243,406	12,643	-	265,532	1,300,477
1909	453,516	7,528	-	486,951	856,857
1910	465,000	15,000	9,841	563,200	1,224,200
1911	509,800	12,400	12,390	606,200	1,138,000
1912	230,600	13,000	5,004	292,400	1,414,800
1913	168,000	38,600	8,467	343,200	1,431,000
1914	310,400	19,600	9,551	392,600	974,000
1915	215,552	24,339	9,304	280,000	1,060,000

Source: Statistical Appendix.

Figure 9.2: Danish West Indies: Public Revenue and Expenditure per head (US$),1820–1915

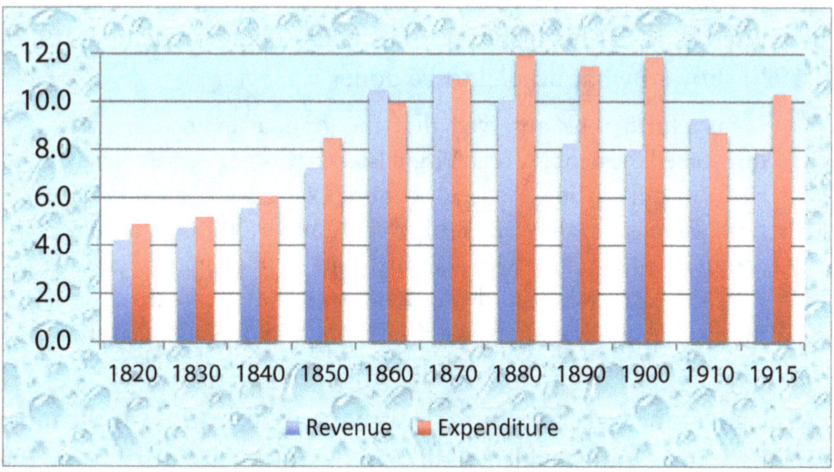

Source: Statistical Appendix.

9.3. Years of Neglect

It may have taken the US 50 years to acquire the DWI, but the federal government still had no development plans for the islands when the transfer was completed. The main purpose had been to prevent the islands, especially St Thomas, falling into the hands of another power. There was no interest at all in the economic resources of the USVI, as the colony would now be called, and no ideas how to develop them.

Even the status of the islanders was unclear. They had expected to be treated like Puerto Ricans who became US citizens in 1917, and the treaty of cession gave them every reason to assume that was the case. However, the US authorities decided after the transfer took place that such an interpretation was erroneous, and the inhabitants of the Virgin Islands were, therefore, defined as 'inhabitants of the Virgin Islands entitled to the protection of the United States'. It was not until 1927 that they were grudgingly allowed to become US citizens and even that concession was not unconditional.[22]

The USVI became a responsibility of the US navy when the transfer took place in 1917 and the first governor was Rear Admiral James Oliver. The Department of State had requested only US$50,000 to cover any unforeseen expenses associated with the transfer, but Congress had raised this to US$100,000 as a precautionary measure.[23] When the new governor expressed shock at the social conditions he encountered, he had to decide on his priorities, taking into account the limited funds at his disposal. An official report on demographics in 1920 showed what needed to be done:[24]

> It may further be observed that the gradual extinction that threatened the people of the Virgin Islands was not a race suicide but a race homicide. Plenty of children were being born in all three islands, at an average of over 30 per 1,000 population, comparing favorably with the birth rate of the United States, which in 1916 was recorded as 24.8 per 1,000 population, but the average life was short, with the enemies of life killing at the average annual rate of 37 per 1,000 population.

The governor was, therefore, clear that public health was the most important issue to be tackled. Unlike in the rest of the Caribbean, the Crude Death Rate (CDR) still exceeded the Crude Birth Rate (CBR) in the last years of the Danish West Indies. The naval authorities, therefore, invested in hospitals, water supply, and sewage to engineer a rapid reduction in the CDR (see figure 9.3). By 1919, the CDR was finally below the CBR, providing the USVI with a natural increase in population for the first time in centuries.[25]

Figure 9.3: DWI/USVI: Crude Death Rate,1896–2016

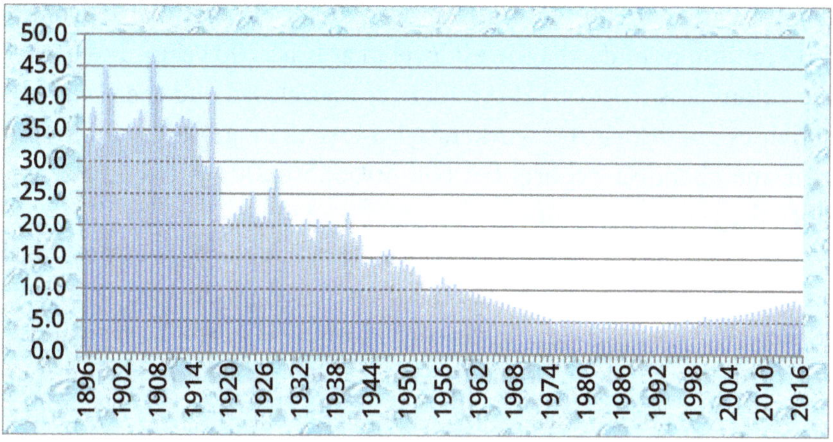

Source: Statistical Appendix.

Unfortunately, there was little for this natural increase to do other than emigrate.[26] The sugar industry on St Croix was subject to a heavy export tax of $8 per ton (reduced to $6 in 1927); the rum industry was largely destroyed by prohibition; the bay rum industry could not expand fast enough to absorb the excess capacity in the rum factories; and St Thomas became less important as an entrepôt.

One of the greatest problems the islands faced was the expectation by the US authorities, even if not fulfilled, that public revenue should cover public expenditure. Under Danish rule, a low tariff on foreign goods (including from the US) had provided the bulk of income.[27] Under naval rule, although the import tariff was left unchanged, imports from the US were no longer 'foreign'. And when re-exports to the US were charged tariff at US ports, the money was not returned to the USVI. Despite the introduction of new taxes, revenue per head did not increase in the first 15 years of US rule.[28] It is small wonder, therefore, that in his annual report for 1925/6, the US governor stated:[29]

> The demands upon the Federal appropriations are so great, the sudden failures in crop returns so serious and so fraught with irremediable danger to the insular finances that the revision of appropriation procedures as relating to the Virgin Islands should command the attention of Congress.

The impact of the Great Depression, combined with continuation of a severe drought that decimated the sugar crop, created an even direr situation for the Virgin Islanders. Sugar exports in 1931 fell to 2.85 million pounds, the lowest level in at least 200 years, and earned the colony less than US$100,000. Factories closed and there were no activities to absorb the workers who lost their jobs. The following year, merchandise exports fell below US$500,000 for the first time since the eighteenth century.

Colonial neglect, at least in such an extreme form, was no longer an option. The US government, following a visit to the islands in March 1931 by President Herbert Hoover (1929–33), transferred responsibility from the US navy to the US Department of the Interior.[30] From now on, governors would be civilians and – unlike their naval counterparts – free to lobby openly for more resources. A homestead programme was introduced to encourage small-scale farming by owner-occupiers, the port facilities on St Thomas were improved and hotel facilities were constructed to enhance the prospects for tourism.

None of this made much difference until after the election of Franklin Roosevelt (FDR) as president at the end of 1932. FDR's priority was a New Deal for the mainland, but it had its echo in the USVI where the state-owned Virgin Islands Company (VIC) was set up in 1934. The VIC accelerated the homestead programme, built hotels, and purchased two sugar mills. In addition, since its creation had coincided with the end of US prohibition, the VIC was able to buy a rum distillery and promote exports once again. The VIC was soon a major employer, and the civilian governors increased the percentage of government jobs filled by locals from ten per cent in 1931 to 75 per cent in 1935. For a few years, there was even net migration inwards.

This unusual example of state-led development created the conditions for an Organic Act for the USVI passed by Congress in 1936. Although it still reserved for Congress the right to annul any

Virgin Islands legislation, it established a constitutional framework and laid the basis to extend the franchise including – for the first time – votes for women. It did not, however, alter the colonial status of the islands whose government was forbidden from incurring bond indebtedness.

The VIC did its best to reverse the economic decline of the islands under US colonial rule, but it could not do much more than that.[31] Private investment, both by islanders and from the mainland, was limited and the outbreak of the Second World War made the USVI even more dependent on the federal government. There was a brief surge in rum exports, as from other Caribbean islands, but these soon fell back to their pre-war levels. Sugar exports also rose in volume during the war years, but the level was still far below what it had been before even the First World War under Danish rule. Percival Reese, a labour leader, complained to visiting Congressmen in 1952 in the following terms:[32]

> Our minimum hourly pay is 40 cents...a laborer in the field in St. Croix receives about $300 to $400 a year...The workers on these islands are not living, but merely existing. Unemployment is at its peak.

In 1953, nearly 40 years after the transfer from Denmark to the US, merchandise exports per head in real terms were still below their level in 1900 and no higher than their level in 1820 (see figure 9.1). Sugar was clearly never going to recover its previous levels and St Thomas' status as a leading entrepôt was not going to be restored. Tourism, it is true, was beginning to emerge as a new industry of some importance, but no one could be sure of its permanence or its ability to compete with other Caribbean locations.

In that same year, however, the prospects for the island began to change with the decision of the federal government to return to the islands' administration the proceeds of the excise duty on rum exported from the USVI to the mainland US. In its first year alone (1953), the amount remitted was US$1.9 million (roughly US$60 for each Virgin Islander) and, by 1960, it had reached US$6.5 million.[33] Public expenditure doubled between 1950 and 1953 and had quadrupled by the end of the decade.

At the same time, the federal government passed, in 1954, a new Organic Act for the USVI, giving the islanders much more responsibility for their own affairs without providing for the direct election of the governor (that would happen in 1969). The islanders would also receive their own representative in Congress (albeit non-voting). Although still a US colony, the USVI now, at least, had a more effective voice in Washington, DC to raise their concerns.

It would take time for the new Organic Act to benefit the colony. In the meantime, many islanders voted with their feet by emigrating. The death rate had been steadily falling under US colonial rule (see table 9.3) while the birth rate had remained stable at around 30 per 1,000. Indeed, by the 1950s, the gap between the two was large enough for the population to grow at two per cent a year in the absence of migration. Yet, there was no growth as a result of persistent outward migration in most years (see table 9.3).

Table 9.3: US Virgin Islands: Demographic Indicators, 1910–50

Year	Population	CBR	CDR	Net Migration
1910	27,412	32.5	33.9	-292
1920	25,017	28.0	21.0	-498
1930	22,000	26.9	22.0	-393
1940	25,000	30.2	22.1	116
1950	26,900	33.5	14.0	-325

Source: Statistical Appendix.

By 1960, the population had recovered to 32,500. Yet, this was still below the level in 1890 and far below the level in the 1790s when St Croix alone had nearly 30,000 inhabitants. Unlike the period of Danish rule, however, when demographic decline was largely due to the excess of deaths over births, it was emigration that prevented the population rising under US administration. Net outward migration during the first four decades of American colonial rule was the norm with a cumulative total of some 8,000 between 1917 and 1960.

9.4. Boom and Bust

The Organic Act of 1954 had paved the way for a more coherent approach by the federal government to its smallest Caribbean colony, but it was the Cuban Revolution that changed US ideas on development. From 1960 onwards, the USVI would experience a period of rapid growth for three decades that led to a tripling of the population, largely through inward migration, and a big rise in living standards.

The dismal economic and social conditions that had so shocked the first US governor in 1917 had disappeared a century later, but by this time the boom years had ended, and the USVI was experiencing once again outward migration, a decline in population, and a stagnant economy with falling living standards. The economic dynamism that had been so marked after 1960 appeared 50 years later to have gone with no one quite sure what would take its place.

The cycle of boom and bust after 1960 is captured in figure 9.4. Growth in GDP per head at constant prices was rapid until 1990.[34] Economic difficulties then emerged in the 1990s with marked variations in annual performance, and the population reached a peak in 2000, after which the numbers started to fall as a result of net outward migration. The economy, at least GDP per head, then increased until 2008 after which there was a deep slump for nearly ten years. The population continued to fall and on present trends will be below 100,000 by the early 2020s – the first time this has happened since 1981.

Figure 9.4: US Virgin Islands: GDP per head (2000 US$), 1960–2015

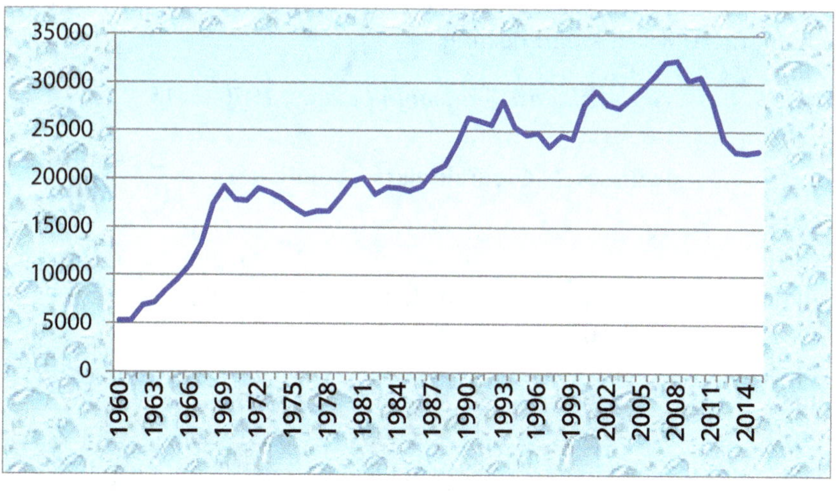

Source: Statistical Appendix up to 2008 and thereafter USVI, Bureau of Economic Research (www.usviber.org).

The growth in service exports and, in particular, tourism has been at the heart of the boom since 1960. With good air connections to the US, easy access for cruise ships, the US dollar as currency, and complete freedom of movement for US travellers, tourism has unsurprisingly prospered in the USVI. And the USVI was a major beneficiary both from the ban on US tourists going to Cuba and of the rise in income per head in the US itself after 1960.

In 1950, there were only 12,650 visitors (see table 9.4), and they spent an estimated US$1.75 million. By 1990, there were nearly two million, and the numbers continued to grow, albeit slowly, in subsequent years. However, the most rapid category of growth was 'excursionists', which consists mainly of cruise ship passengers. Their numbers quadrupled between 1970 and 2015 while overnight visitors (tourists) only grew by 70 per cent. Since cruise ship passengers spend much less than overnight visitors, this led to almost no rise in total expenditure by visitors (see table 9.4) even if the absolute amount spent (US$1.2-US$1.3 billion) was large.

Spending by cruise ship passengers and tourists actually peaked in 2007 (at US$1,512.6 million), after which the US financial crisis led to a sharp fall in spending. Indeed, this peak had still not been reached ten years later despite the recovery in the US economy. And much of the cruise ship passenger spending goes on imports, especially jewellery, which does not generate much employment. Tourism-related employment also peaked in 2007 (at 8,778), after which, there was a small decline.

Table 9.4: US Virgin Islands: Tourism Indicators, 1950–2015

	Tourists	Excursionists	All Visitors	Expenditure (US$mn)
1950			12,650	1.75
1960			124,400	24.78
1970	372,400	451,600	824,000	122.1
1980	380,000	837,400	1,217,400	293.5
1990	462,500	1,349,000	1,811,500	697.0
2000	545,900	1,849,900	2,395,800	1,205.9
2010	572,300	1,958,900	2,531,200	1,223.3
2015	641,600	2,001,400	2,643,000	1,324.4

Source: USVI, Bureau of Economic Research (www.usviber.org/).

If tourism was the main driver of the economy after 1960, merchandise exports were not far behind. This time, however, it was not sugar that led the way. Indeed, sugar exports continued to decline in importance, although rum remained profitable and increased in sales. Instead, the driver was petroleum exports as a result of the oil refinery established on St Croix in 1966.

This refinery was a joint venture between the Hess Corporation and Petróleos de Venezuela (PDVSA) called HOVENSA. Crude oil was imported, in the main from Venezuela, and exported to the US as refined petroleum. The value of exports reached US$181.7 million in 1970, dwarfing all other goods in importance, and had accelerated ten years later to US$4.1 billion. Thirty years later, in 2010, they had a value of nearly US$10 billion.

This would be the peak. The problem of securing supplies, the deterioration in relations between the US and Venezuela, shrinking margins, and violations of the Clean Air Act led to the closure by HOVENSA of the oil refinery in 2012. Overnight the value of USVI merchandise exports dropped dramatically, falling to US$326 million in 2015.

The only remaining merchandise export of importance was now rum.[35] Exports (in proof litres – P.L.) had already reached 6.1 million in 1970 and rose steadily by 2000 to 16.6 million. Soon afterwards, the USVI government – with the blessing of the federal government – started to use part of the rum excise duty rebate (see below) to offer incentives to multinational companies to increase production. This decision led to an explosion in exports, which had reached nearly 50 million P.L. by 2015.[36]

The rum excise taxes returned to the USVI by the federal government (known as 'cover-over') have played a crucial role in the islands' development. In a typical year, they average 25–30 per cent of the USVI's income from internal revenue (income taxes, import duties, etc.). How the rebate works has been explained as follows:[37]

> For every $13.50 in excise taxes per gallon produced in a territory [e.g., USVI] and sold stateside, $13.25 is reimbursed to the territory. Of that amount, $10.50 is authorised permanently by law, while the remaining $2.75 must be authorised periodically by Congress through legislation. Therefore, the more rum a

territory produces and sells to the US mainland, the more funds that territory's government receives.

For half a century from their inception in 1953, the cover-over rum excise taxes were relatively uncontroversial. Starting in 2008, however, the USVI government increased the share going directly to the multinational companies to encourage them through various subsidies to increase production and sale to the US mainland.[38] It was, however, in clear defiance of the rules of the World Trade Organisation (WTO) as was made clear on numerous occasions by other Caribbean rum exporters. Yet, they failed to take their protest to the appellate bodies of the WTO knowing that the defendant would be the powerful US government rather than the weaker USVI administration.

Puerto Rico, of course, protested as the expansion of rum production in the USVI was at its expense. When protests failed, Puerto Rico responded by increasing *its* subsidies to the rum companies, to which the USVI response was a further round of subsidies for the multinationals. The result was a race to the bottom, in which everyone lost out except the rum companies themselves.

The fiscal damage to the USVI from the subsidies was enormous. In addition, the USVI had used the cover-over income as security for government debts and to contract additional loans to build new rum facilities and improve public infrastructure to the benefit of the companies. When the costs of servicing these debts were taken into account, little of the cover-over income remained. In 2016, according to one estimate, only US$20 million of the US$231 million remitted in cover-over supported the budget:[39]

> About $86.28 million went to pay interest and principal on more than $1.3 billion in debt secured by those revenues. The territory is paying for projects at Diageo and Cruzan [the two multinational rum companies], financed with special bonds secured by the federal rum revenues. These ate up another $23.2 million in principal and interest, according to the terms spelled out in the loan documents. Nearly all the remainder – a little more than $100 million – went as a direct cash payment to Diageo and to Cruzan's parent company Beam Suntory.

Ten years after the global financial crisis, the USVI authorities had still not been able to put the economy back on a sustainable growth path. The local economy had been overwhelmed by a combination of lower US GDP per head, a reduction in tourist expenditure, the closure of the oil refinery, and a debt burden that had become increasingly onerous to service.

Many islanders voted with their feet and emigrated. Indeed, net outward migration had been happening almost continuously since the mid-1970s as a result of a mismatch between islanders' educational qualifications and job opportunities. Yet, the scale of outward migration had, at first, been concealed by a relatively high birth rate. As the population aged (the younger adults tending to be the first to emigrate), the birth rate fell and by 2016 was down to ten per 1,000 – only a little higher than the death rate (eight per 1,000). Net outward migration now implied a decline in the size of the population, something that started to happen in 2000.

As a US territory, the USVI is unable to default on its debt, cannot devalue, and has no independent monetary policy. Many islanders, therefore, concluded that the problem could only be resolved with a change in the constitutional relationship, still governed by the 1954 Organic Act. In 2010, a fifth attempt at writing a separate constitution for the USVI was attempted when delegates were elected to a constitutional convention and a draft constitution was adopted.

The draft was sent to the US president, who remitted it to Congress for the final decision. However, President Barak Obama's memorandum attached to the draft made it clear that there was little chance of success since it noted:[40]

> (1) the absence of an express recognition of United States sovereignty and the supremacy of federal law; (2) provisions for a special election on the USVI's territorial status; (3) provisions conferring legal advantages on certain groups defined by place and timing of birth, timing of residency, or ancestry; (4) residence requirements for certain offices; (5) provisions guaranteeing legislative representation of certain geographic areas; (6) provisions addressing territorial waters and marine resources; (7) imprecise language in certain provisions of the proposed constitution's bill of rights; the possible need to repeal certain federal laws if the proposed USVI constitution is adopted; and (9) the effect of congressional action or inaction on the proposed constitution.

So damning was this memorandum that there was little chance of it being overruled by Congress, and the draft constitution was therefore rejected. The USVI, therefore, remains a US colony, unable to resolve its own problems but without the influence to ensure that the federal government takes whatever steps are needed to resolve its deep-seated economic problems.

NOTES

1. St John and St Thomas had been occupied by the Danish in the seventeenth century, while St Croix was purchased from France in 1733 on condition it not be sold to any other power without French approval.
2. Because of the importance of the re-export trade, I have used merchandise exports rather than domestic exports before 1960. This means adjusting re-exports from current to constant prices. I have used the import price index in the Statistical Appendix to do so.
3. See S. Green-Pedersen, 'Demographic Responses,' in *The Abolition of the Atlantic Slave Trade*, ed. W. Eltis and J. Walvin (Madison, WI: University of Wisconsin Press, 1981), 244.
4. The law only banned the trade in slaves in vessels flying the Danish flag, but this effectively ended the legal trade. See W. Westergaard, *The Danish West Indies under Company Rule (1671–1754): With a Supplementary Chapter, 1755–1917* (New York, NY: The Macmillan Company, 1917), 247.
5. On slave demographics at this time, see H. Johansen, 'Slave Demography of the Danish West Indian Islands,' *Scandinavian Economic History Review* XXIX, no. 1 (1981): 1–20.
6. The British had first occupied the islands in 1801, but had returned them to Denmark the following year as a consequence of the Treaty of Amiens.
7. In 1815, there were 24,339 slaves on St Croix, 4,848 on St Thomas, and 2,445 on St John. See Johansen, 'Slave Demography of the Danish West Indian Islands,' 3.
8. On maronnage in St Croix, see L. Roopnarine, 'Maroon Resistance and Settlement in Danish St. Croix,' *Journal of Third World Studies* (September 2010): 1–21.
9. In 1845, the CBR for slaves was 40 and the CDR was 50. See Statistical Appendix.
10. See Bulmer-Thomas (2012), 79, figure 4.1.
11. See Westergaard, *The Danish West Indies under Company Rule (1671–1754)*, 253.
12. The average tariff rate in 1850 was four per cent. This can be obtained by dividing trade taxes collected by the value of merchandise imports. See Statistical Appendix.

13. See Statistical Appendix.
14. See Bulmer-Thomas, *The Economic History of the Caribbean since the Napoleonic Wars*, 147, table 6.2.
15. Governor Peter von Scholten was put on trial on his return to Denmark and stripped of his pension, although he was eventually acquitted. He died in 1854.
16. See L. Roopnarine, *Indian Indenture in the Danish West Indies, 1863–1873* (New York, NY: Palgrave Macmillan, 2016), 16. The Danish West Indian dollar ('dalar') replaced the rigsdaler in 1849. It was in turn replaced by the US dollar in 1917 roughly at par. Thus, 50 dalars were worth approximately US$50.
17. Buddhoe, sometimes confusingly called Moses Gottlieb, went to Trinidad, but it is not known what happened to him subsequently. There is as yet no full-length biography of this remarkable man.
18. The Labour Act is reproduced in full in J.P. Knox, *A Historical Account of St. Thomas, W.I.* (New York: C. Scribner, 1852), 248–55, Appendix B.
19. See Roopnarine, *Indian Indenture in the Danish West Indies, 1863–1873*, 25–33.
20. See P. Jensen, *From Serfdom to Fireburn and Strike: The History of Black Labor in the Danish West Indies, 1848–1916* (Christianstad: Antilles Press, 1998), 144.
21. See Westergaard, *The Danish West Indies under Company Rule*, 256.
22. Only those physically present on the islands on March 31, 1917 were entitled to US citizenship in 1927, thereby excluding those working or living in other islands. This restriction was finally lifted in 1932.
23. See S. McMahon, 'You Pay for What You Get: the U.S. Virgin Islands, 1917–1936,' *The Journal of Caribbean History* 41, nos. 1 and 2 (2007): 114.
24. See United States Department of Commerce, *Birth and Mortality Statistics of the Virgin Islands of the United States, 1901–19* (Washington, DC: United States Department of Commerce, 1920), 20.
25. In that year (1919), the CDR fell to 20.1 while the CBR was 28. See Statistical Appendix.
26. Rothschild Francis, a Virgin Islander, captured the sense of despair in a series of letter published by the New York Times in 1923.
27. See C. Tooke, 'The Danish Colonial Fiscal System in the West Indies,' *American Economic Association* 1, no. 3 (1900): 144–67 and L.H. Evans, *The Virgin Islands: From Naval Base to New Deal* (Ann Arbor, MI: J.W. Edwards, 1945), 189–202.
28. In 1917, the first year of US rule, public revenue per head was US$9.50. Fifteen years later, in 1933, the number was US$7.70. See Statistical Appendix.

29. See US Department of the Interior, *The Governor of the Virgin Islands to the Secretary of the Interior: Annual Report 1926* (Washington, DC: US Department of the Interior, 1926), 9.
30. See I. Dookhan, *A History of the Virgin Islands of the United States* (Epping: Caribbean Universities Press for the College of the Virgin Islands, 1974), 271–72.
31. On the VIC, see G K. Lewis, *The Virgin Islands: A Caribbean Lilliput* (Evanston, IL: Northwestern University Press, 1972), *passim.*
32. Quoted in W. Boyer, *America's Virgin Islands: History of Human Rights and Wrongs* (Durham, NC: Carolina Academic Press, 1971), 219.
33. See R.M Paiewonsky and I. Dookhan, *Memoirs of a Governor: A Man for the People* (New York, NY: New York University Press, 1990), 495.
34. The USVI uses Gross Territorial Product rather than Gross Domestic Product to measure the national accounts, but the two are essentially the same.
35. For many years, watch exports to the US were also important. These reached nearly four million in number by 1980, but had declined to 42,000 by 2015 when the last assembly factory closed.
36. As a result of the incentives, Diageo – one of the largest drinks companies in the world – moved its production base from Puerto Rico to the USVI.
37. See D. Suárez, 'Puerto Rico's Unlimited Generosity Towards Rum Companies,' *Centro de Periodismo Investigativo*. February 1, 2017.
38. See D.A Austin, *Economic and Fiscal Conditions in the US Virgin Islands* (Washington, DC: Congressional Research Service, 2018), 5–6.
39. See B. Kossler, 'The V.I. Budget Crisis: Part 15, Rum and Congress,' *St. Thomas Source*, August 7, 2017.
40. See statement of Jonathan G. Cedarbaum, Deputy Assistant Attorney General, US Department of Justice, to US Congress on consideration of the proposed Virgin Islands constitution from the fifth constitutional convention.

PART IV:
The English-speaking Countries

Chapter 10
JAMAICA

Jamaica's status as the jewel in the British imperial crown, which once seemed unassailable, changed rapidly after the French Revolution. The successful slave revolt in neighbouring Haiti posed an existential threat to the planters, as did the freeing of slaves in all the French colonies in 1794. The end of the trade in slaves by Great Britain in 1807, with effect from 1808, undermined the economic model on which the planters relied. The Jamaican slave revolt in 1831 was a warning of things to come if emancipation did not occur soon.

What followed was a period of rapid economic decline. Emancipation of the slaves in 1834 and the subsequent termination of the privileged position enjoyed by Jamaican sugar and its derivatives (molasses and rum) in the British market ended once and for all the plantocracy's special status in the British Empire. Exports per head fell almost continuously for half a century after 1820 (see figure 10.1). Indeed, the decline had begun 15 years earlier.

The fall in exports per head may have ceased by the end of the 1860s, but it was not followed by a recovery. Instead, there was a period of some 70 years in which exports per head at constant prices remained largely unchanged (see figure 10.1) and far below the level in 1820 (yet alone 1805). Thus, Jamaica experienced no growth in exports per head from the Napoleonic Wars to the end of the Second World War.

This long period of stagnation took place despite a diversification of the economy away from sugar. Such had been the dominant position of sugar, however, that the expansion of other exports simply compensated for the decline in the volume of sugar produced. And given the high correlation between exports per head and GDP per head, at least after 1850, there are strong grounds for concluding that the Jamaican economy on a per capita basis experienced no growth at all for more than a century after the end of slavery (see figure 10.2).[1]

Figure 10.1: Jamaica: Exports per head at constant prices (1900=100), 1820–2016

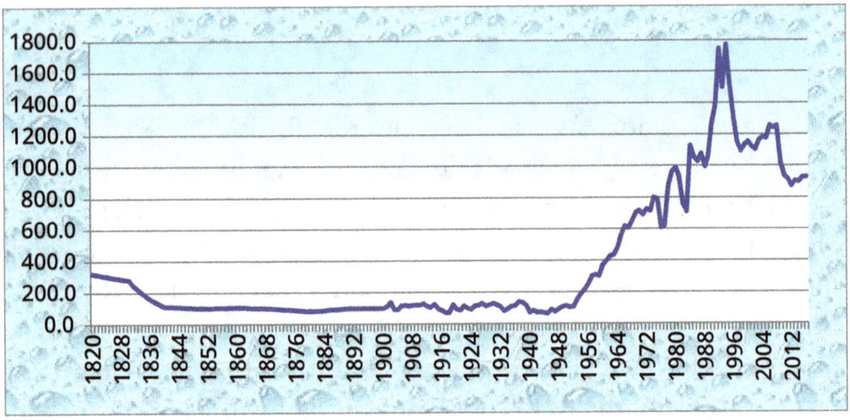

Source: Statistical Appendix up to 2008; World Bank, World Development Indicators thereafter.

Figure 10.2: Jamaica: GDP per head at constant prices (1900=100), 1832–2016

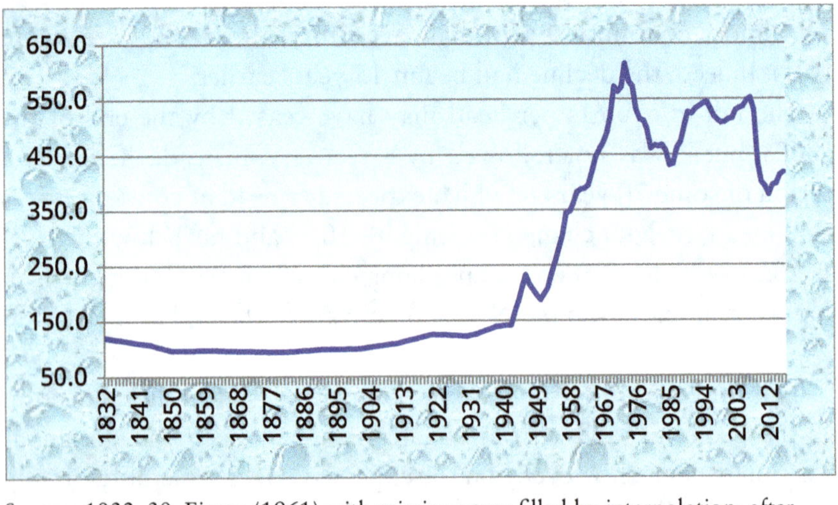

Source: 1832–30, Eisner (1961) with missing years filled by interpolation; after 1930, Maddison (2003) and World Bank, World Development Indicators.

Growth from the 1940s onwards was rapid (see figure 10.2). As in other parts of the Caribbean, it was driven by the diversification and growth of exports. In Jamaica, this included minerals (especially bauxite) and services (above all tourism). For the first time since the end of the eighteenth century, Jamaica appeared to have put its economic travails behind it.

Unfortunately, the period of growth ended a decade after independence in 1962. It was, therefore, relatively brief. By the 1970s, Jamaica was once again facing severe economic difficulties that have still not been fully resolved. Some of the problems were familiar to students of Jamaican economic history and included mass unemployment, net outward migration, high levels of private indebtedness, and falling commodity prices. However, some of them were new, especially currency collapse, high levels of inflation, and unsustainable external public debt.

10.1. Economic Decline

Before the Napoleonic Wars, Jamaica had attracted investments from some of the most ambitious and well-connected individuals in Great Britain and Ireland. They had made fortunes, primarily out of sugar, and reinvested part of the profits in the island. However, these absentee landowners also had substantial commercial interests in the British Isles. As the tide turned against their privileged position in the Caribbean, they focused more of their attention on their business interests elsewhere.

The case of Sir John Rae Reid is fairly typical.[2] Born into a wealthy merchant family in Scotland, he was the recipient of a large amount of compensation for 505 slaves on the Garbrand and Mullet Hall Estate in 1834. By that time, however, he was a partner in the trading house of Reid Irving and a member of parliament for Dover. He would go on to become a director of the London & Bristol Railway Company and governor of the Bank of England, by which time his Jamaican interests probably seemed like a distant memory.

The first warning sign for these absentee proprietors was the act of 1807 abolishing the slave trade from March 1, 1808. At a time when slave deaths exceeded slave births, this act was supposed to force plantation owners into better treatment of their labourers so that the death rate would fall, and slavery could continue indefinitely through natural growth. This demographic change, indeed, is what happened in some islands where most planters were resident.

It did not happen in Jamaica, where the slave death rate remained stubbornly high after the end of the slave trade right up to emancipation (see table 10.1). In fact, the number of deaths *rose* while the number of births *fell*. And as the slave population itself was falling, the Crude Death Rate (CDR) rose quite significantly. So, far from increasing, the slave population dropped in the quarter century before emancipation from 347,000 in 1810 to 311,070 in 1834.[3]

The local representatives of the absentee Jamaican planters, as table 10.1 indicates clearly, were not prepared to make the changes on the estates that would have reduced the number of deaths. With their extensive interests outside Jamaica, the planters looked instead to new and more profitable ventures. A long process of capital flight began, resulting in a fall in all the key economic indicators. This economic decline predated emancipation itself.

Table 10.1: Jamaica: Slave Births and Deaths, 1817–32

Years	Births	Deaths	Net Births	CBR	CDR
1817–20	30,057	30,765	-708	29.1	29.8
1820–23	28,702	32,293	-3,591	28.2	31.7
1823–26	28,427	30,846	-2,419	28.4	30.8
1826–29	26,825	30,805	-3,980	27.4	31.4
1829–32	27,331	32,757	-5,426	28.7	34.4
Total	141,342	157,466	-16,124		

Source: Higman (1984, 610) and Statistical Appendix.

Table 10.2: Jamaica: Principal Exports by Value (US$), 1820–40

	Sugar	Molasses	Rum	Coffee	Domestic Exports	Re-Exports
1820	11,231,370	60,483	1,507,260	4,246,671	17,992,570	2,919,855
1830	6,700,882	18,725	1,400,203	2,475,897	11,622,556	1,886,122
1840	4,942,763	1,880	1,175,852	1,395,464	8,324,865	975,588

Source: Statistical Appendix.

The numbers speak for themselves (see table 10.2). By 1840, shortly after the end of the apprenticeship period, the value of sugar, molasses, rum, and coffee exports had all collapsed, compared with just 20 years before. In just two decades, the value of domestic exports had gone from nearly US$18 million to US$8.3 million. The same was true of re-exports, which fell from nearly US$3 million in 1820 to under one million US dollars in 1840.

The decline had, in fact, started even before 1820 with the peak year for the volume of sugar exported being reached in 1805, rum in 1806, and coffee in 1814.[4] Long before the planters started to blame the decline in domestic exports on their former slaves' unwillingness to work on the estates, the planters themselves had shown their lack of interest through capital flight, disinvestment, and sales of their properties in Jamaica.

The act emancipating slaves was passed in 1833 and came into effect on August 1, 1834. At this point, the Jamaican slave owners became eligible for over a quarter of the £20 million (some £17 billion in current prices) voted as compensation by the British Parliament.[5] There were 13,118 claims, most of which were successful, but very little of the money was reinvested in Jamaica. Instead, it was used in the UK to pay off debts or diversify into other enterprises.

The case of Robert Gordon is fairly typical:[6]

> Robert Gordon owned two plantations, the 185-acre Paisley Estate and Windsor Lodge, both in St. James, and consigned his sugar to Hibbert and Company. In 1827, Gordon's mortgage account stood at £11,098 with an interest rate of 5 per cent per annum. Apparently he kept abreast of the interest payments and the principal remained the same until 1835. Soon after the commissioners began their work, the Hibberts [who controlled the mortgage] submitted their uncontested claims against the estates. By April 1836 they had collected the indemnity for the 520 slaves and reduced Gordon's mortgage by £9,383.

The period of apprenticeship, scheduled to last six years, was a failure from the point of view of both planters and former slaves. It was, therefore, ended in 1838, and the estate workers were now free to leave. Some stayed, because they would need to find new accommodation and provision grounds if they moved. However, many left beginning the flight from the estates that has been chronicled by so many scholars.[7] Thus, Jamaica experienced both capital and labour flight with the difference being that almost all the workers stayed on the island. New villages were formed and food production for local consumption – in many cases a form of import substitution – rose rapidly after 1850.[8]

The exportable surplus of the island inevitably fell. Yet, the planters and their representatives placed all the blame on the former slaves. In response to a question about the agricultural distress in Jamaica from the Select Committee on West India Colonies held on June 16, 1842, William Burge replied:[9]

> I consider, and so do my constituents, that the principal, and indeed the only cause of that distress, is the inadequate supply of labour. The inadequacy consists in the number of the population engaged in agricultural labour being less than that engaged in labour during slavery, and in the insufficiency of the work performed by this diminished number of the labouring population in return for the wages paid them.

The solution called for by the planters was inward migration, both to increase the supply of labour and to drive down wages, which had risen as a result of the labour shortage on the estates. Parliament was receptive, even if unwilling to provide a subsidy, and schemes were soon put in place. First to arrive were Africans, this time voluntarily, soon followed by indentured labourers from India and China.[10] From the end of slavery to the First World War, 53,940 migrants came to Jamaica with two-thirds from India.[11] Not all stayed, but the population started to recover and by 1861 had reached 441,264 – ten per cent above its level in 1810.[12]

The Jamaican Assembly had hoped that immigration would revive the fortunes of the estates, especially those devoted to sugar. This did not happen, however, and this time the blame could not be put on the former slaves who refused to dedicate as much time to their previous owners. Instead, global competition was blamed as a result of the removal of the imperial preferences granted to the British West Indies in the British market. This had started in 1826 with the admission of sugar from Mauritius on equal terms, then from India in 1836, and finally from all countries with the phasing out of sugar preferences from 1846 to 1854.[13] From now on Jamaican sugar would have to compete with slave-grown sugar from Brazil and Cuba as well as sugar grown with free labour from many other countries.

The volume of sugar exports per head did, indeed, continue to fall after 1830. However, prices were not at first to blame (see figure 10.3). Indeed, sugar prices doubled in the 1830s and by 1850 were still at their level 20 years earlier. It was not until the competition from European beet sugar became intense in the last quarter of the nineteenth century that sugar prices fell precipitately. And sugar growers in many other Caribbean countries managed to increase exports before 1870, suggesting that the problem was not prices but the lack of investment by the estate owners in Jamaica itself.

Rum exports also continued to fall, as did coffee, but other exports did not perform so badly (see table 10.3). Indeed, there was a significant increase in the volume of logwood, ginger, and pimento exports after 1830. These three commodities, which contributed only five per cent to the total value of domestic exports in 1830, were contributing nearly 20 per cent by 1870. However, the collapse of sugar, molasses, rum, and coffee overwhelmed the impact of growth in these other exports and re-exports also continued to contract. Thus, merchandise exports were valued at only US$6 million in 1870 compared with US$21 million in 1820.

Figure 10.3: Jamaica: Sugar Export Volume per head and Prices (1830=100), 1830–70

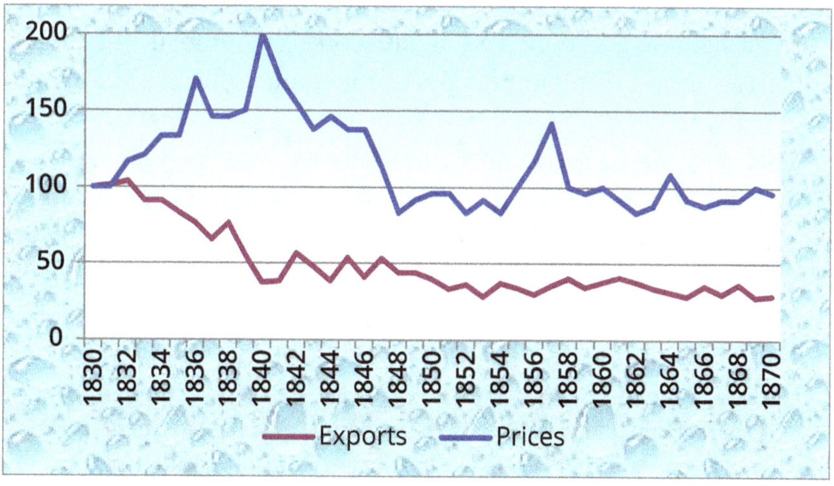

Source: Derived from Eisner (1961, 204).

Table 10.3: Jamaica: Non-sugar Exports by Volume, 1830–70

	Rum (gal)	Coffee (lb)	Logwood (lb)	Ginger (lb)	Pimento (lb)
1830	3,641,520	16,616,761	16,710,400	548,821	4,671,827
1840	1,198,471	7,207,289	21,535,360	464,294	3,244,181
1850	1,391,065	5,929,414	9,098,880	684,189	3,840,300
1860	1,709,636	5,939,555	33,526,080	736,981	5,726,868
1870	1,340,950	6,894,169	193,062,375	858,069	6,225,332

Source: Statistical Appendix.

Some sugar estates had switched to other commodities, but a part of the non-traditional exports was coming from the small farms established by former slaves after the end of the apprenticeship period. This was the first sign of a change in the Jamaican economic model from its dependence on large-scale sugar estates, and the small farmers were also contributing to coffee exports for the first time. And in logwood, easily available throughout the mountainous regions of the island, the small farmers had access to a valuable resource even if it was harvested in a non-sustainable way.[14]

The role of small farmers would after 1870 become much more important, but they could not reverse the downward spiral of the Jamaican economy as long as it was still dependent on sugar estates whose owners had shown no desire to invest in modernisation and expansion.[15] As a result, conditions on the island for many Jamaicans were intolerable and they were made worse by outbreaks of cholera in the 1850s and rising import prices for staples after the start of the US Civil War.

This was the background to the famous letter in January 1865 from a Baptist minister, Edward Underhill, to the British Colonial Secretary. In this long letter, Underhill drew attention to the imbalance between the supply and demand of labour:[16]

> The labouring class is too numerous for the work to be done. Sugar cultivation on the estates does not absorb more than 30,000 of the people, and every other species of cultivation (apart from provision growing) cannot give employment to more than another 30,000. But the agricultural population of the island is over 400,000, so that there are at least 340,000 whose livelihood depends on employment other than that

> devoted to the staple cultivation of the island. Of these 340,000 certainly not less than 130,000 are adults, and capable of labour.

The letter received so much attention that the British government was forced to respond, but the crass and insensitive reply only made matters worse:[17]

> I request that you will inform the Petitioners that their Petition has been laid before the Queen, and that I have received Her Majesty's command to inform them, that the prosperity of the labouring Classes, as well as of all other Classes, depends, in Jamaica, and in other Countries, upon their working for wages, not un-certainly or capriciously, but steadily and continuously, at the times when their labour is wanted, and for so long as it is wanted; and that if they would use this industry, and thereby render the Plantations productive, they would enable the Planters to pay them higher Wages for the same hours of work than are received by the best Field Labourers in this Country; and as the cost of the necessaries of life is much less in Jamaica than it is here, they would be enabled, by adding prudence to industry, to lay by an ample provision for seasons of drought and dearth; and they may be assured that it is from their own industry and prudence, in availing themselves of the means of prospering that are before them, and not any such schemes as have been suggested to them, that they must look for an improvement in their condition; and that Her Majesty will regard with interest and satisfaction their advancement through their own merits and efforts.

This reply, like Underhill's letter, received widespread publicity and created what can only be described as a pre-revolutionary situation. It just needed a spark to ignite the flames, and this soon came in the form of the Morant Bay Rebellion in October 1865.[18] The reaction of the colonial state was brutal, but effective, and the rebellion ended with severe loss of life.[19] However, the British government finally accepted that the *status quo* had to end. The Jamaican Assembly was forced to abolish itself, and the island became a Crown Colony under direct British rule.

10.2. Diversification without Growth

When the Jamaican Assembly ended in 1866, it left behind a dismal legacy. It had fought vigorously to defend the narrow sectarian interests of the sugar estates, and yet the industry had still crumbled long before the collapse of world prices brought about by the expansion of beet sugar; opportunities for diversification were thwarted by a lack of public infrastructure with the railway network limited to a mere 42 kilometres, most of which had been built in the 1840s; public expenditure per head had fallen from US$5 in 1820 to US$2.9 in 1860, leaving very little to be spent on education for the expanding population of young people.

The legacy of the Jamaican Assembly had been graphically captured by the letter from Edward Underhill to the Secretary of State for the Colonies portraying the underemployment, poverty, and poor health of the vast majority of the population. The initial response by the British government – to defend the *status quo* – not only failed to work, but had even exacerbated the situation. Thus, the officials in charge after Crown Colony rule was imposed had no choice but to adopt a different approach.

The priorities identified were infrastructure, education and finance, all of which required putting government income on a more solid basis. Revenue per head had nearly doubled to US$5.70 by 1900. Spending per head more than doubled over the same period and had reached US$5.90 by the end of century. However, both revenue and spending per head were still only US$10 at the end of the 1920s, an indication of how difficult it was to increase government income in an economy subject to long-run stagnation.

With public finance on a stronger footing, the governor of Jamaica purchased in 1879 the existing 42 kilometres of railways, and the system was extended to 105 kilometres by 1885. The railways were then transferred to a US consortium, which expanded the system to nearly 300 kilometres by the end of the century. Meanwhile, the colonial state focused on public roads, which had been seriously neglected under the Jamaican Assembly. By 1900, Jamaica had nearly 6,000 kilometres of all-weather roads, which were much admired by one visitor from the US:[20]

> [Jamaica has] roads such as no country district in the United States possesses, which are built to grade, splendidly macadamized, well drained and cared for.

Education was another area that had been woefully neglected by the Jamaican Assembly. In 1840, shortly after the end of the apprenticeship period, a mere 14,881 children were in school.[21] This was four per cent of Jamaica's population at the time, and it had only risen to five per cent on the eve of Crown Colony government. Furthermore, registration did not necessarily mean regular attendance and many of these children failed to complete elementary school.

After the Morant Bay Rebellion, education received much more attention from the Jamaican government. By 1880, there were 66,686 children in school, representing over 11 per cent of the Jamaican population.[22] Public spending on education quintupled in these years, and spending per pupil also rose sharply. By 1900, the numbers in school had reached nearly 90,000. This, however, was still only 11 per cent of the Jamaican population and by no means was it all of the school-age children, suggesting that public education was no longer such a high priority.

What did remain a priority was the financial system and the need to increase the opportunities for savings and investment on the island. The Colonial Bank had been granted a charter in 1836 by King William IV 'for the purpose of carrying on the business of a Banker in Jamaica and the other West India Islands and British Guiana, and not elsewhere'. A number of banks had then followed, but these all collapsed within a few years.[23] Savings Banks had also been established in Jamaica in 1837, but the Secretary of one such bank committed a series of frauds causing a panic among account holders in all similar institutions.[24]

Crown Colony rule brought an immediate change. A government savings bank was established in 1870 with branches throughout Jamaica. By 1910, there were over 40,000 depositors. The Bank of Nova Scotia, headquartered in Canada, entered Jamaica in 1889 and the Canadian Bank of Commerce some 20 years later. And when the Colonial Bank merged with Barclays Bank in 1925, Jamaica could claim to have much stronger financial institutions than in the years of rule by the Jamaican Assembly.

These changes to infrastructure, education and finance were all long overdue, but they could not reverse the decline of the sugar industry. Even the most modernised plantations struggled to cope with the precipitate fall of prices in the last quarter of the nineteenth century – a consequence of the rise in beet sugar production in Europe and North America. The volume exported continued to fall and by 1900 the value of sugar exports had dropped below US$1 million (see table 10.4), by which time sugar contributed less than ten per cent of the value of domestic exports.

The decline in the importance of sugar would never be fully reversed. Jamaica now ceased to be a sugar island in the classic sense. Instead, its economic fortunes would depend on the export of other commodities. The most important of these, for many years, was bananas, which had been shipped speculatively in a tiny quantity by Captain Lorenzo Baker on a return voyage from South America to Boston in 1870.

Jamaica would now join a handful of countries shipping bananas in limited quantities to the US. By 1880, the country was exporting over 350,000 bunches, but the value (some US$150,000) was still small (see table 10.4). However, the creation in 1885 of the Boston Fruit Company and its merger with other banana companies into the United Fruit Company in 1899 changed the outlook completely. By 1890, Jamaica was shipping 3.7 million bunches with a value of some US$1.5 million and the numbers would double each decade until the First World War (see table 10.4).

Table 10.4: Jamaica: Sugar and Banana Exports, 1860–1910

	Sugar (lb)	Bananas (bunches)	Sugar (US$)	Bananas (US$)
1860	67,070,901		2,821,665	
1870	61,614,112		2,479,561	
1880	52,248,933	363,770	2,029,376	152,783
1890	42,072,128	3,744,082	1,194,824	1,557,150
1900	33,040,784	8,248,485	808,133	3,012,757
1910	37,270,315	15,768,262	1,016,619	6,488,115

Source: Statistical Appendix. All years are three-year averages.

By 1890, bananas had become Jamaica's most important export, and it would remain so in almost all years until the Second World War. However, other exports would also play their part. Indeed, Jamaican exports at the start of the twentieth century had become quite diversified with rum, cigars, coffee, cacao, logwood, logwood extract, ginger, pimento, coconuts, copra, oranges, and grapefruits all making significant contributions. Several of these even became more important than sugar in the years before the First World War. And the proximity of Jamaica to the US meant that tourism began to make its appearance as a commercial industry before the end of the nineteenth century.

Jamaica, therefore, diversified, but it was diversification without growth in income per head as the new exports could not yet compensate for the fall in the importance of sugar and the rise in population. As figures 10.1 and 10.2 showed (see above), this long period leading up to the Second World War were years of stagnation in real exports and real GDP per head. And public revenue and expenditure per head in real terms also stagnated after the initial increase following Crown Colony rule.[25]

The Jamaican Assembly had not bothered to collect accurate vital statistics. When these finally became available in 1879 under Crown Colony rule, they showed a society in which the natural rate of growth of population was around one per cent. This had risen to 1.5 per cent by 1900 and two per cent by 1930, an increase that was almost entirely due to the fall in the death rate.

The population did rise, but nothing like as fast as might have been expected from the natural rate of increase. Instead, there was net outward migration in many years (see figure 10.4).

Figure 10.4: Jamaica: Net Migration, 1880–1950

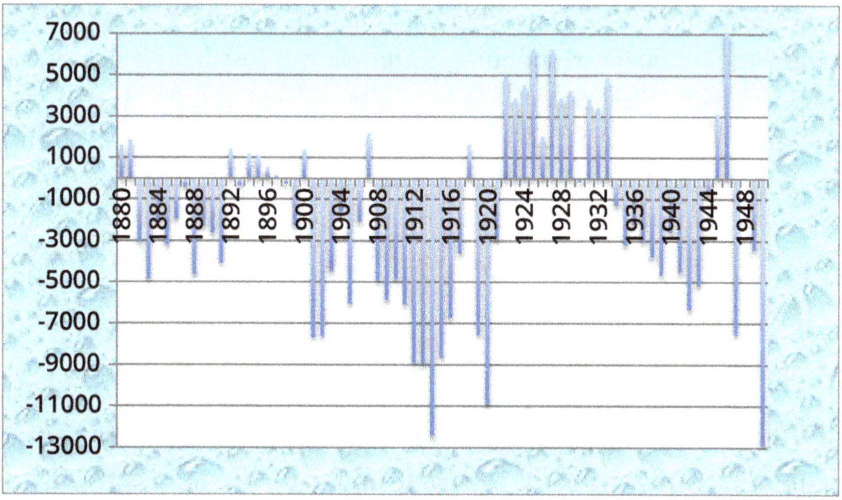

Source: Statistical Appendix.

Jamaicans left for Costa Rica after 1870 to build the railways and work in the banana industry; they left for Panama after 1900 to work on the construction of the canal; they left for Cuba after 1910 to work in the sugar industry and in domestic employment; and they left for Europe to fight in the First and Second World Wars.[26]

On those rare occasions when there was net inward migration, there was usually a very specific reason. Thus, Jamaicans returned from Cuba in the 1920s as the sugar industry stopped growing. And, of course, they returned from Europe after the two world wars. Cumulative net migration outwards, however, was much more important than inwards, which is why the Jamaican population grew slowly and only exceeded one million in 1929 – just as the Great Depression was beginning.

The Great Depression hit Jamaica hard, especially as it coincided with an outbreak of Panama disease on the banana plantations. All exports were affected with the value of domestic exports falling by half between 1929 and 1933 to US$11 million. Unemployment soared and wages were cut, but outward migration became more difficult because of immigration restrictions imposed by other countries. Economic and social pressures in Jamaica then became unbearable.

Labour unrest started in earnest in 1935, but it was the strikes and riots in 1938 that changed Jamaica. Worker agitation transformed itself into a demand for trade union rights, and the political parties were formed that have dominated Jamaican politics ever since. The British government, responding to unrest not just in Jamaica but in other parts of the British West Indies as well, established the Moyne Commission. It reported in 1940 on the shocking state of affairs in Jamaica and elsewhere.[27] However, its recommendations for the amelioration of economic and social conditions could not be fully implemented until after the Second World War.

10.3. Growth without Equity

The Second World War led to a shortage of shipping, which restricted what Jamaica could sell and buy from abroad. Banana exports were particularly affected and had slumped to 289,000 bunches by 1943 compared with more than 20 million just before the war. However, sugar imports were deemed a strategic necessity by Great Britain so that exports from Jamaica were less affected. This helped the value of exports to recover, and they had almost reached their 1939 value of US$20 million again by 1945.

If the war years were economically challenging for Jamaica, the political advances were substantial. Universal suffrage was adopted in 1943 and in 1945 the British government announced it wished to hold a conference on Federation of the British West Indies (BWI) with a view to self-government on the Dominion model. The meeting was held in Montego Bay in 1947 and the following year a report was issued by the Standing Committee stating:[28]

> We start from the assumption that the main underlying purpose of our task is to seek the shortest path towards a real political independence for the British peoples of the region, within the framework of the British Commonwealth – what is meant in fact by 'Dominion Status'. We assume further that we have been charged with this task because there is general agreement that this object cannot be attained without some form of federal association within the territories concerned, but that with Federation its attainment becomes practicable.

The British government now had a strong incentive to provide economic incentives for Jamaica and other countries in the BWI to stay on the path towards federation. One consequence was the Commonwealth Sugar Agreement in 1951 that provided a guaranteed market at realistic prices for Jamaica among others. The volume of sugar now soared, reaching nearly 800 million pounds in 1960, four times higher than in 1940. Even more important, the value of sugar exports in this period rose ten-fold to reach US$36.5 million in 1960.

Other agricultural exports, such as bananas, could not match this performance and some actually fell in volume terms as sugar once again took over land used for growing other crops. The number of oranges exported, for example, fell from some 50 million in 1940 to less than ten million in 1960. Yet, despite this, sugar's share of the value of domestic exports did not rise as might have been expected and was less than a quarter in 1960.

The reason was the rise of the bauxite industry. The 'red ferruginous earth' had been noted by geologists as early as 1869, but it was not until the 1940s that multinational companies began surveying, acquiring land and preparing for production. The first export of bauxite was made in 1952, but even then officials were sceptical about the impact. The World Bank, for example, predicted at the end of that year that output might eventually increase to two million tonnes.[29]

In the end, the impact of the new industry was far greater than had been expected. Alumina, the first stage in the transformation of bauxite into aluminium, was being exported by 1955. Two years later, Jamaica had become the world's largest exporter of bauxite with production capacity of nearly five million tonnes. Although Jamaica would cede this position in 1971 to Australia, it would remain the world's second largest exporter and in 1974 became the second largest exporter of alumina as well.

The rapid growth of bauxite/alumina exports meant that by 1960 the industry was responsible for 50 per cent of domestic exports – more than twice the value of sugar. Although in years to come the fiscal contribution of the multinationals would come under scrutiny, the impact of a small royalty on production (all of which was exported) meant that public revenue rose rapidly. Between 1950 and 1960, public revenue per head at constant prices almost doubled, and public expenditure per head rose even faster as the new income stream allowed the Jamaican government – still under colonial rule – to justify spending in excess of income.[30]

Figure 10.5: Jamaica: Net Migration, 1952–2016

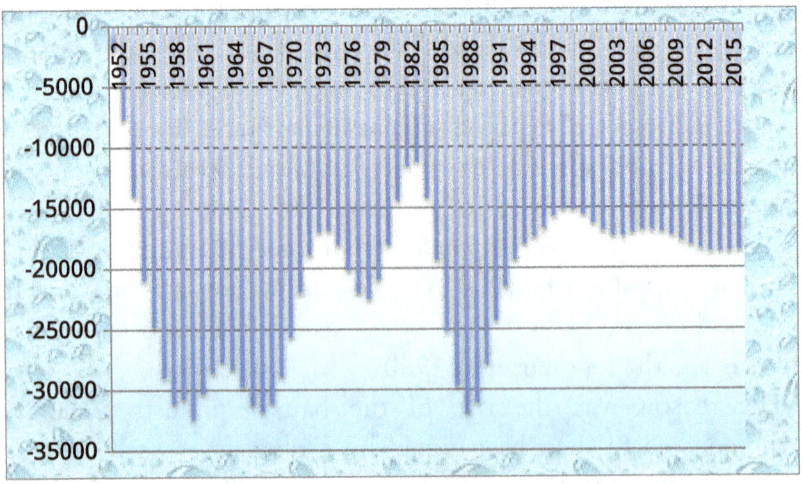

Source: Statistical Appendix and World Bank, World Development Indicators.

The World Bank may have underestimated the scale and impact of mineral exports, but it was correct to warn against the lack of employment opportunities that would be created by the new industry. With the birth rate rising rapidly after the Second World War, while the death rate continued to fall, the pressure to leave became strong – especially as the UK was keen to attract migrants from the region. From 1952 onwards (see figure 10.5), there has not been a single year in which net migration has not been outwards. And this included the years of high growth of the economy before the 1970s. Jamaica, whose population had reached its first million in 1929, did not reach its second million until 1975 despite a high natural rate of increase.

The Federation of the West Indies finally came into existence on January 3, 1958, but the British government's joy at the prospect of adding another Dominion to the Commonwealth was short-lived. Disquiet among many Jamaicans with the federal system led to a referendum, in 1961, in which a small majority of the electorate voted to leave. Jamaica became independent the following year and the Federation soon collapsed.

Independence in 1962 took place at a time of rapid economic growth. There was, therefore, no need for the government to take unnecessary risks and public policy – fiscal and monetary – was relatively conservative. In particular, the currency remained the Jamaican pound until 1969, when it was replaced by the Jamaican dollar. The Bank of Jamaica, established in 1960 as a central bank, ensured that the Jamaican currency was at par with the British pound. As this was the era of fixed exchange rates under the Bretton Woods system, this meant that the Jamaican currency only changed value against the US dollar if the British pound was devalued and the Jamaican authorities followed suit (as in 1967).

The result was a stable currency for 15 years after independence in which the Jamaican currency was worth more than the US dollar. Even after the devaluation of the British pound in 1967, when the peg to sterling was maintained, the Jamaican currency was still worth US$1.2. And when the Bretton Woods system collapsed in 1971, the Bank of Jamaica soon established a new currency peg – this time to the US dollar – in which the Jamaican dollar was worth US$1.1.

This system survived until 1978, which meant that Jamaica had the ideal currency environment for several decades after the Second World War in which to promote international tourism during the age of jet travel. The island, of course, had been no stranger to wealthy visitors before the war, including many celebrities from the arts and literary worlds, but the numbers were small. Even in 1947, there were still only 53,000 visitors and most of these were short-term.[31]

A Jamaican Tourist Trade Development Board had been established in 1922, but after independence this became the Jamaican Tourist Board with an associated Ministry of Tourism. Growth was rapid with nearly 415,000 visitors by 1970. In that year, service exports (almost entirely derived from tourism) were valued at US$158 million, which was roughly half the value of merchandise exports. Jamaica was well on its way to becoming an economy dominated by exports of services, although it would not be until 1985 that service exports exceeded goods exports by value.

With exports surging as a result of mining and tourism, a stable currency and inflation under control, the government formed by the Jamaican Labour Party (JLP) after independence felt it had strong grounds for optimism. However, this optimism was severely dented as a result of major riots in 1968. Clearly, the Jamaican model based on free markets, acceptance of foreign capital and conservative macroeconomic policies was not working as intended.

The trigger for the riots was the decision by Prime Minister Hugh Shearer to ban the re-entry of Walter Rodney, a Guyanese lecturer employed by the University of the West Indies at Mona. Very quickly it became clear that it was not only middle-class intellectuals who had major grievances with the government. Rioting and looting by slum-dwellers in Kingston, the capital and largest city by far, showed the limited impact of the trickle-down economics practised by the pro-business government.

In truth, the government should not have been surprised. Land concessions to the mining companies and acquisitions by the multinational companies in agriculture coupled with a rising population had pushed the number of farms under five acres to nearly 80 per cent of the total by 1969, with an average size of 1.5

acres.[32] This was too small to make a living, and in the 15 years before 1969 some 150,000 left the countryside to live in Kingston. In the capital, work was scarce leading to very high rates of un- and underemployment and the growth of a gang culture that occupied an unhealthy symbiotic relationship with the political party system.

The growth of the economy, therefore, concealed a high degree of inequality and injustice. GDP per head at constant prices had increased by an average of 4.8 per cent per year between 1940 and 1970, an extraordinary achievement by comparison with the previous 150 years. Yet, dissatisfaction with the outcome ran deep in Jamaican society, and comparisons were soon made between the riots in 1968 and those in 1938.

This time there would be no Moyne Commission. Instead, it would be left to the political parties to provide a response. With elections in 1972 ejecting the JLP from power and bringing the People's National Party (PNP) into government, it was left to the new prime minister, Michael Manley (son of the conservative former premier Norman Manley), to articulate an appropriate response. And that response would prove to be anything but conservative.

10.4. Secular Stagnation

Voters going to the polls in 1972 could not have known that year would see the highest value ever for Jamaican GDP per head (at 2010 $US). Since then GDP per head has fallen sharply (1973–85), recovered modestly (1986–95), and then fluctuated (1996–2017) around a value that is still ten per cent below the level in 1972. Jamaican governments may have experimented with models of socialism, state capitalism, and free markets, but none have succeeded in permanently shifting the economy away from nearly 50 years of secular stagnation.

During this long period, the Jamaican economy has been subject to numerous external shocks, including sharp increases in the oil price and steep falls in the price of its main exports, but the same has been true of many other Caribbean economies that have proved more successful at weathering the storms. Jamaica, like other countries, has also been subject to IMF and World Bank conditionality during many of the past 50 years without any significant benefit in terms of the long-run sustainable rate of growth of GDP per head. It is has also been the recipient of both extremely harsh and very favourable treatment by the US government, depending on which government was in power.

Jamaica, in common with other Caribbean countries, has also faced significant changes in its external trading arrangements. CARICOM was launched in 1973, but – despite its ambition of creating a single market and economy – has never achieved its goals. Preferential access to the British market was replaced in 1975 with privileged access to the EEC under the Lomé Convention and its successors, but this was later eroded by changes imposed unilaterally by the EU. The Caribbean Basin Initiative (CBI) gave Jamaica special access to the US market from 1984, but this in turn was undermined as the US signed preferential trade agreements with countries outside the Caribbean.

The list of what has been responsible for Jamaica's dismal performance in recent decades is, therefore, a long one. It includes a hostile external environment in many years, international financial institutions and foreign governments with their own agendas, multinational companies with no real commitment to the country, a domestic business class that has shown little dynamism, and a political elite characterised by sharp sectarian divisions and operating in a party system corrupted by the large-scale purchase of votes. Trying to establish which of these has been the most damaging is an almost impossible task.

When Michael Manley was first elected as prime minister in 1972 on a radical agenda promoting redistribution of income and social justice, the economic environment was still favourable. This deteriorated very quickly, but the radical agenda remained in place. This, in turn, put huge strains on fiscal policy that could only be financed by an accommodating monetary policy. What followed was a fall in the exchange rate, a rise in inflation, a surge in public debt, and a confrontation with the Jamaican and foreign representatives of the established capitalist order.

When Manley lost power in 1980 and Edward Seaga became prime minister, it was widely assumed that Jamaica would return to its earlier high growth path. Yet, despite Seaga's market-friendly policies and strong support from the US government and the international financial institutions, this did not happen. When Seaga was replaced as prime minister by Manley in 1989, the economy was still suffering from many of the weaknesses that had first emerged after 1972. Jamaica, it would seem, was facing structural rather than cyclical impediments to growth. Neither Manley (1989–1992), no longer committed to a radical agenda, nor any of his successors have been able to find an answer.

Soon after becoming prime minister for the first time, Michael Manley had to deal with the impact of the 1973/4 quadrupling of oil prices. For a country almost wholly dependent on imported energy, this was a severe blow. Manley's response was an increase in the bauxite levy that improved the receipts in US dollars from the industry. Coupled with the substantial increase in world sugar prices at the time, this helped to protect the balance of payments, and the government felt sufficiently confident to press ahead with its ambitious plans for economic and social reform.

This required a large increase in government spending, and in 1976 the Bank of Jamaica Act was amended to allow the government to increase its borrowing to 30 per cent of expected revenues in any given year. The fiscal deficit increased from five per cent of GDP in 1972 to 24 per cent in 1976, and the Jamaican government, which had previously financed its deficits externally on concessional terms, now started to accumulate a substantial domestic public debt as well.

Inevitably, this put intense pressure on the exchange rate, which had been pegged to the US dollar in 1973. Therefore, the government was acutely conscious of the political risk from devaluation. Following re-election in 1976, however, the Manley government was forced to seek balance of payments assistance from the IMF. The currency peg was now ended, and the exchange rate against the US dollar would begin its precipitate decline (see figure 10.6) from J$1.78 when Manley left office in 1980 to nearly J$140 forty years later.

The collapse of the nominal exchange rate may have started during Manley's second administration (1976–80), but – as figure 10.6 shows – it has continued during the mandate of all other leaders. In the words of Owen Jefferson, former senior deputy governor of the Bank of Jamaica:[33]

> Jamaica's traditional pattern of exchange rate adjustment was to use monetary austerity to keep the par value stable for as long as possible. When the rate could no longer be defended, there would be an adjustment and a continuation of tight monetary policies. The recurring result would be depletion of foreign reserves, subsidization of imports and penalization of foreign exchange earners.

This pattern only ended in September 1991 when exchange controls were abolished and the exchange rate was free to float. Its value, which had been pegged at J$6.50 as recently as November 1989, had fallen to J$33 within five years. Since then, it has depreciated in almost every year without interruption (see figure 10.6).

Other countries facing similar problems, and there were many, had reacted by developing new sources of foreign exchange earnings through non-traditional exports. Jamaica was slow to do so. Exports are still dominated by traditional goods and services such as alumina and tourism. The most significant addition to the export list in the last 50 years was clothing, which was made possible by the tariff concessions under the Caribbean Basin Initiative (CBI). However, this sector had dwindled to insignificance by 2010 as a result of competition from cheaper sources. Non-traditional exports, therefore, consist mainly of food and drink, but these accounted for less than ten per cent of total exports of goods and services in 2017.[34]

Figure 10.6: Jamaica: Official Exchange Rate to US Dollar, 1972–2018

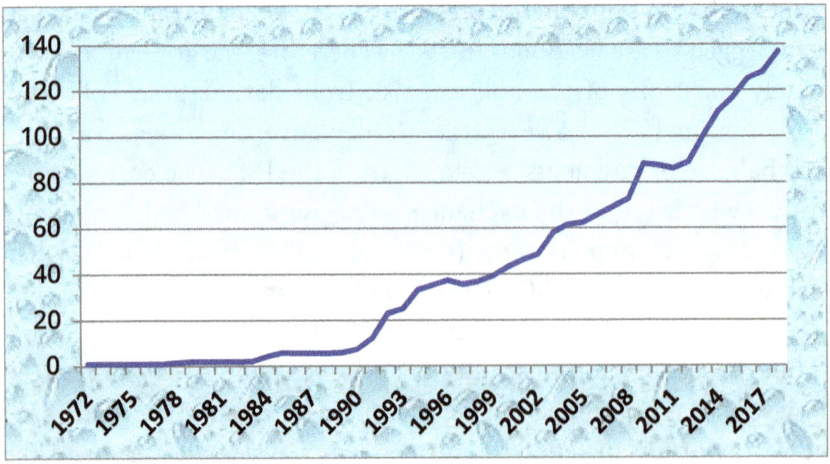

Source: World Bank, World Development Indicators.

Throughout much of the period of secular stagnation that started in the early 1970s, Jamaica has been under the tutelage of the international financial institutions – especially the IMF. The relationship with the fund was at first tense, as Jamaican governments were not only reluctant to accept the medicine but also sceptical about the diagnosis.[35] Over time, however, the resistance of the authorities crumbled, and Jamaica became a willing model for IMF prescriptions.

The fund now considers Jamaica a success based on the application of its favoured policies, including an exceptionally large primary fiscal surplus. The operation may have been successful in the eyes of the IMF, but the patient nearly died in the view of most commentators. For example, the Economic Commission for Latin America (ECLAC), the inter-governmental body operating under UN auspices and by no means a radical organisation, concluded that the dismal growth rates achieved under IMF surveillance had become endemic and that 'achieving stronger growth than this will depend on improved tourism receipts, lower energy costs, and higher remittance flows.'[36] Jamaica, of course, has very little control over any of these variables. In particular, remittances (already enormous) will only increase if there is further outward migration – a dismal recipe for a country's future.

Figure 10.7: Jamaica: Public Debt Service as % age of GNI and Exports, 1976–2016

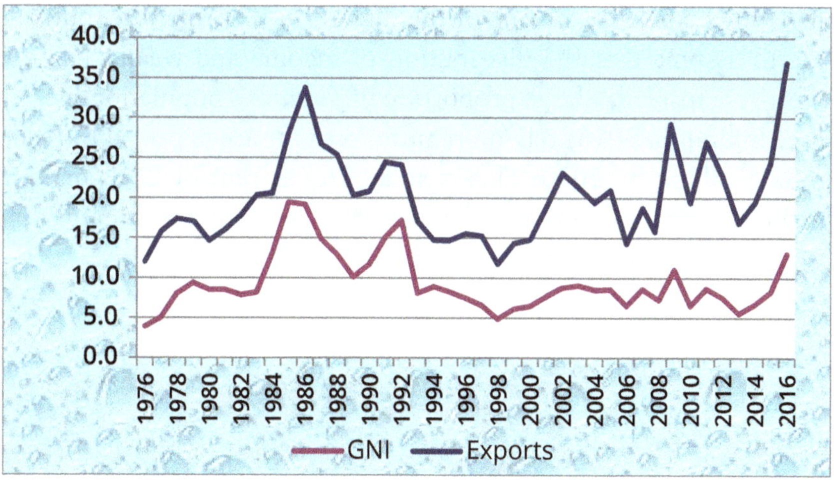

Source: World Bank, World Development Indicators.

Of all the reasons why the international financial institutions have been unable to put Jamaica back on a high growth path, perhaps the most important is the size of the debt burden.[37] Jamaica's income per head is too high to qualify for official debt reduction schemes under the Heavily Indebted Poor Country (HIPC) Initiative and its geopolitical status too weak to force its private creditors to accept a large 'haircut' on the nominal value of the commercial debt. Meanwhile, the debt owed to the international financial institutions, a large part of the total, is considered sacrosanct and cannot be adjusted.

After many years of IMF supervision, the public debt was still more than 100 per cent of GDP in 2018, and its servicing (see figure 10.7) constitutes an enormous proportion of both Gross National Income (GNI) and exports of goods and services. Furthermore, these proportions at first *increased* rather than decreased during the period of intense fund surveillance since 2013. Jamaica has, therefore, joined a small group of countries caught in a low-level equilibrium trap caused by a debt burden that can only be lifted through faster growth – a growth that is unattainable under the macroeconomic restrictions imposed by the international financial institutions.

Social conditions in Jamaica, therefore, remain deeply unsatisfactory. In 2018, the unemployment rate was still in double digits, youth unemployment exceeded 25 per cent, net migration outwards remained high, and income per head was stagnant. No measures of income inequality have been published since 2004, when the Gini coefficient was one of the highest in the Americas, but it is safe to assume that the distribution of income and wealth has not improved. Instead, a large proportion of Jamaica's population (nearly three million in 2018) rely on remittances that are expected to reach US$2.5 billion by 2020. This is some 16 per cent of GDP, making Jamaica one of the countries that are most dependent on what is sent back by family members living abroad.

NOTES

1. From 1830 to 1850, there was a structural change in the Jamaican economy in which the share of exports in GDP declined sharply. See G. Eisner, *Jamaica, 1830–1930: A Study in Economic Growth* (Manchester: Manchester University Press, 1961), 237. From 1850 to 1930, the share was largely unchanged.
2. See https://www.ucl.ac.uk/lbs.
3. See Statistical Appendix.
4. See *Report from the Select Committee on West India Colonies* (London: 1842), 325.
5. Compensation paid for Jamaican slaves was £6,121,446 out of total compensation of £20 million, of which £16,356,661 was paid to owners of slaves in the British West Indies. See H. Beckles, *Britain's Black Debt: Reparations for Caribbean Slavery and Native Genocide* (Kingston, Jamaica: University of the West Indies, 2013), 155 and N. Draper, *The Price of Emancipation: Slave-ownership, Compensation and British Society at the End of Savery* (Cambridge, MA: Cambridge University Press, 2010), 139.
6. See K.M. Butler, *The Economics of Emancipation: Jamaica and Barbados, 1823–43* (Chapel Hill, NC: University of North Carolina Press, 1995), 55.
7. See, for example, J. Phillippo, *Jamaica: Its Past and Present State* (London: John Snow, 1843); D. Hall, *Free Jamaica, 1838–1865: An Economic History* (New Haven, CT: Yale University Press, 1959); M.C. Campbell, *The Dynamics of Change in a Slave Society* (Cranbury, NJ: Associated University Presses, 1976; and E. Brodber, *The Second Generation of Freemen in Jamaica, 1907–1944* (Gainesville, FL: University of Florida Press, 2004).
8. See Eisner, *Jamaica, 1830–1930: A Study in Economic Growth*, table 8.1 and table 8.2.
9. See *Report from the Select Committee on West India Colonies*, 332.
10. On immigration from Africa, see M.E. Thomas, *Jamaica and Voluntary Laborers from Africa, 1840–1865* (Gainesville, FL: University of Florida Press, 1974). For China and India, see W. Look Lai, *Indentured Labor, Caribbean Sugar: Chinese and Indian Migrants to the British West Indies, 1838–1918* (Baltimore, MD: Johns Hopkins University Press, 1993).
11. See Look Lai, *Indentured Labor, Caribbean Sugar*), 276, table 5 and table 6.
12. See Statistical Appendix.
13. The phasing out of imperial preferences for sugar was supposed to have ended in 1848, but special pleading by the planters secured a delay until 1854.

14. Logwood, from which a natural dye can be extracted, had a variety of uses. The most important was as a colouring agent in the European and North American textile industry.
15. The British government passed in 1854 the Encumbered Estates Act in order to make it easier for the planters in Jamaica and the rest of the West Indies to sell their lands to others who might be more interested in modernisation.
16. See https://scholar.library.miami.edu/emancipation/jamaica4.htm.
17. See Hall, *Free Jamaica, 1838–1865*, 244.
18. See G.J. Heuman, *The Killing Time: The Morant Bay Rebellion in Jamaica* (Knoxville, TN: University of Tennessee Press, 1995).
19. Governor Edward John Eyre was responsible for the suppression of the rebellion and the execution of George William Gordon, a member of the Jamaican Assembly. His brutal tactics led him to face multiple charges in the UK, but he was exonerated on all of them, and the state paid him a full pension.
20. See R.T. Hill, *Cuba and Porto Rico, with the Other Islands of the West Indies: Their Topography, Climate, Flora, Products, Industries, Cities, People, Political Conditions, etc.* (New York, NY: The Century Co., 1898), 217.
21. See Statistical Appendix.
22. See M.K. Bacchus, *Education as and for Legitimacy: Developments in West Indian Education between 1846 and 1895* (Waterloo, Canada: Wilfrid Laurier University Press, 1994), 34–35.
23. See K.E.A. Monteith, *Depression to Decolonization: Barclays Bank (DCO) in the West Indies, 1926–1962* (Kingston, Jamaica: University of the West Indies Press, 2008), 19–20.
24. See A.E. Aspinall, *The British West Indies: Their History, Resources and Progress* (London: Pitman, 1912), 363–64.
25. Public revenue and expenditure per head (1930 US$) in 1900 had reached US$10.90 and US$11.20 respectively. Thirty-five years later, the figures were exactly the same. See Statistical Appendix.
26. See E.M.L. Petras, *Jamaican Labor Migration: White Capital and Black Labor, 1850–1930* (Boulder, CO: Westview Press, 1988), *passim.*
27. The British government did not make the report public until 1945 to prevent its portrait of the conditions in the British West Indies being used as German propaganda in the Second World War.
28. See 'Background to West Indian Federation,' *The World Today* 6, no. 6 (June 1950): 263.
29. See IBRD, *The Economic Development of Jamaica* (Baltimore, MD: Published for International Bank for Reconstruction and Development by the Johns Hopkins Press, 1952), 65.

30. See Statistical Appendix.
31. See IBRD, *The Economic Development of Jamaica*, 90–91.
32. See T. Munroe, and D. Robotham. *Struggles of the Jamaican People* (London: WLL, 1977), 169–70.
33. O. Jefferson, *Stabilization and Stagnation in the Jamaican Economy, 1972–97: Some Reflections on Macroeconomic Policy over the Past Twenty-five Years* (Kingston, Jamaica: Canoe Press, 1999), 201.
34. They did, however, account for about 20 per cent of exports of goods.
35. See M. Pologone, E. Rangel-González, and L. Blanco-González, 'Wrong Variable: Foreign Variables and Monetary Policy in Jamaica,' *Social and Economic Studies* 63, no. 1 (2014): 57–87.
36. See ECLAC, Economic Survey of Latin America and the Caribbean 2018, section on Jamaica, 1.
37. This had reached over US$16 billion by the end of 2016, representing US$5,616 per person.

Chapter 11
TRINIDAD AND TOBAGO

Trinidad and Tobago became a unified British colony in 1889 and independent in 1962. For almost a century, the production of goods has been largely synonymous with the energy sector, which is located in Trinidad. At the beginning of the nineteenth century, however, when Trinidad was ceded to Great Britain by Spain, it was sugar that dominated the economy of both islands, and this was more important in Tobago. And today in the service economy, the outstanding feature is the success of Tobago in international tourism. Thus, the fortunes of the two islands have fluctuated with the changing global environment for trade in goods and services.

Tobago had first become a British colony in 1666, although its possession was not secured until the end of the eighteenth century. It was a classic sugar economy producing raw sugar, molasses, and rum for export before the Napoleonic Wars. However, the plantocracy, largely non-resident, soon lost interest in response to the end of the slave trade, new opportunities elsewhere, and finally the end of slavery itself. The sugar sector survived, but it was a pale shadow of its former self. Underinvestment made it impossible to achieve the reduction in costs needed to compete when the world price of sugar fell and many Tobagonians emigrated – including to Trinidad. Annexation by Trinidad in 1889 and the loss of fiscal autonomy in 1899 were the logical outcomes.

If Trinidad was the poor relation at the time of the British invasion in 1797, that would soon change. Sugar exports soared, despite a brief slump after emancipation, thanks to an abundant supply of land and immigrant labour until the collapse of world prices towards the end of the nineteenth century. Trinidad by then, however, had developed an important smallholding sector based primarily on cacao exports.

This, together with the asphalt from the pitch lake and a few other non-traditional exports, helped Trinidad to avoid the worst effects of the depression that afflicted the sugar industry in other British West Indian colonies.

The unified colony of Trinidad and Tobago faced an uncertain future until the start of oil exports just before the First World War. This gave the colony an asset unlike any other in the British West Indies. Within a generation, sugar had become the junior partner as the colony made the sometimes painful transition to becoming a major energy exporter. The Second World War emphasised the geopolitical role it would now play in the energy decisions of the oil multinationals and the Western alliance. By the end of the 1950s, Trinidad and Tobago had many of the characteristics of an advanced economy, and its colonial status was increasingly anachronistic.

Independence, after a brief period in the Federation of the West Indies, brought further gains for the energy sector. However, efforts to diversify the economy away from its dependence on oil and gas proved frustrating. Excessive ambition and mismanagement would, in due course, lead to economic crisis, a deep recession, and major riots. The surge in world energy prices eventually allowed Trinidad and Tobago to stabilise the economy and return to a sustainable, if less ambitious, growth path encapsulated in *Vision 2020*. This addressed some of the accumulated problems, but still left many islanders feeling excluded or marginalised.

11.1. Tobago: The Nineteenth Century

When Tobago was ceded by France to Great Britain under the Treaty of Paris in 1763, it still had a small Amerindian population. Their ancestral lands, together with the rest of the island, were then surveyed by the Commissioners for the Sale of Lands in the Ceded Islands and, by 1768, some 77 British individuals had purchased properties. Only 20 were resident, the others either living in Great Britain or in the rest of the British West Indies.

The main export crop produced, at first, by these British landowners was not sugar but cotton. Indeed, the quality of Tobago's cotton became legendary and was praised as 'the finest quality ever brought to the English market, or probably ever grown'.[1] However, France recaptured Tobago in 1781 during the US War of Independence. The brief period of French rule coincided with the slave revolt in Haiti, leading to a collapse in sugar production and a shortage of sugar on the world market. This boosted the fortunes of sugar in other islands, and Tobago planters had begun the switch from cotton even before the island was taken by Great Britain in 1793.

By the end of the eighteenth century, Tobago had become completely dependent on sugar exports. Sugar was, at first, a profitable crop, leading to the expression 'as rich as a Tobago planter'. However, 1799 would turn out to be the peak year for the volume of sugar exports. As in Jamaica, the planters lost interest both in sugar and the island itself over the next few decades. The evidence given by William Robert Keith Douglas, an absentee landlord and member of parliament, in 1832 to the Select Committee on the State of the West India Colonies captured their mood:[2]

> The consequence of this [abolition of the slave trade] was, that the surplus produce of this country going to the Continent of Europe was brought into immediate competition with the production of countries raising produce; under such different circumstances, the inequality of the competition, as regards slave labour, by countries still carrying on the Slave Trade, began from the first moment of that competition to press against our planters, and subsequently the increased supplies, together with the greater advantages which foreigners have had in raising those supplies, has pressed down the prices, and been a very main cause of producing that distress and derangement which our planters now suffer under.

Soon after giving this statement, Douglas, a wealthy Scottish landowner and younger brother of the Marquess of Queensbury, received nearly £11,000 in compensation following the emancipation of his 576 slaves.[3] This huge sum (nearly £10 million in current prices) was not reinvested in Tobago but used in the UK for a variety of purposes and to support his political interests even though he left the House of Commons in 1832.

The colony was an island in which the slave population under British rule had been built up quickly through slave imports. However, the death rate among these slaves was among the highest in the Caribbean.[4] This changed very little before emancipation. The number of slaves, therefore, fell after abolition, although they always accounted for around 90 per cent of the total population.

The demographics of Tobago were fragile. The Amerindian population had all but disappeared by the end of the Napoleonic Wars, only one family being recorded in 1812. The white population was a mere 439 even in 1807 and outnumbered by the free blacks. In 1810, there were 18,000 slaves out of a population of 19,600, but this had fallen to 15,050 out of a population of 16,000 in 1820. On the eve of emancipation, there were 11,765 slaves out of a population of 13,198.

The population continued to fall, reaching a low point of 11,721 a few years later. However, the death rate improved dramatically after emancipation. By 1840, births exceeded deaths and, for the rest of the century, the natural rate of increase was positive. The population started to grow and had recovered its 1810 level by the mid-1890s. In 1900, just after full union with Trinidad, it had reached 20,000.

The increase in the population was nothing like as fast as implied by the difference between births and deaths. In every five-year period after 1850, net migration was outwards (see figure 11.1) and reached in many years more than one per cent of the population. Indeed, without outward migration the population in 1900 would have been 27,000 – one-third higher than the actual level.

Figure 11.1: Tobago: Net Migration (%age of population), 1851–1900

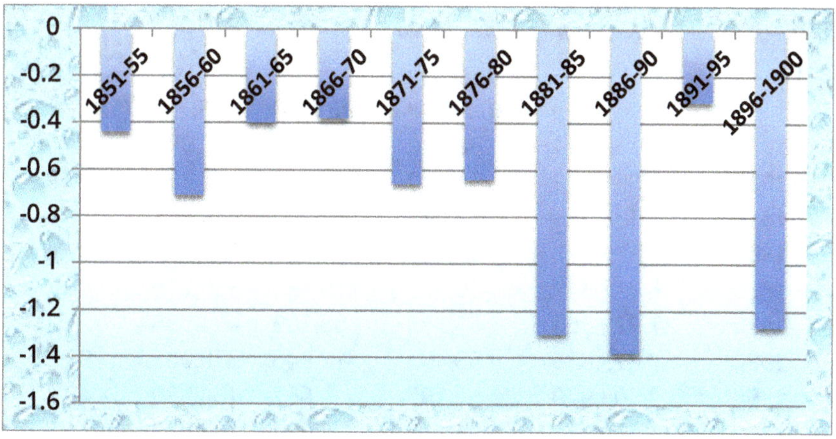

Source: Statistical Appendix.

Figure 11.2: Tobago: Exports per head (1860 US$), 1820–1900

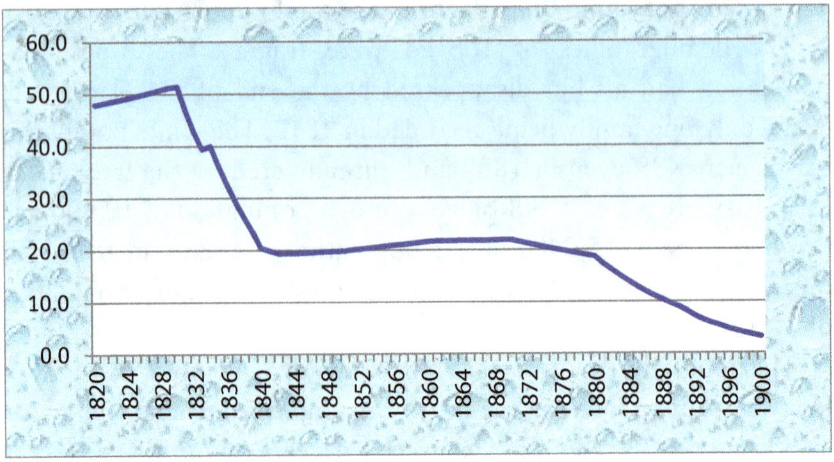

Source: Statistical Appendix.

Most emigrants went to Trinidad, and the main reason for their departure was the decline of the export sector in Tobago. After a brief period of rising exports per head after 1820, the numbers collapsed (see figure 11.2). Between 1830 and 1840, there was a dramatic fall in exports per head and another collapse after 1880. Domestic exports per head, which had been nearly US$50 in 1820, had fallen to less than US$10 at the time of annexation by Trinidad in 1889 and to less than US$5 ten years later when Tobago lost all autonomy. This was one of the most spectacular declines in the export sector both in the British West Indies and in the Caribbean as a whole.

Table 11.1: Tobago: Domestic Exports, 1820–1900

	Sugar (lb)	Molasses (gallons)	Rum (gallons)	Exports (US$)	to UK (%)
1820	15,138,144	30,940	357,770	666,960	94.6
1830	12,651,072	158,420	379,029	567,758	90.9
1840	4,562,656	32,040	132,750	419,988	99.0
1850	5,856,935	15,925	96,126	256,166	97.0
1860	6,992,347	9,633	118,890	330,219	91.0
1870	7,829,360	64,775	88,589	404,535	96.1
1880	7,613,835	58,403	17,943	375,087	91.7
1890	3,503,920	53,107	4,667	134,599	40.1
1900	1,119,762	16,162	8,387	58,732	41.7

Source: Statistical Appendix.

The fall in exports was, of course, due to the decline of the main industry (sugar, molasses, and rum). The volume of sugar exports (see table 11.1) fell between 1820 and 1830, but it was a modest decline with both molasses and rum exports increasing. Indeed, exports per head, in this decade, actually rose as a result of population decline (see figure 11.2). In the 1830s, however, following emancipation and the end of the apprenticeship period, there was a precipitate fall. Absentee landlords lost interest in their estates and many of the former slaves left to work for themselves on small farms.

In an effort to lower costs, the planters had started to introduce the *metayage* system in 1842. This system, which was widely used in other parts of the Caribbean after the end of slavery, was defined by Kaye Dowland in 1849 as follows:[5]

> The general terms of the Metairie System are that the Renter cuts his Canes, and has them conveyed to the Mill, and that he finds the Boilerman and Mill Gang all at his own expense. That the cultivation be under the control of the Proprietor, who shall supply at his own Cost, Stock and Carts and Machinery necessary to grind the canes, and make the sugar in the usual manner. The Sugar, when made to be divided in equal portions, and the Proprietor to have all Rum and Molasses. Renter to furnish his own barrels or Vessels.

Following a major hurricane in 1847 and the collapse of the West India Bank in the same year, the *metayage* system became the dominant system despite the fact that it had no legal status until 1888. It helped to effect a modest recovery in the volume of sugar exported until 1880 (see table 11.1), after which exports once again collapsed as a result of the fall in prices. When the West India Royal Commission took evidence from Tobago residents in 1897, the sugar industry had virtually disappeared. A local committee, in its explanation to the commissioners, put all the blame on prices and none on themselves:[6]

> Private friends in the United Kingdom assure us that they are ashamed to consume sugar at the present low prices, knowing as they do that it means the ruin of their old West Indian Colonies. We take this as an index that if the present critical condition of the West Indian sugar industry be clearly laid before the British public they will readily acquiesce in whatever measures may be deemed necessary for its revival. We venture to add that

> the only possible remedy, in our opinion, is to neutralize the beet sugar bounties in the way most convenient to the British Government.

These pleas fell on deaf ears, and the trade links between Tobago and Great Britain began to wither. Even by 1890, less than half of domestic exports were going to the UK (see table 11.1). Instead, Tobago had turned to other activities, especially raising livestock, which found a market in Trinidad. This could not reverse the economic decline of Tobago, however, and the value of exports by the end of the century did not even reach US$60,000 – less than ten per cent of what it had been in 1820 (see table 11.1). Labourers continued to emigrate in large numbers.

The decay of its major industry, on which public revenue was so dependent, meant that Tobago's constitutional status was bound to come up for revision. Tobago had become a Crown Colony in 1876, and a few years later the British government had proposed a federal government with Grenada, St Lucia, and St Vincent. This was roundly denounced in Tobago, although the alternative – union with Trinidad – was not much welcomed either. However, the dismal state of the Tobagonian economy led to the annexation of Tobago by Trinidad in 1889.

Annexation left Tobago in charge of its own public revenue and expenditure. However, economic decline continued so that by 1898 revenue had fallen to £8,213 (US$2 per head of population and one of the lowest in the Caribbean).[7] Tobago was now, in effect, bankrupt and the only way forward was complete union with Trinidad. This took place in 1899, leaving Tobago with no fiscal autonomy at all. From now on, both before and after independence, Tobago would be the junior partner in the new country of Trinidad and Tobago.

11.2. Trinidad: The Nineteenth Century

Nominally Spanish for nearly three centuries, Trinidad was never a priority for Spain's rulers. Its capital, St Joseph, in 1772 had a population of only 326 Spaniards and 417 Amerindians.[8] This would soon change, however, as a result of the decision by the Spanish crown in 1783 to permit immigration by Roman Catholics who were subjects of any country in alliance with Spain. The first to respond were French subjects in the rest of the Caribbean. They brought slaves with them, and 14 years later the population of Trinidad was 17,643 – almost the same as Tobago – made up of 2,086 whites, 4,466 free people of colour, 1,082 Amerindians, and 10,009 slaves.

Trinidad became British following a successful invasion in 1797. Unlike many other islands in the Caribbean, however, it was not returned to the former sovereign power at the Treaty of Amiens in 1802. Instead, Trinidad was ceded by Spain to Great Britain and became a Crown Colony, although at first it retained Spanish laws and the majority of the population spoke French. With the arrival of new settlers and their slaves from other parts of the British Caribbean, this would be transformed. By 1810, the population had reached 35,270 – almost double that of Tobago – of whom 26,200 were slaves.[9]

The French and British settlers were attracted by the offer of fertile land with good prospects for growing sugar cane. For this, however, they needed labour and therefore slaves. The decision by the British Parliament in 1807 to abolish the slave trade was seen as a potential disaster by these landowners. With the death rate among slaves far higher than the birth rate, there was no chance of the labour force expanding and every reason to think it would shrink.

Fortunately for these new settlers, the abolition law had a loophole that allowed owners in other parts of the British West Indies to bring their slaves with them when migrating to Trinidad.[10] Over 7,000 slaves were brought in between abolition and emancipation, in many cases using a generous interpretation of the loophole. As a result, the slave population declined only slowly and was still in excess of 20,000 in 1834 when slavery was ended. Because free migration had continued, however, the population in that year was some 44,000 so that slaves made up less than 50 per cent. This was different from the situation in the 'old' British West Indian colonies, where slaves constituted 80–90 per cent of the total.

There were some 2,000 claims for compensation by slave owners in Trinidad, but the amounts claimed were small compared with longer established colonies. The largest claim was for 234 slaves by William Hardin Burnley, who also successfully claimed for 202 slaves on another estate. His son, William Frederick, would go on to become a successful Glasgow merchant and marry into another family that also had received compensation for ownership of slaves in Trinidad.[11]

The birth rate in Trinidad did not normally exceed the death rate until the 1870s. Indeed, there were many years when the death rate exceeded 50 per 1,000 as a result of outbreaks of diseases such as cholera.[12] Yet, the population rose rapidly and had reached 110,000 by 1871 and nearly 250,000 by 1900. The increase was mainly due to net inward migration, which averaged two to three per cent of the population in most years (see figure 11.3).

Figure 11.3: Trinidad: Net Migration (%age of Population), 1846–1900

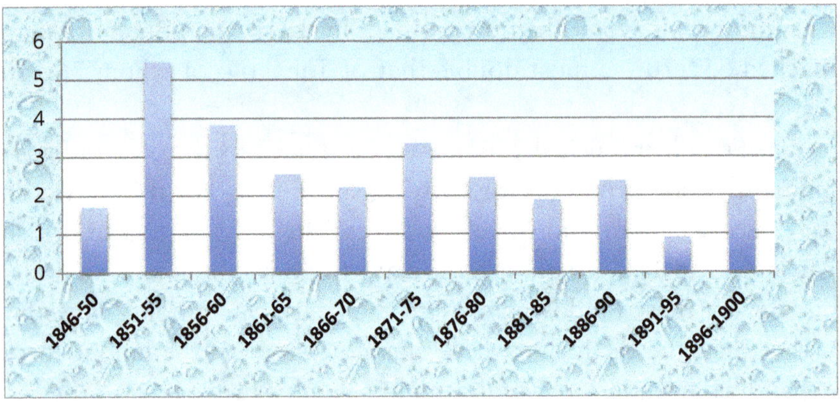

Source: Statistical Appendix.

The case for mass immigration had, in fact, been made by the planters as soon as slavery ended. A shortage of labour, they argued, had led to wage rates in Trinidad that were higher than in other parts of the British West Indies. Meanwhile, squatting – while in theory subject to legal sanctions – went largely unpunished as the planters had few effective means of coercion. And vagrancy laws were simply ignored while a culture of contracts was hard to establish. Giving evidence in 1842 to the Select Committee on West India Colonies, the same William Hardin Burnley stated:[13]

> The supply of labour has diminished considerably amongst the original labourers of the estates; but very nearly, probably, to the exact amount, the deficiency has been supplied and filled up by immigration; so that I presume, from what is stated in the Trinidad evidence, that the amount of labour at the present moment is pretty nearly what it was at the first period of

> emancipation; that is, with reference to field labour; but we find with reference to manufacturing labour, that is not the case; and we are of the opinion that unless contracts for labour can be entered into, no number brought into the island will give us that continuous labour in crop time which will be found necessary to take off the crops.

Voluntary immigration initially was from Africa itself, but it was not long before the planters resolved to find a solution to their problems in indentured labour from Asia, especially British India. Between 1845 and 1917, when the Indian government ended the practice, the numbers arriving had reached 143,939 with only a small number returning at the end of their contractual period of indenture.[14] By 1891, Indians accounted for 31 per cent of the total population. Their passage was subsidised by the local government, which dedicated up to one-fifth of public revenue on immigration schemes.[15]

Figure 11.4: Trinidad: Exports per head (1860 US$), 1820–1900

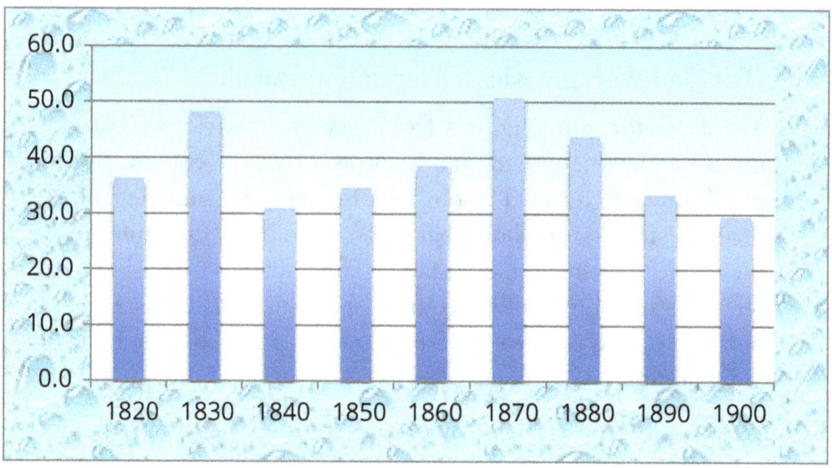

Source: Statistical Appendix.

Trinidad, therefore, had one of the highest rates of inward migration in the Caribbean in the nineteenth century. And it was both cause and effect of the sustained rise in exports during the century. This increase was so strong that Trinidad, despite a six-fold increase in population between 1820 and 1900, was able to increase exports per head in many years (see figure 11.4). It was only during the 1830s, when the colony was adjusting to the end of slavery and apprenticeship and during the years at the end of the century when sugar prices were collapsing, that exports per head fell. As a result, exports per head in 1900 were similar to their level in 1820.

Trinidad avoided the fate of many other Caribbean colonies in the nineteenth century. It witnessed a steep rise in population and exports, while public expenditure per head was high by the standards of the day (in fairness, so was taxation).[16] For four decades after 1840 it had experience a big expansion in the volume of sugar exported, in contrast to Jamaica and many other colonies, while at the same time avoiding the risk of becoming too dependent on this one commodity.

Sugar expansion ended after 1880 (see table 11.2) and the planters were quick to blame the bounties offered to sugar beet producers in continental Europe, the 30 per cent customs duties applied by Venezuela[17] and the taxes raised by the local government to finance the immigration schemes. They did, however, cut their costs sharply even if their methods were exceedingly brutal. Walter Mills, for example, gave evidence to the Royal Commission in 1897 on behalf of the Trinidad Working Men's Association stated:[18]

> The Protector of Immigrants had to increase the rice ration of the coolie by one pound, and he proved that the coolies were physically unfit for field labour because they were underfed. He brought statistics to show that in other colonies the ration of the coolies was much more than in Trinidad. It is surprising to see when the immigrants are landed here such well set, strong, bulky men, and in a few months they get to be debilitated and are sent into the hospitals.

Sugar was, therefore, no longer the engine of growth, but other exports would rise in importance. Ever since the arrival of the French planters, cacao had been grown. Not subject to economies of scale, cacao was an ideal crop for smallholders able to purchase crown land. It was also a particularly attractive crop for Indian labourers at the end of their period of indenture. As a result, the volume of exports rose steadily at first and spectacularly after 1870 (see table 11.2). And by 1900 the value of cacao exports was greater than that of sugar.

Table 11.2: Trinidad: Principal Exports by Volume, 1820–1900

	Sugar (lb)	Molasses (gal)	Rum (gal)	Cacao (lb)	Coffee (lb)	Asphalt (tons)
1820	30,000,000	153,930	53,270	1,780,379	347,399	
1830	41,390,804	1,074,960	4,320	1,057,885	108,863	
1840	31,201,940	704,890	2,420	2,457,486	36,288	85
1850	41,145,243	828,677	33,300	4,561,444	131,480	
1860	59,683,307	615,421	151,550	5,494,121		1,565
1870	105,644,747	1,896,309	19,426	6,743,606		5,661
1880	122,312,739	1,568,105	34,540	11,150,117		24,364
1890	109,736,453	1,931,674		14,094,662		84,319
1900	89,987,164	761,283	25,226	30,383,808	19,152	158,752

Source: Statistical Appendix

The other export of importance by the end of the century was asphalt from the famous pitch lake. Exports rose rapidly after 1860 (see table 11.2) in response to global demand. Although Trinidad would lose its monopoly before the end of the century (Venezuela would become another supplier), the value of exports was nearly US$860,000 by 1900, making it the third most important commodity for Trinidad. And asphalt was one of the reasons why less than half of Trinidad's exports by the end of the century went to the UK, the US having becoming a major destination as well.

11.3. Trinidad and Tobago: Before Independence

By 1900, one year after full unification, Trinidad and Tobago had avoided the pitfalls of most British Caribbean colonies whose fortunes had sunk in line with the sugar price. Non-traditional exports, including asphalt and the world famous Angostura bitters,[19] were contributing nearly 15 per cent of domestic exports, and there was a thriving entrepôt trade valued at nearly US$2 million despite the problems with Venezuela.

Even more important, smallholdings in cacao had given the colony an alternative to cane sugar as a principal source of export earnings. These, in turn, not only paid for imports but also provided the basis for a level of public revenue that both financed immigration schemes and public services such as education. Indeed, Trinidad and Tobago now boasted one of the finest schools in the Caribbean (Queen's Royal College) and, at the start of the twentieth century, 11 per cent of the population were in full-time education compared with only 3.2 per cent in 1870.[20]

The unified colony had a population of 268,449 in 1900. And it was growing fast thanks to a combination of natural increase and net inward migration. The natural rate of increase – births less deaths – was around one per cent at the start of the twentieth century and would rise to three per cent just before independence due mainly to a fall in the death rate. By contrast, the birth rate barely changed at all.

While other Caribbean colonies experienced high levels of net outward migration at the beginning of the twentieth century, as a result of depressed conditions at home and job opportunities in Panama and Cuba, Trinidad and Tobago witnessed the opposite (see figure 11.5). This would change in the First World War, when volunteers left for the front in 1914 and after the Indian Legislative Council in 1916 called on its government to end indentured labour 'at the earliest opportunity'. Yet, despite this, Trinidad and Tobago experienced net inward migration in most years during the inter-war period, and the population approached 500,000 when the Second World War started.

Figure 11.5: Trinidad and Tobago: Net Migration,1900–60

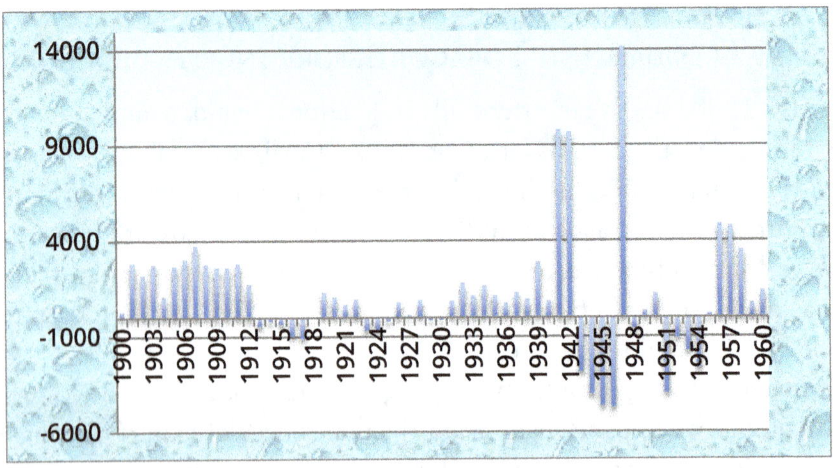

Source: Statistical Appendix.

The promising economic performance at the start of the century took place despite a series of difficult problems. The depression in the sugar industry continued. The disputes with Venezuela – over the Antillean surtax, maritime boundaries, and smuggling – did not end with the assumption of power by President Vicente Gómez (1908–35). On the contrary, the development of the oil industry in Venezuela with British capital meant that the British government was likely to sacrifice the colony's interests in the event of any conflicts.

It was, therefore, fortunate for Trinidad and Tobago that the oil industry was established early on. The first oil well had been drilled in 1857 close to the pitch lake, but production did not begin until 1908. From then onwards, development was steady, if unspectacular, and the colony was exporting nearly 14 million gallons on the eve of the First World War. Because of the low price per gallon (just over two cents), however, the contribution to export earnings was still small.

This soon changed. By 1917, the contribution was ten per cent, by 1922 it was 20 per cent, and by 1929 it was over 40 per cent. Then, as the value of other commodities collapsed in the Great Depression, oil started to contribute more than half of export earnings, reaching two-thirds on the eve of the Second World War. Petroleum refining developed in line with crude oil production, earning the colony increased revenue, and from 1930 onwards Trinidad was importing Venezuelan oil for refining on the island.[21]

Figure 11.6: Trinidad and Tobago: Exports per head (1930 US$), 1900–60

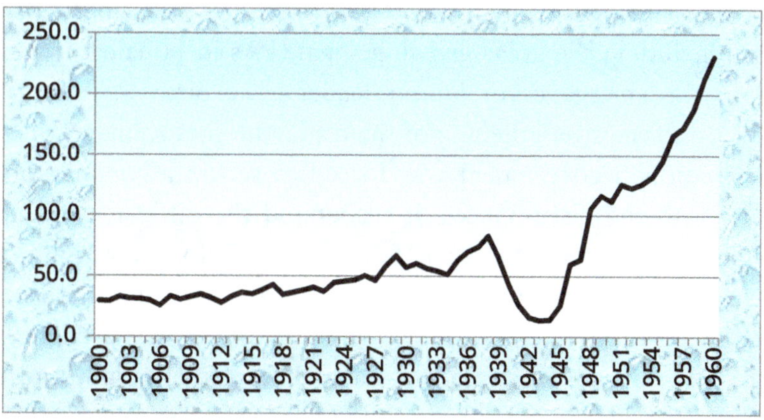

Source: Statistical Appendix.

Thanks to the oil industry, Trinidad and Tobago experienced a steady rise in exports per head after 1900 – at least until the Second World War (see figure 11.6). Although there was a modest recovery in the sugar industry, helped above all by the application of British imperial preference in the inter-war period, the rise in exports per head was largely due to the oil industry. By contrast, cacao exports peaked in 1921 and fell steadily thereafter. They were hit first by the decision of the colonial government to end almost entirely sale of crown lands for agricultural purposes (preferring to reserve it for oil exploration) and then by the advent of disease.

Trinidad and Tobago had now transitioned from a sugar to an oil economy. However, as other countries had found out the hard way, oil could bring foreign exchange to pay for imports and public revenue to pay for government spending, but it was not good at creating jobs. Trinidad and Tobago was, therefore, not exempt from the labour unrest that afflicted many British West Indian colonies in the 1930s, leading to the creation of the Moyne Commission just before the Second World War.

Trinidad, as opposed to Tobago, had been no stranger to unrest long before the 1930s. There had been riots in Port of Spain in 1881 and 1884 as a result of police brutality during Carnival celebrations, and in 1903 there were major disturbances over the (lack of) water supply.[22] However, it was the riots in 1937 that shook Trinidad to the core. These began in the oilfields over the failure of pay to keep up with the rising cost of living, but soon spread to other parts of the island, including the areas growing sugar.[23] As in Jamaica, it would lead to the emergence of labour leaders, the birth of nationalist politics, and the strengthening of the trade union movement.

The colonial government was forced to set up a commission of inquiry into the disturbances. It recognised the difficult conditions facing many workers and their families, but before any significant measures to ameliorate the situation could be implemented, the Second World War erupted. In September 1940, the British government had offered the US administration a naval base on Trinidad, and the economy would become subject to the needs of the allied war effort in the next five years.[24]

The result was a collapse of all the main exports (see table 11.3). The volume of sugar exports fell by half between 1939 and 1943, cacao by two-thirds between 1940 and 1943 and asphalt by four-fifths between 1939 and 1942. The biggest fall of all was found in oil, but this was a consequence of the oil and its derivatives being sold to the US naval base at Chaguaramas and therefore no longer being considered exports. And the refined oil not only went into the ships, assembled in Trinidad for the Atlantic convoy, but also into the planes that used Trinidad for refuelling. This reinforced even further Trinidad and Tobago's status as an oil economy.

Table 11.3: Trinidad and Tobago: Principal Exports, 1939–45

	Sugar (lb)	Cacao (lb)	Asphalt (tons)	Oil (gallons)	Exports (US$)
1939	256,144,000	16,800,000	66,000	359,000,000	24,708,600
1940	173,152,000	24,864,000	29,000	198,000,000	18,322,720
1941	242,592,000	18,816,000	26,000	48,000,000	12,404,340
1942	188,944,000	10,080,000	12,000	14,000,000	8,684,650
1943	121,856,000	8,064,000	12,000	12,000,000	8,128,510
1944	123,424,000	10,640,000	17,000	13,000,000	8,886,150
1945	132,944,000	7,728,000	11,000	118,000,000	15,725,060

Source: Statistical Appendix.

The refining of imported crude oil became increasingly important, and by the end of the 1950s more oil was being refined from imported than domestic sources. By then, Texaco, a US company, had entered the market to join the established British firms, and new opportunities were presenting themselves. The exploitation of natural gas was underway and a fertiliser plant was opened in 1960. And the energy companies were contributing directly about one-third of government revenue throughout the 1950s while being responsible for nearly half of all fixed investment.[25]

The colony's dependence on the energy industry was confirmed with the publication of the first estimates of the national accounts. In 1952, oil (together with the much less important asphalt) contributed 28.6 per cent to GDP at factor cost, while agriculture, forestry, and fishing was only 17.8 per cent (see table 11.4). By 1961, the year before independence, the oil share had risen further while agriculture had fallen to 11.3 per cent despite the boost to sugar exports from the Commonwealth Sugar Agreement in 1951.

Table 11.4: Trinidad and Tobago: GDP at Factor Cost (Percentage), 1952–61

	1952	1955	1958	1961
Agriculture, forestry, fishing	17.8	17.6	13.7	11.3
Oil and asphalt	28.6	29.2	32.4	30.5
Manufacturing	13.6	12.4	12.7	13.8
Construction	2.7	3.0	4.5	5.2
Transport and distribution	12.6	14.5	16.6	17.0
Public utilities	3.6	3.1	2.7	3.8
Government	10.5	10.2	8.8	9.8
Ownership of dwellings	2.6	2.3	1.6	2.1
Banking and finance	2.1	1.5	2.1	2.1
Other Services	5.9	6.2	4.9	4.4

Source: Mulchansingh (1971, 96), table II.

The oil boom was confined to Trinidad with no developments on Tobago. However, Tobagonians moved in large numbers to Trinidad during these years. By 1960, the population of Trinidad and Tobago, which had been born in Tobago, was 45,103.[26] The number of those living on the smaller island was only 27,208 in 1946 (33,333 in 1960). And commodity exports in the post-war period were essentially limited to cacao, copra, livestock, fresh vegetables, and coconut fibre with a combined value in 1950 of little more than US$1 million. Tourism, which would become the main source of employment after independence, was still in its infancy.

Trinidad, if not Tobago, had experienced fast economic growth and massive structural change combined with a high level of income per head. Yet, political change had lagged behind. The colony had participated in 1958 – with no great enthusiasm – in the Federation of the West Indies promoted by the British government, but refused to continue in it after Jamaica withdrew in 1961. Decolonisation followed swiftly, and Trinidad and Tobago became independent the following year, with Eric Williams as the first Prime Minister.

11.4. Trinidad and Tobago: After Independence

Although independence established Trinidad and Tobago as a sovereign state, the government chose at first to follow a cautious path. Both monetary and fiscal policies were highly conservative, the Queen remained Head of State,[27] and the multinational energy companies were assured they had nothing to fear. The only significant change – and it was a very positive one – was the improvement in the relations with Venezuela, whose government in 1966 finally dropped the Antillean surtax that had caused so much resentment for nearly a century.[28]

This sense of caution was perhaps understandable in view of the delicate ethnic balance in the new state. Both Afro-Caribbeans and Indo-Caribbeans supported independence, but political parties had formed on ethnic lines, and the first government led by Eric Williams' People's National Movement (PNM) did not want to take any measures that might suggest preference for those of African descent.

Those of Indian origin, constituting around 40 per cent of the population, may have been reassured. However, outward migration started to become a major issue with independence and affected both major ethnic groups. There was not a single year after 1960 when net migration was inward (see figure 11.7).

Figure 11.7: Trinidad and Tobago: Net Migration, 1961–2016

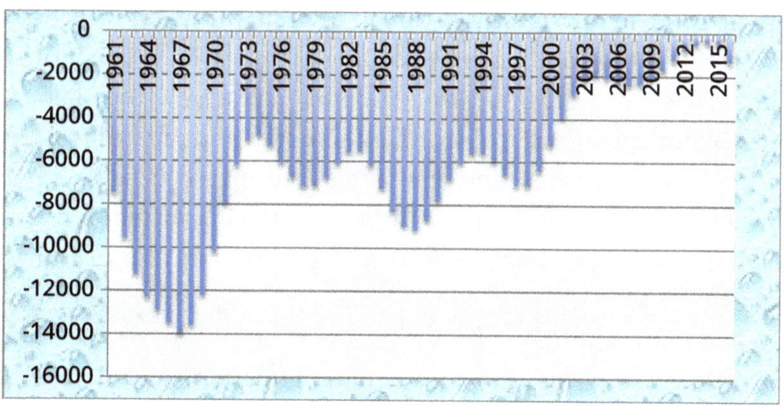

Source: Derived from World Bank, World Development Indicators.

Although the numbers migrating peaked in 1967, it remained high until after 2000 when new arrivals from Venezuela reduced the net outflow significantly. Thus, Trinidad and Tobago, whose population was 880,000 in the year of independence, experienced only a modest demographic expansion in the next decades despite a birth rate that only fell below 20 per 1,000 in the 1990s.

Gradually, the government became less conservative. Having inherited a currency system based on sterling, the administration established a central bank in 1964 and introduced for the first time a Trinidad and Tobago dollar ($TT). This, however, was pegged to sterling at 4.80 (making it worth 1.71 to the US dollar), and the government decided to stick with the pound after the British devaluation in 1967. This devalued the TT dollar to the US dollar, and the collapse of the Bretton Woods system after 1971 led to a fluctuating currency until the TT dollar was pegged to the US dollar in 1976 at 2.40.

The peg could not be maintained as a result of domestic inflation, but Trinidad and Tobago avoided the fate of Jamaica where the currency collapsed soon after the fixed rate system was ended. The value of the TT dollar depreciated steadily against the US dollar, with intervening short periods of stability and had 'only' fallen to 6.73 by 2018. This was almost entirely due to the energy sector, which ensured a strong supply of foreign exchange to pay for imports.

Energy was, indeed, a priority for all administrations before and after independence. Three development plans (1958–62, 1962–68, 1968–73) outlined ambitious projects for the economy, all of which were dependent on increased income from the energy sector. To facilitate this, the government encouraged increased production and refining of hydrocarbons through fiscal incentives, together with downstream operations in processing activities and public investment in infrastructure. Firms were encouraged to invest in new activities using cheap energy as a key raw material. This included not just production of organic and inorganic chemicals but also of iron and steel.

When BP withdrew from Trinidad and Tobago (it would later return) to focus on more profitable activities elsewhere, the government acquired a strong presence in the energy sector. However, the industry was still dominated by foreign multinationals, making the fiscal system crucial to the division of resources between the private and public sectors. Tensions over the revenue split eased with the steep rise in energy prices from 1973 onwards, after which the government of Trinidad and Tobago enjoyed a huge increase in income from taxes and royalties on the companies. Since government spending could not be cut quickly or easily, this created the potential for fiscal problems if the price of oil fell sharply.

Administrations after independence were united in their desire to diversify the economy so that it would not be over-dependent on oil and gas. The resource-based industrialisation at Point Lisas was part of this, as were more traditional attempts at import-substituting industrialisation (ISI) through high tariffs on manufactured goods. The ISI strategy was taken a step further in 1973 when Trinidad and Tobago became a founding member of CARICOM designed to foster import substitution at the regional level. Services were also targeted, especially tourism, which was seen as a means by which Tobago, in particular, could share in the benefits of economic growth. From the 1990s onwards, non-tourism exports also became a priority with an emphasis on financial services, insurance, and logistics.

High levels of unemployment throughout the post-independence period, riots in 1970, and persistent net outward migration were a harsh reminder that diversification away from energy dependence was easier said than done. And the economy remained vulnerable to energy price falls. As Terrence Farrell noted in his major study of the economy called pessimistically *The Underachieving Society*:[29]

> In the model of development driven by natural resources, failure to 'break out' of the traditional 'equilibrium' structure causes the economy to fall back into that traditional structure when the resource boom collapses. This seems to have been the case with Trinidad and Tobago. The period of resource-based industrialization had not effected sufficient transformation of the structures of the production and consumption so that when the boom collapsed, the economy reverted essentially to preboom conditions.

Macroeconomic performance after independence demonstrates this clearly. A long period of rapid growth of GDP per head came crashing to a halt in the early 1980s (see figure 11.8), when energy prices started to fall. This led to a long and deep recession that only ended in 1993. It was 2001 before the previous peak of GDP per head (in 1982) was again reached, leading to a loss of nearly two decades. A rise in energy prices then led to a restoration of rapid growth in GDP per head, before another recession after 2008 that was also caused by falling energy prices.

Figure 11.8: Trinidad & Tobago: GDP per head (2010 US$), 1960–2017

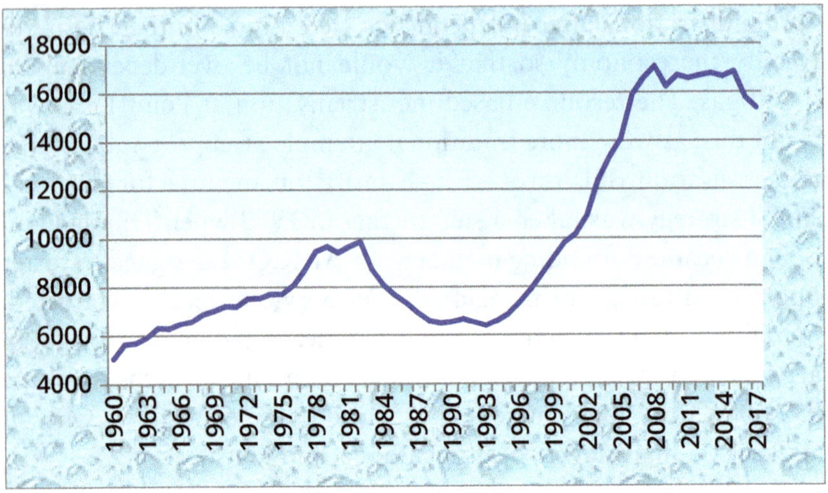

Source: World Bank, World Development Indicators.

The recession that started in the early 1980s, shortly after the death of Eric Williams, was caused by the drop in energy prices. However, it was exacerbated by the need to cut government spending in response to the drop in public revenue. These spending plans were difficult to reverse, leading to a sharp rise in the fiscal deficit, a rise in public external indebtedness, a weakening of the currency, a rise in inflation, and an increase in the rate of unemployment. Reluctantly, and after much prevarication, the government turned to the International Monetary Fund (IMF) for help in 1988.

The IMF's conditions for financial assistance included many of the measures that the government had been reluctant to adopt. This time, however, they could not be postponed. Public sector employment was curtailed, spending was cut, devaluation accelerated, and state enterprises were dismantled or sold. Trinidad and Tobago's economy stabilised, but it was now less diversified and even more dependent on world energy prices. Thirty years later, in 2018, the IMF was forced to recognise this reality while paying lip service to the idea of diversification in the future:[30]

> The economy is slowly recovering from a prolonged recession driven by energy supply shocks and low energy prices. With signs of improvement driven by energy sector growth from the second half of 2017, the economy is expected to return to positive growth in 2018 as the recovery takes hold in the non-energy sector. Good progress is being made in implementing fiscal consolidation. As growth gathers pace, policies should focus on completing the fiscal adjustment, while insulating the economy from future commodity price swings within a medium-term fiscal policy framework, and on creating an enabling environment for the non-energy sector as an engine of growth.

Energy has made Trinidad and Tobago a rich country by the standards of Latin America and the Caribbean. And, unlike some other energy producers in the region, it has not squandered the resources made available through taxation and royalties. It has also used available resources to give shape to a long-term strategic view of the country's future, first through five-year plans and later through the document *Vision 2020*.[31] Strategy, however, has been hostage to the cycles in energy production and prices so that the recession after 2008, while not as severe as the decade 1983–93, has taken a heavy toll on GDP per head (see figure 11.8) and has notably dampened ambitions.

The twin island state, despite energy abundance, suffers from many of the economic and social problems that afflict other countries in the region. These include high rates of unemployment, high levels of crime, unsatisfactory health indices, and poor quality of education at many levels. There is also, it is safe to assume, a high degree of income and wealth inequality, as happens frequently in oil-and gas-rich countries.[32] The government understandably sees its priority as increasing, or at least maintaining, earnings from the upstream and downstream energy industries, but it cannot insulate the country against the inevitable downturns. And with the day soon coming when hydrocarbon deposits may have to be left in the ground due to restrictions on burning fossil fuels, time is running out.

NOTES

1. See S. Craig-James, *The Changing Society of Tobago, 1838–1938: A Fractured Whole*, vol. 1 (Arima, Trinidad and Tobago: Cornerstone, 2008), 5.
2. See *Report from Select Committee on the Commercial State of the West India Colonies* (London: 1832), 79.
3. See https://www.ucl.ac.uk/lbs/search.
4. See Statistical Appendix.
5. Quoted in Craig-James, *The Changing Society of Tobago, 1838–1938*, 160.
6. See *Report of the West India Royal Commission* (London: 1897), 355.
7. See Craig-James, *The Changing Society of Tobago, 1838–1938*, 295.
8. See E.E. Williams, *History of the People of Trinidad and Tobago* (London: Andre Deutsch, 1964), 28.
9. See Statistical Appendix.
10. See D. Eltis, 'The Traffic in Slaves between the British West Indian Colonies, 1807–1833,' *The Economic History Review*. 25, no. 1 (February 1972): 55–64.
11. See https://www.ucl.ac.uk/lbs/search.
12. In 1854, the CDR reached 104, one of the highest ever recorded in the Caribbean, as a result of an outbreak of cholera.
13. See *Report on the Select Committee on West India Colonies* 1842, 53.
14. See B. Samaroo, 'The Immigrant Communities,' in *General History of the Caribbean. Vol. IV: The Long 19th Century*, ed. K.O. Laurence (Paris: UNESCO, 2011), 249.
15. See K.O. Laurence, *A Question of Labour: Indentured Immigration into Trinidad and British Guiana, 1875–1917* (New York, NY: St Martin's Press, 1994), 526–27.
16. In 1880, for example, public expenditure per head was £3 5s. 4d. This was more than three times higher than Jamaica. Only St Croix and St Thomas in the Danish West Indies came close. See *Report of the West Indian Royal Commission* (1884), part iv, appendix xx.
17. These were the same as applied to Curaçao (see chapter 8) and raised the costs of any imports to Trinidad routed through Venezuela. See K. Singh, *British-Controlled Trinidad and Venezuela: A History of Economic Interests and Subversion, 1830–1962* (Mona: University of the West Indies, 2010), 59–88.
18. See *Report of the West India Royal Commission* 1897, 304.
19. The company had started in Venezuela, but moved to Trinidad in 1875.
20. See Statistical Appendix.
21. See V. Mulchansingh, 'The Oil Industry in the Economy of Trinidad,' *Caribbean Studies* 11, no.1 (1971): 78.

22. See E.E Williams, *History of the People of Trinidad and Tobago*, 180–88.
23. See O.N. Bolland, *On the March: Labour Rebellions in the British Caribbean, 1934–39* (Kingston, Jamaica: Ian Randle Publishers, 1995), 90–96.
24. See F.A. Baptiste, 'The Exploitation of Caribbean Bauxite and Petroleum, 1914–1945,' *Social and Economic Studies* 37 (1988): 107–42.
25. See Mulchansingh, 'The Oil Industry in the Economy of Trinidad,' 73–100.
26. See Craig-James, *The Changing Society of Tobago, 1838–1938*, 230.
27. Until 1976, when Trinidad and Tobago became a republic within the Commonwealth.
28. See S.D. Ryan, *Eric Williams: The Myth and the Man* (Kingston, Jamaica: University of the West Indies Press, 2009), 623.
29. See T. Farrell, *The Underachieving Society: Development Strategy and Policy in Trinidad and Tobago, 1958–2008* (Mona, Jamaica: University of the West Indies Press, 2012), 173.
30. See https://www.imf.org/en/News/Articles/2018/07/06/mcs070618-trinidad-and-tobago-staff-concluding-statement.
31. This strategic plan was published in 2007.
32. There have been no published official statistics on income inequality or the distribution of income since 1992.

Chapter 12
GUYANA

When Holland ceded the Dutch colonies of Berbice, Essequibo, and Demerara in 1814, they had already been under British rule for a decade. However, with the exception of the act abolishing the slave trade in 1807, the three colonies had remained largely subject to Dutch law. Only gradually did Great Britain impose its own colonial system on its new acquisitions, merging Demerara and Essequibo in 1822 and adding Berbice in 1831 to form the colony of British Guiana.

Before and after the unification of the three formerly Dutch colonies, British Guiana faced an intense labour shortage. The land was deemed very suitable to cultivate sugar, but this required huge inputs of labour to drain swamps, build dykes, and prepare the soil before planting could even take place. Meeting the planters' demand for labour after abolition of the slave trade, and even more so after emancipation, was a high priority for the colonial state throughout the nineteenth century.

The efforts to build a dynamic sugar economy in South America based on a seemingly inexhaustible supply of land, immigrant labour, and British capital were only partially successful. Exports per head (see figure 12.1) fell after 1830 and did not recover until the middle of the century. From then onwards, there was growth although – when adjusted to a *per capita* basis – the increase was very modest. This continued until the First World War, by which time the economy had become much less dependent on sugar and its derivatives as a result of the exploitation of non-traditional exports.

After the First World War, British Guiana experienced a long and sustained period of growth in exports per head that lasted with only minor variations until independence in 1966 (see figure 12.1).

This was largely due to non-traditional exports, especially bauxite, at a time when the sugar industry faced a series of crises. During this period, the labour shortage started to resolve itself through a sharp fall in the death rate, which meant that the colony was able to adjust to the end of indentured labour from British India after 1917.

Figure 12.1: Guyana: Exports per head at constant prices (1900=100), 1820–2016

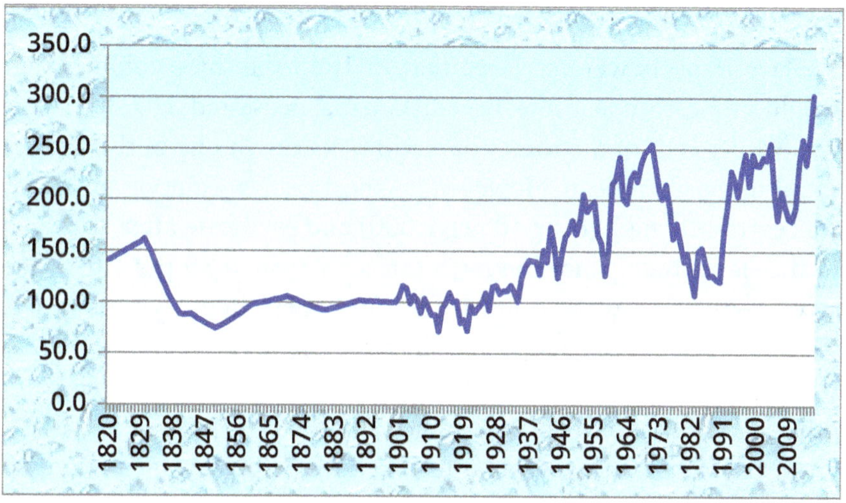

Source: Statistical Appendix, 1820–2008; World Bank, World Development Indicators thereafter.

After independence, Guyana – as it was now called – faced a major economic collapse for which internal factors were largely responsible. The drop in exports per head in the two decades after independence (see figure 12.1) was spectacular and brought with it currency collapse, massive outward migration, and severe hardship for most of those that remained.

The economy eventually stabilised and recovery proceeded until another downturn soon after the start of the new millennium. The subsequent growth of the economy was rapid, however, and the country's economic prospects were significantly enhanced by the discovery of vast reserves of oil. These were expected to come on stream by 2020, providing a huge boost to exports and public revenue with a much smaller impact on employment.

12.1. From Abolition to the First World War

Capitalists from Great Britain were quick to move into the new territories after they were captured from Holland. They did this by buying existing estates from their Dutch owners, taking over those that had been abandoned or starting new plantations on land made available by the British crown. All this required slaves and until 1808 they were able to import slaves from Africa as the Dutch settlers had done before them.

Slave imports were so large that in 1810 the three colonies that would come to constitute British Guiana possessed 107,300. This was 94 per cent of the total population, making it one of the highest ratios in the Caribbean. However, the mortality rate among the slaves was extremely high (over 40 per 1,000) and even rose after abolition of the slave trade. Since the birth rate was around 30 per 1,000, the slave population was bound to decline unless imports took place. This is, indeed, what happened, since the planters – as in Trinidad – took full advantage of the loophole in the law to bring in slaves from other parts of the British West Indies.

Nearly 10,000 slaves came in this way before emancipation, so the slave population of British Guiana declined only slowly.[1] It was above 100,000 in 1820 and nearly 90,000 in 1830, when slaves still represented some 90 per cent of the population. In 1834, when slavery ended, the number was 83,545, and all of these were then subject to compensation claims by their former owners.

One of the biggest claimants was the absentee owner Sir John Gladstone. Born in Scotland, he had moved to Liverpool in 1786 and his business interests at first centred on India. However, he was one of the first British planters to buy a sugar estate in Demerara after the British occupation in 1803 and he went on to buy several others – the last in 1826. By 1828, his personal wealth, estimated at £40,000 in 1799, had risen to over £500,000, suggesting that his investments, in sugar, in the Caribbean during the years of slavery had been profitable.

He made several claims, all successful, for 1,702 slaves and was paid over £80,000 in compensation.[2] He was a strong defender of both the slave trade and slavery during his time in politics, something which his son (the future British Prime Minister) preferred not to advertise later in life. He then used his considerable wealth, part of which had come from slave compensation, to invest in railways before becoming a director of the Royal Bank of Scotland.

John Gladstone did not stay long in British Guiana after emancipation. However, before he sold his estates, he was the first to experiment with indentured labour from Bengal in British India, a region he knew well because of his business activities. The experience was not a success, and the mortality rate among the Indians on his estates became something of a scandal.[3] Yet, it would pave the way for the mass immigration to British Guiana of indentured labourers over the next 80 years.

The scale of net inward migration was astonishing. As figure 12.2 shows, there was never a single five-year period before 1900 in which net inward migration was not positive, including years when the main export commodity (sugar) was in deep crisis. Although most of the migrants came from British India, not all did so with others from Africa, China, Madeira, and other parts of the West Indies. By 1851, the migrants represented half the labour force on the estates, and by the end of the century, they were a large majority. By 1911, the estate population of 71,000 was almost entirely Indian.[4]

Figure 12.2: Guyana: Net Migration (%age of Population), 1836–1900

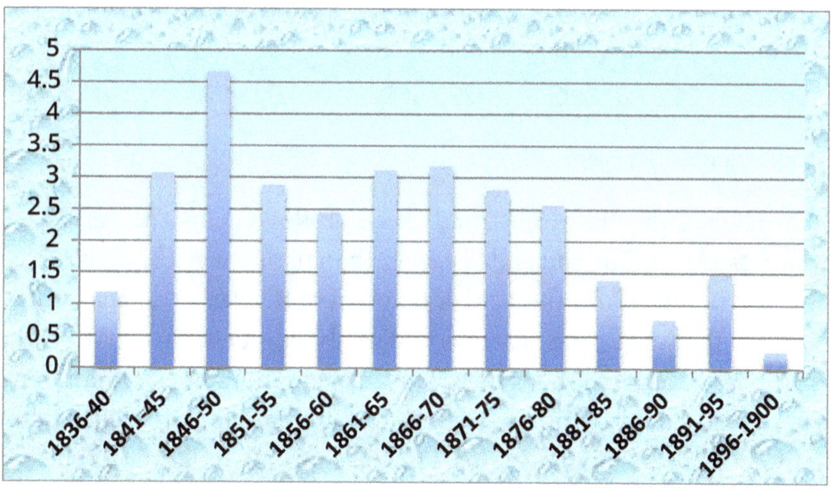

Source: Statistical Appendix.

The birth rate in British Guiana only exceeded the death rate on a regular basis from the 1920s onwards while frequent outbreaks of cholera and other diseases led to exceptionally high numbers of deaths in several years throughout the nineteenth century. Yet migration on the scale shown in figure 12.2 was bound to increase the population eventually despite the high mortality rate. Indeed, the number of people in the colony, which had briefly dipped below 100,000 at the time of emancipation, steadily rose thereafter and had reached nearly 310,000 on the eve of the First World War. The ethnic balance of the country between Afro- and Indo-Guyanese was now firmly established.[5]

Table 12.1: Guyana: Sugar, Molasses and Rum exports, 1820–1900

	Sugar (lb)	Molasses (gallons)	Rum (gallons)	Share in Exports (%)
1820	73,015,789	1,159,283	3,176,734	58.3
1830	101,180,900	2,920,076	2,278,417	89.0
1840	60,037,510	1,734,515	1,171,609	94.6
1850	81,643,996	486,491	1,068,259	91.7
1860	127,932,000	139,475	1,925,910	93.4
1870	185,549,280	1,349,950	1,827,607	94.8
1880	213,002,496	843,220	1,834,070	96.4
1890	252,402,528	1,048,005	1,416,077	87.0
1900	212,228,800	230,063	4,023,828	75.9

Source: Statistical Appendix.

Emancipation in 1834 had been followed by a period of apprenticeship. This had ended earlier than planned in 1838, by which time the planters and the British colonial authorities had reluctantly accepted that the former slaves could not be compelled to work on the estates in a country where there was such an abundance of land and where land could be purchased cheaply by individuals or groups of individuals to form villages. This meant that only migration schemes could deliver the potential of the colony as Mungo Campbell, giving evidence in 1842 to the Select Committee on West India Colonies, explained:[6]

> Such are the natural resources of British Guiana, and the vast and superior machinery there established, that I am of the opinion that if it were afforded an adequate supply of labour, the colony is capable of competing with any country in the world in tropical productions, but particularly in sugar.

Campbell's words would prove prescient. Between 1840 and 1890 (see table 12.1), British Guiana quadrupled the volume of sugar exported. The share of earnings from sugar, molasses, and rum in domestic exports, which had been less than 60 per cent in 1820 (coffee and cotton were still important), soon jumped above 90 per cent and stayed there until the last years of the nineteenth century. The colony, like so many others, became almost entirely dependent on the fortunes of one commodity.

British Guiana may have been one of the lowest cost producers of sugar in the Caribbean, but it was not exempt from the global pressures in the last part of the nineteenth century that crippled the industry in so many countries. Giving evidence to the Royal Commission in 1897, a representative of the Planters' Association stated:[7]

> There is great fear of the extinction of the sugar industry in this colony, as proprietors cannot carry on at present low prices, and no financial assistance can be obtained to enable them to carry on estates during a period when losses are incurred. The uncertainties, as to the future of sugar, caused by the operation of bounties, entirely destroys the credit of the industry in this colony. It is certain, if no early improvement takes place, the majority of estates will be cropped. The present critical condition of the sugar industry is entirely owing to low prices. The average net value of one ton of first sugar during 1896 was 9l. 15s., the lowest average price for sugar ever yet realised.

Planters' associations are hardly objective and the sugar industry did not disappear. Nevertheless, the steady growth from 1840 to 1890 had gone into reverse by 1900 (see table 12.1) with the volume of exports down to the levels 20 years earlier. Since prices had fallen so sharply, the value of sugar exports in 1900 was close to the level in 1860. And since export earnings paid for imports that provided the bulk of public revenue, which in turn financed public expenditure, the crisis in the sugar industry at the end of the nineteenth century threatened a big reduction in colonial spending.

In the end, public revenue and expenditure experienced only a small decline. This, however, was due to an increase in taxation, in particular a doubling of average tariff rates between 1880 and 1900 (from 11.3 to 23.5 per cent).[8] This increased the cost of living and reduced living standards, since the planters were in no condition to raise wage rates. This led to social unrest, resulting, in many cases, in strikes and violent confrontation with the authorities. The riots of 1905 were especially noteworthy as they spread to many parts of the country and provided a case study in colonial repression as documented by Walter Rodney in his history of the Guyanese working people.[9]

British Guiana did not experience the kind of economic collapse suffered by some British Caribbean colonies before the First World War. Sugar benefited after 1902 from a new market in Canada made possible by the Dominion's adoption of imperial preference. Mainly, however, the survival of the economy was made possible by export diversification. Rice production, the staple of the Indian population, had expanded so rapidly that more than five million pounds were being exported by 1860. Fifty years later, exports had reached 12 million pounds. And, as in Trinidad, smallholders had some success in producing cacao and coffee for export. Timber exports reached five million board feet just before the war started.

The major change, however, was the export of three products that were highly unusual in the British Caribbean: gold, diamonds, and balata. Gold had started to be exported in the 1880s and by 1900 had reached 108,522 troy ounces. This would be the peak for many years, but exports declined only slowly before the First World War. The diamond boom came later (in the 1920s), but the industry's exports earned US$100,000 in 1902 – a not insignificant figure at the time. And balata exports exceeded one million pounds for the first time in 1908. By 1913, the last normal year before the war, non-traditional commodities provided one-third of earnings from domestic exports.

Except for the ending of indentured immigration from India, the First World War changed little in the colony. The sugar industry reversed its decline as its exports, including rum, were now so important for the war effort. By 1918, as the war ended, the industry was once again responsible for 80 per cent of export earnings. More significant was the switch of British Guiana from a net importer to a net exporter of people. The population actually fell between 1910 and 1920 and this was not due to volunteers going to the front (they had returned by the end of 1919). Instead, continued high death rates, coupled with a lack of immigrants willing to take the place of indentured workers from Asia, gave the colony its first major experience of net outward migration.

12.2. From the First World War to Independence

With the war over, it looked as if British Guiana would once again revert to its previous status as a sugar colony. This was not only due to the decline in non-traditional exports during the war years but also to the exceptionally powerful role now played by Bookers' Sugar Estates, a subsidiary of the British multinational company Booker Brothers, McConnell and Company, Ltd.

Josias Booker had come to British Guiana in 1815 as a plantation manager. Joined by two relatives, they then bought the estate that Josias had managed. With the fall in the price of sugar plantations after emancipation, Booker Bros. then acquired other estates.[10] The concentration of sugar estates in their hands proceeded without drawing much opprobrium in the nineteenth century, and it entirely escaped the attention of the 1897 Royal Commission, but by the end of the First World War the company's dominance was too great to ignore.

In 1934, Jock Campbell, a descendant of one of the founders of Bookers Bros., joined the holding company registered in the UK and oversaw developments in British Guiana until his retirement as chairman in 1967. While recognising and partially addressing the appalling conditions faced by workers on the company's estates, he still had no intention of reversing the monopolistic position of the group in the colony.[11]

Soon after the end of the Second World War, Bookers' Sugar Estates owned 15 out of 19 estates and had 'understandings' with the others. In addition, the company had interests in British Guiana in rum and gin manufacture and distribution, foundry operations, store-keeping, drug manufacture, printing, balata collection, petroleum marketing, insurance agencies, coastal and trans-Atlantic shipping as well as numerous interests in smaller companies.[12]

Thanks to Bookers' influence in the colony and the 1951 Commonwealth Sugar Agreement, for which Jock Campbell had lobbied hard, the sugar industry remained the most important industry up to independence – especially in terms of employment. The volume of exports doubled in the 40 years after the First World War, while earnings trebled thanks to higher prices. The industry survived the Great Depression and was helped by the imposition of imperial preference by Great Britain in 1932. Shortly before independence, sugar, molasses, and rum still accounted for more than 50 per cent of the value of domestic exports.

Yet, there was some export diversification in the years after the First World War. The colony experienced a diamond boom in the 1920s when exports regularly exceeded 100,000 carats and, in one year (1923), the value of exports was nearly US$5 million. Rice exports, after a long period of fluctuating sales, finally took off in the Second World War after the Japanese invasion of many British colonies in Asia and both production and exports soared when the war was over. Timber exports also increased in value after the war, earning more than US$2 million in many years.

It was bauxite, however, that proved to be the most important non-traditional export – at least in terms of value and contribution to public revenue. The industry began in the First World War, as in Suriname, with the entry of a Canadian company. The first exports took place in 1923 and on the eve of the Second World War bauxite exports were contributing 20 per cent of domestic exports. This share jumped sharply in the war, when bauxite became a strategic resource of vital importance for the allied war effort. In the 1950s, the share averaged one-quarter when the industry was briefly the second most important producer in the world, and almost all output came from the Demerara Bauxite Company, a subsidiary of the Aluminium Company of Canada.[13]

The leading capitalists in British Guiana, who controlled the sugar and bauxite industries among others, were foreigners. After the arrival of the last indentured labourers in 1917, however, labour was overwhelmingly domestic. Yet a classic class struggle between foreign capital and domestic labour never erupted as workers and their trade union organisations were divided on ethnic lines. Disputes did occur, especially in 1939 when a strike on the Leonora Sugar Estate led to riots across the country, but lack of unity among the labour force undoubtedly delayed the rise of nationalism that other British colonies experienced at this time.[14]

Guyanese workers and their families experienced considerable hardship in the Great Depression. The value of domestic exports, for example, fell by half between 1927 and 1932. However, much of this decline was due to the collapse in the volume and value of diamond exports. Sugar also experienced a fall in the value of exports as a result of the drop in world prices, but the volume of exports was virtually unchanged as Booker Sugar Estates was able to exploit its dominant position to cut costs and increase efficiency.

The cost cutting exercise, of course, included the wages of the largely Indo-Guyanese labour force. This led to sporadic labour unrest, but it was never generalised. And by 1935, the value of sugar exports was back to the level before the Great Depression. Together with the earnings from increased bauxite exports, British Guiana ended the decade of the 1930s with the value of exports close to their peak before the Great Depression. And the Royal Commission, appointed in 1938 to look at social and economic conditions across the British Caribbean, was able to recommend measures that would benefit the colony in the post-war years.

The importance of exports to the standard of living in the colony was finally demonstrated, in 1942, with the preparation of the first complete set of national accounts by Frederic Benham. This showed that domestic exports accounted for half of British Guiana's GDP. This was high even by British Caribbean standards. And since average labour productivity in the export sector was much greater than in the rest of the economy, this export share explained why GDP per head was relatively high. However, Benham also calculated that nearly seven per cent of GDP consisted of income paid abroad – mainly in the form of dividends of companies operating in British Guiana and paid to foreign shareholders.[15]

By 1948, the monetary value of the colony's GDP had doubled compared with 1942, and by 1952 it had trebled.[16] British Guiana was enjoying an economic boom based on export-led growth. Indeed, sales abroad of commodities, including sugar and rice, were so strong that the share of agriculture and forestry in GDP was close to 30 per cent in 1951, with mining adding another ten per cent. And the boom would continue with the value of exports jumping from nearly US$50 million in 1953 to over US$100 million a decade later.

Explaining developments in the previous decade to a British audience, the Evans Report in 1948 concluded:[17]

> It must be emphasized at the outset that during the period from 1939 until the present time British Guiana...has enjoyed a yield of revenues and a scale of public expenditure hitherto unparalleled in its financial history. The war years have in fact been years of apparent prosperity standing out in marked contrast to the years of depression which preceded the appointment of the Royal Commission of 1938.

Yet this growth could hardly be called development as the colonial structure of British Guiana restricted the benefits to a small group. The World Bank, for example, noted one of many peculiarities about the economy when it stated:[18]

> There is an unusual and rather paradoxical relationship between local savings and investment. Most of the liquid savings held in banks and other institutions were invested outside the colony while, on the other hand, the bulk of the private investment in the economy comes from external sources.

The 'commanding heights' of the economy were, therefore, firmly in foreign hands when the British government finally agreed to a new constitution in 1953 providing for universal suffrage. The newly formed People's Progressive Party (PPP), led by Dr Cheddi Jagan, was in a strong position to contest the first elections held under the new constitution and swept to power with more than half of the popular vote while winning 18 out of 24 seats in the National Assembly. The PPP's stated aim, never disguised, was to advance towards independence on the basis of an economic model that shifted power from foreign to domestic control.

Jagan's government moved swiftly to alter the balance of power away from capital towards labour, especially on the sugar and rice estates. It also introduced a bill that would, if implemented, have required employers to recognise trade unions.[19] These measures, moderate by any standards, convinced the Eisenhower administration in the US that the PPP was hoping to move an independent Guyana into the Soviet sphere of influence.[20] Under US pressure and stoked by lurid accusations in the British and Guyanese press, the governor suspended the Constitution on October 9, 1953 – only 133 days after the inauguration of the PPP government.

British Guiana would now endure more than a decade of political turmoil before independence in 1966. Although Jagan would win elections in 1957 and again in 1961, it was – in his own words – 'office without power'. A civil service strike in 1963, financed by the CIA, destroyed his ability to govern, and the colonial authorities the following year imposed a system of proportional representation on the country that allowed the People's National Congress (PNC), a largely Afro-Guyanese party formed in 1955 by Forbes Burnham, to come to power despite the fact that the PPP, a mainly Indo-Guyanese party, had won the most votes.[21]

12.3. Economic Crisis

The political and constitutional crisis before independence led to serious financial difficulties for the government, and the colonial authorities commissioned a report on the position in 1963. The author, K.C. Jacobs, concluded:[22]

> No other conclusion is possible than that assistance will be required first to pay off the bank overdrafts at the end of 1963 and secondly to make possible a budget in 1964 which, instead of imposing more cuts which might be disastrous, allowed for the restoration to normal of provisions in the Estimates and the filling of vacancies in the establishment which have been kept unfulfilled to reduce expenditure, to the detriment of efficiency and in the long run economy...The orderly and systematic conduct of Government affairs and its services cannot be expected when there is the necessity constantly to count the money in the till or look up the overdraft in the passbook and to alter course according to what is found.

GDP per head fell between 1961 and 1963 (see figure 12.3). However, it then recovered as the new government formed at the end of 1964 had the strong support at first of the business community as well as the British and US governments. GDP per head then recovered and grew rapidly in the first half of the 1970s thanks to exceptionally high prices for the main commodity exports. The peak was reached in 1976, after which there was a catastrophic decline until 1990 (see figure 12.3). In these 15 years, Guyana's GDP per head fell by nearly one-third leaving income per head at the same level as in 1963. It was one of the sharpest declines eve recorded in the Caribbean and it had devastating consequences.

The administration formed by Forbes Burnham's PNC in 1964 governed in coalition with Peter D'Aguiar's pro-business United Force (UF). It also had the support of the US government that had no wish to see radical economic policies adopted. The four years of coalition, therefore, gave no hint of what was to come. On the contrary, the private sector thrived both before and after independence in 1966 as the coalition reversed the more radical policies of the previous Jagan administrations.

In 1968, however, the situation changed dramatically. The coalition government ended with the withdrawal of the UF, and Burnham was able to secure an outright majority in that year's election thanks to the manipulation of the vote of Guyanese living abroad. Burnham made clear that there would now be a change of economic strategy with a shift to 'cooperative socialism'.

Figure 12.3: Guyana: GDP per head (2010 US$), 1960–90

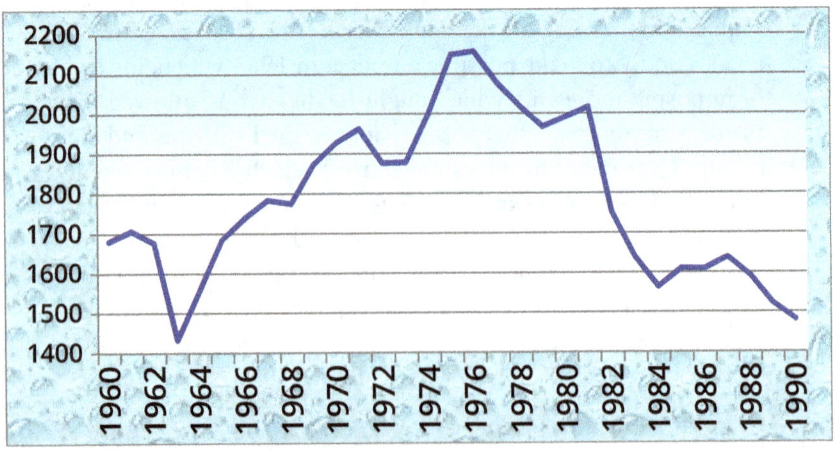

Source: World Bank, World Development Indicators.

He, therefore, announced that the country would become the Cooperative Republic of Guyana (it did so in 1970), and that the highest court would no longer be the Privy Council in London. It would be replaced by a local court of appeal that was more likely to be sympathetic to the change of direction thanks to government patronage over judicial appointments.

Cooperative socialism implied that the commanding heights of the economy would be nationalised and replaced by cooperatives of workers and farmers. The nationalisation programme did, indeed, go ahead, but what replaced private sector firms were not so much worker-led cooperatives as traditional state-owned enterprises. Thus, the foreign-owned bauxite industry was taken over in 1971 and the Booker sugar estates in 1976. In between these years, large swathes of the distribution, manufacturing, communications, transport, agricultural, and financial sectors were brought into the public sector.

The government's economic strategy also favoured import substitution over export promotion. This required the aggressive use of tariffs and quotas as well as the rationing of scarce foreign exchange. In a small economy such as Guyana, this was always going to be a risky strategy, but the inefficiencies were, at first, disguised by the export boom in the middle of the 1970s made possible by the high world price of the main commodity exports. Sugar, rice, and bauxite – the three commodities that accounted for nearly all domestic exports – enjoyed exceptionally high prices that disguised the fall in output as a result of the nationalisation programme and the drop in productivity.

The foreign owners were fully compensated for nationalisation of their assets, which required additional borrowing by the government. The ratio of external debt to Gross National Income (GNI), a mere 33 per cent in 1970, therefore started to rise. By 1975, the ratio had doubled, but this was mild compared to what would now happen (see figure 12.4). With GDP per head starting to fall after 1976 and public spending continuing to rise, foreign borrowing soared. By 1980, the ratio of external debt to GNI had reached 150 per cent; nearly 400 per cent by 1985; and over 700 per cent by 1990.

Figure 12.4: Guyana: External Debt to GNI (%), 1970–91

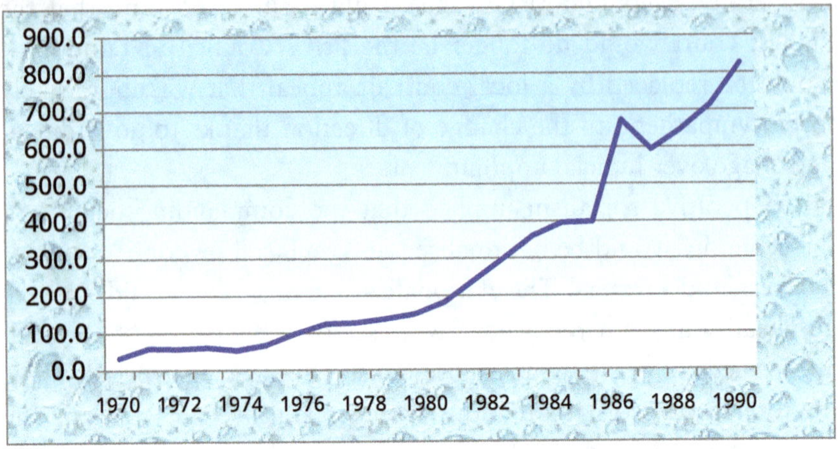

Source: World Bank, World Development Indicators.

The debt crisis was mirrored by a balance of payments crisis that began with the fall in export prices after 1975. This was exacerbated by the decline in production of the main export commodities. Bauxite production fell by more than half in the 1970s, while the volume of sugar exports fell by one-third. Rice at first bucked the trend, but the volume of exports also declined sharply after 1978. Import prices surged in the 1970s, a common experience throughout the world following the collapse of the Bretton Woods system of fixed exchange rates, and the position was even worse for those countries such as Guyana dependent on oil imports after the energy price rises in 1973/4 and 1978/9. By the end of the 1970s, the deficit on the current account of the balance of payments was over 20 per cent of GDP.[23]

The government attempted to ration foreign exchange, but this just accelerated the growth of a black market. Having started after independence with a currency (the Guyanese dollar) pegged to the pound sterling, the government switched to a peg to the US dollar in 1976 at 2.55. The peg survived to 1980, although the spread of the black market by then had rendered it almost meaningless. The annual rise in the cost of living had reached double digits by 1978 and would stay there with few exceptions until 1996. And in one year, 1991, annual inflation exceeded 100 per cent.

The deterioration of the economy in the second half of the 1970s made it inevitable that the government would need to go to the IMF.

Guyana had, in fact, signed ten standby arrangements with the fund in the decade after 1967, but these were either unused or of short duration. A three-year Extended Fund Facility (EFF) signed in mid-1979 signalled a new approach, when the IMF focused exclusively on demand reduction to eliminate macroeconomic imbalances. This was, however, a complete failure, and the programme was suspended before completion. The same fate awaited another EFF reached, along with a similar agreement with the World Bank, in 1980 despite the fact that the IMF now recognised the need for policies to increase supply rather than merely reduce demand.

Perhaps the most serious consequence of the economic crisis was the rise in net outward migration. Although there had been years of outward migration before the Second World War, there had been no clear trend. By 1960, however, the birth rate had reached 40 per 1,000 and the death rate was down to ten. This natural increase, equivalent to a population growth of three per cent a year, began to put a severe strain on the labour market even before the economic crisis and net outward migration was persistent throughout the years of growth leading up to the mid-1970s (see figure 12.5).

Figure 12.5: Guyana: Net Migration,1960–2015

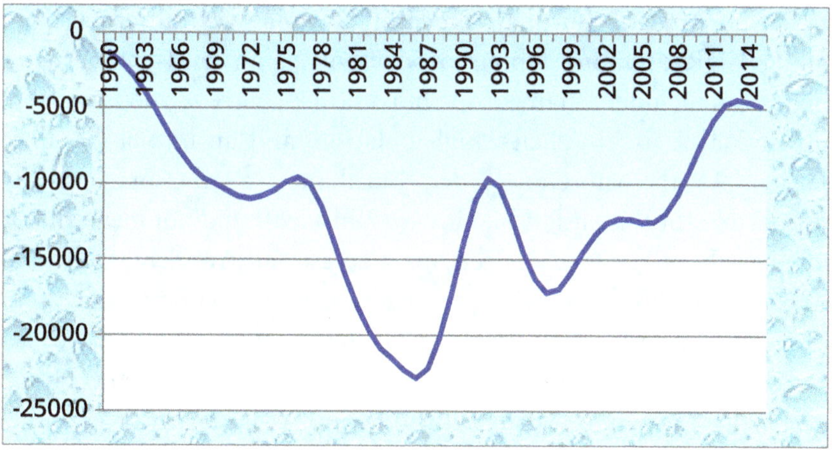

Source: Statistical Appendix.

The economic crisis after 1976 led to a sharp rise in net outward migration, which reached a peak in the mid-1980s. Emigration was so large in these years (see figure 12.5) that the absolute size of the population started to fall from its peak in 1981, when it had reached 781,732. It continued to decline until 2009, by which time it was 745,693. This was the same figure as in 1975, nearly 35 years earlier.

The cumulative impact of net outward migration from 1960 to 2015 was 660,000 – almost as large as the population itself and proof of the terrible social cost of the economic crisis in Guyana. Guyanese in Canada, the UK, the US, and many other countries may have maintained family ties to their home country, sending back large sums in remittances, but they lost faith in their government and its economic model in the first two decades after independence.

12.4. Recovery, Growth and Oil

Forbes Burnham died in August 1985 after more than 20 years as Guyana's leader. He had started as the premier of a British colony before becoming the first prime minister of an independent Guyana in 1966 and, from 1980, president of the country. This would normally have been a political legacy worthy of celebration, but Burnham's was tarnished both by electoral fraud after 1964 and by the economic crisis that overwhelmed the country after 1976 – not to mention the massive abuse of human rights.

At the time of Burnham's death, Guyana was suffering from falling GDP, declining labour productivity, high levels of outward migration, including many of the most skilled, currency depreciation, unsustainable fiscal deficits, high inflation, and an intolerable debt burden. As the supreme leader, Burnham was the man mainly responsible for this situation. However, his death did not mean that it could easily be reversed. Indeed, his successor as president, Desmond Hoyte, soon discovered that the macroeconomic conditions would continue to deteriorate if drastic measures were not adopted.

These measures were finally adopted in 1988, when the Hoyte government announced an ambitious Economic Recovery Programme (ERP). This included liberalising foreign exchange regulations, allowing exporters to retain part of their foreign currency earnings; lifting price controls on many goods and services; terminating import restrictions on most goods; providing tax incentives for private investors and a promise that 'it is no part of Government's policy to nationalize property...The era of nationalizations is therefore considered to be at an end.' The ERP had been drawn up in consultation with the IMF and World Bank. Soon after it was implemented, an Extended Credit Facility and a Standby Arrangement were signed with the fund, and loans were made available. The same happened with the World Bank and other official lenders. In particular, a Donor Support Group, led by Canada and the Bank for International Settlements, provided US$180 million to help Guyana pay arrears on servicing its external debt.

Guyana now had the external funding to ease the pain of its stabilisation and adjustment programme that saw the official exchange rate fall from ten to the US dollar in 1980 to 125 in 1992. Inflation inevitably soared, reaching a peak of 135 per cent in 1991. The impact on income distribution of such a sharp rise in prices cannot be measured due to the absence of official statistics, but it can safely be assumed that inequality became more extreme. By 1990, however, the economy had finally reached its nadir after 15 years of decline and was poised for a recovery.

No recovery could be sustainable without tackling the external debt, which had reached 825 per cent of GNI in 1991 (see figure 12.4). The funds provided by the Donor Support Group had been the first step in clearing debt payment arrears, but it would take many more years for the debt itself to be rescheduled and eventually reduced. Much of this was made possible by Guyana's eligibility for the Heavily Indebted Poor Country (HIPC) Initiative launched by the IMF and World Bank in 1996.

HIPC came with onerous conditions before the debt could be reduced. These included free market policies favoured by the international financial institutions, which had been rejected by almost all governments since 1953.[24] Yet so desperate were the circumstances that Guyana did manage to meet these conditions, and by 2000 the ratio of external debt to GNI had fallen to 208 per cent. This was still dangerously high, but by 2006 it was down to 82 per cent. And ten years later, it had fallen to 47 per cent. This was a manageable ratio and came with a low average rate of interest as so much of the debt had been received on concessional terms.

The rigorous application of the ERP, a shock adjustment programme designed to deliver short-term pain before long-term gain, finally ended the steep decline of GDP per head. The economy started to recover after 1990 (see figure 12.6). So great had been the distortions and inefficiencies in the Guyanese economy that the rate of growth, at first, was rapid and above the trend line of the period from 1990 to the present (see figure 12.6). And the elections of 1992, the first free and fair ones for decades, brought Cheddi Jagan back to power – this time as president – without any damaging effect on growth as the PPP was now committed to market-friendly policies.

A comparison of the poverty headcount ratio between 1992 and 1998 showed the progress Guyana had made. The country had never officially calculated poverty until 1992, when the scale of the problem was first revealed. The poverty headcount ratio in that year, for example, was one-third, assuming a cut-off of US$1.90 per day (2011 prices); nearly two-thirds, assuming a cut-off of US$3.20; and an extraordinary 85 per cent, assuming a cut-off of US$5.50 (see table 12.2). By 1998, all three ratios had dropped sharply.

Despite the optimism surrounding Guyana after 1990, the period of rapid growth had, in fact, already ended by 1997. What followed was almost a decade of anaemic economic performance (see figure 12.6), in which GDP per head barely registered any increase.

Figure 12.6: Guyana: GDP per head (2010 US$), 1990–2017

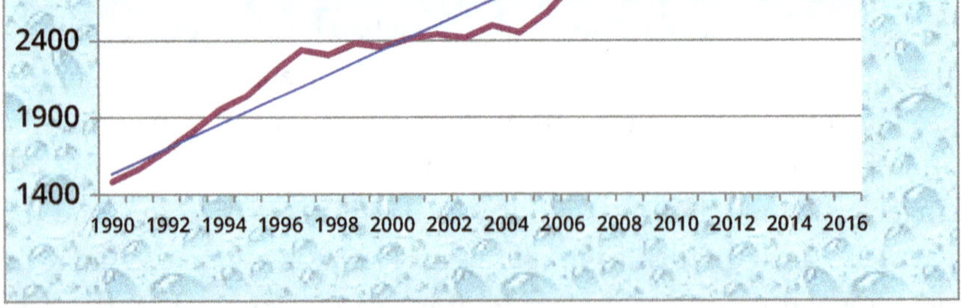

Source: World Bank, World Development Indicators.

Table 12.2: ***Guyana: Poverty Headcount Ratio (Percentage of Population), 1992–98***

	1992	1998
Poverty headcount ratio at $1.90 a day (2011 PPP)	33.9	14.0
Poverty headcount ratio at $3.20 a day (2011 PPP)	61.2	29.5
Poverty headcount ratio at $5.50 a day (2011 PPP)	85.4	56.4

Source: World Bank, World Development Indicators. PPP means Purchasing Power. Parity.

Net outward migration continued at high levels in the period (1997–2005), exceeding 10,000 in every year (see figure 12.5). Despite market-friendly policies, an open invitation to foreign investors, and cautious fiscal policy, something was clearly not working in the Guyanese economy.

The main problem, as so often in the past, was export performance. Encouraged by the ERP, exports had surged and, by 1991, earnings from goods and services were greater than GDP. The ratio of exports of goods and services then stayed above 100 per cent for the next few years, providing Guyana with a welcome period of export-led growth. What happened to exports, especially commodities, was therefore bound to have a disproportionate impact on the economy as a whole.

Between 1997 and 2005, the main commodities exported fell in volume. Sugar, rice, bauxite, and rum suffered this fate due either to falling prices or production problems or both.[25] All of these except sugar also experienced a drop in value. Bauxite was particularly badly hit with the value of dried bauxite exported falling sharply. Only molasses, shrimp/prawns, and timber/plywood experienced an increase.

The key commodity exported, however, was gold. The entry of a Canadian company (Guyana Goldfields Inc) had pushed annual production from around 2,000 kg to 14,605 kg in 1998.[26] This made it by far the most important Guyanese export by value, and the official figures did not even include some of the earnings of the pork-knockers producing gold in the interior of the country under dangerous and environmentally unsustainable conditions.[27] By 2005, however, the volume of production had fallen to 6,405 kg with an immediate impact on foreign exchange earnings, public revenue, and capacity to import.

Fortunately for Guyana, this would be the low point. Gold, rice, and rum surged in volume and value from 2006. In ten years, the volume of rice exports rose by 200 per cent. In the seven years after 2010, the volume of rum exports trebled. Yet, it was gold that had the greatest impact with production reaching 22,167 kg in 2016, following the entry of another foreign firm. Guyana was now predominantly a gold exporting country, with the precious metal accounting for around 50 per cent of exports of goods.

With exports of services (mainly tourism) still small, Guyana's destiny appeared to be in the hands of two foreign companies responsible for almost all recorded gold exports.[28] Yet, in 2015, after decades of exploration, Guyana was able to announce the discovery by ExxonMobil of offshore oil deposits in commercial quantities.[29] Although production (by at least four companies) was not expected to start until 2020, the impact on the economy was soon felt through the expansion of construction and ancillary industries. Guyana, therefore, experienced a decade of rapid growth from 2006 (see figure 12.6) that is expected to continue into the future as the country makes the transition to being an oil-exporting country.

Guyana's new status is attracting migrants for the first time in decades even if net migration is still outwards (see figure 12.5).[30] Macroeconomic conditions have improved dramatically with a stable currency, low rate of inflation, moderate fiscal deficits, and a manageable debt to GDP ratio. Yet many Guyanese are understandably concerned about the impact of oil given the low levels of administrative efficiency and the high levels of corruption. Guyana may have won the commodity lottery, but the experiences of neighbouring Venezuela and Trinidad and Tobago are a salutary reminder that oil booms do not necessarily bring social progress or improvements in income distribution.

NOTES

1. See D. Eltis, 'The Traffic in Slaves between the British West Indian Colonies, 1807–1833,' *The Economic History Review*. 25, no. 1 (February 1972): 55–64.
2. See https://www.ucl.ac.uk/lbs/.
3. See G.W. Roberts, 'A Life Table for a West Indian Slave Population,' *Population Studies* 5 (1952): 238–42.
4. See J. Mandle, *The Plantation Economy: Population and Economic Change in Guyana, 1838–1960* (Philadelphia, PA: Temple University Press, 1973), 21.
5. In the 1891 census, there were 144,619 Afro-Guyanese and 105,463 Indo-Guyanese. See B.L Moore, *Race, Power, and Social Segmentation in Colonial Society: Guyana after Slavery, 1838–1891* (New York, NY: Gordon & Breach Science Publishers, 1987), 274.
6. See *Report of the Select Committee on West India Colonies* (London: 1842), 162.
7. See *Report of the West India Royal Commission* (London: 1897), 562.
8. See Statistical Appendix.
9. See W. Rodney, *A History of the Guyanese Working People, 1881–1905* (Baltimore, MD: The Johns Hopkins University Press, 1981), 190–216.
10. See M. Swan, *British Guiana: The Land of Six Peoples* (London: HMSO, 1957), 85.
11. See C. Seecharan, *Sweetening Bitter Sugar: Jock Campbell – The Booker Reformer in British Guiana 1934–1966* (Kingston, Jamaica: Ian Randle Publishers, 2004), 302–487.
12. See R.T. Smith, *British Guiana* (London: Oxford University Press, 1962), 60 and 82–87.
13. See IBRD, *The Economic Development of British Guiana* (Baltimore, MD: Published for International Bank for Reconstruction and Development by the Johns Hopkins Press, 1953), 352.
14. See O.N. Bolland, *On the March: Labour Rebellions in the British Caribbean, 1934–39* (Kingston, Jamaica: Ian Randle Publishers, 1995), 170–89.
15. See F. Benham, 'The National Income of British Guiana, 1942,' *Development and Welfare in the West Indies*, Bulletin No. 17 (1947): 21. Bridgetown, Barbados.
16. See IBRD, *The Economic Development of British Guiana*, 93.
17. See *Report of the British Guiana and British Honduras Settlement Commission* (Evans Commission) (London: 1948), 58.
18. See IBRD, *The Economic Development of British Guiana*, 88–89.
19. See Latin America Bureau, *Guyana: Fraudulent Revolution* (London: LAB, 1984), 33.

20. See S. Rabe, *US Intervention in British Guiana: A Cold War Story* (Chapel Hill, NC: University of North Carolina Press, 2005), 75–104.
21. The PNC allied with a small pro-business party to secure more seats than the PPP.
22. See K.C. Jacobs, *British Guiana: Report on the Financial Position* (London: HMSO, 1964), 6.
23. See C.Y. Thomas, 'Guyana: The IMF-World Bank Group and the General Crisis,' *Social and Economic Studies* 31, no. 4 (1982): 27, table 7.
24. The main exception is the coalition government from 1964 to 1968.
25. See www.statisticsguyana.gov.gy.
26. See www.ceicdata.com/en/indicator/guyana/gold-production.
27. See International Human Rights Clinic, *Gold Mining in Guyana: The Failure of Government Oversight and the Human Rights of Amerindian Communities* (Cambridge, MA: Human Rights Program, Harvard Law School, 2007), 1–73.
28. The two foreign firms (Guyana Goldfields and Troy Resources) were responsible for 70 per cent of declared gold production, the remainder coming from pork-knockers. Undeclared gold production is unknown, but it is thought to be substantial.
29. The offshore area announced by ExxonMobil to contain large oil deposits is in the area claimed by Venezuela and still the subject of dispute between the two countries.
30. Many of these migrants have come from Venezuela following the deterioration in economic and social conditions in that country since 2010.

Chapter 13
BELIZE

This chapter focuses on Belize before independence.[1] The country is, in many ways, unique in the Caribbean and not just because it is located on the mainland of Central America. The settlers who arrived in the seventeenth century had to run their own affairs for approximately 100 years before the country became a British settlement. This makes Belize different from other imperial dependencies in the Caribbean. In addition, until the second half of the twentieth century, the basis of the economy was forestry rather than agriculture.

The British government acknowledged Spanish sovereignty over Belize until nearly two decades after the collapse of Spanish authority in Central America and Mexico. The settlement was, therefore, under constant threat until Spain ceded minimal usufruct rights under the Treaty of Paris in 1763.[2] These rights were extended by Anglo-Spanish treaties in 1783 and 1786, but the territorial threat did not disappear. Since Belize was not a sovereign British territory, however, the settlers were not at first subject to British Navigation Laws.

The first part of this chapter explores the development of the settlement up to the middle of the nineteenth century. During and after the Napoleonic Wars, the settlers ignored the boundaries established in the Anglo-Spanish treaties and unilaterally extended the area from which timber could be extracted. Logwood (from which a dye was extracted) and later mahogany provided the basis of the economy, and Belize had achieved by 1820 the highest domestic exports per head in the Caribbean. Yet, the prosperity of the settlement now no longer rested on forestry alone, as Spain had been unable to prevent a clandestine re-export trade with Central America from emerging and belatedly gave it legitimacy in 1819. When Spanish authority collapsed in the region in 1821, Belize was exceedingly well placed to take advantage of its new role as an entrepôt centre.

Gradually, the British government established its authority over the settlement, which finally became a colony in 1862. Far from ushering in a period of renewed prosperity, colonialism proved to be an uninspiring experience. The second part of this chapter then examines the decline of the economy up to 1900 as a result of stagnant mahogany exports and a reduced entrepôt trade. Official efforts to shift the basis of the economy towards agriculture were thwarted by the structure of private landholdings, the dismal state of infrastructure, and a lack of vision by the imperial government.

There was a brief revival in the fortunes of the colony in the first years of the twentieth century, but this came to an abrupt end in 1914. The third part of the chapter then examines the fall of the economy during an extremely difficult period that culminated with devaluation at the end of the 1940s. These years included the end of logwood exports and the emergence for the first time of surplus labour. There were riots in Belize on several occasions during this period, and the authorities were forced to take steps that would eventually help the colony to shift away from forestry.

13.1. Prosperity without Sustainability: From Settlement to Colony

It is not known when the British first settled in Belize. However, the first settlers likely came from different parts of the Caribbean in the first half of the seventeenth century. In the second half, their numbers increased as a result of the logwood trade which – at £50–60 per ton – offered phenomenal profits. By 1672, the Jamaican governor could speak with pride of the achievements of the logwood cutters in the Bay of Honduras, and by the first years of the eighteenth century they had established such strong trading links with Boston that a pew was reserved for them in the Great North Church.[3] Ironically, the settlement also benefited from the successful Spanish efforts to oust British logwood cutters in the Yucatán peninsula, as many of those forced out moved to Belize where the logwood trade then concentrated.

The British government, at first, imposed an import tax of £5 per ton on logwood. As exports increased, prices fell and the tax became burdensome. Since they were not subject to British Navigation Laws

(Belize was not yet a colony), the settlers could sell their logwood wherever they could find a market. Some logwood was shipped direct to continental Europe. However, the trade with Boston was the most important (and New England traders then exported much of the logwood to consumers outside the UK without paying tax). Nonetheless, prices fell so low after 1750 that mahogany exports provided a welcome alternative and had overtaken logwood in terms of value by the last quarter of the eighteenth century. Mahogany extraction, however, is much more labour-intensive than logwood, and this explains the increase in the Belizean import of slaves.[4]

Logwood grows in dense clumps that make it relatively easy to extract in large quantities. Mahogany was quite different as it averages one tree per acre in its natural state and takes around 100 years to reach full maturity. There was no attempt at forest management, which was perhaps understandable when property rights were still unclear. However, forest practices remained largely unchanged until well into the twentieth century and the rise of mahogany exports was inconsistent with any notion of sustainability of the forest resources.

The rise of mahogany had a further undesirable consequence. The Baymen, as the settlers were known, had distributed logwood cutting rights among themselves through a system that, at first, limited each settler to one 'location' based on a river frontage of 2,000 yards and extending half way back to the next navigable stream or river. This relatively democratic system did not work for mahogany as the trees grow to maturity so sparsely. As a result, mahogany locations were issued on the basis of a river frontage of three miles, and cutters were allowed two locations on each river. The 'principal families', then, abused the system by issuing locations in the names of other family members or even servants. It was estimated that about a dozen families held almost all the land in locations by the beginning of the nineteenth century.[5] When locations were turned into freeholds by British officials after 1858, the concentration of private land in a few hands was to prove a major obstacle to economic development.

The unsustainable nature of mahogany cutting in Belize was, at first, disguised by the unilateral extension of the settlement's boundaries southwards in the first three decades of the nineteenth century. This was not sanctioned by any treaty, but it gave the settlers access to untouched forests, as there were no Spanish and only a small number of Maya in the area. The British superintendents, who resided in the settlement from 1789, connived at this territorial extension. From 1817, however, the superintendent refused to accept new claims to private ownership in view of the uncertain position in international law.

The volume of mahogany exports rose after 1820 (see figure 13.1). Before then, mahogany had been mainly used in furniture and shipbuilding. However, the use of mahogany in railway carriages provided a great stimulus. The peak of mahogany extraction in Belize was in the1840s when annual exports occasionally exceeded ten million feet. The cost of mahogany extraction then increased as the settlers had to go further inland to secure the trees. Logwood exports also prospered as the rapidly expanding textile industry was still entirely dependent on natural dyes, and Belize was one of the main suppliers to the whole of Europe and North America.

By the 1820s, Belize had by far the highest merchandise exports per head of all Caribbean countries. However, this would prove to be the peak. Not only was there no increase in the value of merchandise exports per head but they also declined even before the country became a colony (see figure 13.2). There were three main reasons for this.

Figure 13.1: ***Belize: Volume of Logwood and Mahogany Exports, 1820–1850***

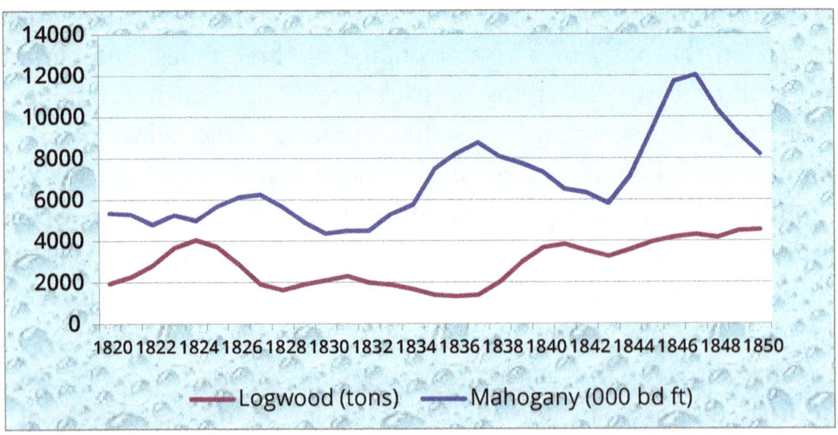

Source: Bulmer-Thomas (2012, 289).

Figure 13.2: Belize: Merchandise Exports per head (US$), 1824–60

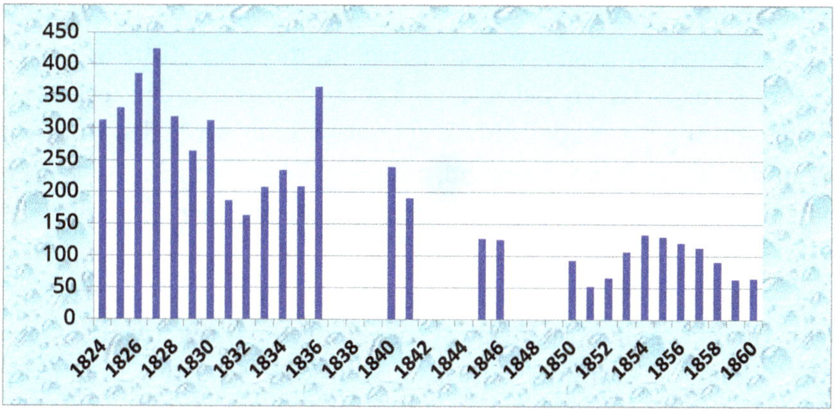

Source: Bulmer-Thomas (2012, 290).

First, the price of mahogany fell. Second, the population of Belize increased after 1830 through net inward migration with the new arrivals playing only a small part in the export sector. Third, re-exports declined after 1840.

The price of mahogany, like other commodities, was exceptionally high at the end of the Napoleonic Wars. Prices subsequently dropped, although the fall was no worse than for many other commodities. With the UK the main market, the British import duty on mahogany then became a controversial issue (Belizean mahogany should have been charged at the foreign duty rate as the settlement was not a colony). Yet, successful lobbying by the exporters and their London agent ensured that Belize was treated *more* favourably than its competitors, including British colonies.[6]

The population of Belize was still less than 4,000 at the end of the Napoleonic Wars. It grew slowly at first, in part, because some slaves escaped to the neighbouring republics where slavery had been abolished.[7] After emancipation, however, the population grew rapidly, reaching over 8,000 by 1841. This may have been partly due to the return of some former slaves. However, it was also due to the inclusion of the inhabitants of the southern districts, as the British authorities became more confident about their claim to these lands. This area included not only the Maya but also the Garinagu who had been expelled from St Vincent by the British in 1797 to Roatán in the

Bay Islands. Many had subsequently made their way to Belize and settled in the south.

When Spanish power was at its height, there was little or no re-export trade between Belize and Central America. This began to change during the Napoleonic Wars, when Spain struggled to assert its authority over its mainland colonies. The entrepôt trade then boomed following the independence of Central America despite the friction caused by runaway slaves. The re-export trade continued after the United Provinces of Central America were dissolved in 1838, with Guatemala in particular maintaining ties with Belizean traders. By the late 1840s, however, these republics were starting to explore alternative avenues of import supply, and this process accelerated with the opening of the Panama railroad in 1855.

The entrepôt trade, at this time, was in two parts. First, Belize imported large quantities of British manufactured goods that were then re-exported to the neighbouring republics. Secondly, Belize imported agricultural products from Central America, such as indigo and cochineal, which were then re-exported (mainly to the UK). Both types of re-exports peaked around 1840 before starting to decline as the Central American states developed direct shipping links with Europe and the US. However, towards the end of the nineteenth century, Belize companies started to extract products from the forests of the neighbouring countries, and these would be re-exported through Belize.

The entrepôt trade accounted for nearly two-thirds of merchandise exports between 1830 and 1860 and had a lasting impact on the currency system of the settlement. Before 1800, Belize had used Jamaican pounds, known as currency, which had a lower value than the pound sterling. The entrepôt trade so flooded the market with coins from Mexico, Central America, Peru, Venezuela, and even Chile that the silver dollar became the *de facto* currency. These silver dollars[8] were then exchanged against the pound sterling at 5:1 – a rate very similar to that of the US dollar under the gold standard (4.87:1). This arrangement, approved by royal decree in 1838, survived until 1887 when the decline in the silver price of gold forced the authorities to revise the currency regime.

The exceptional position of Belize in the 1820s meant that the settlement would remain one of the richest Caribbean countries for some decades despite the problems outlined above. Indeed, by 1850, only the Danish West Indies with its vast re-export trade had overtaken Belize in terms of merchandise exports per head. It is true that there was virtually no domestic production in Belize, agriculture having been forbidden by the terms of the Anglo-Spanish treaties, but as a consequence most of the small population was, at first, engaged in export trades where labour productivity tended to be highest. The first full-time agriculturalists (apart from the Maya who had never abandoned farming) were the migrants who came in the nineteenth century.

The settlers were responsible for their own taxation through the Public Assembly that had been in force since the earliest days. Public revenue per head (see figure 13.3) was modest in comparison with the high level of exports per head. In particular, taxes on imports were relatively low as neither of the dominant groups among the settlers (exporters and merchants) had any desire to raise them and, for most of the time, imports destined for Central America and Mexico were free of duty.

Figure 13.3: ***Belize: Public Revenue per head (US$), 1808–60***

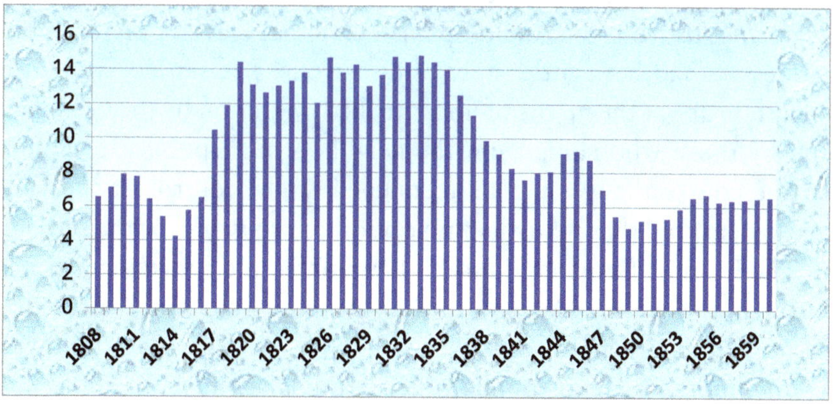

Sources: Revenue from Colonial Department (1836), Martin (1843), Gibbs (1883), Bristowe (1890), and Burdon (1931). Population data are from Statistical Appendix.

These arrangements were deeply unsatisfactory for the British superintendents. The Baymen did not always agree on social and economic policies (the exporters, for example, were strongly opposed to a land tax). Yet, they were often united against the British officials, sent to the settlement, who threatened the traditional privileges that they fought to preserve. Indeed, the superintendent had to insist that British laws abolishing the slave trade in 1807 applied to Belize, and that slaves should be subject to the same process of registration as in the British colonies.

The end of the slave trade presented the settlers with the same issue as other employers in the Caribbean – how to resolve the chronic shortage of labour. In Belize, however, the problem was exacerbated by the number of runaway slaves. Following the end of the apprenticeship period in 1838, the cutters moved swiftly to a system of advance payments for mahogany and logwood workers (almost all former slaves), which pushed them into debt and tied them to the employer for years. Furthermore, the advance had to be spent in the stores, many of which were owned by the employers, where goods were sold through the 'truck' system.

Pernicious though it was, the advance and truck system survived until labour scarcity ended at the beginning of the twentieth century. However, from the point of view of the employers, it was much more effective than the alternatives. The settlers had secured a number of *emancipados* from the Anglo-Spanish Court in Havana in 1836, but the results had been little short of disastrous. The settlers were also uncertain about the merits of uncontrolled migration by the Garinagu and by those who came from the neighbouring republics, although in due course they would be reconciled. Tight control of the land market ensured that many had no option but to work for the settlers.

The Baymen for generations had appointed their own magistrates through the Public Assembly, but the superintendent succeeded in appointing them directly himself in 1833. This was followed by the appointment of public officials on salary in the 1840s. The superintendent did not interfere with locations acquired before 1817 between the Sibun and Hondo rivers, and these would be converted to freehold titles after 1858. However, British officials established that all land south of the Sibun River (about half the settlement) should be Crown lands even before Belize became a colony. Thus, the settlement was divided in two parts: a northern half where a small number of 'monied cutters' monopolised the use of the land and a southern half where there was little or no private ownership of land.

In 1854, the superintendent finally succeeded in replacing the boisterous Public Assembly with a tame Legislative Council with tax-raising powers. The low customs duties favoured by the settlers would be gradually replaced by rates similar to those in the rest of the British Caribbean. The following year, the Laws in Force Act was passed and British officials then moved quickly to legitimise landholdings in Belize. Although the 1858 Honduras Land Titles Act never received the royal assent, a register of land titles was established anyway, and a revised act was passed in 1859. From this point onwards, owners of freehold titles could buy and sell in much the same way as in other British colonies.

The decision by the British to accelerate the shift to colonial institutions had been preceded by the Clayton-Bulwer Treaty of 1850 with the US. Although its wording was ambiguous, it would become clear by 1856 that the US would not oppose British sovereignty over Belize. All that remained were boundary treaties with Guatemala and Mexico. The former signed and ratified a treaty in 1859, but political unrest in the Yucatán peninsula ruled out a treaty with Mexico until 1893. The Anglo-Guatemalan Treaty of 1859 would turn out to be a poisoned chalice, but this would not become clear for some years. The British authorities, therefore, proceeded to demarcate most of the boundary, and Belize became the colony of British Honduras in 1862.

13.2. Colonialism and Economic Decline

One of the first problems the new colony had to address was the wave of migration from the Yucatán peninsula after 1847. This was a consequence of the *Guerra de las Castas*, which was to last half a century and involved not only a struggle between the Maya Indians, the landowners, and the Mexican state but also major conflicts between the different Maya groups. Without an officially recognised boundary between Belize and Mexico, the conflict spread across the border on many occasions while thousands of Yucatecans chose to make their home in northern Belize as both economic and political refugees.

There was no official population figure after 1845 until 1861. However, contemporary estimates suggested the population had jumped to nearly 20,000 by 1857, and the 1861 census confirmed a figure in excess of 25,000. For a country that had recorded a population of less than 4,000 in 1816, this was a huge increase; yet, it did not end labour scarcity as most of the new arrivals became squatters on private land and concentrated on subsistence agriculture. Indeed, within a few years of the census, the colony was importing indentured labour from China and India as well as workers from Barbados (with disappointing results in all cases).[9]

A large part of the problem was the low natural rate of growth of the population. Although births had exceeded deaths among the slave population just before emancipation, it was only by a small margin. This low birth rate almost certainly continued for many decades so that the increase in population was mainly due to the inward migration from Mexico and Guatemala. Furthermore, when reliable figures on births and deaths became available from 1886 onwards, it suggested that the natural rate of growth was still close to zero. It was only after 1894 that the births finally exceeded deaths by a significant margin.

British officials, therefore, saw no reason to relax the policy of restricting access to land that the Colonial Office – and the private landholders – had exercised even before establishing the colony. Crown lands in the south were not, at first, made available in small parcels at low prices while private lands in the north were almost never sold to small farmers. Colonial policy was, therefore, in line with that preferred by the large landowners, who complained constantly of labour shortage despite the population growth and who restricted access to their own land as vigorously as possible.

Landholdings had been highly concentrated even before the last of the Anglo-Spanish treaties in 1786. However, it would become much more concentrated after the colony was established. By this time (c.1860), it had become normal for exporters in Belize to have associations with merchants in the UK and, in one case, this had been formalised in a London-quoted company established under the provisions of the 1856 British legislation permitting limited liability. This enterprise, the British Honduras Company, was formed in 1859 and from the moment of its creation owned well in excess of one million acres of freehold land.[10] When it became in 1875 the Belize Estate and Produce Company (BEC), it would own more than half of all freehold land in the country.

The BEC, like General Motors in the US in the twentieth century, considered its interests synonymous with that of the country as a whole, and colonial officials saw no reason to disagree. Its influence on colonial policy included not only land and labour but also taxation and the exchange rate. It was represented in all the colonial assemblies and could count on direct access to the governor. Furthermore, it was influential in the UK through its shareholders, and at least one of its directors sat in Parliament, so that the British government had to take heed of its interests as well.

What BEC could not do was prevent the crisis in the mahogany industry that was brought about by the decline in demand and the fall in price after the mid-1860s. This was a consequence of the switch to iron in ships and the end of the boom in railway carriage construction in the UK. The company, therefore, switched back to logwood and other cutters followed suit (see figure 13.4). By 1870, the value of logwood exports had overtaken that of mahogany, although both were below their levels at the beginning of the century.

Figure 13.4: ***Belize: Volume of Logwood and Mahogany Exports, 1856–1900***

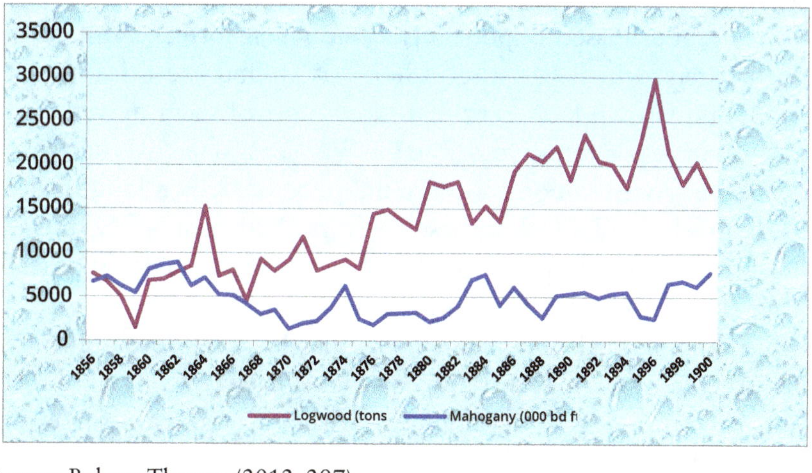

Source: Bulmer-Thomas (2012, 297).

The mahogany crisis in the 1860s had been temporarily disguised, in Belize, by the boom in re-exports to the Confederacy during the US Civil War (1861–65). Legal exports soared, but illegal exports probably increased as well since part of the trade consisted of munitions. Britain – officially neutral in the Civil War – tried to stop the contraband, but the efforts of colonial officials were not successful as Belizean merchants had been trading guns to the Maya insurgents in Yucatán for years and were adept at concealing the trade.

As the re-export boom ended, officials finally concluded that the colony's long-term salvation depended on the development of agricultural exports alongside timber extraction. It had been clear for years that the rate of extraction of mahogany was beyond what was sustainable in the long-run. Belize, on the other hand, had an abundance of land suitable for agriculture. Yet, the Colonial Office was unclear how to proceed, and British officials missed many opportunities to promote the diversification of the economy.

The first missed opportunity had come with the arrival of migrants before the colony was even established. Neither the Garinagu nor the Yucatecans, yet alone the *emancipados* or returning former slaves, were initially offered Crown lands on favourable terms so that a small-scale peasantry could not take root. The minimal development in small-scale agriculture that did take place was a result of squatting. Furthermore, these squatters were far from Belize City,[11] the only significant urban centre, so that no marketable surplus was offered and the colony continued to depend on imported foodstuffs.

The second missed opportunity came when former Confederate soldiers arrived in Belize after 1865, but found the price of both private and Crown land exorbitant and most of them moved on to other countries or returned to the US.[12] At least one governor asked permission from London to lower the price of Crown land or even make it freely available, but these overtures had been firmly resisted. The notion of labour scarcity had taken such a firm hold that officials were not prepared to take any chances.

The third missed opportunity was the (lack of) development of infrastructure. Private sector and colonial elites were convinced there could be no long-term development without a railway connecting Belize with Guatemala. When a US entrepreneur, Walter Regan, came with a serious offer in 1884 and surveyed a route that would have passed through the south-west corner of the colony, there was almost universal enthusiasm. However, the Colonial Office dithered as it wanted to ensure that any railway would meet the terms of the British obligation to Guatemala under the 1859 boundary treaty. The railway to Guatemala was, therefore, never built.

Colonial officials were reluctant to use public resources to pursue developmental goals. Public revenue per head was higher than in most other British colonies, but the threat from Yucatán meant that, in many years, much of this was absorbed by military expenditure. Indeed, the danger was so severe in the second half of the 1860s that the Legislative Assembly (responsible for raising taxes) abolished itself in 1870 and Crown Colony government was introduced in April 1871. This backward step had been taken to oblige the British government to absorb more of the cost of colonial defence, since the members of the Assembly had no wish for the land tax they had passed in 1867 to be anything other than temporary.[13]

Public debt under colonialism was first issued in 1863, but it remained at very modest levels and was used primarily to make improvements to Belize City. Frustration with the slow progress in infrastructure development finally persuaded the private sector to finance a tramway a few miles up the Stann Creek valley. This opened in 1892 and promoted banana exports (see below). When the shipping line carrying bananas was purchased by the United Fruit Company in 1900, the colonial government was lobbied to build a full-scale railway down the whole length of the valley to the nearest seaport.

Belize still had no all-weather roads and the 90-mile journey from Belize City to San Ignacio on the western border took many days by boat. The northern frontier was also inaccessible except by water, and the south remained very isolated. Yet, despite the dismal state of infrastructure, the first small steps towards export diversification had been taken by the end of the nineteenth century. This had little to do with colonial policy and initially had nothing to do with the landowners either, but it was welcome and much needed all the same.

The first significant step was the establishment of a sugar industry by the Yucatecan refugees in the north of the country. While most refugees engaged in self-sufficient agriculture, a small number experimented with sugar and rum production around the town of Corozal. In 1857, the first small shipment of sugar was made, but this was not repeated until 1862. By then, the British Honduras Company had turned some of its idle lands into sugarcane plantations and the growth of sugar exports was rapid. The Confederate settlers, especially in the Toledo district, also contributed to the growth of the industry.

The next step was the development of a banana industry centred on the Stann Creek Valley. The first regular shipment was made in 1882, and within a few years, exports had increased rapidly. The trade was, at first, in the hands of small-scale farmers, who were able to take advantage of the steamships that were now calling regularly from New Orleans following a decision of Governor Barlee in 1878 to transfer the mail subsidy away from the Jamaica route. A British Honduras Syndicate was formed out of several smaller firms and soon multinational companies started calling at Belize to buy bananas. As the century ended, and even before the railway was planned, the prospects for banana exports looked bright.

Colonial officials could take some credit for the next two examples of non-traditional exports. Rubber (*castilloa elastica*) had started to be exported in 1882, but it was at first harvested from the wild. A small botanic garden had been established in the grounds of Government House in 1892, and rubber seedlings were distributed throughout the country.[14] Shortly afterwards, a small export trade in cacao and coffee was started. None of these products amounted to much in volume or value terms, but they did at least show that Belize could produce agricultural goods for export.

Ironically, it was a forest product (chicle) that proved the most enduring and successful non-traditional export as the nineteenth century ended. The bleeding of the sapodilla tree produces a latex, which is the basis of chewing gum and was much in demand in the US. It served the needs of the large estates perfectly, and they started to add chicle to their traditional exports from 1894 onwards.

By no means was all the chicle exported by Belize produced in the country. By the late nineteenth century, the landowners had so exhausted their forest reserves that they were cutting logwood and mahogany across the borders in Guatemala and Mexico. Chicle was soon added to the list, and re-exports once again became vital to Belize. The traditional re-export trade to Central America and Yucatán had not entirely ended – indeed, merchants did a thriving trade, supplying the forest workers across the borders – but it had changed character.

The rise of non-traditional exports took place as the currency question became especially awkward. The silver dollars (*sol*) circulating in the colony served their purpose well enough until the silver price of gold started to fall after 1873. By 1880, it was no longer possible to maintain the fiction of a fixed rate of exchange against sterling, and the Treasury each year converted *sol* to sterling at a different rate. In 1887, by royal decree, the Guatemalan silver dollar was made the legal tender of the colony, although other silver dollars were still accepted up to small amounts.[15] However, this was only a temporary measure as the silver price continued to fall. Finally, bowing to pressure from different interest groups, the US gold dollar was made legal tender in 1894.

Belize was now effectively on the gold standard, but nominal wage rates had to be reduced so that exports could remain competitive. The average reduction was 30 per cent, which brought nominal wage rates back approximately to their level in 1892. This caused much grumbling and some rioting (including by the police force in the northern district). From this point onwards, in common with the surrounding republics, Belize enjoyed a period of economic recovery that lasted with only minor interruptions up to the First World War.

Yet, the deep structural flaws remained in place. There was no forest management by either the public or private sector so that timber exports were unsustainable over the long-term. Mahogany trees were increasingly difficult to find and expensive to extract (hence the search for cheaper alternatives in Guatemala and Mexico). Chicle was also not being harvested in a sustainable fashion. With the rise of the German chemical industry and the development of aniline dyes in the 1890s, logwood faced a synthetic competitor at the end of the century for the first time. Bananas, as elsewhere in Central America, were at the mercy of diseases for which there were no known cures. And there were still no roads, so that efforts to diversify the economy and encourage agricultural exports were seriously impeded.

The Belize economy, by 1900, had lost its privileged position in the Caribbean (it had been ranked first in 1850 in terms of domestic exports per head and second – behind the Danish West Indies – in terms of merchandise exports per head). By 1900, it had fallen to fourth position in terms of merchandise exports per head and sixth position in terms of domestic exports per head. These rankings were by no means disastrous, but more worrying was the *absolute* decline in the Belizean position since domestic exports per head in 1900 were roughly half what they had been in 1850, while merchandise exports per head were only one-third of their earlier value.

13.3. The Fall of the Economy: 1900–50

The Belizean economy made some progress in the first years of the twentieth century. The first bank was established in 1903.[16] A new market had been found for mahogany in the US; chicle had been added to the list of principal exports; bananas were expanding and the re-export trade was recovering. Agricultural exports only contributed 20 per cent to domestic exports, and Crown land leased to farmers (large and small) was less than one per cent of the colony's surface area, but the authorities could convince themselves that a start had been made in diversifying the economy away from timber.

In the next few decades, however, Belize's position would seriously deteriorate and by 1950 it would be ranked fourteenth in terms of domestic exports per head, placing it in the bottom half of all Caribbean countries. The four decades after 1910 were, therefore, critical ones for Belize and mark the years when the economy – still heavily based on forest products exploited in an unsustainable fashion – started to fail.

Although the period coincided with two world wars and the Great Depression, this was also true of all other countries. Thus, the *relative* decline of the Belize economy needs to be explained as well as its *absolute* fall. Furthermore, the relative deterioration continued through the 1950s. As an illustration, the growth of domestic exports per head at constant prices is shown in table 13.1 for three periods, and it demonstrates clearly how poorly Belize performed not only in relation to the British colonies, but also relative to other subregions. Indeed, over the whole period from 1900 to 1960, domestic exports per head at constant prices fell and the Belizean performance was worse than all the other subregions shown.

Table 13.1: ***Belize: Comparison of Annual Rate of Change of Domestic Exports per Head (1930 Prices), 1900–60***

				Dependencies:				
	Belize	**Hispaniola**	**Cuba**	**British**	**French**	**Dutch**	**US**	**Caribbean**
1900–20	-0.3	-0.3	1.3	0.5	1.5	0.3	6.8	2.0
1920–40	-0.6	-1.2	-3.7	0.3	0.0	10.2	0.4	-1.2
1940–60	-0.5	2.1	2.2	7.0	0.7	1.8	4.2	3.6
1900–60	-0.5	0.2	-0.1	2.6	0.7	4.0	3.8	1.5

Source: Statistical Appendix.

The outbreak of the First World War in August 1914 was, of course, a serious blow for Belize. The mahogany shipped to the US since the 1890s may have reduced the importance of the British market, but the UK was still a major customer and continental Europe (including Russia) was also important for logwood. Demand from Europe for timber fell immediately, but mahogany exports to the US also plummeted because contractors in Mexico, fearful of losing their concessions, had over-supplied the US market following the outbreak of revolution in December 1910.

The slump in demand for exports in the early years of the war reduced the need for labour. In the 1914/15 season, forestry requirements were roughly half what they had been the previous year. For the first time ever, the colony experienced surplus labour, a situation made worse by the return of those workers who had migrated to Panama after 1903 to build the canal. Belize suffered net migration outwards in every decade after 1900, a complete reverse of what had happened in the nineteenth century. The mahogany industry was rescued, however, by the decision of the British Admiralty to place a large order in 1916. This was used not just in shipbuilding but also to make propellers for the Royal Air Force.

When the war ended, traditional sources of demand for mahogany returned, and exports rose to previously unheard of levels (see figure 13.5). Prices, as for other commodities in the Caribbean, fell sharply in 1921, but in Belize they soon recovered. And Belize now had a new and unexpected source of additional income as a result of US prohibition (1919–33). Re-exports, mainly of whisky imported from Canada, soared to destinations from which they could be smuggled into the US.

While Belize was benefiting from the boom in mahogany exports and the brief revival of the entrepôt trade, its other main commodity exports were facing ever more dismal prospects. The most serious case was logwood, which as late as 1900 was almost equal in value to mahogany. The First World War hit the trade hard (see figure 13.5) and it never recovered. The textile industry now preferred the cheaper aniline dyes sold by chemical firms and Belizean logwood exports would fade away in the 1920s after 250 years of continuous exploitation. The trees were, and still are, available in abundance, but the market had changed forever. The last shipments were made in the Great Depression.

Chicle faced a similar problem, although it was not as severe. Even before the First World War, manufacturers of chewing gum had been diluting chicle with cheaper substitutes – mainly from Asia where they could be obtained at one-third the cost. When peacetime conditions returned, manufacturers had grown accustomed to the cheaper substitutes. The 1920s were, therefore, a difficult time for the industry in Belize and exports fell.

Figure 13.5: Belize: Volume of Logwood and Mahogany Exports, 1900–50

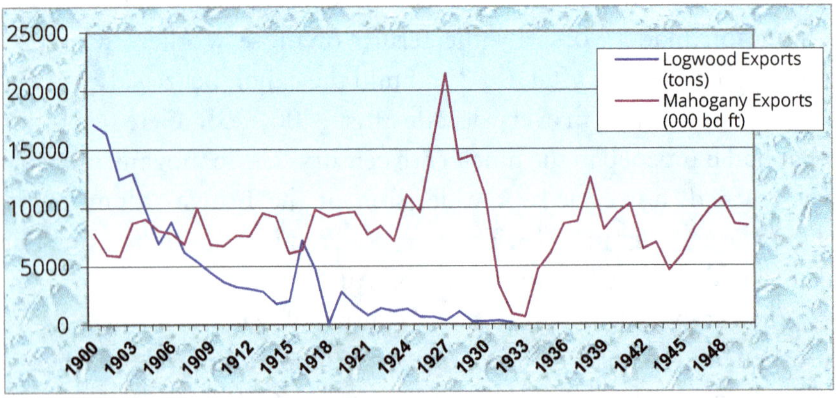

Source: Statistical Appendix.

The banana industry faced no competition from cheaper substitutes and much had been expected from its development, especially after the opening of the Stann Creek Railway in 1911. However, Panama disease soon entered Belize, and exports started to decline from 1917. This was no different to other parts of Central America, but the banana companies in the republics had dealt with the threat by opening new plantations. This option was more difficult in Belize – not because of a shortage of land but because there were no transport and port facilities. As the multinational companies lost interest in Belize, ships called less frequently, and exports became dependent on smallholders with no marketing expertise.

The authorities could no longer postpone introducing policies that should have been adopted much earlier. Following a critical report on the state of the colony's forest resources, a Forestry Department was finally established in 1922, some Crown lands were turned into forest reserves, and a public loan was taken out to establish timber on a sustainable basis through conservation on public and private lands (an income tax was finally introduced in 1920 to service this debt). Mahogany was made a priority as the rate of extraction was far in excess of what the colony could sustain, and the aim was to raise the density of mahogany trees from one to 40 per acre on conserved land. Finally, the land tax was also increased in the 1920s (first to 1.5 and then to 2.0 cents per acre).

Even before the establishment of the Forest Department, an Agricultural Commission had been set up in 1917. It emphasised the need for improved infrastructure, particularly roads, if there were to be any chance of export diversification. However, its recommendations were ignored on the grounds of cost, and the first steps in road-building would not be taken until 1925. Progress was so slow, however, that the road from Belize City to Corozal near the Mexican border was not finished until 1938, while that to San Ignacio close to the western frontier would not be completed until after the Second World War.

By the end of the 1920s Belize was, therefore, vulnerable. Despite the efforts at diversification, the colony's prosperity still hinged on forest products, and mahogany was once again the leading commodity – responsible for nearly 70 per cent of domestic exports.

Mechanisation, using tractors instead of oxen and short-haul logging railways, began in the 1920s, and this increased the rate of extraction. However, it reduced the need for labour. Furthermore, many firms started to hire labour for six months a year rather than 11 months as before. Employment peaked in 1924, but mahogany extraction carried on rising until 1927 (see figure 13.5) at a rate that was not only far too high for Belize but also saturated the world market.

Some pinned their hopes on marine products as a solution to the problem of export diversification. Belize, after all, has extensive rivers and coasts as well as offshore islands (cayes). Marine products began to be exported in the 1920s with a small sponge industry at Turneffe Island, lobster (canned and fresh) on Ambergris Caye, and turtleshell throughout the coastal district, but the contribution of these products to domestic exports was still tiny when world trade started to shrink at the end of the decade. Marine exports then disappeared to re-emerge after the Second World War.

With the start of the Great Depression, and shortly afterwards (in 1931) a devastating hurricane, the Belize economy went into a tailspin. The main problem for Belize was the global collapse in the demand for mahogany after 1929. Exports from Belize fell in one year from 14 to 11 million feet before collapsing to 3.3 million feet in 1931 (see figure 13.5). Two years later, they had fallen to 636,000 feet, their lowest level since the eighteenth century. The fall in demand for chicle was not so precipitate, but by now the logwood had gone and bananas were of negligible importance. Domestic exports per head fell to $5.8 in 1932 (the worst year) compared with $34.6 on the eve of the First World War and $48.8 in the boom year of 1920 (see figure 13.6).

Belize faced an additional problem in the Great Depression, which most other Caribbean countries were able to avoid. Imperial preference since 1919 had helped the UK to retain a significant share of the Belize market, but the colony's currency was tied to the US dollar. When, therefore, Great Britain abandoned the gold standard in 1931 and devalued its currency, the Belize dollar was immediately *revalued* against the pound sterling. This helps to explain the astonishing collapse in the volume of Belizean exports after 1930. The decision by the US to abandon the link with gold in 1933, thereby devaluing the US dollar against sterling and other European currencies, then helped Belize to recover from the depression.[17]

Figure 13.6:* *Belize: Exports per head (US$),1850–1950

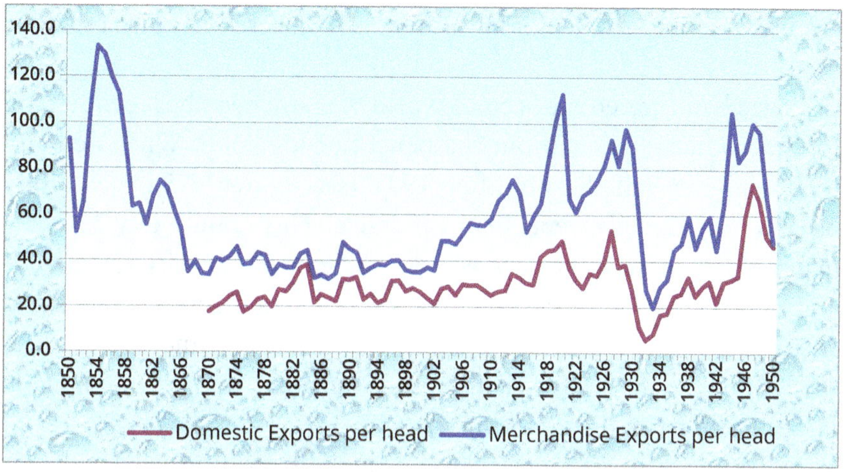

Sources: 1900–50 from Statistical Appendix. Earlier years derived from *Parliamentary Papers* and Statistical Appendix.

The 1931 hurricane caused a significant loss of life and damage to property.[18] A loan was hastily agreed with the British Treasury to provide mortgages for those who had lost homes and businesses, but the impact of the depression on public revenue was so severe that the colonial government was forced to accept a loan-in-aid from the British Treasury in the fiscal year 1932/3. Although modest in size, it brought with it fiscal control from London.

Embarrassing though this was, it had a silver lining. The British officials, now in charge of public finances, were shocked by the poor state of infrastructure. From 1932 onwards, therefore, Belize received a stream of Colonial Development Funds and loans-in-aid that continued after the Second World War. These were spent, in large part, to give the colony the rudiments of an all-weather road system, although the roads were barely passable in the wet season.

Treasury control also helped to improve fiscal effort. Import duties had been steadily raised in the 1920s (to a maximum of 20 per cent) as a consequence of the introduction of imperial preference (yields would otherwise have fallen). They were raised again after the hurricane to a maximum of 25 per cent and customs duties then continued to provide the bulk of public revenue until 1946, when a new income tax law was forced through a reluctant assembly by the use of the governor's reserve powers. The land tax was increased in the 1930s, but the large landowners (including BEC) refused to pay the increase and the Colonial Office then lowered it to its previous rate.

Belize had entered the Second World War still heavily dependent on forest products, but without the benefit of logwood. When demand for mahogany fell sharply after 1941 (see figure 13.5), the colony became increasingly dependent on chicle. This commodity, the raw material for chewing gum, was close to being a necessity for the US, and demand fell less precipitately than for mahogany. Banana and coconut exports, on the other hand, were reduced almost to nothing as shipping space was used for other purposes and citrus virtually disappeared from the export list.

Belize, therefore, found itself in a difficult position when the war ended, a position not helped by increasing friction with Guatemala.[19] The infrastructure was slowly improving, and the 1946 census showed that nearly 30 per cent of the labour force was now in agriculture. However, private land was still tightly controlled by a tiny number of landowners, principally BEC, and the first national income estimates confirmed the modest position that Belize now held among even the British Caribbean colonies.[20] The colonial authorities seemed at a loss how to proceed and yet they were unwilling to encourage local participation in any shape or form. It was not until after devaluation, which took place on the last day of 1949, that the political situation would start to change and the economic diversification of the Belizean economy could truly begin.

NOTES

1. During the period considered here, Belize was known by many different names. It was the 'British Settlement in the Bay of Honduras' until the early nineteenth century, when it became known in British sources as the 'Bay of Honduras' or even on occasions 'Honduras'. It became 'British Honduras' in 1862 and 'Belize' in 1973.
2. This gave the settlers the right to cut logwood, but the area in which they could do so was not clearly defined. See R.A. Naylor, *Penny ante Imperialism: The Mosquito Shore and the Bay of Honduras, 1600–*

1914: A Case Study in British Informal Empire (Rutherford, NJ: Fairleigh Dickinson University Press, 1989), 55.

3. It is still called the Bay Pew and the inscription, dated 1727, reads: 'This Pew for the use of the Gentlemen of the Bay of Honduras'. A few years later, in 1740, the merchants of Belize donated timber for the steeple.
4. The first reference to slaves in Belize is in 1724, when they were said to have only recently arrived, while the total number was only 120 as late as 1745. See A. Shoman, *13 Chapters of a History of Belize*. 2nd ed. (Belize City, Belize: Angelus Press, 2011), 28–29.
5. The evacuation of the Mosquito Shore in 1787, as agreed in the Anglo-Spanish Treaty the previous year, had swollen the Belize population and threatened the dominant position of the established cutters. They, therefore, protected their position by ruling that only those with four slaves were entitled to a mahogany work, thereby excluding most of the new arrivals from access to timber. See O.N. Bolland, *The Formation of a Colonial Society: Belize, from Conquest to Crown Colony* (Baltimore, MD: Johns Hopkins University Press, 1977), 32–33.
6. See N. Dobson, *A History of Belize* (Port of Spain, Trinidad and Tobago: Longman Caribbean, 1973), 131–32.
7. It was abolished by the United Provinces of Central America in 1824 and by Mexico in 1829.
8. They were known collectively as *sol*, which was the name of the Peruvian silver dollar. See L. Bristowe and P. Wright, *The Handbook of British Honduras for 1889–90* (Edinburgh: Blackwood, 1980), 205–10.
9. Many of the Chinese were so badly treated that they fled across the border and joined the Santa Cruz Maya in Mexico. See Bolland, *The Formation of a Colonial Society*, 143.
10. This was about one-fifth of the whole colony. See Bolland, *The Formation of a Colonial Society*, 186–87.
11. When the country was known as British Honduras, and even before, the main town was called 'Belize'. It became 'Belize City' when the country's name was changed to Belize in 1973.
12. See D.C. Simmons, *Confederate Settlements in British Honduras* (Jefferson, NC: McFarland, 2001), 48–53.
13. In this they were disappointed as the land tax was made permanent in 1871, albeit at a very low rate.
14. See B. Bulmer-Thomas and V. Bulmer-Thomas, *The Economic History of Belize: from 17th Century to Independence* (Benque Viejo del Carmen, Belize: Cubola, 2012), chapter 5.
15. See Bristowe, *The Handbook of British Honduras*, 205–10.
16. Its name was the Bank of British Honduras. It was purchased by the Royal Bank of Canada in 1912.

17. It could not prevent serious riots in 1934, however, as a consequence of high levels of unemployment. See O.N. Bolland, *Colonialism and Resistance in Belize: Essays in Historical Sociology* (Benque Viejo del Carmen, Belize: Cubola Productions, 1988), 167–76.
18. It was the first hurricane to hit Belize City for 80 years, there was no early warning system and the public was completely unprepared.
19. Guatemala had unilaterally abrogated the 1859 treaty in 1939 and later closed the border. The situation became so tense in 1948 that Britain despatched a gunboat and war was considered a real possibility. The closure of the border had a very negative impact on the re-export trade.
20. The first reliable estimate was made for 1946. See N.S. Carey Jones, *The Pattern of a Dependent Economy: The National Income of British Honduras* (Cambridge: Cambridge University Press, 1953).

Chapter 14
BARBADOS AND THE EASTERN CARIBBEAN

Barbados and the eastern Caribbean countries of Antigua and Barbuda, Dominica, Grenada, St Kitts and Nevis, St Lucia, and St Vincent and the Grenadines form the subject of this chapter. The seven were British colonies by the time the Napoleonic Wars ended and all are now independent. The first to become independent was Barbados in 1966 and the last was St Kitts and Nevis in 1983.

The British never gave up on the idea of some kind of union as a prelude to dominion status until the collapse of the Federation of the West Indies in 1962. As a result, the Leeward Islands Federation – including Antigua and Barbuda, Dominica (until 1940), and St Kitts and Nevis – survived from 1871 to 1956. The Windward Islands Federation, including Barbados (until 1885), Grenada, St Lucia, and St Vincent and the Grenadines, had an even longer history.

The idea that these islands were too small to stand on their own was shared not just by the colonial authorities but by many islanders themselves. Only Barbados has been sufficiently self-confident since 1885 to eschew any form of union with the other islands, proceeding to independence in 1966 and then making its own monetary arrangements. Elsewhere, the end of the sterling area brought an early experiment in monetary union and the formation of the Eastern Caribbean Central Bank (ECCB), with its own currency pegged to the US dollar.[1] The experiment was highly successful, leading to low inflation in all the member states. This has provided the necessary, if not sufficient, conditions to remain internationally competitive in the face of external shocks and cycles in the domestic economy.

Unlike Barbados, the other countries in this chapter all joined Petrocaribe, the scheme launched by the Venezuelan government in 2005 to provided subsidised oil and cheap loans to member states.

All took full advantage, allowing them to implement projects that would otherwise have been impossible or would have entailed more costly loans. However, Petrocaribe was undermined first by the fall in oil prices after 2014 and secondly by the economic crisis in Venezuela, making it impossible for the Bolivarian republic to meet its obligations. Member states, however, have been left with a debt to Venezuela.

14.1. Barbados

Barbados had begun its life as a British colony in the seventeenth century, producing tobacco for export with European indentured labour. It was not long, however, before it switched to exporting sugar with African slave labour. It would soon become the Caribbean island most specialised in sugar and its by-products, so that at the end of the Napoleonic Wars 96 per cent of its domestic exports came from the industry.

Despite specialisation in sugar, exports per head in 1820 were below average for the Caribbean. After nearly two centuries of intense sugar production on a small island, the soil was exhausted and yields were below those elsewhere. Yet, the planters had such a tight grip on the political economy of the colony that no serious effort was made to diversify.

Figure 14.1: ***Barbados: Exports per head at constant prices (1900=100), 1820–2016***

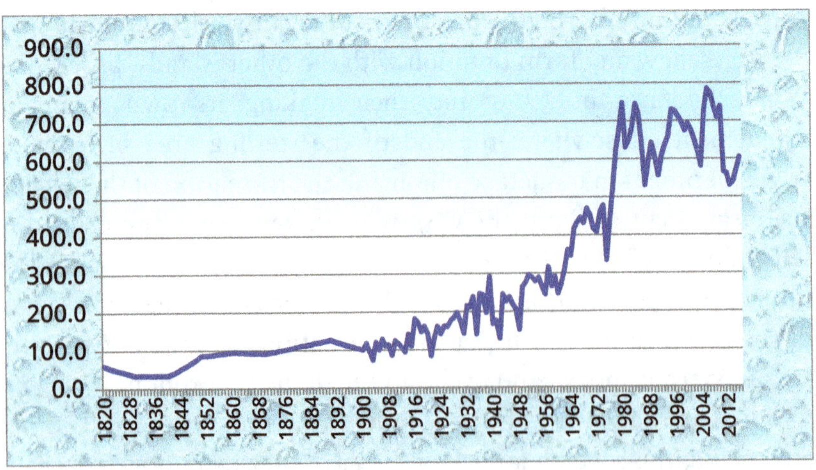

Source: Statistical Appendix to 2008; UNNA thereafter.

The planters were able to survive the abolition of the slave trade because the slave birth rate was higher than the death rate. By 1833, on the eve of emancipation, the number of slaves had actually increased over the previous 25 years and still accounted for 75 per cent of the population. And, unable to squat or buy smallholdings, the former slaves after emancipation had little choice but to emigrate or stay on the plantations.[2]

Many did emigrate, but those that remained made it possible for the planters to increase both yields and production of sugar through the adoption of more intensive use of the land. After a small drop between 1820 and 1840, exports per head recovered rapidly in the next 50 years until the fall in the world sugar prices took its inevitable toll in the 1890s (see figure 14.1).

The sugar crisis at the end of the century was a matter of great concern to the Royal Commission sent in 1897 to investigate conditions in the West Indies. The commissioners referred to the abundant labour supply in Barbados. While correct, this could not disguise that emigration had started as soon as the apprenticeship period had ended in 1838. From then onwards, Barbadians had left in their thousands. At first, they went to other British colonies in the Caribbean. However, as soon as opportunities appeared – in Costa Rica, Cuba, Panama, and the US – they left for jobs there as well.

***Figure 14.2:* Barbados: Net Migration (% of Population), 1851–2015**

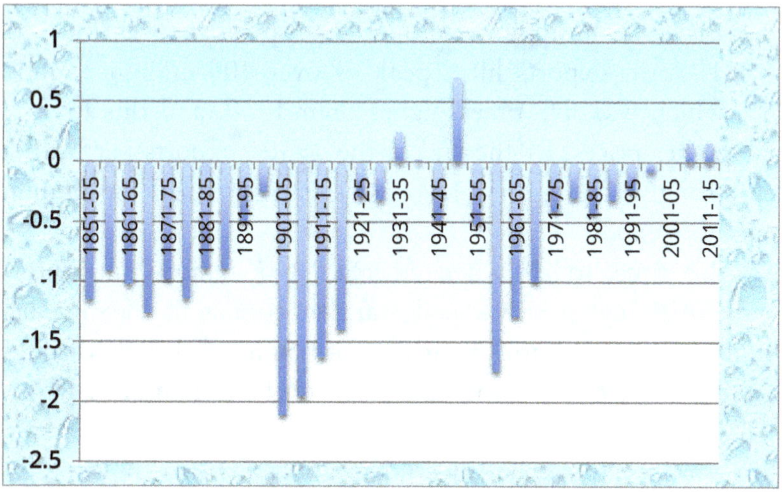

Source: Statistical Appendix and World Bank, World Development Indicators.

The scale of the net outward migration was astonishing. In almost every five-year period from 1850 onwards, Barbados experienced a loss of people (see figure 14.2). And the main exception (1946–50) was simply due to the troops returning home at the end of the war. It was only at the end of the period shown here – from 2006 onwards – that Barbados experienced net inward migration, but the scale of immigration has been tiny.

Emigration on this scale meant that the population was bound to grow slowly. Indeed, if it were not for births almost invariably exceeding deaths by a large margin, the population would have fallen significantly. From roughly 100,000 in 1829, it had risen to only 194,500 by 1900. It then went into decline, such was the scale of emigration, before reaching its nadir of 155,000 in 1921. Since then, the population has grown very slowly to reach 285,000 in 2016.

The sugar crisis continued into the twentieth century and exports per head (see figure 14.1) stagnated despite the new market that opened up in Canada as a result of the Dominion's application of imperial preference. The First World War, however, gave a huge boost to the sugar and rum industries in Barbados and exports soared. Although prices quickly fell after the war, there was still no real desire, on the part of the planters and the colonial legislature, to diversify away from dependence on sugar.

The decision not to diversify appeared to have been vindicated when the UK adopted imperial preference at the Ottawa conference in 1932 and the Commonwealth Sugar Agreement went into force in 1951. Sugar exports hit a peak of over 400 million pounds in 1957, which was five times higher than 1930, and this time with much higher prices. By the end of the 1950s, exports per head had risen strongly (see figure 14.1) and sugar remained the dominant commodity export.

By this time, tourism had emerged as a major contributor to growth. Although tourists had started arriving in the nineteenth century, it was not until the advent of commercial flights from the US and Europe that it was able to reach large numbers. In 1952, the Barbados Hotel Association was formed, and it was not long before service exports had overtaken goods exports by value. With the addition of cruise shipping in the 1990s, together with the decline of the sugar industry, Barbados had become the quintessential Caribbean economy, dependent primarily on service exports.

The impact of tourism on economic growth was at first positive. GDP per head rose rapidly in the 1960s (see figure 14.3). However, as a tourist-dependent country, Barbados was vulnerable to external events such as the two oil shocks in the 1970s and the debt crisis of the 1980s. In addition, Barbados soon lost its 'first mover' advantage as other Caribbean countries were quick to follow in its footsteps as a pioneer of tourism.

Governments in Barbados now accepted the need to diversify. Sugar exports were replaced with a series of assembly operations as well as oil refining. CARICOM provided an opportunity for a modest amount of import-substituting industrialisation. Service exports were expanded to include non-tourist activities such as call centres, finance and insurance. However, Barbados was badly affected by the global financial crisis in 2008 (see figure 14.3).

Figure 14.3: Barbados: GDP per head (2010 US$), 1960–2017

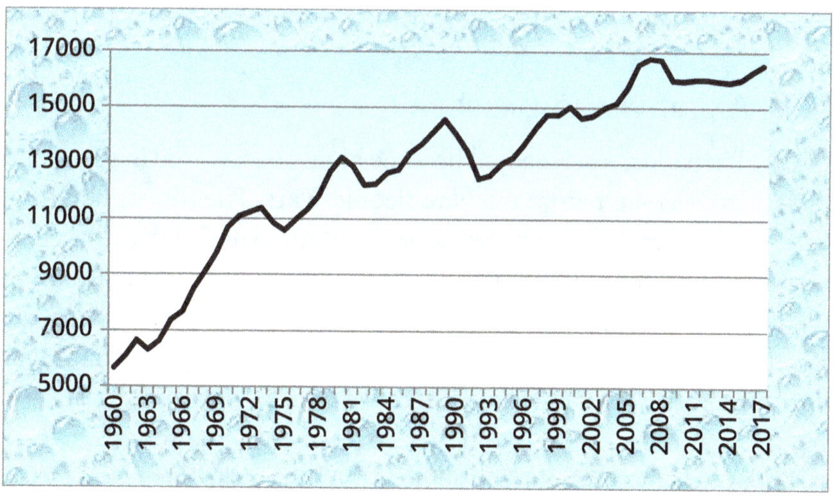

Source: World Bank, World Development Indicators from 1974 onwards; earlier years from Statistical Appendix.

Unable to expand exports significantly and unwilling to curtail public spending, Barbados experienced a steep rise in public debt – both internal and external – which had reached 157 per cent of GDP by mid-2018. The new government, elected in May 2018, felt it had no choice other than to go the International Monetary Fund (IMF) and negotiate an Extended Fund Facility. The IMF offered its usual medicine:[3]

> Over the last decade, Barbados's economy has experienced low growth, while fiscal and external imbalances have gradually widened to reach an unsustainable situation, with very high debt and very low reserves. The authorities' reform program seeks to address these challenges with a combination of front-loaded fiscal consolidation, measures to boost growth, and debt restructuring, while protecting social spending.

Barbados had replaced dependence on sugar with dependence on tourism. For many years, it reaped a handsome dividend in terms of fast economic growth, although it was not fast enough to reverse net outward migration. Yet, it ended in a decade of stagnation with no guarantee that the IMF medicine will restore growth in the future. It was a bitter lesson in one of the harsh realities of Caribbean economics: export diversification, of goods and services, is a permanent feature of small, open economies if they are to achieve sustainable long-run economic growth of GDP per head.

14.2. ANTIGUA AND BARBUDA

Like Barbados, Antigua had become highly specialised in sugar and its derivatives long before the Napoleonic Wars. The forests had been cleared to make way for sugar cane and little was left for any other purposes. The population, a mere 40,000 shortly after the abolition of the slave trade in 1808, was nearly 90 per cent slaves leaving the planters in constant fear of revolts.[4] At the same time, marronage was almost impossible for the slaves because of the destroyed forests and the fact that most of the island was covered with plantations.

With slave deaths each year higher than births, the slave population declined after the trade's abolition. It had fallen to 28,635 in 1834 when slavery ended on both Antigua and Barbuda,[5] but still accounted for nearly 80 per cent of the population. At this point, the slaves might have expected a period of apprenticeship but this – uniquely among British colonies – was waived by the colonial authorities. The planters were so confident that the slaves would be forced to remain on the estates that they did not see the need for apprenticeship.

What the planters had not anticipated was the competition among themselves for workers. For those who stayed on the island, estate work may have been inevitable, but they were free to move to different plantations. Wage rates for skilled and unskilled workers rose rapidly, raising the possibility that the sugar industry would be destroyed by rising costs.[6] Nicholas Nugent, a planter, explained to the select committee on West India colonies in May 1842:[7]

> When our labour was at 6d. per day…I collated many documents in the presence of different philanthropic gentlemen who visited the colony at different times to see how the thing was working, and I think we made it out that the free labour system was the cheaper of the two; but as the price of labour has now risen 50 per cent we are now to take a different view of the matter, and I rather think that our expenses are just at this moment somewhat beyond the amount of slave labour.

Draconian measures were then adopted by the planters to reduce both predial and skilled wage rates sharply between 1842 and 1850. As a result, the sugar industry survived. Indeed, it would expand up to 1890 after which – as elsewhere in the British Caribbean – it succumbed to the impact of low world prices caused by European bounties and no imperial preference.

Figure 14.4: ***Antigua: Exports per head at constant prices (1900=100), 1820–2016***

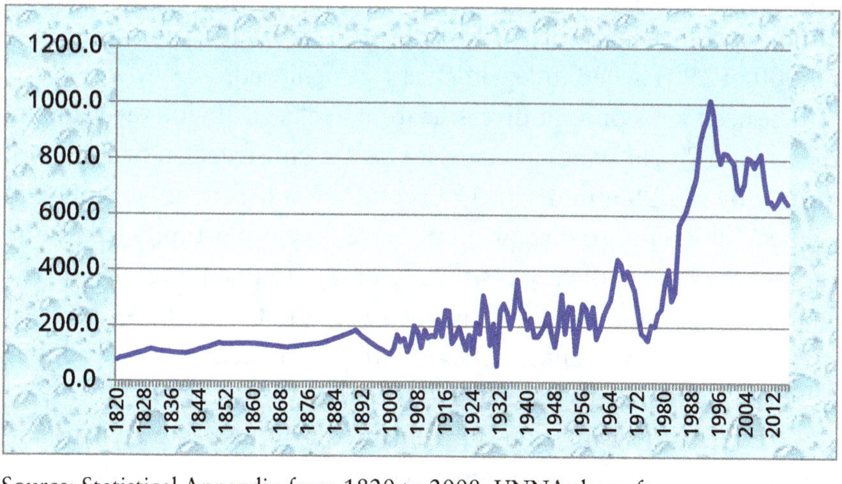

Source: Statistical Appendix from 1820 to 2008; UNNA thereafter.

The difficulties faced by sugar at the end of the nineteenth century meant that exports per head fell sharply after 1890 (see figure 14.4). Indeed, by 1900, they were back to their level in the mid-1820s. This was not only due to the decline in the volume of sugar exported but also to the virtual disappearance of the rum industry. From exports of 200,000 gallons in 1850, rum sales had fallen to 24 gallons in 1900.

The sugar industry did recover after 1900, helped by Canadian imperial preference, and cotton exports began again in 1904. Sugar remained the dominant export for the next 50 years, but there was no great boost from either the First World War, British imperial preference after 1932, or even the Commonwealth Sugar Agreement in 1951. Sugar was too dependent on water, and the island suffered from long periods of drought, making it an unsuitable crop for the twin-island economy. As a result, exports per head (see figure 14.4) showed little growth before the 1960s.

The size of the population barely changed in the century after slavery was abolished. At 35,000 in 1900, it was still below the level in 1810 as a result not only of net outward migration but also a death rate that frequently exceeded the birth rate. Births finally exceeded deaths on a consistent basis after 1912, but by then net outward migration had accelerated. As a result, the population continued to fall and reached its low point (29,512) in 1921. From then onwards, thanks to a drop in the death rate, the population started to rise, although it was not until 1952 that it reached 50,000, and it was only 73,000 in 1981 when independence was achieved.

The need for economic diversification had been obvious even before the Second World War. However, it was the construction of a modern airport by the US military in 1941[8] and the subsequent development of the Mill Reef tourist resort that created the opportunity to expand rapidly the export of services through mass tourism after 1960. The share of agriculture in GDP dropped precipitately from 44 per cent in 1950 to 18.2 per cent in 1963 and to 6.6 per cent in 1973.[9] By the 1990s, tourist arrivals exceeded 200,000 per year.

Overnight tourism, soon supplemented by cruise ship arrivals and specialist events such as Antiguan sailing week, became as dominant as sugar had been before.[10] The direct contribution to GDP by the end of the century was estimated at 16 per cent, but adding the indirect contribution boosted this figure to 60 per cent. GDP and GDP per head rose rapidly between 1960 and 2000, raising average incomes and reversing net outward migration in the 1990s.

Antigua and Barbuda would then discover that dependence on tourism was as risky as sugar monoculture. Overnight tourist arrivals barely increased after 2000, and the industry was no longer the engine of growth that it had been 50 years before. Attention focused on the export of non-tourist services, with special consideration given to offshore finance. When this collapsed as a result of the criminal activities of Allen Stanford, owner of the Bank of Antigua, the government promoted internet gambling. This, however, was effectively undermined by the US government despite a ruling of the World Trade Organisation in favour of Antigua and Barbuda.[11]

In desperation, the government then promoted the sale of economic citizenship.[12] In their own words:

> For small island developing countries such as Antigua and Barbuda, the decision to adopt this programme was made to bolster the economy in the face of declining revenues from tourism, a contraction of the overall economy as a direct consequence of the global financial crisis, and ineligibility for official development assistance and concessional financing to support development due to the country's classification as an upper middle income country. These factors posed and continue to pose an existential threat to the viability of our economy.

The sale of economic citizenship has brought in considerable public revenue, but it has provoked a negative reaction from the OECD whose rich member states fear the programme will be used for tax evasion.[13] Antigua and Barbuda, despite commendable efforts to diversify service exports, has found that it is almost as difficult to achieve as diversifying commodity exports in a previous age.

14.3. Dominica[14]

Dominica was ceded to Great Britain by France in 1763. Both European powers, therefore, broke their earlier promise to preserve the island and its indigenous inhabitants from imperial rivalry. The Caribs were soon reduced to a small reservation in order to provide the planters with access to land for commodity exports, but the British found out – as the French before them – that the topography of the island with its rugged mountains and steep valleys made monoculture both difficult and inadvisable.

The planters did produce sugar, but they always produced other crops as well. The French had introduced coffee during their period of rule, and at the end of the Napoleonic Wars this was more important than sugar. Most of the slaves – 18,255 in 1815 (85 per cent of the population) – worked on the coffee plantations. These estates were able to take advantage of the hilly landscape to export a high quality product.

Deaths exceeded births among the slave population in 1820, but this had been reversed by 1830. The slave population, therefore, declined only slowly after the abolition of the slave trade and by 1833, the year the emancipation law was passed by the British Parliament, it still accounted for 75 per cent of the population of 18,550. As the relative price of sugar rose compared to coffee between 1820 and 1830, there was a switch from coffee to sugar (see table 14.1).

Table 14.1: Dominica: Domestic Exports, 1820–1900

	Sugar (lb)	Coffee (lb)	Cacao (lb)	Limejuice (gal)
1820	4,742,080	1,974,635	6,859	
1830	6,256,992	1,365,932	112	
1840	3,663,856	88,729	5,171	
1850	6,835,752	61,144	31,472	
1860	7,594,125	20,120	113,460	
1870	7,646,264	12,909	214,265	
1880	6,731,256	6,488	533,114	19,803
1890	5,406,923	0	631,100	58,286
1900	239,680	4,407	1,036,173	112,857

Source: Statistical Appendix.

Emancipation led to a flight of former slaves from the estates, with many acquiring smallholdings in the mountains. The export of both sugar and coffee, therefore, fell sharply between 1830 and 1840 (see table 14.1). Coffee would continue to decline in importance, unable to compete on price with other countries such as Brazil after Great Britain ended imperial preference, but sugar once again expanded, reaching a peak in terms of volume by 1870. The fall in prices then led to a steep drop, especially after 1890, and in 1908 the last sugar was exported.[15]

With both sugar and coffee exports disappearing, the islanders had no choice but to experiment with other crops. Two were found to be well suited to the climate and topography while simultaneously providing profitable opportunities for smallholders. The first was cacao, which expanded in every decade after 1830 (see table 14.1). The second was juice made from limes, which by 1900 had become the most important commodity export by value.

Cacao and limejuice exports helped to alleviate the economic pain caused by the collapse of coffee and the decline of sugar. However, they could not fully compensate and exports per head had fallen significantly by the end of the nineteenth century (see figure 14.5). Net outward migration had been almost continuous after the end of slavery, and yet the population had experienced a small increase (to 28,432 in 1900). This was almost entirely due to a high birth rate and a relatively low death rate.[16]

Figure 14.5: Dominica: Exports per head at constant prices (1900=100), log scale,1820–2016

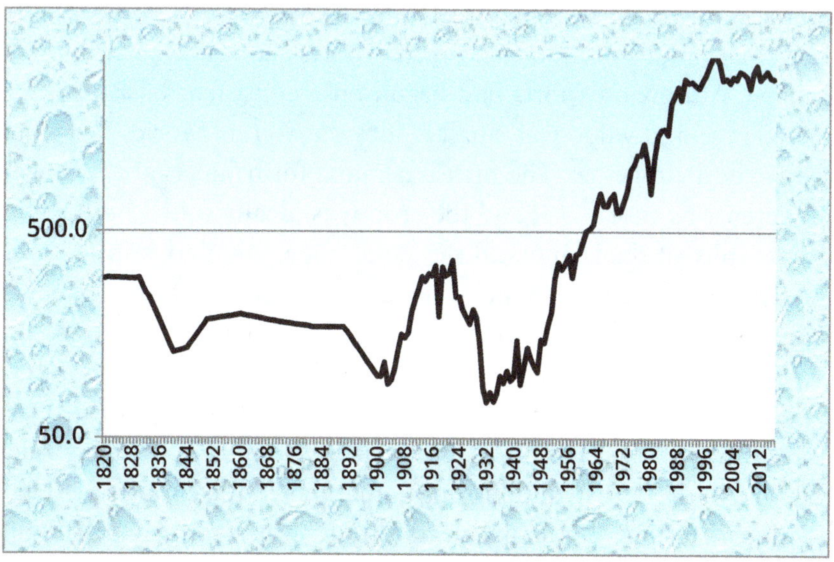

Source: Statistical Appendix to 2008; UNNA thereafter.

The new century brought no change in the fortunes of the sugar industry, which continued to decline. And cacao exports would soon suffer from the spread of disease, from which the industry never fully recovered. Experiments were made with banana exports, but they were soon abandoned (the industry only became a success after the Second World War). Vanilla exports were also tried, but never brought in much revenue. Coconut and copra exports provided an income for some smallholders, but it never amounted to a large share of exports.

Yet, exports per head did rise sharply in the first two decades of the twentieth century (see figure 14.5). This was almost entirely due to the expanded lime industry, which was soon exporting not just limejuice, including in concentrated form, but also barrels of green limes, lime oil, and citrate of lime. By 1919, the value of exports in US dollars was three times greater than in 1900, and almost all of this came from the lime industry.

Unfortunately, lime would prove as ephemeral as sugar had been before. The last shipment of citrate of lime was made in 1923, and both barrels of green lime and concentrate stopped being exported in 1939. Exports per head fell below even their level in 1900, but were then rescued after the Second World War by an unlikely source that pushed export per head rapidly upwards even before a modern tourist industry was created (see figure 14.5).

The commodity that transformed exports per head was the humble banana. Although exports had begun on a consistent basis in 1929, the volume and value was small before the Second World War when they ceased altogether. The British demand for bananas after the war, however, was enormous, and the crop was ideally suited both to the topography of the island and the smallholders that constituted such a large part of the rural population. By the end of the 1950s, bananas were responsible for two-thirds of the value of domestic exports, and exports per head had surpassed their previous peak (see figure 14.5).

Banana exports today are a shadow of what they once were as a result of the erosion of preferences Dominican farmers once received in the British and European markets.[17] Yet, exports per head continued to soar for many years due to tourism growth. Despite the absence of an airport capable of accommodating large jets, the industry grew rapidly after the 1950s until numbers started to peak in the 1990s. Although cruise ships then softened the blow, it was clear that tourism was no longer the engine of growth that it had once been.

In an understandable attempt to maintain the growth of exports per head through diversification, Dominica started in the 1990s to experiment with non-travel service exports. The most successful has been education through providing medical education to foreign students. However, the experiment with offshore financial services was much less successful, provoking, as it did, the ire of OECD countries concerned by the use of Dominica for tax evasion. And the sale of economic citizenship, despite bringing in much needed revenue, risked the same fate.

Exports per head, therefore, stopped growing after 1998 (see figure 14.5). Heavy increases in public expenditure ensured that there was some growth in the economy as a whole, but GDP per head increased very slowly, and Dominica was soon saddled with a large public sector debt that by 2000 had reached 100 per cent of GDP.[18]

Dominica has been much more successful than most Caribbean countries at continually diversifying its exports, first of goods and later of services. Yet, this has not been sufficient to ensure a long-run sustainable rise in living standards. Instead, there have been periods – sometimes long ones – when income per head has risen rapidly followed either by falls or stagnation. Perhaps this is the inevitable fate of small open economies, and yet it is frustrating for the island's inhabitants, thousands of whom have migrated for what they hope will be a better life elsewhere.[19]

14.4. Grenada

Grenada, like Dominica, became a 'ceded isle' when it was transferred to Great Britain from France under the Treaty of Paris in 1763. The French planters had used slaves to produce sugar, but they had also grown cacao – a crop that was better suited to the topography – and cotton. Thus, Grenada was never a classic case of sugar monoculture under the French. This remained the case under British rule, although the planters at first tried to increase sugar production. By 1820, they were exporting 32 million pounds, and this accounted for nearly 80 per cent of the value of domestic exports (even more when molasses and rum are included), while cotton and cacao exports had dwindled.

The British planters relied on slaves for estate labour and in 1810, shortly after the abolition of the slave trade, slaves numbered 27,900 out of a total population of 29,850. With deaths among the slave population exceeding births, the slave population fell and had dropped to 23,645 at the time of emancipation in 1834. Yet this was still over 90 per cent of the population, which continued to fall until 1837 when it reached its lowest level of 21,858.

The population then increased and had reached 32,671 at the time of the census in 1851. This was not due to inward migration, since many of the former slaves started to emigrate as soon as they could. Instead, it was due to a big drop in the death rate after the end of slavery. By the early 1850s, for example, the CDR was less than 20 although a cholera epidemic in 1854 raised it temporarily to 74. With a CBR around 40, Grenada could now expect births to exceed deaths in normal years by a substantial margin.

By 1840, the volume of sugar exported had fallen by two-thirds compared with 1820. Exports of molasses, rum, and cotton had also declined sharply. Only cacao experienced any increase as a result both of estates switching to cacao and many former slaves establishing smallholdings on land purchased or rented from the planters. Yet cacao could not compensate for the decline in other commodities, and exports per head dropped precipitately after 1820 (see figure 14.6).

In the 1840s, the nutmeg tree was first introduced to Grenada. Although nutmeg and mace exports would, in due course, change the economy of what would become known as the 'spice island', it was, in fact, many years before that would happen. Thus, the Grenadian economy remained dependent on a declining sugar industry that still accounted for over half the value of domestic exports in 1870. Yet nothing could save the industry. Molasses exports ended in the 1870s, rum exports in the 1880s, and sugar in the 1890s.[20]

In an effort to provide some metropolitan support for the struggling island, the British imposed Crown Colony rule in 1877. However, it made little difference. The Royal Commission established in 1882 to report on the finances of numerous colonies concluded two years later:[21]

> Considering the large sums of money which have been spent on the roads in Grenada during the five years past, their present condition is most disappointing. Spending four or five times as much money on this service as any other of the sister islands, the road system should be very much the best. This is by no means the case, and there can be no doubt that the money has been in many cases most injudiciously spent. Nor is this to be wondered at, for when we were in the island the Inspector of Schools, who had no professional qualifications for the post, was acting as head of department...The want of roads is particularly unfortunate in Grenada, where there are numbers of small estates inland which, with improved means of communication, could supply abundant produce for shipment.

Figure 14.6: Grenada: Exports per head at constant prices (1900=100) 1820–2012

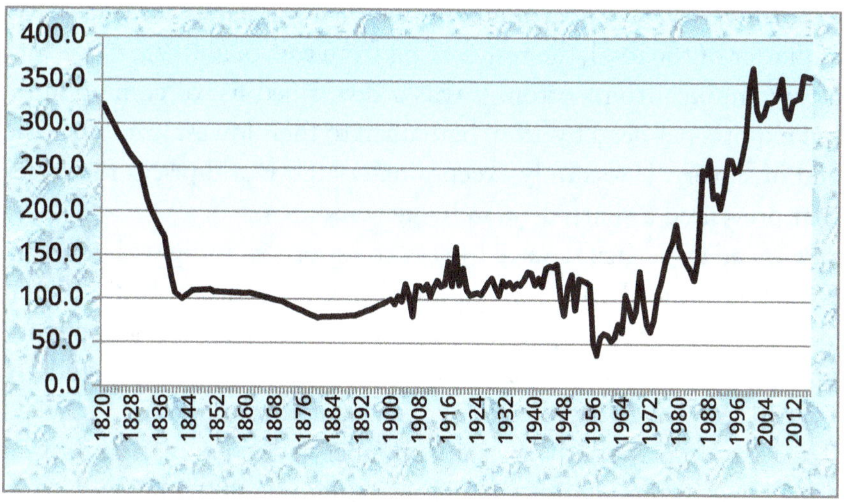

Source: Statistical Appendix from 1820 to 2008; UNNA thereafter.

Exports per head reached their lowest point almost as these words were being written (see figure 14.6). For the next 40 years, there was a modest improvement made possible, at first, by the rapid growth of cacao exports. Their volume increased ten-fold between 1860 and 1900 to exceed 10 million pounds, when they accounted for nearly 90 per cent of the value of domestic exports. They would continue to grow and performed well in the First World War before disease, as in so many countries, took hold in the 1920s.

Cacao exports, unlike sugar, did not end. By 1960, the volume exported was still four million pounds, but the industry was struggling after 1920. What prevented a sharp decline in living standards was that new commodities were introduced to the export list. Spices – nutmeg and mace – were first exported in the 1860s, but it was not until the new century that they contributed significantly to export earnings. The volume exported expanded rapidly in the 1920s and 1930s, compensating for the drop in cacao exports. The peak for nutmeg came in 1950 (mace in 1953), when Grenada was the world's largest exporter. After that, there was a steep drop; Grenada fell below Indonesia as the main source of nutmeg.

The other new commodity export was bananas. First exported in the 1930s, they ceased in the Second World War. They started again in 1949 with the UK as the main market, and by the end of the 1950s exports were valued at around one million US dollars. This was nearly a quarter of the total, the rest coming from cacao, nutmeg, mace, and a tiny amount from cotton. It was a diversified list of commodities, but exports per head by 1960 had fallen to their lowest level since the end of slavery. It was only exceptionally high world prices for spices that prevented a sharp drop in living standards.

Grenada was then rescued by service exports, starting with tourism. Exports per head rose rapidly after 1960 (see figure 14.6), as did GDP per head. Yet the population rose only slowly with net outward migration persistent before and after independence in 1974. Indeed, from 1850 to 2016, cumulative net outward migration reached 92,445 – almost exactly the same number as the population itself in 1962. And the population had reached only 105,000 50 years later.

Uncertainties created by the coup in 1979 that brought Maurice Bishop to power as the head of the New Jewel Movement led to a steep decline in exports per head, and the downward trend was exacerbated by the US-led invasion in 1983 to overthrow the government.[22] Yet exports per head were soon above their pre-1979 level once again, and Grenada looked set to reap a handsome dividend. Exports per head continued to grow rapidly and finally surpassed their 1820 level at the end of the 1990s (see figure 14.6).

Unfortunately for Grenada, exports per head peaked in 2000 as tourism ceased to be an engine of growth. The island had already experimented with diversifying services through establishing a medical school and adding new non-travel services, including a Citizenship by Investment Programme. This added substantially to public revenue and made possible an expansion of public spending and employment. GDP per head, after a brief drop between 2008 and 2012 as a result of the global financial crisis, therefore carried on rising.

14.5. St Kitts and Nevis

St Kitts, often called St Christopher until the name was officially changed in 1986, was the first Caribbean island to be settled by the British. However, sovereignty was disputed with France and Spain for decades. It was only after the Napoleonic Wars that British control was assured. The colonial authorities then annexed Anguilla to St Kitts in 1825 and Nevis in 1882. When Anguilla attempted to secede after 1967, separation was reluctantly accepted by the British government after many delays. St Kitts and Nevis then proceeded to independence in 1983 without Anguilla.

The constitutional status of St Kitts and Nevis may have changed frequently, but there was no doubt until recently about the economic model. These were sugar islands, in which the export of sugar, molasses, and rum provided the main activities for centuries. As British colonies, all metropolitan policies were seen through this prism: how they would react on the sugar industry.

A particularly strong source of complaint for the planters after the Napoleonic Wars was the export duty of 4.5 per cent applied to the 'old' colonies but not the new ones.[23] Yet this complaint was soon overtaken by the planters' fear of the impact of the end of the slave trade in 1808 and emancipation in 1834. With slave deaths higher than births, the planters in St Kitts had seen the number of slaves drop from 20,800 just after abolition to 17,525 in 1834, while Nevis had experienced a reduction from 10,400 to 8,840. So the concern of the planters on both islands was that, as soon as the apprenticeship period was over, the former slaves would emigrate. To discourage this, 'strong arm' tactics appear to have been used, as the emigration agent from British Guiana discovered:[24]

> On returning to St. Kitt's [sic] we proceeded immediately to take the coals on board; and that I might not be charged with disrespect to the authorities, I called on the officer who administered the Government...My reception was cold and repulsive, and the conversation which followed sufficiently proved how little favour I had to expect in that quarter, as it ended in a threat to seize the vessel...We waited a few days in the expectation of the labourers coming, whose names had been enrolled; only a few of them, however, came, and said that false accounts had been made out against them for moneys which they did not owe, in order to prevent their going away....

Figure 14.7: St Kitts and Nevis: Exports per head at constant prices (1900=100), log scale, 1820–2016

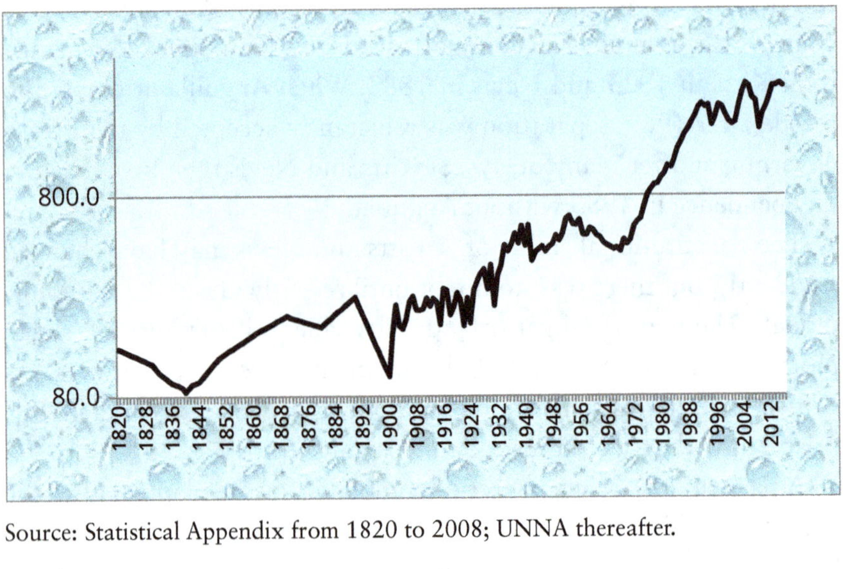

Source: Statistical Appendix from 1820 to 2008; UNNA thereafter.

Not even the strongest tactics could completely stop emigration, and the populations of both St Kitts and Nevis continued to fall, reaching their lowest points around 1840.[25] This was also the nadir for domestic exports per head (see figure 14.7) as the volume of sugar exported expanded on both islands for the next 50 years. Indeed, sugar exports on Nevis increased from 1.3 million pounds in 1840 to 9.5 million in 1890, while on St Kitts it went from 7.3 million to 32.7 million.[26]

Not even the most efficient estates could survive the collapse in sugar prices from the 1880s onwards. The industry on St Kitts and Nevis was, therefore, badly affected (see figure 14.7), but it survived and the volume of exports again expanded after 1900, although rum had by now ceased to be exported from Nevis and would end from St Kitts after the First World War. With sugar exports of 40 million pounds in 1928, St Kitts and Nevis was now more specialised in sugar than ever before, although a small cotton industry had been established with exports beginning in 1902.

The extreme dependence on sugar meant that the reaction of the planters to the fall in prices during the Great Depression was to *increase* exports, which reached 80 million pounds by 1939. With only one factory on St Kitts to process sugar cane, however, the estates were at the mercy of the prices set by the board of the St Kitts Sugar Factory. The fall in prices was then passed on by planters to workers whose wages were sharply reduced in 1932. Tensions rose and riots erupted in 1935. This did not lead to restored wage rates, but the restrictions on trade unions were at least lifted in 1940.[27]

Sugar dependence continued after the Second World War as no other commodities had emerged. The Commonwealth Sugar Agreement in 1951 assured better prices, but work was insufficient for a population among whom the death rate had fallen sharply. Therefore, net outward migration accelerated, and the population of St Kitts and Nevis only reached 50,000 in the late 1950s when the country joined the short-lived Federation of the West Indies.

By this time, it was clear that tourism would finally provide a means for the twin islands to diversify their economies. Sugar survived for a while, but the industry was finally closed in 2005 when the St Kitts and Nevis Sugar Diversification Foundation was established. By then, it was the export of services, especially overnight tourism and cruise ships, which was driving the economy and raising exports per head (see figure 14.7).

Tourism may have provided an alternative to sugar, but it still did not create jobs in sufficient quantities. The population started falling again after 1960 as net outward migration exceeded net births. It reached its lowest point in 1990 when it was a mere 40,834. By this time, St Kitts and Nevis had been independent for seven years, making it one of the smallest members of the United Nations. As late as 2016, the population was still less than 55,000.

The need for further diversification was clear, and the government was the first in the Eastern Caribbean to establish a Citizenship by Investment Programme. This started in 1984 and brought in much needed public revenue that allowed the state to expand public sector employment. It risked reputational problems, but the programme survived. In 2014, it generated fees equivalent to 14.2 per cent of GDP. This, however, was the peak as competition from other states in the region then lowered the income raised significantly. St Kitts and Nevis was, therefore, not immune to the need for further diversification, especially as overnight tourism had ceased to be an engine of growth after the global financial crisis in 2008/9.

14.6. St Lucia

Although the British had coveted St Lucia in the seventeenth century, it was the French who controlled it when the Anglo-French war broke out in 1793. The following year, the French assembly abolished slavery, but the impact on the island was short-lived as the British seized control a few weeks later. British control was only assured in 1796, but the island was restored to France in 1802 when Napoleon re-established slavery in the French Empire. When the British again seized the island in 1806, they kept slavery as the foundation of the estates although they ended the trade in slaves two years later. The island was then ceded by France to the UK in 1814.

The slave population (18,500 in 1810) had been falling ever since abolition of the slave trade and had reached 13,275 in the year of emancipation. This was some 80 per cent of the total population so the future of the island depended on what the former slaves chose to do after the end of the apprenticeship period in 1838. By this time, births exceeded deaths and few chose to emigrate. The British authorities note with relief:[28]

> Owing to the high wages and other advantages enjoyed by the St Lucia labourers, few, if any, have emigrated to the other islands; and although the supply of labour is wholly inadequate to the demand, yet the work of the estates under cultivation has no where been arrested.

The 'other advantages' to which the British official referred included the *metairie* system, known at the time as cultivating in halves. This had developed quickly after the end of slavery and applied especially to sugar (it was less important on the cacao estates). The former slaves provided their labour while the planter furnished the land and machinery before the output was shared between the two.

The *metairie* system, which eventually died out, was one of the reasons why the volume of sugar exports recovered fairly quickly.[29] From ten million pounds exported in 1820, the volume dropped precipitately to 4.3 million in 1830. From then onwards, it grew in every decade until 1880, when it reached 14.5 million. With the volume of cacao exports also expanding in every decade of the nineteenth century, St Lucia was nothing like as dependent on sugar as many other islands, although coffee – an important export in 1820 – had disappeared by the middle of the century.

Such a rapid expansion of the volume of exports required additional labour, but it was not available in sufficient quantities despite the population reaching nearly 40,000 by 1880 (double what it had been in 1840). Twenty years later, however, it was a different story. The collapse of sugar prices had led to a steep fall in the volume of sugar and molasses exported (rum had ceased to be exported). This led to a depression on St Lucia that affected everyone, not just those in the export sector. John Quinlan, a land surveyor, explained to the Royal Commission:[30]

> St Lucia contains a population of more than 6,000 peasant proprietors; allowing three men to each property you have 18,000 men. The evidence given shows that these peasants suffer more than the agricultural labourers, and that they are in need of pecuniary assistance. They are not lazy; their small properties were purchased with moneys that came to them from share of sugar as metayers of the old sugar estates, before the depression and long before the works were opened on the Panama Canal [French scheme]. When the depression came they risked their lives in search of money at Panama. They now risk it with the same object at the Cayenne [French Guiana] gold fields.

Exports per head fell sharply after 1880 as a consequence of the sugar crisis (see figure 14.8). However, they soon recovered. This was a consequence of export diversification made possible by the presence of a large peasant sector willing to experiment with new crops. In addition to sugar and cacao, St Lucia after 1900 started to export bananas, coconuts, coconut oil, copra, green lines, limejuice, and lime oil.

With the exception of the Second World War, when all but sugar exports were sharply curtailed, these commodity exports helped to sustain the level of exports per head for many years. And when St Lucia was rocked by riots in the 1930s, they did not take place on the estates but in the coaling station at the capital, Castries, as visiting ships started to switch from coal to oil. Yet, some of these commodities, such as those based on limes, were not competitive on the world market after the war and eventually disappeared. By contrast, banana exports boomed and by 1957, for the first time, had overtaken sugar in terms of their value.

Figure 14.8: St Lucia: Exports per head at constant prices (1900=100), log scale, 1820–2016

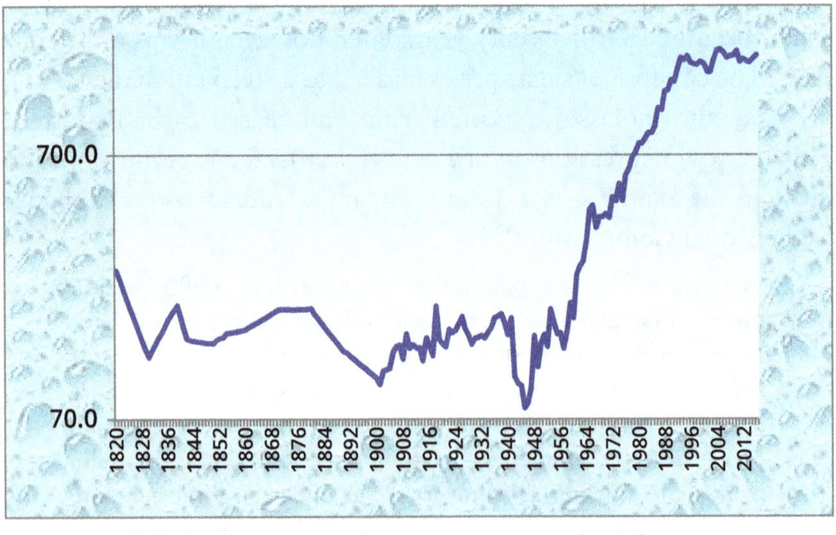

Source: Statistical Appendix from 1820 to 2008; UNNA thereafter.

Bananas and sugar, together with cacao, coconut oil and copra, provided the bulk of St Lucia's commodity exports for many years until changes in EU preferences led to their decline. By then, tourism was well established and led to a steep rise in exports per head (see figure 14.8). And, unlike some neighbouring countries, St Lucia has had some success in increasing visitor numbers even after the global financial crisis in 2008/9, although not at a rate to make much impact on the high rates of unemployment (especially among the youth). Yet the island is peculiarly sensitive to natural disasters and these have taken a heavy toll, as the IMF itself noted in its 2018 Article IV Consultation:[31]

> A small island in the Atlantic hurricane belt, St Lucia is very vulnerable to natural disasters and climate change...Besides significant human and social costs, extreme weather and other catastrophic events have major macroeconomic and fiscal implications, with an average annual cost estimated at 1.5 percent of GDP, of which 1 percent is borne by the government.

The government of St Lucia has done its best to address the risks to its economic model from climate change, but the cost is high and expected to rise as the mean global temperature increases. A Citizenship by Investment Programme was eventually introduced in 2016, but competition from other countries means that the revenues are unlikely to be as great as expected. The prospects for St Lucia, as indeed for other Eastern Caribbean countries, are therefore deeply problematic.

14.7. St Vincent and the Grenadines

St Vincent and the Grenadines, ceded by France in 1763, was a British colony until independence in 1979. However, British control before 1800 was challenged both by France and by the indigenous Caribs. It was only after the Caribs had been defeated in battle in 1796 and deported to Roatán, off the coast of Honduras, the following year that British sovereignty was assured.

By the time the slave trade was ended in 1808, the most productive lands had been formed into plantations with a small number of owners. These estates were worked by the slaves whose number in 1810 was 27,400 (91.2 per cent of the population). With slave deaths much higher than births, the slave population had dwindled to 22,250 by the time of emancipation. This was 82 per cent of the population, which in 1834 was estimated at 27,148.

The estates were largely dedicated to sugar cane in order to produce sugar, molasses, and rum, although as early as 1820 a small amount of arrowroot was also being exported. The productivity, at first, was high, with the value of exports per head in that year being US$77.5, the second highest in all the Caribbean.[32] This degree of specialisation in exports depended on a captive labour force, which ended once the apprenticeship period was over. At that point, many of the former slaves moved on to smallholdings in the interior either as owners, renters, or squatters, and the estates soon faced a labour shortage.

Labour scarcity, at least at the wage rates offered on the estates, was the principal complaint of the planters and their agents to the Royal Commission in 1842. Hay McDowall Grant, in charge of eight estates as attorney or agent between 1831 and 1841, explained:[33]

> Since the labourers became free, many of them prefer gaining their livelihood in other ways than by the cultivation of sugar such as hiring land for the cultivation of provisions, travelling about the country as hucksters or sellers of goods, and working in towns and villages as jobbers or day labourers; also many women who used to work, refuse to labour now on the plea of being married.

The proposed solution, immigration from Africa, India, Portugal, and other places, was tried. Yet, it was notably unsuccessful with domestic exports per head falling severely until the end of the century (see figure 14.9). In the terse remarks in 1883 of one planter, W.M. Smith:[34] 'Immigration in St. Vincent is now played out, and the contributions levied in aid are grudgingly given, and it is now regarded as an expensive idea to be got rid of as quietly and as early as possible.' Indeed, the tax burden had increased as the fixed costs of public administration under Crown Colony rule did *not* fall in line with exports per head.[35]

The brunt of the collapse in exports per head was, of course, due to sugar whose volume exported fell from 39.5 million pounds in 1820 to 1.3 million in 1900, by which time molasses exports had ceased altogether and only 9,231 gallons of rum were shipped abroad. Two years later, in 1902, a volcanic eruption caused immense damage by killing 1,680 people (3.4 per cent of the population) and destroying numerous estates. If it were not for the rise in production of arrowroot, from which starch is made, the decline of exports per head would have been even more dramatic.

Figure 14.9: St Vincent: Exports per head at constant prices (1900=100), log scale, 1820–2016

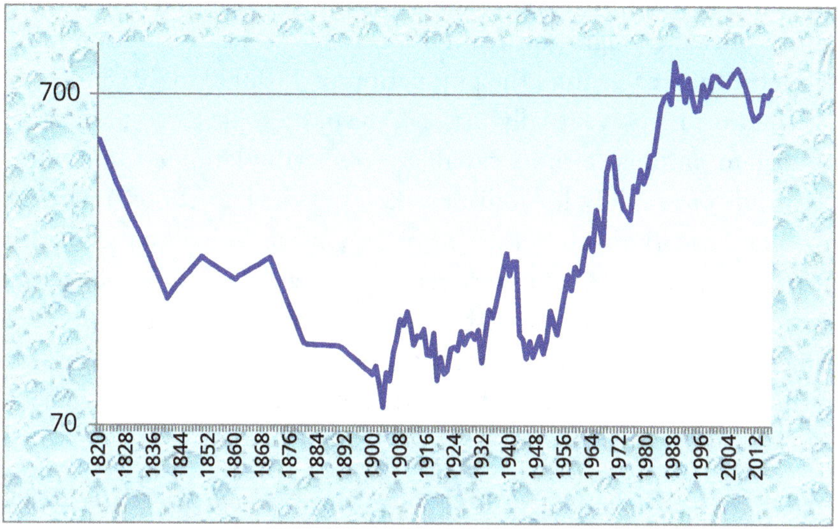

Source: Statistical Appendix, 1820-2008; UNNA thereafter.

Sugar did not survive and contributed little to export earnings from St Vincent after 1900; they had ceased altogether in the Grenadines by the end of the nineteenth century. Arrowroot, cacao, and cotton then took sugar's place. Copra was added in the First World War, but cacao exports ended in 1938, and all exports suffered in the Second World War when exports per head fell back sharply (see figure 14.9). Bananas would be exported for the first time in 1954, but rose rapidly in importance and pushed arrowroot into second place by 1957.

Mass tourism was slow to develop, although the Grenadines became a niche market in the 1950s. Even in the 1960s exports per head were still far below their level in 1820. And the lack of dynamism in the export sector was reflected in the labour market, with the demand for labour unable to match the supply. Empty land in the interior was soon used up, and the felling of trees not only left the island denuded but also deprived future generations of peasant farmers of a valuable source of income.

With a relatively low death rate after the end of slavery and a very high birth rate from the 1860s onwards, emigration was always a risk. However, the scale was shocking even by Caribbean standards.

In every decade since 1850, net migration has been outwards (see figure 14.10). The migrants left for Trinidad, French Guiana, Panama, Canada, the UK, and for the US. The cumulative amount of net outward migration from 1850 to 2018 has been 140,000 – significantly greater than the population of 110,000 in 2018.

Mass tourism eventually arrived, despite the absence until 2017 of an international airport capable of receiving large jets, and GDP per head rose rapidly for four decades after the late 1960s. It stalled, in common with much of the Caribbean, in the global financial crisis in 2008/9, but struggled to recover subsequently. With no increase in overnight visitors, no citizenship by investment programme, and no mineral exports, St Vincent and the Grenadines was forced to rely on an unreliable combination of Venezuelan support and an increase in cruise ship passengers.

Figure 14.10: St Vincent: Net Migration (% of Population), 1850–2018

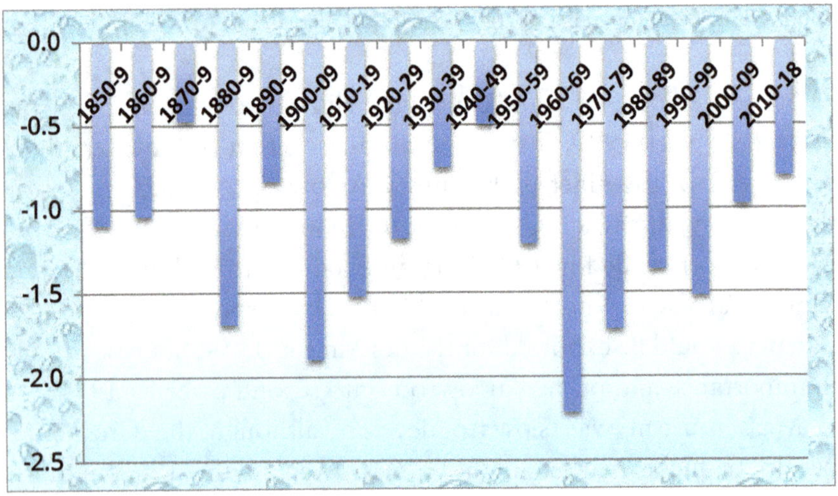

Source: Statistical Appendix to 2008; World Bank, WDI thereafter.

The new airport is now in operation, with its construction having left the government with a heavy debt burden after nearly ten years. Few would deny that it was needed, since it is difficult to compete in international tourism without appropriate infrastructure. Yet, even an increase in overnight visitors may not be sufficient, as other Caribbean countries have discovered, to achieve the kind of long-run sustainable growth for which all countries yearn. Therefore, new thinking on growth dynamics in St Vincent and the Grenadines is needed.

NOTES

1. The ECCB was formed in 1983. Its members are not just the countries listed in this chapter (excluding Barbados), but also Anguilla and Montserrat.
2. See H. Beckles, *A History of Barbados* (New York, NY: Cambridge University Press, 2006), 147–51.
3. See www.imf.org/en/News/Articles/2018/10/01/pr181370-imf-exec-board-approves-us-290-million-ext-arr-under-ext-fund-facility-barbados.
4. These figures include Barbuda, the private property of the Codrington family, although Barbuda was not annexed to Antigua until 1860 when the twin islands became the colony of Antigua and Barbuda.
5. Barbuda was joined to Antigua in 1860.
6. See D. Hall, *Five of the Leewards, 1834–1870* (Caribbean Universities Press: Ginn and Co. Ltd, 1971), chapter 3.
7. See *Report from the Select Committee on West India Colonies* (London: 1842), 216.
8. This was part of the lend-lease agreement with the UK signed in 1940.
9. See G. Nicholls, 'Reflections on Economic Growth in Antigua and Barbuda,' *Integration & Trade* 5, no. 15 (2001): 138, table 10.
10. For a few years Antigua and Barbuda was also a significant exporter of refined oil using imported crude, but this ended before independence.
11. See A. Cooper, *Internet Gambling Offshore: Caribbean Struggles over Casino Capitalism* (New York, NY: Palgrave Macmillan, 2011), 95–123.
12. The sale of citizenship is not treated in the balance of payments as a service export, although in practice that is what it is.
13. In October 2018, the OECD listed the Citizenship by Investment Programme of Antigua and Barbuda, along with those of other Eastern Caribbean states, as potentially being of high risk to the Common Reporting Standard demanded by OECD/G20 countries. See http://www.oecd.org/tax/automatic-exchange/crs-implementation-and-assistance/residence-citizenship-by-investment.
14. The official name of Dominica, a republic in the Commonwealth, is Commonwealth of Dominica.
15. A small shipment was made in 1921, but that was the only year. See Statistical Appendix.
16. See Statistical Appendix.

17. Preferences for Caribbean bananas in the EU were eroded as a result of a legal challenge through the WTO by US banana companies. Sugar preferences ended when the quotas for beet sugar production in the EU were lifted in 2017.
18. Fiscal prudence, supported by membership of the ECCB, had brought this down to 75 per cent two decades later.
19. The population peaked in 1981 (at 75,375), since when there has been a small decline.
20. See Statistical Appendix.
21. See *Report of the West India Royal Commission* (London: 1884), 27, part II.
22. There are many books and articles on this episode, although little has been written on the economic policy of the Bishop administration.
23. The 'new' colonies were the ceded islands from 1763 onwards.
24. Quoted in *Report from the Select Committee on West India Colonies* 1842, 232.
25. For St Kitts, the lowest point was 1839 when the population was 21,578. For Nevis, it was 1840 when the population was 7,330.
26. Export statistics for St Kitts after 1825 included Anguilla. However, these were always tiny. Their value in 1845, for example, was only US$6,000. See V. Bulmer-Thomas, *The Economic History of the Caribbean since the Napoleonic Wars* (Cambridge: Cambridge University Press, 2012), 508. No deduction has, therefore, been made.
27. See O.N. Bolland, *On the March: Labour Rebellions in the British Caribbean, 1934–39* (Kingston, Jamaica: Ian Randle Publishers, 1995), 66.
28. See *Report from the Select Committee on West India Colonies* 1842, 745.
29. The system did not survive the collapse in sugar prices after 1880 and had died out by 1900.
30. See *Report from the Select Committee on West India Colonies* (London: 1897), *Appendix C Volume III Proceedings, Evidence and Documents relating to the Windward Islands, the Leeward Islands and Jamaica*, 80.
31. See International Monetary Fund (IMF), *Direction of Trade Statistics (DOTS)* (Washington, DC: IMF, 2018), *St Lucia: Article IV Consultation*, Washington DC, 54.
32. See Bulmer-Thomas, *The Economic History of the Caribbean since the Napoleonic Wars*, 79, figure 4.1.
33. See *Report from the Select Committee on West India Colonies* 1842, 28.
34. See *Report of the West India Royal Commission* (London: 1884), 117, part II.
35. St Vincent and the Grenadines became a Crown Colony in 1877, adding a layer of bureaucracy to what already was there.

Chapter 15

The Bahamas and the British Overseas Territories

The six countries considered in this chapter (the Bahamas and the five British Overseas Territories located in the Caribbean) had all become British colonies long before the Napoleonic Wars. Consisting of a single or many small islands, each country faced severe logistical and administrative problems, leading Great Britain – as the colonial power – frequently to change the administrative arrangements.

Geography did not create a natural division between the islands of the archipelago north of the Greater Antilles, so the British from their first occupations in the seventeenth century claimed all of them without distinction. Thus, the Turks Islands were considered a division of the colony of the Bahamas, as were the Caicos Islands, after Spain ceded sovereignty in 1783. When the complexity of this arrangement became intolerable for all concerned, the Turks and Caicos Islands were merged with each other and then separated from the Bahamas in 1848 while the Bahamas continued as a British colony before becoming independent in 1973.

The Turks and Caicos Islands, following their merger by Great Britain, then became a dependency of Jamaica. That arrangement survived until 1962, when Jamaica alone became independent. The Turks and Caicos Islands would then continue, by choice, as a British colony before becoming, after many constitutional changes, a British Overseas Territory (a colony in all but name) in 2002.

A similar history befell the Cayman Islands, which was a dependency of Jamaica until 1962. When Jamaica became independent, the Cayman Islands chose to remain a British colony before becoming, in due course, a British Overseas Territory. Anguilla, as shown in the previous chapter, had no wish to proceed to independence with St Kitts and Nevis and had effectively 'seceded' by the end of the 1960s before also becoming an Overseas Territory in 2002.

The British Virgin Islands (BVI) and Montserrat, despite their small size and tiny populations, were not merged with other colonies until the Leeward Islands Federation was created in 1871. Montserrat (unlike BVI) joined the Federation of the West Indies in 1958, but neither had any wish to proceed to independence after the collapse of the Federation in 1962. Both, therefore, remained colonies before eventually becoming British Overseas Territories in 2002.

15.1. BAHAMAS

British settlers arrived in the Bahamas in the seventeenth century, disputing sovereignty with Spain for more than a century. The British presence, however, was minuscule until the end of the US War of Independence in 1783, when many loyalists moved to the colony from Georgia and Florida with their slaves and trebled the population.[1] By 1810, the population was 12,782, of which 8,500 – two-thirds – were slaves.[2] This was much higher than the proportion of slaves before the arrival of the new settlers, as the earlier settlers had struggled to find employment for their slaves in the absence of a plantation economy (sugar did not thrive on the thin soil of the Bahamas).

The new settlers hoped to change this and brought with them knowledge of the cotton industry. Estates were acquired from the colonial authorities on generous terms and cotton exports – not unknown before 1783 – were soon expanding. However, the ecology of the Bahamas was not suited to this crop and exports soon peaked. In addition, cotton diseases took their toll on many estates. Cotton did not disappear, but it had ceased to be an engine of growth even before the abolition of the slave trade in 1808.

The end of the legal trade in slaves did not trouble the slave owners unduly. The number of slave births was higher than the number of deaths throughout the period leading up to emancipation in 1834. In addition, most slave owners had to rent out their slaves to others in order to find work for them. And, finally, the location of the archipelago, so close to Cuba, meant that African slaves captured by the British navy close to the Spanish island were taken to the Bahamas where they were usually employed as indentured labourers.

The population of the Bahamas, therefore, increased and had reached 16,271 by 1832. The number of slaves fluctuated, but was roughly the same at the time of emancipation as it had been at the time of abolition of the slave trade. As a result, slaves as a proportion of the population had fallen to 50 per cent by the time of emancipation. The other 50 per cent consisted of 'old' settlers, 'new' settlers (mainly from Georgia and Florida), free people of colour, and recent immigrants from Africa.

This small population needed exports to survive. Cotton had not prospered, while sugar was not considered feasible. By 1820, however, salt had become established as the main source of exports and fresh fruits (especially pineapples) were growing in importance (see table 15.1). Still, these commodities were a meagre source of earnings, bringing in only US$150,000 in 1820, which was barely US$10 per head. And since slave compensation by the British government after 1834 was based on the value of domestic exports, this meant that slave owners received less per slave than any other British colony.[3]

Yet, the population continued to grow after emancipation and had reached 20,000 by 1850. And the Bahamas, despite births exceeding deaths by a large margin, avoided the mass outmigration in these years that afflicted many other British colonies. This was due less to the staple exports in these years, none of which except pineapples showed much dynamism, and much more to three other features of the Bahamanian economy.

Table 15.1: Bahamas: Domestic Exports by Volume, 1820–1900

	Cotton (lb)	Sponge (lb)	Fruit (units)	Salt (bushels)
1820	76,648		134,590	500,000
1830	81,000		241,158	567,167
1840	110,075		325,832	532,521
1850	130,000	704	491,676	687,210
1860	155,225	574,896	1,564,868	332,789
1870	37,468	332,043	4,142,072	599,114
1880	42,831	470,213	4,474,128	332,147
1890	64,926	908,945	5,080,700	138,990
1900		1,165,406	8,497,069	

Source: Statistical Appendix.

The first was the presence of a thriving re-export trade, the value of which exceeded the value of domestic exports in most years and which was particularly important during the US Civil War when Bahamanians traded with the Confederacy in defiance of the Unionist blockade. The second was the growth of a small-scale peasantry on many islands that provided opportunities for domestic use agriculture (DUA). The third was the business of salvaging wrecks, which was an outgrowth of the privateering and piracy for which the Bahamas had once been famous.

Wrecking, as it was called, was a skilled economic activity that benefited the individuals involved as well as the colonial authorities that sold the licences and auctioned the goods. Ever since the arrivals of Europeans, sailing ships had been wrecked on the reefs surrounding the numerous islands that make up the Bahamas. An American visitor during the War of 1812 noted:[4]

> The white inhabitants are of two classes, called *residents* and *wreckers*. The residents are chiefly loyalists and their descendants who emigrated from the southern states of the America, at the close of the war. The wreckers are those persons and their slaves, who are employed in rescuing Shipwrecked vessels, and their crews and cargoes, from the waves.

So important was wrecking to the Bahamas that the colonial authorities came to list it in the trade statistics as a source of imports (see table 15.2). In 1860, for example, the value of the cargo from the wrecks was almost half of the value of imports from all sources although, of course, the goods had not been purchased from foreigners but auctioned to islanders and then re-exported in some cases.

After 1860, wrecking was temporarily eclipsed by an even more profitable source of income. This was importing from the blockaded ports in the US (see table 15.2). The value of these imports jumped from £92,800 in 1860 (the last year before the Civil War) to £3,772,389 in 1864 (the final year before the war ended). Thereafter, imports from the US quickly fell back to their pre-war level. Many of those involved in running the blockade then returned to their previous trade of wrecking, although this would now be much less profitable as a result of improvements in navigation and the shift to steam from sail.

Table 15.2: ***Bahamas: Imports (£) by Origin, 1859–66***

	UK	USA	From Wrecks	Other	Total
1859	29,879	92,360	69,811	21,116	213,166
1860	25,442	92,800	102,890	12,897	234,029
1861	51,025	136,002	66,519	21,038	274,584
1862	762,627	352,520	49,178	85,997	1,250,322
1863	1,054,775	2,932,945	50,666	256,930	4,295,316
1864	1,218,914	3,772,389	51,414	303,395	5,346,112
1865	417,326	808,898	28,017	216,226	1,470,467
1866	52,124	133,706	107,660	35,132	328,622

Source: Statistical Abstract for the Several Colonial and Other Possessions of the United Kingdom (various years).

Figure 15.1: Bahamas: Net Migration (% of Population), 1850–2016

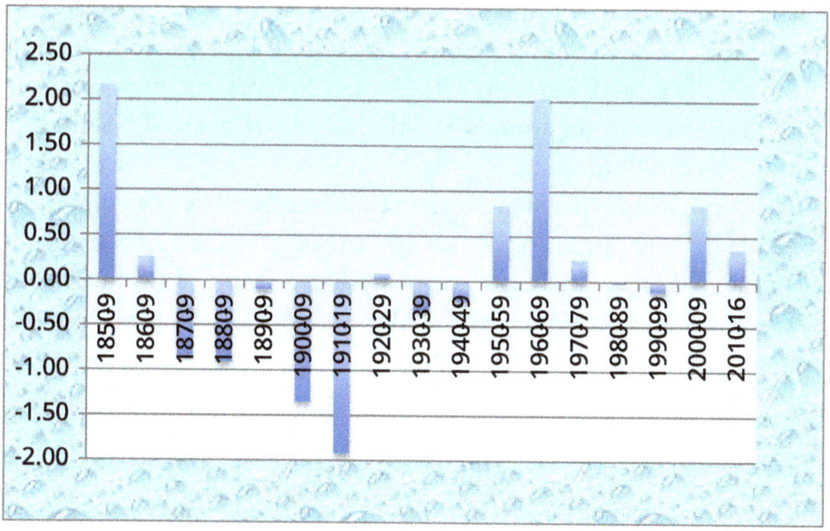

Source: Statistical Appendix.

Both wrecking and running the blockade swelled the population of the Bahamas in the 1850s and 1860s. Net migration was inward in those two decades (see figure 15.1), but from then onwards there were 80 years of net outward migration with one minor exception (the 1920s) when a small number of migrants returned. From 1870 until the start of mass tourism in the 1950s, the Bahamas experienced a deep depression that drove thousands to leave the country for work elsewhere.

These were the years when Bahamanians settled in Key West in the Florida Keys, in Coconut Grove in Miami, and many other places.

The long depression was, in large part, due to the difficulty of finding new sources of export earnings after the US Civil War had ended. By 1890, both cotton and salt were each generating less than US$10,000 in exports and would cease altogether by 1900 (see table 15.1). In that year, export earnings came from pineapples (fresh and tinned), sisal, tortoise shell, and sponge. Of these, sponge was by far the most important, generating more than half of domestic exports, but the latter was not even $1 million, and re-exports had by then dwindled into insignificance.

The rise of the sponge industry was matched by the decline of wrecking. The same merchants in Nassau, as well as white Bahamanians from Harbour Island and Abaco, now leased their ships to spongers instead of wreckers while taking one-third of the value of the catch. By the end of the nineteenth century, the volume of sponge exports exceeded one million pounds (see table 15.1), with half going to the US. The peak came in 1912 when the volume exported was more than two million pounds and the value was nearly US$850,000 (two-thirds of all domestic exports).

The sponge industry then went into decline, hit first by competition from plastic substitutes and then by disease. At the same time, the pineapple industry virtually disappeared as a result of US tariffs and an overworked soil. Once again, the search was on for profitable commodities to add to the export list. Lumber exports began in 1906, tomatoes in 1924, fish in 1933, shell and straw work in 1939, pit props in 1952, and pulpwood in 1957. There was even an attempt to revive the salt industry after the Second World War. Yet, none of this made much impact, and domestic exports per head at constant prices were lower in 1960 than they had been in 1900.[5]

Until the rise of mass tourism after the Second World War, the economy of the Bahamas was, therefore, in a long period of stagnation punctuated only by brief periods of prosperity. One such was a few years after 1919 when the Volstead Act was passed in the US, ushering in prohibition. Almost overnight, re-exports boomed as Bahamanian merchants imported alcohol for resale via contraband routes to the US. The peak years were 1922 and 1923, when recorded re-exports were valued at more than US$7 million.

The bootleg trade not only created fortunes for a small number of Bahamanians but also boosted public expenditure because of the high taxes on imported liquor. Infrastructure improved and a number of wealthy foreigners began to settle on the islands after the end of prohibition. In addition, direct flights started from Miami in 1929. And the airports constructed during the Second World War by the US military provided additional means for civilians to reach the Bahamas when the war ended. By 1949, the annual number of visitors reached 32,018, a high figure for the Caribbean at the time.

This was not yet mass tourism, but the direction of travel was clear. Unable to raise living standards by exporting commodities produced locally, the Bahamas was going to depend on a combination of re-exports and exports of services. And the results were spectacular. By 1966, the annual number of visitors had reached 750,000, real estate was booming on many islands, Freeport had been established on Grand Bahama, which offered tax concessions to numerous companies, and financial services catering to legitimate companies (as well as tax-evading entities and individuals) were mushrooming.

The population, less than 80,000 in 1950, had jumped to nearly 170,000 20 years later. This was partly due to natural increase, the death rate having fallen below ten per 1,000 by the mid-1950s, but also to net inward migration after decades of emigration (see figure 15.1). Oil refining facilities, established at the end of 1960s, provided a further boost to job creation and led to competition for labour that drove up wages.

The way was now clear for Bahamas to become independent from the UK, which it did in 1973. The currency had already been pegged at par to the US dollar in 1966, providing incentives for companies and individuals in the neighbouring country to expand business and tourism in the Bahamas. A central bank provided assurances of financial stability, although for a time it was powerless to prevent Colombian drug traffickers from exploiting the geographical isolation of the outer islands.

The Bahamas, it seemed, had solved the puzzle with which all Caribbean countries had grappled since the end of slavery by replacing domestic exports with services and re-exports of merchandise. By the new millennium, tourism directly and indirectly accounted for two-thirds of GDP, and by 2017 the Bahamas was host to six million visitors.[6] Financial services were responsible directly and indirectly for a further 15 per cent of GDP. And yet, as figure 15.2 shows, GDP per head at constant prices was the same in 2017 as it had been in 1970.

Figure 15.2: Bahamas: GDP per head (2010 US$), 1960–2017

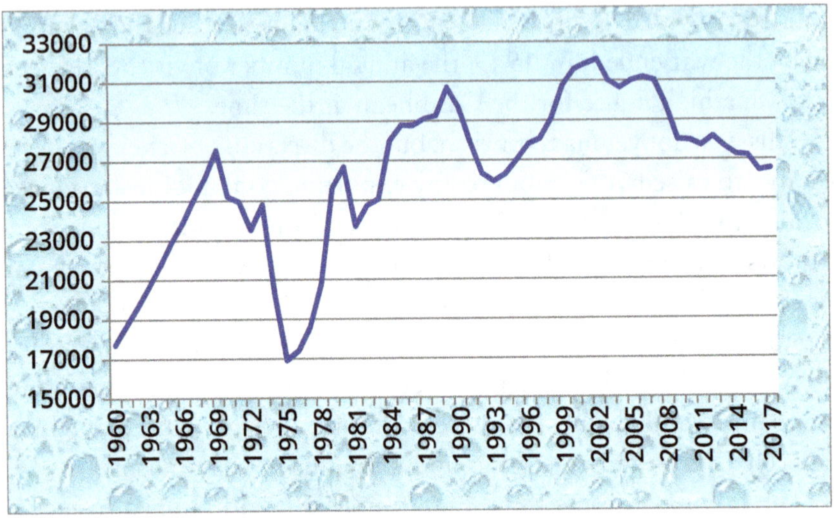

Source: World Bank, World Development Indicators.

The Bahamas economy since independence has been subject to a series of cycles that have brought brief booms and busts without laying the foundation for a sustained improvement in living standards. At first, this could be ignored since the first slump after independence coincided with the two oil crises in the 1970s (see figure 15.2), about which the Bahamas could do little, and the economy soon recovered. By the end of the 1990s, however, as the Bahamas weathered a sustained attack by the Organisation for Economic Co-operation and Development (OECD) and other international institutions on its financial services industry, it was no longer possible to ignore the risks to the economy from over-reliance on finance and tourism. As was astutely noted in 2001 by a researcher at the Central Bank of the Bahamas:[7]

> The challenge perhaps is not the mere concentration on services, but that the model itself did not seem to evolve fast enough to keep pace with the changing times, nor has it fully exploited

> opportunities that the human infrastructure developed in support of existing industries can provide. The tourism industry is still largely just a hotel industry, and the events of the past 24-months exposed the financial services industry as one that seemingly too did not manage to keep up with the pace of change.

Despite this warning, GDP per head steadily declined in subsequent years (see figure 15.2). This was largely due to the performance of exports, which accounts for some 40 per cent of GDP. Exports of goods and services at constant prices did, at first, increase after 2000, but they peaked in 2013 and subsequently fell. And when adjusted for population growth, they were no higher in 2017 than they had been 20 years earlier. In addition, the non-export economy was adversely affected by a series of natural disasters and bankruptcies among major companies, the most serious of which closed the construction of the Baha Mar tourist complex for many months.[8]

Despite the disappointing performance of the economy after 2000, there was once again net inward migration (see figure 15.1). This was mainly due to the arrival of large numbers of Haitians, although migration from Jamaica and the US was also important. The population, which had been 181,000 at the time of independence, had doubled by 2010 and was close to 400,000 in 2018. This was 30 times larger than the figure 200 years before, and it demonstrated the extraordinary demographic transformation that the Bahamas has experienced in the last two centuries.

It would be churlish to deny that the Bahamas has been relatively successful in making the transition to an economy based primarily on the exports of services. Indeed, so dependent on services is the economy that the Bahamas never joined the Caribbean Single Market and Economy, although it is a member of CARICOM. And, at the time of writing, it had still not joined the World Trade Organisation whose focus is mainly on goods. Yet, this transition has rendered the Bahamas vulnerable to changes in the global economy over which it has no control. With its financial services industry subject to regulations created elsewhere and its tourism industry facing intense competition from cheaper destinations, the Bahamas may need to find other sources of dynamism to maintain rising living standards in the future.

15.2. TURKS AND CAICOS ISLANDS

The Turks Islands were used in the eighteenth century by settlers from Bermuda to extract salt using slave labour. This, together with their strategic position on the trade routes to and from the Caribbean, led to competition among European powers. However, their status as a British territory was finally recognised by other European states in 1764, after which they were declared a dependency of the Bahamas. The Caicos Islands, largely uninhabited until the arrival of loyalists from the southern US seeking to establish cotton plantations with slave labour, also became part of the Bahamas.

In 1810, the Turks and Caicos Islands, still dependencies of the Bahamas, had a population of 1,718, of which 1,500 were slaves. The end of the slave trade, however, did not lead to a decline in the slave population as the birth rate was higher than the death rate. In addition, although the cotton plantations on the Caicos Islands were already in decline, the salt ponds on Grand Turk and Salt Cay were still profitable, and salt started to be extracted from South Caicos as well. Some slaves were transferred from the Bahamas to these salt works after abolition so that the slave population of the Turks and Caicos Islands was almost exactly the same in 1834, the year of emancipation, as in 1810. And the population, as a whole, had grown to 2,266.[9]

Heavy taxation on salt, levied from Nassau in the Bahamas without reference to the price on the world market,[10] generated deep resentment. In 1848, the British government separated the Turks and Caicos Islands from the Bahamas and made them responsible for their own affairs subject to the governor of Jamaica. This led to a temporary boost to the economy, with the volume of salt exports trebling between 1840 and 1860. Although often assumed to be 'primitive', salt extraction was quite sophisticated as the following description in 1918 made clear:[11]

> Salt ponds vary in size and are sometimes as large as five acres, while the pans are from one quarter of an acre to one acre in extent. The sea passes through sluices, entering by wide canals into the common storage reservoirs and then into the private reservoirs. The water now goes to the 'weak or No. 1 pond' until the salometer indicates 60. In this pond a great deal of the

> impurities are precipitated, and the water turns a saffron hue. By the time the brine has reached the strength of 60, the water has been reduced in quantity more than half of the original sea water, and it is now passed into the 'strong or No. 2 ponds'. The brine stays in this latter pond for about twenty days, until the strength of the pickle has increased to 90. The pickle is now pink in color and but one-sixth part of the original sea water. Having reached a strength of 90, it is turned into the 'making pans', where after ten to fifteen days, the salt commences granulate around the margins and bottoms of the pond. After twenty to twenty-five days more the salt is ready to be raked.

This was the industry on which the economy of the Turks and Caicos Islands rested until the last salt pond closed in 1964. Given the fluctuations in world prices and the problems posed by heavy rain, monoculture based on salt was bound to be extremely risky. Other commodity exports were, therefore, tried – especially on the Caicos Islands. A sponge industry was established in the late nineteenth century, but over-exploitation meant that exports declined precipitately after 1900. Conch was exported, especially to Haiti, but the value in most years before the Second World War was less than US$10,000. Sisal was also cultivated for export, but it never generated much income.

The economic fortunes of the Turks and Caicos Islands, therefore, depended too heavily on salt exports, and the risks did not change with the imposition of Crown Colony rule as a dependency of Jamaica in 1874. Domestic exports per head at constant prices peaked in 1860 and a century later had fallen by half.[12] Net migration, which had been inward in the first decade after separation from the Bahamas, then turned outward for the next century (see figure 15.3), with the greatest net outflow of islanders in the 1950s and 1960s. The population, a mere 5,257 in 1900, was still only 5,633 in 1970. Indeed, were it not for a birth rate that far exceeded the death rate in almost all years, the population would have actually fallen.

When Jamaica became independent in 1962, the prospects for the Turks and Caicos Islands appeared bleak. However, the islands' fortunes were transformed by replacing commodity exports with services. Net migration turned inwards after 1970 (see figure 15.3), with most of the migrants coming from Haiti, and the population had reached 35,000 by 2016.

Figure 15.3: Turks & Caicos Islands: Net Migration (% of Population), 1850–2016

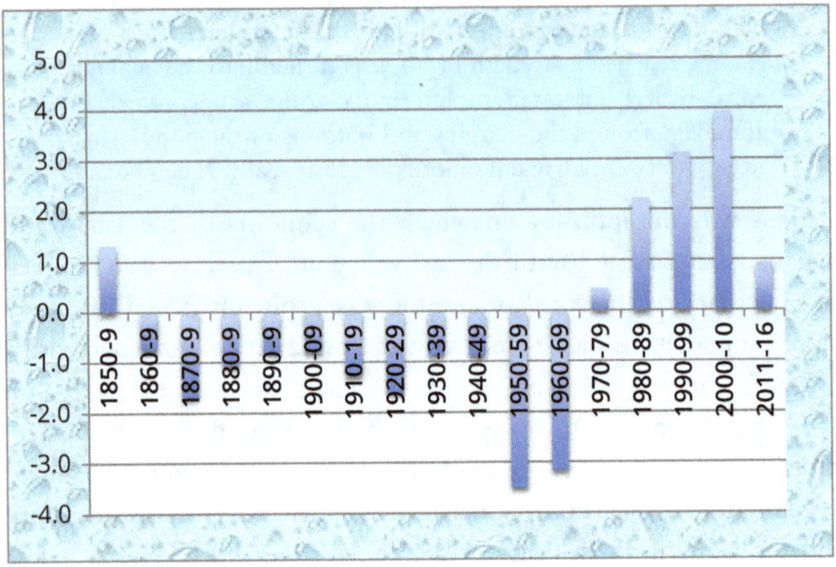

Source: Statistical Appendix and World Bank, World Development Indicators.

The most important service export has been tourism, including property development. From almost no visitors in 1960, the numbers have grown rapidly, reaching 1.3 million in 2016 of which one-third stayed overnight. Helped by airfields constructed by the US military in the 1950s and with the US dollar as the official currency, the tourism industry has transformed the Turks and Caicos Islands despite the impact of numerous hurricanes, the global financial crisis in 2008/9, and relatively high costs.

The second most important service export has been finance. After rapid growth in the 1980s and 1990s, however, the industry suffered a setback in 2000 when it was listed by the OECD as one of 17 tax havens.[13] Strenuous efforts subsequently helped partially to restore the reputation of the islands' financial services, but they have ceased to be an engine of growth. Corruption scandals at the highest level of government, leading to the imposition of direct rule by the British government from 2009 to 2012, have not helped.[14]

Tourism and financial services lifted GDP per head at constant (2010) prices to US$28,675 in 2008. In the next eight years, however, it fell to US$23,121. The economy is now as dependent on tourism as it once was on salt, and the need for diversification is just as pressing. Tourism may have fostered a standard of living that was inconceivable when salt was the main industry, but – as a global industry with many suppliers – it is just as fickle.

15.3. Cayman Islands

The Europeans who came to the Cayman Islands in the eighteenth century were, at first, interested in exploiting logwood and mahogany using slave labour. A cotton industry was then established, but – as in the Bahamas – this was in decline by the time the slave trade was abolished. However, the number of slaves did not diminish as their birth rates were much higher than their death rates, and the conditions of work (most were in households) were less onerous than on plantations.

When the emancipation law was passed in 1833, the slave owners assumed they would be entitled to compensation. However, no slave registry had been taken as the islands' relationship as a dependency of Jamaica had never been formalised (and would not be so until 1863). Registration was, therefore, hastily arranged in early 1834, and the number of slaves was recorded as 985 – some 60 per cent of the population. The owners, most of whom owned only a small number of slaves, then claimed £40,000. However, they received only £20,000. And to compound their woes, the governor of Jamaica on a visit in 1835 declared an immediate end to the apprenticeship period.

The decline of logging and the cotton industry left Caymanians in search of a new staple with which to finance their essential needs. They found it in turtling, which had long been exploited by the islanders in the coastal waters. This time, however, they would need to go further afield and many migrated temporarily or permanently to the Bay Islands off the coast of Honduras and other cayes off the coast of Nicaragua. A description of the Cayman Islands' main industry in the 1880s showed the importance of turtling:[15]

> Their livelihood depends on the capture of turtle, loggerheads being the most common, then hawksbill and the green turtle.

> The tortoise shell of the hawksbill and the soup meat, and eggs are all cured and carried to Jamaica markets by schooners.

The need to exploit waters far from the Cayman Islands made turtling a risky profession. Spain banned Cayman Islanders from Cuban waters in the 1870s, and Nicaragua would do the same in the 1890s. Both disputes would eventually be resolved after intervention by the British authorities, but there was understandable relief when a new commodity was found to be exported. This was phosphate, leading to the establishment of two companies in the 1880s, but both had collapsed by the early 1890s.[16] When the Cayman Islands, therefore, started producing their own trade statistics for the first time after 1900,[17] turtling was once again responsible for nearly all domestic exports.

The value of these domestic exports in 1900 was a mere US$34,000. Despite the high levels of emigration after the end of slavery, the population had increased to 5,000 thanks to the excess of births over deaths. So exports per head were less than $7. Although efforts would be made to establish new export industries, including coconuts and rope, turtling still accounted for more than half the value of all domestic export earnings after the Second World War.

This was no basis for a dynamic economy and, at constant prices, domestic exports per head were lower in 1960 than they had been in 1900. The population barely increased over these years, reaching 7,865 in 1960 as net outward migration almost wiped out the increase due to the excess of births over deaths. The only source of growth was public revenue and expenditure, which, expressed in real terms, rose rapidly. Public spending per head at 1930 prices, for example, quadrupled from US$2.40 in 1900 to US$10.20 in 1938 before jumping to US$27.50 in 1960.[18]

Public revenue may have risen rapidly, especially after the Second World War, but nearly all of it came from customs duties thanks to an increase in the number of visitors and the associated rise in imports. By contrast, there were no taxes on income or capital. In other countries, this would have been seen as a serious fiscal weakness, especially after Jamaica became independent in 1962 and the Cayman Islands chose to remain a British colony. However, the authorities – British and Caymanian – saw the lack of direct taxation as an opportunity to enter the offshore business by marketing the colony as a tax haven.

By 1970, the transformation of the Cayman Islands into a British colony dependent on the export of services was well under way. The number of visitors arriving both for vacation and non-vacation purposes had reached 22,900 (it had been only 3,440 in 1963) and would exceed 100,000 by the end of the decade. New registrations for 'exempt' companies, i.e., those whose proposed activities were to be carried out mainly outside the Cayman Islands and which would receive exemption from all tax that might be imposed on other companies, reached 148 in 1970 and nearly 1,000 at the end of the decade. Last, but not least, a Cayman Island (CI) dollar was introduced in 1972 and fixed at CI$1=US$1.20 in 1974 where it remains today.

A fixed exchange rate, tax exemption and British colonial status then brought about one of the fastest rates of economic growth of any Caribbean country ever recorded. Based entirely on the export of services (tourism and financial services), the Cayman Islands became one of the richest countries in the world with a GDP per head that reached US$76,195 at its peak (see figure 15.4). And the population, still less than 10,000 in 1970, had jumped to 60,000 by 2016 thanks to a high level of net inward migration.

Figure 15.4: Cayman Islands: GDP per head (2010 US$), 1970–2016

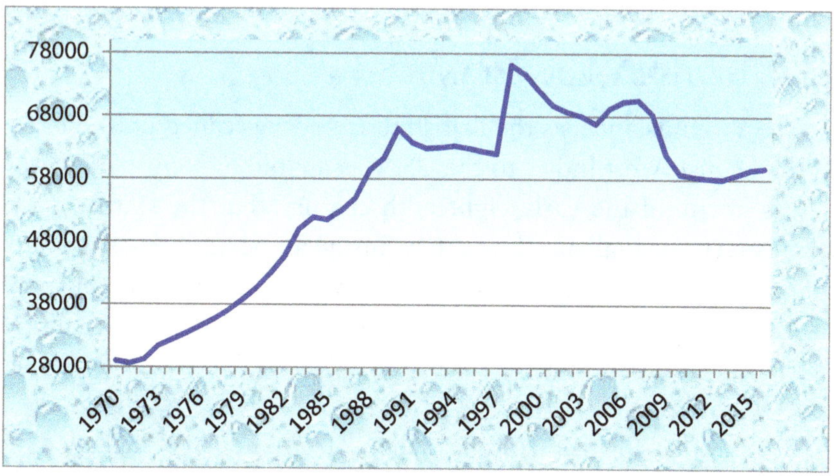

Source: UNNA.

Unfortunately for the Cayman Islands, the economic model that had looked so durable after 1970 lost its dynamism in the new millennium when the tide turned against tax havens. Rich countries became concerned about of the loss of tax revenue and the use of such havens for money laundering from illegal activities. The number of visitors to the Cayman Islands continued to rise, exceeding two million in 2016, but the net income from financial services went into decline. And as one of the few Caribbean countries where financial service exports are more important than tourism, this hit the Cayman Islands hard. By 2016, GDP per head had fallen by more than 20 per cent from its peak.

The Cayman Islands are still a rich country even after deducting the income that accrues to non-residents.[19] However, the special circumstances that transformed the islands' economy after the Cayman Islands ceased to be a dependency of Jamaica have now changed. The islands' authorities have worked hard to ensure that they are compliant with all the demands of OECD countries on tax havens and avoided being placed on any blacklist until 2020. Yet even if a large financial services industry survives, it will no longer be an engine of growth. Furthermore, tougher regulation has been passed into law by the British government that has ultimate control over Overseas Territories. This requires the government of the Cayman Islands to provide full disclosure about the ownership of offshore entities, making its status as a tax haven less attractive for many firms, trusts, and individuals.

15.4. British Virgin Islands

The Virgin Islands, as the British territory was called until the sale of the Danish West Indies to the US, was an 'old' colony.[20] However, it was not until the early eighteenth century that the status of the islands went unchallenged by other European powers. At that point, numerous British settlers arrived with their slaves with the purpose of exporting cotton and sugar. By 1810, shortly after the abolition of the slave trade, the population was 8,780 of which 7,500 (85 per cent) were slaves.

As in other British colonies, the cotton industry struggled to compete with exports from cheaper sources and by 1820 domestic exports consisted entirely of sugar. Although the number of slaves fell steadily to 5,135 in the year of emancipation, the planters did not lack for labour as many Africans captured on the high seas by the British navy were indentured in the Virgin Islands. However, the planters still complained bitterly about their prospects, so much so that, in a barely literate memorial of 1832, they asked the British government to nationalise their slaves:[21]

> Your Memorialists further crave permission with all humility to suggest, in case it shall be deemed most expedient, in spite of every remonstrance and explanation, to emancipate the slaves and make a full compensation for all losses sustained thereby, on a fair principle of justice, the propriety of pausing until an experiment be made, which the Virgin Islands, from their insulated situation and small extent, (the proprietors of property therein being willing, for the general good, to aid in the promotion thereof by consenting to transfer their right and title in and to such property, real and personal, at a fair valuation, payable immediately, or by instalments, with interest, in three, four, or five years,) will afford an opportunity of doing, as the measures already pursued have deteriorated property in this country beyond all precedent, at comparatively small expense, and with due caution, little risk, the effects of which will be sufficiently manifest, in the course of a year or two, to prove what would be the consequences of perfecting the measure on a general scale, not only as regards the good of the nation, but also the welfare of that particular class of people.

The British government was not swayed by this pathetic plea for special treatment, but the planters did receive £72,950 in compensation for their slaves. This substantial sum was not reinvested in the islands, as the sugar industry was now in terminal decline and exports had virtually ceased by the 1850s.[22] A small export trade in cattle and livestock (mainly to the Danish West Indies) now took its place, but the economy was clearly suffering. Public revenue per head in 1850 was a mere US$1, a cholera epidemic struck in 1853, and, in that same year, a major riot took place triggered by a head tax on cattle.

The population steadily fell although in most years births exceeded deaths. By 1900, it had fallen to 4,846, almost half what it had been in 1810, and the cause was the high rate of net outward migration (see figure 15.5). This continued after 1900, although the population did at least increase modestly and had reached 8,000 in 1960 – still below its level 150 years before. It was not until the 1980s that net migration turned inwards and the population started to increase rapidly, exceeding 30,000 for the first time in 2015.

Figure 15.5: British Virgin Islands: Net Migration (% of Population), 1850–2016

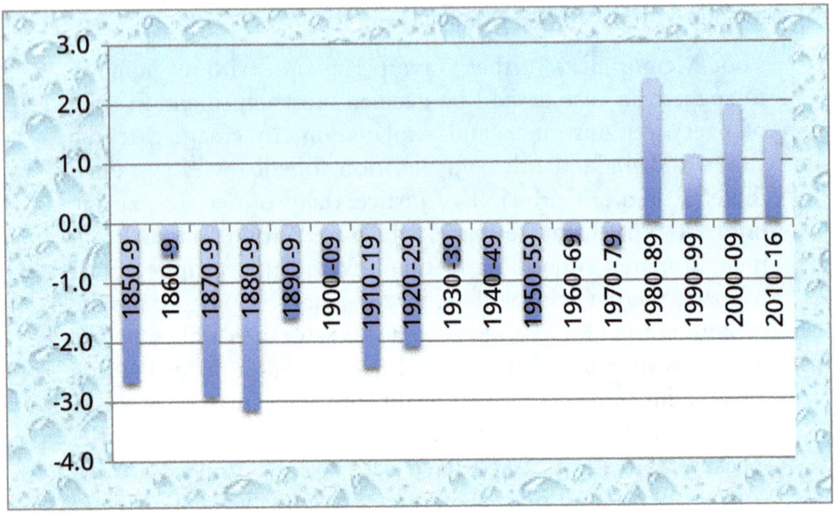

Source: Statistical Appendix and World Bank, World Development Indicators.

The Virgin Islands joined the Leeward Islands Federation in 1871, and the scale of the economic problems was soon made apparent in a report on the federation's finances:[23]

> This group of Islands has no public debt, but suffers from a chronic inability to make revenue cover expenditure…The term Civil Establishments is hardly applicable to the Administration of these small and sparsely-populated settlements, although there is still kept up the semblance of an independent Legislature and separate Administrative Departments. The President's residence, the Court House, the Legislative Council Chamber, and the small accommodation which the Administration of the Islands requires are all contained in one tumble-down building near the shore at Road Town in Tortola.

Public finances slowly improved under the federation, but domestic exports per head did not. In the first few years of the federation, the only exports were cattle, charcoal, goats, horses, and sheep with a gross annual value of around US$25,000. An attempt was made to revive sugar and cotton exports after 1900, but neither was successful. By 1960, exports per head at constant prices had still not reached their level in 1820.[24] At that time, the only bank in operation was the Government Savings Bank. The prospects for the colony, which had refused to join the Federation of the West Indies in 1958 and which clung desperately to the US dollar as its currency, appeared grim indeed.

The international airport built on Beef Island, after it had been connected to Tortola by bridge, brought modern tourism to the BVI in the 1960s, and the impact was dramatic. By 2016, the BVI was receiving more than 400,000 overnight visitors with an additional 700,000 coming on cruise ships. This would have been sufficient in itself to raise income per head rapidly, but the tourism industry was soon eclipsed by exports of a different kind.

These were financial services, an industry that first became established in the 1970s. With the passage of the International Business Companies (IBCs) Act in 1984, granting tax exemptions to offshore companies, the stage was set for explosive growth.[25] By the start of the new millennium, over 500,000 IBCs had been formed, and GDP per head at 2010 prices had reached US$44,000 with financial services accounting for a quarter of the total.

Yet, as in other Caribbean countries dependent on the export of financial services, this would be the peak. Beginning with the onslaught in 2000 from the OECD and many of its member states, followed by the global financial crisis in 2008/9 and the release of the Panama and Paradise Papers a few years later,[26] the industry went into decline. By 2016, GDP per head at 2010 prices had fallen to US$29,000 – one-third below its peak in 2001. The authorities may have ensured that the BVI financial services were compliant with all OECD conditions needed to avoid blacklisting, but the industry was no longer an engine of growth and was unlikely ever to be so again.

15.5. Montserrat

Although French forces had captured Montserrat in 1782, the island was returned to the British by the Treaty of Paris the following year. By then, British and Irish settlers had developed sugar, cotton, and arrowroot industries using slave labour, the conditions of which had led to a major – if unsuccessful – slave revolt in 1768. British sovereignty over the island went uncontested after 1783, so the island remained in British hands throughout the Anglo-French Wars.

In 1810, soon after the slave trade was abolished by Great Britain, the population of Montserrat was 7,650 of which 6,800 (88.9 per cent) were slaves. Deaths among the slaves, at first, exceeded births, but by 1830 this had been reversed.[27] As a result, the slave population was still 6,400 (87.1 per cent of the population) in 1834 when the slaves were emancipated.

If the free and slave populations were largely unchanged in size between abolition and emancipation, the same was not true of the composition of exports. Arrowroot and cotton had disappeared, so Montserrat had become an island whose exports depended wholly on the products of the sugar industry. Large numbers of slaves were held by a relatively small number of slave owners, among whom the largest was Queely Shiel. He claimed for 375 slaves on his Montpelier and Hope Estates, a share of 256 slaves on the Richmond and Grove Estates, and nearly 250 slaves on three other estates.

The volume of sugar exports (three million pounds in 1820) had fallen in half by 1840, but then recovered despite having to pay the 4.5 per cent export duty applied to the 'old' colonies. By 1870, the volume exported was back to its level in 1820 and by 1880 it had reached four million pounds. From then onwards, however, there was a precipitate decline with only 500,000 pounds being exported in 1900, by which time Montserrat had the lowest value of exports per head in the whole of the Caribbean.[28] Joseph Allen, giving evidence to the Royal Commission, painted a dismal picture:[29]

> Every sugar estate in the island has suffered by the fall in price, estates are heavily taxed...estates are overvalued for land tax... [Joseph Allen] has tried other cultivation, but has no money to employ labour...Labourers are employed on some estates taken off from manufacturing the crop, and are paid not in money but in sugar; the sugar is valued at 14s. 6d. a barrel, but they can only get 8s. 6d. for it. They have no other employment, so they have to take what they can get.

With sugar in decline (the last shipment would be made in 1928), the estate owners were forced to try other exports. Livestock was one commodity shipped to other islands, but it never earned much. Lime exports were started in the late nineteenth century by the Montserrat Company and from which came exports of green limes, limejuice (raw and concentrated), citrate of lime, and lime oil. Yet, the industry was never large enough to make much of an impact and virtually disappeared after the 1930s. Only the cotton industry, revived after 1900, prevented Montserrat from continuing to have the lowest exports per head in the Caribbean, and even cotton struggled once the Second World War had ended.

The dire state of the export economy was reflected in public finance, which even in 1870 – when sugar exports were performing well – only generated US$2.8 per head in public revenue. Montserrat agreed to join the Leeward Islands Federation the following year, in the hope that this would change the poor state of the island's public finances, but it did not. Instead, there were regular complaints about the cost of the federation and the poor quality of management of public expenses. The Royal Commission in 1884 duly noted:[30]

> These [public] works have throughout been badly managed. They were entrusted in the first instance to unprofessional hands in the Island, and consequently difficulties arose, mistakes were made, and for a time they were suspended; but they have now been placed under the supervision of the Civil Engineer of Dominica, and it is hoped will soon be brought to a successful conclusion.

Exports per head at constant prices did recover after 1900, but they reached a peak in 1935 after which the cotton and lime industries went into decline. Emigration was a constant feature of Montserrat life from emancipation – or at least the end of apprenticeship in 1838 – onwards. However, a high birth rate meant that there was a modest increase in population in the second half of the nineteenth century and the total was 12,217 in 1900. Yet, from then onwards, there was no increase at all, as outward migration matched the excess of births over deaths, and the population was still only 12,000 in 1960.

With such a small population, independence was not considered viable by the islanders who opted to remain a colony. Yet Montserrat, despite its dependent status, was allowed to join CARICOM after its foundation in 1973 and later became a member of the Eastern

Caribbean Central Bank (ECCB), joining the Eastern Caribbean Currency Union (ECCU) as well. And, as the public infrastructure improved, Montserrat was able to make the transition from an exporter of goods to an exporter of services relatively easily.

Figure 15.6: Montserrat: GDP per head (2010 US$), 1970–2016

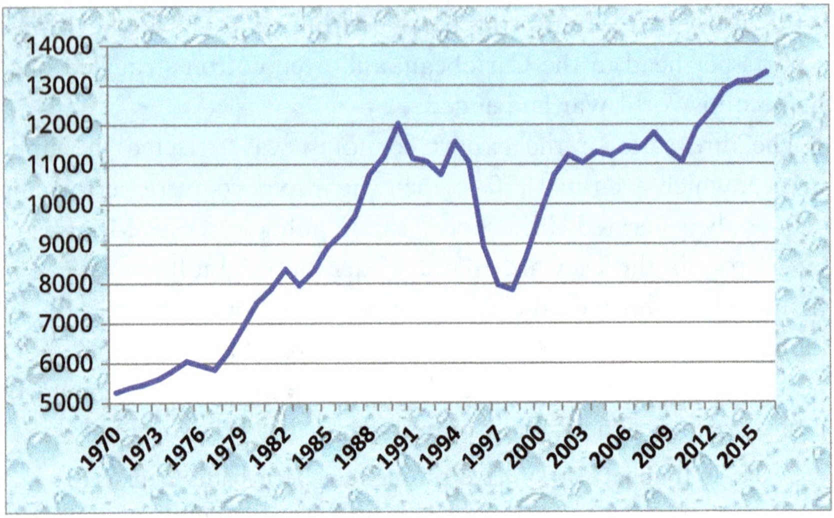

Source: UNNA.

The main service provided was tourism and, by the mid-1990s, it had helped Montserrat to double GDP per head from its 1970 level (see figure 15.6). In 1995, however, the long dormant volcano in the south of the island (La Soufrière) erupted and destroyed the capital Plymouth. The government was forced to create an exclusion zone that included the airport and evacuation of the island had reduced the population of the island to 4,400 by 2002 since the volcano showed continued signs of activity.

As the colonial power, the British government expected all the islanders to leave. However, the few that remained were eventually joined by others. By 2016, the population had reached 5,000. Confined to the northern third of the island, the population size was helped by constructing a new airport, returning international visitors, and exporting telecommunications, and computer and information services. By 2011, GDP per head had recovered its previous peak and soon exceeded it (see figure 15.6).

The habitable part of the island of Montserrat was already small before La Soufrière erupted, but was made much smaller when the government established the exclusion zone. Without the external assistance made possible by being a British Overseas Territory, the islanders could not have survived. Yet, survive they did, and there is no reason why GDP per head should not continue to rise as the prospects for increasing tourism are good – especially when the exclusion zone is lifted. Montserrat may be the poorest of the British Overseas Territories in the Caribbean, but it is not poor by comparison with the rest of the region.

15.6. Anguilla

British settlers and their slaves first arrived in Anguilla in 1650, but British sovereignty over the island was disputed until the end of the Napoleonic Wars. Long before then, however, the island had been used to export a variety of commodities including cotton, indigo, and sugar. Of these, cotton was the most important export, as frequent periods of drought made sugar an unreliable staple. In 1787, for example, cotton represented 40 per cent of the value of exports, while sugar was only 15 per cent.[31]

By the time the trade in slaves ended in 1808, the sugar economy had declined even further. The population in 1810 was only 2,300, of which 1,700 were slaves. However, the slave population actually increased in the next two decades so that there were 2,260 at the time of emancipation in 1834 (this was mainly due to a birth rate among the slaves that was much higher than the death rate). There were eight claims for more than 50 slaves with the Lake, Gumbs, and Hodge families particularly prominent.

The slaves worked the sugar and cotton plantations, but were also used in the salt works that became an important industry after 1800. Indeed, Anguilla briefly became a free port in 1824 to facilitate the trade before annexation by St Kitts the following year brought an end to this privilege. A severe drought, followed by famine in 1832, was the prelude to emancipation and apprenticeship, after which Anguilla became perhaps the most neglected colony in the Caribbean. All the main commodity industries struggled, sugar disappeared entirely, and the value of domestic exports in 1845 was a mere US$6,000. In the

1860s, phosphate was extracted from Sombrero to the north of the main island, but this industry was short-lived, and in 1890 another drought and famine struck the island.

Emigration was the norm after the end of the apprenticeship period, although the population did not decrease as a result of the high birth rate and relatively low death rate. With the shrinking of the export sector, raising revenue became harder and harder with no subvention from St Kitts. When the Royal Commission on public finance considered the matter, it found gross revenue in 1883 of only £750 (US$3,645), which – among a population of 3,315 in that year – was barely $1 per person. The commissioners, suggesting that the merger of St Kitts and Nevis the previous year had raised other priorities, concluded:[32]

> This Small Island...will no longer be looked upon as in any sense a separate settlement. It will be both more economical and more satisfactory in every way to regard it simply as a district enjoying the same administration and laws and paying the same taxes as the other portions of the Colony.

Table 15.3: Anguilla: Vital Statistics and Cotton Exports, 1911–17

	CBR	CDR	Cotton (lb)		
			Anguilla	Nevis	St Kitts
1911	48.3	18.1	148,595	344,395	329,322
1912	54.1	17.6	97,142	165,329	322,168
1913	46.1	16.5	112,138	166,477	374,594
1914	34.6	19.1	94,372	268,542	372,633
1915	36.8	14.1	33,750	305,154	397,567
1916	43.2	14.8	49,620	99,173	131,859
1917	33.2	19.1	49,399	196,915	106,285

Sources: Jones (1976, 33) and Burdon (1920, 21).

By the time of the census taken on December 31, 1920, the population had reached 4,219. This was partly due to healthy vital statistics in the previous decade (see table 15.3) but also to a revival of the cotton industry in 1904 that in the next few years rivalled that of both St Kitts and Nevis. Anguillan cotton exports, however, peaked in 1911, after which there was a steady decline (see table 15.3). By the early 1950s, only 60 acres of cotton were planted and Anguilla had become an economy of small farmers in which livestock, especially poultry, played a large part.

Anguilla had joined the Leeward Islands Federation in 1871 as part of St Kitts, and the Federation of the West Indies in 1958 as part of St Kitts and Nevis. The two federations had helped to shield Anguilla from complete dependence on St Kitts, but the collapse of the West Indies Federation in 1962 and the preparation of St Kitts and Nevis for associated statehood with Great Britain changed the calculus of Anguillans. A movement for separation gained momentum, leading to the launch of the Anguillan revolution in 1967 and the second declaration of independence two years later.

Anguilla was placed under direct rule by the UK, but it would take a further 11 years before St Kitts and Nevis in late 1980 yielded to British pressure to let Anguilla leave the three-island state. St Kitts and Nevis then proceeded to independence in 1983. Anguilla's colonial status was no longer challenged by the majority of its inhabitants, and the island would become, in 2002 a British Overseas Territory with a population in that year of nearly 12,000.

Long before this, Anguilla had made the transition to becoming an economy dependent on the export of services. Anguilla joined the ECCB and benefited from the currency stability provided by the monetary union. The island's government also joined the Caribbean Development Bank, giving Anguilla access to soft loans for infrastructure development. And grants from the British government also helped to transform public services.

Tourism, held back at first by the lack of air connections, was slower to develop than in the neighbouring islands, but the completion of the Wallblake International Airport in 1974 gave a big boost. In 2016, the year before Hurricane Irma did terrible damage, the number of overnight visitors was nearly 80,000, with many more coming on cruise ships. As a result GDP per head at constant prices rose rapidly after 1970 (see figure 15.7).

Aware of the dangers of being over-dependent on tourism, the Anguillan government took steps to diversify exports with special attention to financial services. This met, at first, with considerable success, especially in the areas of offshore insurance and mutual funds intermediaries. However, the designation of Anguilla as a tax haven by the OECD led to the island's government making a series of commitments in favour of greater transparency in order to avoid being tarnished as uncooperative.

Figure 15.7: Anguilla: GDP per head (2010 US$), 1970–2016

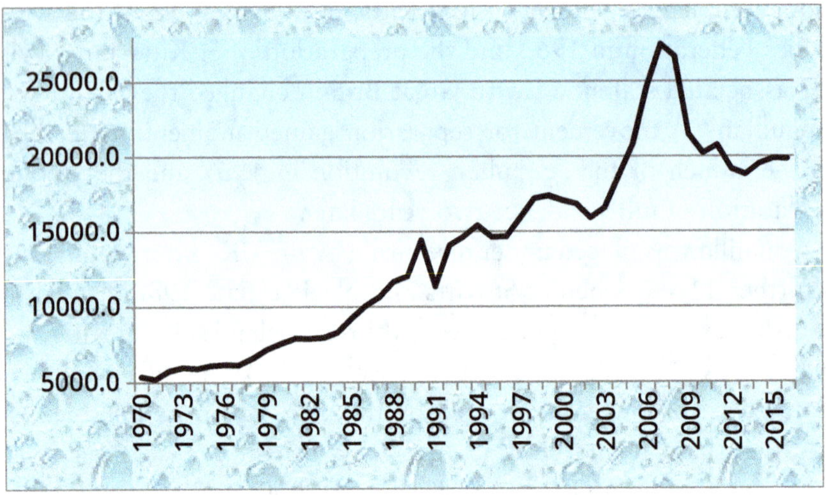

Source: UNNA.

This, together with the impact of the global financial crisis in 2008/9, led to a decline in service exports and a fall in GDP per head (see figure 15.7). Yet, the financial services industry survived and is responsible for roughly 20 per cent of all exports (the rest coming mainly from tourism). And the sector was much less severely affected by Hurricane Irma in 2017 than tourism, which was badly hit by damage to hotels and other facilities.

Anguilla is now a relatively rich Caribbean country in sharp contrast to the situation in the nineteenth century. The population had reached nearly 15,000 before Hurricane Irma, some five times greater than 200 years before, but this time with an exceptionally low death rate. Still, its fragile ecosystem and vulnerability to hurricanes suggest that economic prosperity is far from assured. Like all other Caribbean countries, the diversification of exports will remain a constant struggle while its dependence on grants from the British government and other sources is unlikely to diminish.

NOTES

1. Florida had been a British colony from 1763 until 1783, when under the Treaty of Paris Great Britain transferred sovereignty to Spain. Most of the British settlers then left for the Bahamas with their slaves.
2. All numbers in this section refer only to the Bahamas and exclude the Turks and Caicos Islands even before separation in 1848. See Statistical Appendix.
3. The average amount of compensation per slave was £12 14s 6d. By contrast, it was close to £50 in British Guiana and Trinidad. See M. Craton, *A History of the Bahamas* (London: Collins, 1968), 203–04.
4. Quoted in H. Johnson, *The Bahamas from Slavery to Servitude, 1783–1933* (Gainesville, FL: University Press of Florida, 1996), 31.
5. See Statistical Appendix.
6. 1.2 million were overnight visitors and the rest cruise ship passengers.
7. See G. Fraser, 'Can the Sir Stafford Sands Model of the Bahamian Economy, Survive Today's Global Economy?' XXXIII Conference of the Caribbean Centre for Monetary Studies, Belize City, Belize, 2001, 29.
8. The Baha Mar complex on the island of New Providence is one of the biggest tourist resorts in the world with 2,200 rooms. It finally opened in 2017.
9. See Statistical Appendix.
10. See Craton, *A History of the Bahamas*, 221.
11. See T. de Booy, *The Virgin Islands: Our New Possessions, and the British Islands* (Philadelphia, PA: J.B. Lippincott Co., 1918), 42.
12. See Statistical Appendix.
13. See Organisation of Cooperation and Development (OECD), *2000 Progress Report: Towards Global Tax Co-operation: Progress in Identifying and Eliminating Harmful Tax Practices* (Paris: OECD, 2000), 17.
14. See P. Clegg, 'The Turks and Caicos Islands: Why Does the Cloud Still Hang?' *Social and Economic Studies* 61, no. 1 (2012): 24–26.
15. Quoted in M. Craton, *Founded upon the Seas: A History of the Cayman Islands and their People* (Kingston, Jamaica: Ian Randle Publishers), 160.
16. See Craton, *Founded upon the Seas*, 167.
17. Before 1900, the trade statistics for the Cayman Islands were included in those of Jamaica.
18. See Statistical Appendix.
19. Gross National Income, which excludes the income of non-residents, is 90 per cent of GDP in the Cayman Islands.
20. This meant it had to pay the export duty of 4.5 per cent.

21. See *Report from Select Committee on the Commercial State of the West India Colonies* (London: 1832), 123–24.
22. This did, however, mean that land prices fell sharply allowing former slaves to buy land more easily. See I. Dookhan, *A History of the British Virgin Islands* (Epping: Caribbean Universities Press for the College of the Virgin Islands, 1975), 127.
23. See *Report of the West India Royal Commission::* (London: 1884), 29.
24. See Statistical Appendix.
25. See R. Darius and O. Williams, 'Impact of Growth in International Business Companies on the British Virgin Islands Economy,' *Social and Economic Studies* 46, nos. 2/3 (1997): 172–73.
26. The Panama Papers were leaked from a law firm in Panama in 2015, while the Paradise Papers were mainly leaked from a company based in Bermuda. The BVI was the host for many of the companies and individuals listed in the leaks as practising tax evasion.
27. See Statistical Appendix.
28. See V. Bulmer-Thomas, *The Economic History of the Caribbean since the Napoleonic Wars* (Cambridge: Cambridge University Press, 2012), 128, figure 5.8.
29. See *Report of the West India Royal Commission* (London: 1897), 152.
30. See *Report of the West India Royal Commission: :* (1984), 26.
31. See C.L. Petty, *A Handbook History of Anguilla* (Anguilla: Colville L.Petty, 1991), 6.
32. See *Report of the West India Royal Commission: Part III: The Leeward Islands* (1984), 25.

Bibliography

Algemeen Bureau voor de Statistiek. *Armoedegrenzen en armoede in Suriname*. Paramaribo: Algemeen Bureau voor de Statistiek, 2010.

Almanak voor de Nederlandsche West-Indische bezittingen: En de kust van Guinea, voor het jaar 1856, 1859–1861. Gravenhage: Gebroeders van Cleef: 1860.

Annuaire de la Guyane. Paris, various years.

Aspinall, A.E. *The British West Indies: Their History, Resources and Progress*. London: Pitman, 1912.

Austin, D.A. *Economic and Fiscal Conditions in the US Virgin Islands*. Washington, DC: Congressional Research Service, 2018.

Ayala, C., and R. Bernabe. *Puerto Rico in the American Century: A History since 1898*. Chapel Hill, NC: University of North Carolina Press, 2007.

Bacchus, M.K. *Education as and for Legitimacy: Developments in West Indian Education between 1846 and 1895*. Waterloo, Canada: Wilfrid Laurier University Press, 1994.

Balch, E.G. *Occupied Haiti: Being the Report of a Committee of Six Disinterested Americans Representing Organizations Exclusively American, Who, Having Personally Studied Conditions in Haiti in 1926, Favor the Restoration of the Independence of the Negro Republic*. New York, NY: The Writers Pub. Co., 1927.

Banco Nacional de Cuba. *Economic Report 1994*. Havana: Banco Nacional de Cuba, 1995.

Baptiste, F.A. 'The Exploitation of Caribbean Bauxite and Petroleum, 1914–1945.' *Social and Economic Studies* 37 (1988): 107–42.

Barberia, L. 'Remittances to Cuba: An Evaluation of Cuban and U.S. Government Policy Measures.' In *The Cuban Economy at the*

Start of the Twenty-first Century, edited by J.I. Domínguez, V.O.E. Pérez, and L. Barberia. Cambridge, MA: David Rockefeller Center for Latin American Studies, Harvard University, 2004.

Barros, J. *Haïti, de 1804 à nos jours*. Paris: Editions L'Harmattan, 1984.

Bassières, E. *Notice sur la Guyane*. Paris: Editions Orphie, 1900.

Beckles, H. *Britain's Black Debt: Reparations for Caribbean Slavery and Native Genocide*. Kingston, Jamaica: University of the West Indies, 2013.

———. *A History of Barbados*. New York, NY: Cambridge University Press, 2006.

Benham, F. 'The National Income of British Guiana, 1942.' *Development and Welfare in the West Indies*, Bulletin No. 17 (1947): 1–28. Bridgetown, Barbados.

Benoit, P.V. *Évolution budgetaire et développement économique d'Haiti*. Port-au-Prince, Haiti: H. Deschamps, 1954.

Bergad, L.W. *Coffee and the Growth of Agrarian Capitalism in Nineteenth-century Puerto Rico*. Princeton, NJ: Princeton University Press, 1983.

Blancpain, F. *Un siècle de relations financières entre Haïti et la France, 1825–1922*. Paris: L'Harmattan, 2001.

Blérald, A.P. *Histoire économique de la Guadeloupe et de la Martinique: Du XVIIe siècle à nos jours*. Paris: Karthala, 1986. *RHS*, 1988.

Bolland, O.N. *Colonialism and Resistance in Belize: Essays in Historical Sociology*. Benque Viejo del Carmen, Belize: Cubola Productions, 1988.

———. *The Formation of a Colonial Society: Belize, from Conquest to Crown Colony*. Baltimore, MD: Johns Hopkins University Press, 1977.

———. *On the March: Labour Rebellions in the British Caribbean, 1934–39*. Kingston, Jamaica: Ian Randle Publishers, 1995.

Boorstein, E. *The Economic Transformation of Cuba: A First-hand Account*. New York, NY: Modern Reader Paperbacks, 1968.

de Booy, T. *The Virgin Islands: Our New Possessions, and the British Islands*. Philadelphia, PA: J.B. Lippincott Co., 1918.

Bosworth, B., and S. Collins. 'Economic Growth.' In *The Economy of Puerto Rico*, edited by S. Collins, B. Bosworth, and M. Soto-Class. Washington, DC: Brookings Institution, 2006.

Boyer, W. *America's Virgin Islands: History of Human Rights and Wrongs*. Durham, NC: Carolina Academic Press, 1971.

Brière, J.-F. 'L'Emprunt de 1825 dans la dette de l'independence haitienne envers la France.' *Journal of Haitian Studies* 12, no. 2 (2006): 126–34.

Bristowe, L., and P. Wright. *The Handbook of British Honduras for 1889–90*. Edinburgh: Blackwood, 1980.

Brodber, E. *The Second Generation of Freemen in Jamaica, 1907–1944*. Gainesville, FL: University of Florida Press, 2004

Brown, L. 'The Three Faces of Post-Emancipation Migration in Martinique, 1848–1865.' *Journal of Caribbean History* 36, no. 2 (2002): 310–35.

Buffon, A. *Monnaie et crédit en économie coloniale: Contribution à l'histoire économique de la Guadeloupe, 1635–1919*. Basse-Terre, Guadeloupe: Société d'histoire de la Guadeloupe, 1979.

Bulmer-Thomas, B., and V. Bulmer-Thomas. *The Economic History of Belize: from 17th Century to Independence*. Benque Viejo del Carmen, Belize: Cubola, 2012.

Bulmer-Thomas, V. *The Economic History of the Caribbean since the Napoleonic Wars*. Cambridge: Cambridge University Press, 2012.

———. *Empire in Retreat: The Past, Present and Future of the United States*. New Haven, CT: Yale University Press, 2018.

Burdon, K.J. *A Handbook of St. Kitts-Nevis*. London: West India Committee, 1920.

Burdon, J.A. *Archives of British Honduras: Being Extracts and Précis from Records, with Maps*. London: Sifton, Praed & Co., Ltd, 1931.

Bureau, G. *La Guyane Méconnue*. Paris: Fasquelle Éditeurs, 1936.

Burtless, G., and O. Sotomayor. 'Labor Supply and Public Transfers.' In *The Economy of Puerto Rico*, edited by S. Collins, B. Bosworth, and M. Soto-Class. Washington, DC: Brookings Institution, 2006.

Butler, K.M. *The Economics of Emancipation: Jamaica and Barbados, 1823–43*. Chapel Hill, NC: University of North Carolina Press, 1995.

Calvo Ospina, H. *Bacardí: The Hidden War*. London: Pluto Press, 2002.

Campbell, M.C. *The Dynamics of Change in a Slave Society*. Cranbury, NJ: Associated University Presses, 1976.

Carey Jones, N.S. *The Pattern of a Dependent Economy: The National Income of British Honduras*. Cambridge: Cambridge University Press, 1953.

Carter, S.B. *Historical Statistics of the United States: Earliest Times to the Present*. New York, NY: Cambridge University Press, 2006.

Central Bureau of Statistics. *Statistical Yearbook of the Netherlands Antilles*. Willemstad, Curaçao: Central Bureau of Statistics, various years.

Centro Dominicano de Promoción de Exportaciones. *Boletín Estadístico* 4, 1988.

Chauleau, L. *Dans les îles du vent: La Martinique (XVIIe-XIXe siècle)*. Paris: L'Harmattan, 1993.

Clarence-Smith, W.G. *Cocoa and Chocolate, 1765–1914*. London: Routledge, 2000.

Clarence-Smith, W.G., and S. Topik. *The Global Coffee Economy in Africa, Asia and Latin America, 1500–1989*. Cambridge, UK: Cambridge University Press, 2003.

Clegg, P. 'The Turks and Caicos Islands: Why Does the Cloud Still Hang?' *Social and Economic Studies* 61, no. 1 (2012): 23–47.

Cleland, H.F. 'Curacao, a Losing Colonial Venture.' *Bulletin of the American Geographical Society* 41, no. 3 (1909): 129–38.

Colonial Department. *Honduras: Account of the Expenses of the Government of Honduras Defrayed by Taxes Raised on the Inhabitants of that Settlement, from the Beginning of the Year 1824 down to the Present Period, so far as the Same can be Made out*. London: Colonial Department, 1836.

Comisión Económica para América Latina y el Caribe (CEPAL). *Estudio económico de América Latina y el Caribe 2009–2010*. Santiago: CEPAL, 2010.

Comptes économiques rapides pour l'Outre-mer. *Estimation du PIB par habitant de Saint-Barthélemy*. Paris: Comptes économiques rapides pour l'Outre-mer, 2014.

———. *Estimation du PIB par habitant de Saint-Martin*. Paris: Comptes économiques rapides pour l'Outre-mer, 2018.

Cooper, A. *Internet Gambling Offshore: Caribbean Struggles over Casino Capitalism*. New York, NY: Palgrave Macmillan, 2011.

Craig-James, S. *The Changing Society of Tobago, 1838–1938: A Fractured Whole*. Arima, Trinidad and Tobago: Cornerstone, 2008.

Craton, M. *A History of the Bahamas*. London: Collins, 1968.
———. *Founded upon the Seas: A History of the Cayman Islands and Their People*. Kingston, Jamaica: Ian Randle Publishers, 2003.
Darius R., and O. Williams. 'Impact of Growth in International Business Companies on the British Virgin Islands Economy.' *Social and Economic Studies* 46, nos. 2/3 (1997): 169–98.
Deere, C.D. et al. *In the Shadows of the Sun: Caribbean Development Alternatives and US Policy*. Boulder, CO: Westview Press, 1990.
Department of State. *Commercial Relations of the United States with Foreign Countries*. Washington, DC: Department of State, 1884.
Dietz, J.L. *Economic History of Puerto Rico: Institutional Change and Capitalist Development*. Princeton, NJ: Princeton University Press, 1986.
van Dijck, P. 'Structural Change and Long-Term Growth: The Suriname Experience.' *Integration & Trade* 5, no. 15 (2001): 275–99.
van Dijck, P. et al. *The Suriname Economy: Experiences of the 1990s and Challenges Ahead*. Amsterdam: CEDLA, 2000.
Dobson, N. *A History of Belize*. Port of Spain, Trinidad and Tobago: Longman Caribbean, 1973.
Domínguez, J.J. *La dictadura de Heureaux*. Santo Domingo, Domincan Republic: Editora Universitaria, UASD, 1986.
Dookhan, I. *A History of the British Virgin Islands*. Epping: Caribbean Universities Press for the College of the Virgin Islands, 1975.
———. *A History of the Virgin Islands of the United States*. Epping: Caribbean Universities Press for the College of the Virgin Islands, 1974.
Dorsey, J.C. *Slave Traffic in the Age of Abolition: Puerto Rico, West Africa, and the Non-Hispanic Caribbean, 1815–1859*. Gainesville, FL: University Press of Florida, 2003.
Draper, N. *The Price of Emancipation: Slave-ownership, Compensation and British Society at the End of Savery*. Cambridge, MA: Cambridge University Press, 2010.
Duany, J. 'Población y migración desde 1815 hasta la actualidad.' In *Historia de Puerto Rico*, edited by L. González Vales and M. Luque de Sánchez. Madrid: Consejo Superior de Investigaciones Científicas, 2010.

Eisner, G. *Jamaica, 1830–1930: A Study in Economic Growth*. Manchester: Manchester University Press, 1961.

Eltis, D. 'The Traffic in Slaves between the British West Indian Colonies, 1807–1833.' *The Economic History Review*. 25, no. 1 (February 1972): 55–64.

Emmer, P.C. 'Between Slavery and Freedom: The Period of Apprenticeship in Suriname (Dutch Guiana), 1863–1873.' *Slavery & Abolition* 14 (1993): 87–113.

Espina Prieto, M. 'Social Effects of Economic Adjustment: Equality, Inequality and Trends toward Greater Complexity in Cuban Society.' In *The Cuban Economy at the Start of the Twenty-first Century*, edited by J.I. Domínguez, V.O.E. Pérez, and L. Barberia. Cambridge, MA: Harvard University, David Rockefeller Center for Latin American Studies, 2004.

Evans, L.H. *The Virgin Islands: From Naval Base to New Deal*. Ann Arbor, MI: J.W. Edwards, 1945.

Farraudière, Y. *École et Société en Guyane Française*. Paris: Sciences Education, 1978.

Farrell, T. *The Underachieving Society: Development Strategy and Policy in Trinidad and Tobago, 1958–2008*. Mona, Jamaica: University of the West Indies Press, 2012.

Federal Reserve Bank of New York. *Report on the Competitiveness of Puerto Rico's Economy*. New York, NY: Federal Reserve Bank, 2014.

Ferguson, J. *The Dominican Republic: Beyond the Lighthouse*. London: Latin American Bureau, 1992.

Firmin, J.-A. *M. Roosevelt, président des États-Unis et la République d'Haïti*. New York, NY: Hamilton Bank Note Engraving and Printing Company, 1905.

Fraser, G. 'Can the Sir Stafford Sands Model of the Bahamian Economy, Survive Today's Global Economy?' XXXIII Conference of the Caribbean Centre for Monetary Studies, Belize City, Belize, 2001.

Gayer, A., P. Homan, and E. James. *The Sugar Economy of Puerto Rico*. New York, NY: Columbia University Press, 1938.

General Accounting Office. *Pharmaceutical Industry: Tax Benefits of Operating in Puerto Rico*. Washington, DC: General Accounting Office, 1992.

Gibbs, A.R. *British Honduras: An Historical and Descriptive Account of the Colony from Its Settlement, 1670*. London: S. Low, Marston, Searle & Rivington, 1883.

Godfrey, M. *Kourou and the Struggle for a French America: War, Culture and Society, 1750–1850*. New York, NY: Palgrave Macmillan, 2015.

Goslinga, C.C. *The Dutch in the Caribbean and in Suriname, 1791/5–1942*. Assen, Netherlands: Van Gorcum, 1990.

Green-Pedersen, S. 'Demographic Responses.' In *The Abolition of the Atlantic Slave Trade*, edited by W. Eltis and J.Walvin. Madison, WI: University of Wisconsin Press, 1981.

Hall, D. *Five of the Leewards*, 1834–1870. Caribbean Universities Press: Ginn and Co. Ltd, 1971.

———. *Free Jamaica, 1838–1865: An Economic History*. New Haven, CT: Yale University Press, 1959.

Hartog, J. *Curaçao, from Colonial Dependence to Autonomy*. Aruba: De Wit, 1968.

———. *St. Maarten, Saba and St. Eustatius*. Aruba: de Wit Stores, 1978.

Heuman, G.J. *The Killing Time: The Morant Bay Rebellion in Jamaica*. Knoxville, TN: University of Tennessee Press, 1995.

Higman, B. W. *Slave Populations of the British Caribbean, 1807–1834*. Baltimore, MD: Johns Hopkins University Press, 1984.

Hill, R.T. *Cuba and Porto Rico, with the Other Islands of the West Indies: Their Topography, Climate, Flora, Products, Industries, Cities, People, Political Conditions, etc.* New York, NY: The Century Co., 1898

Hiss, P.H. *Netherlands America: The Dutch Territories in the West*. New York, NY: Distributed by Duell, Sloan & Pearce, 1943.

Hoefte, R. *In Place of Slavery: A Social History of British Indian and Javanese Laborers in Suriname*. Gainesville, FL: University Press of Florida, 1998.

Huberman, L., and P.M. Sweezy. *Cuba: Anatomy of a Revolution*. New York, NY: Monthly Review Press, 1960.

IBRD. *The Economic Development of British Guiana*. Baltimore, MD: Published for International Bank for Reconstruction and Development by the Johns Hopkins Press, 1953.

———. *The Economic Development of Jamaica*. Baltimore, MD: Published for International Bank for Reconstruction and Development by the Johns Hopkins Press, 1952.

Institut National de la Statistique et des Études Économiques (INSEE). *antianEchos*, no. 1. Paris: INSEE, 2007.

———. *Conjuncture Guyane*, no. 3. Paris: INSEE, 2017.

Inter-American Development Bank (IDB). *Country Program Evaluation: Suriname 1980–2004*. Washington, DC: IDB, 2006.

International Bureau of the American Republics. *Haiti: A Handbook*. Washington, DC: International Bureau of the American Republics, 1893.

International Human Rights Clinic. *Gold Mining in Guyana: The Failure of Government Oversight and the Human Rights of Amerindian Communities*. Cambridge, MA: Human Rights Program, Harvard Law School, 2007.

International Labour Organisation (ILO). *Growth, Employment and Social Cohesion in the Dominican Republic*. Geneva: ILO, 2013.

International Monetary Fund (IMF). *Direction of Trade Statistics (DOTS)*. Washington, DC: IMF, 2018.

———. *Suriname: Selected Issues: IMF Country Report, 05/142*. Washington, DC: IMF, 2005.

Jacobs, K.C. *British Guiana: Report on the Financial Position*. London: HMSO, 1964.

Jefferson, O. *Stabilization and Stagnation in the Jamaican Economy, 1972–97: Some Reflections on Macroeconomic Policy over the Past Twenty-five Years*. Kingston, Jamaica: Canoe Press, 1999.

Jensen, P. *From Serfdom to Fireburn and Strike: The History of Black Labor in the Danish West Indies, 1848–1916*. Christianstad: Antilles Press, 1998.

Joachim, B. *Les racines du sous développement en Haïti*. Port-au-Prince: Impr. H. Deschamps, 1979.

Johansen, H. 'Slave Demography of the Danish West Indian Islands.' *Scandinavian Economic History Review* XXIX, no. 1 (1981): 1–20.

Johnson, H. *The Bahamas from Slavery to Servitude, 1783–1933*. Gainesville, FL: University Press of Florida, 1996.

Jones, S.B. *Annals of Anguilla, 1650–1923*. Belfast: Christian Journals, 1976.

Knox, J.P. *A Historical Account of St. Thomas, W.I.* New York: C. Scribner, 1852

Kossler, B. 'The V.I. Budget Crisis: Part 15, Rum and Congress.' *St. Thomas Source*, August 7, 2017.

Krueger, A., R. Teja, and A. Wolfe. *Puerto Rico: A Way Forward.* San Juan: Gobierno de Puerto Rico, 2015.

Lacerte R. 'Xenophobia and Economic Decline: The Haitian Case, 1820–1843.' *The Americas* 37, no. 4 (1981): 499–515.

Latin America Bureau. *Guyana: Fraudulent Revolution.* London: LAB, 1984.

Laurence, K.O. *A Question of Labour: Indentured Immigration into Trinidad and British Guiana, 1875–1917.* New York, NY: St Martin's Press, 1994.

Léger, J.N. *Haiti: Son histoire et ses détracteurs.* New York, NY: Neale Pub. Co., 1907.

Lewis, G K. *The Virgin Islands: A Caribbean Lilliput.* Evanston, IL: Northwestern University Press, 1972.

van Lier, R.A.J. *Frontier Society: A Social Analysis of the History of Surinam.* The Hague: Martinus Nijhoof, 1971.

Look Lai, W. *Indentured Labor, Caribbean Sugar: Chinese and Indian Migrants to the British West Indies, 1838–1918.* Baltimore, MD: Johns Hopkins University Press, 1993.

Lozano, W. *Los Trabajadores del Capitalismo Exportador.* Santo Domingo, Dominican Republic: Banco Central de la República Dominicana, 2001.

MacDonald, A. 'Lost and Forgotten? Official Colonial Statistics: Experience in Constructing Historical Statistics for Surinam.' *Statistical Journal of the United Nations* 14 (1997): 121–30.

Mackenzie, C. *Notes on Haiti: Made during a Residence in That Republic.* London: H. Colburn and R. Bentley, 1830.

Maddison, A. *The World Economy: Historical Statistics.* Paris: OECD, Development Centre, 2003.

Mam-Lam-Fouck, S. *Histoire de la Société guyanaise. Les annéés cruciales: 1848–1946.* Paris: Editions Caribéennes, 1987.

———. *La Guyane française au temps de l'esclavage, de l'or et de la francisation (1802–1946).* Petit-Bourg: Ibis Rouge, 1999.

———. *Histoire générale de la Guyane française: Des débuts de la colonisation à l'aube de l'an 2000: les grands problèmes guyanais, permanence et évolution.* Cayenne, French Guiana: Ibis rouge éditions, 2002.

Mandle, J. *The Plantation Economy: Population and Economic Change in Guyana, 1838–1960.* Philadelphia, PA: Temple University Press, 1973.

Marquetti, H. 'La Economía del dólar: balance y perspectivas.' *Temas*, no. 11 (1998): 51–62.

Marte, R. *Estadísticas y documentos históricos sobre Santo Domingo, 1805–1890*. Santo Domingo, República Dominicana: Museo Nacional de Historia y Geografía, 1984.

———. 'Sociedad y economía en Santo Domingo, 1795–1844.' In *Historia de la República Dominicana*, edited by F. Moya Pons. Madrid: Consejo Superior de Investigaciones Científicas, 2010.

Martin, R.M. *History of the Colonies of the British Empire in the West Indies, South America, North America, Asia, Austral-Asia, Africa, and Europe*. London: Allen and Routledge, 1843.

McMahon, S. 'You Pay for What You Get: the U.S. Virgin Islands, 1917–1936.' *The Journal of Caribbean History* 41, nos. 1 and 2 (2007): 109–41.

Mesa-Lago, C. *Market, Socialist, and Mixed Economies: Comparative Policy and Performance: Chile, Cuba, and Costa Rica*. Baltimore, MD: Johns Hopkins University Press, 2000.

Monreal, G.P.M. *Development Prospects in Cuba: An Agenda in the Making*. London: Institute of Latin American Studies, 2002.

Monteith, K.E.A. *Depression to Decolonization: Barclays Bank (DCO) in the West Indies, 1926–1962*. Kingston, Jamaica: University of the West Indies Press, 2008.

Moore, B.L. *Race, Power, and Social Segmentation in Colonial Society: Guyana after Slavery, 1838–1891*. New York, NY: Gordon & Breach Science Publishers, 1987.

Morris, E. 'Cuba's New Relationship with Foreign Capital: Economic Policy-Making since 1990.' Journal of Latin American Studies 40, no. 4 (2008): 769–92.

Moya Pons, F. 'Evolución de la población dominicana.' In *Historia de la República Dominicana*, edited by F. Moya Pons. Madrid: Consejo Superior de Investigaciones Científicas, 2010.

Mulchansingh, V. 'The Oil Industry in the Economy of Trinidad.' *Caribbean Studies* 11, no.1 (1971): 73–100.

Munroe, T., and D. Robotham. *Struggles of the Jamaican People*. London: WLL, 1977.

Navarro, J. *Creating Tropical Yankees: Social Science Textbooks and U.S. Ideological Control in Puerto Rico, 1898–1908*. New York, NY: Routledge, 2002.

Naylor, R.A. *Penny ante Imperialism: The Mosquito Shore and the Bay of Honduras, 1600–1914: A Case Study in British Informal Empire*. Rutherford, NJ: Fairleigh Dickinson University Press, 1989.

Nicholls, D. *Economic Dependence and Political Autonomy: The Haitian Experience*. Montreal: McGill University, Centre for Developing-Area Studies, 1974.

———. *From Dessalines to Duvalier: Race Colour, and National Independence in Haiti*. Cambridge, MA: Cambridge University Press, 1979.

Nicholls, G. 'Reflections on Economic Growth in Antigua and Barbuda.' *Integration & Trade* 5, no. 15 (2001): 105–44.

Oficina Nacional de Estadísticas (ONE). *Anuario Estadístico de Cuba 2009*. Havana: ONE, 2010.

Organisation of Cooperation and Development (OECD). *2000 Progress Report: Towards Global Tax Co-operation: Progress in Identifying and Eliminating Harmful Tax Practices*. Paris: OECD, 2000.

Paiewonsky, R.M., and I. Dookhan. *Memoirs of a Governor: A Man for the People*. New York, NY: New York University Press, 1990.

Panday, R.M.N. *Agriculture in Surinam, 1650–1950: An Inquiry into the Causes of Its Decline*. Amsterdam: H.J. Paris, 1959.

Pérez, L. 'Cuba, c.1930–59.' In *The Cambridge History of Latin America*, vol. vii, edited by L. Cambridge, MA: Cambridge University Press, 1990: 419–56.

Perloff, H.S. *Puerto Rico's Economic Future: A Study in Planned Development*. Chicago: University of Chicago Press, 1950.

Pétot, J. *L'or de Guyane: Son histoire, ses hommes*. Paris: Editions Caribéenes, 1986.

Petras, E.M.L. *Jamaican Labor Migration: White Capital and Black Labor, 1850–1930*. Boulder, CO: Westview Press, 1988.

Petty, C.L. *A Handbook History of Anguilla*. Anguilla: Colville L. Petty, 1991.

Pew Research Center. *Hispanics of Dominican Origin in the United States, 2011*. Chicago, IL: Pew Research Center, 2013.

Phillippo, J. *Jamaica: Its Past and Present State*. London: John Snow, 1843.

Plante Fébure, J.M. *West-Indië in het Parlement, 1897–1917: Bijdrage tot Nederland's koloniaal-politieke geschiedenis*. S Gravenhage: M. Nijhoff, 1918.
Plummer, B.G. *Haiti and the Great Powers, 1902–1915*. Baton Rouge, LA: Louisiana State University Press, 1988.
Pologone, M., E. Rangel-González, and L. Blanco-González. 'Wrong Variable: Foreign Variables and Monetary Policy in Jamaica.' *Social and Economic Studies* 63, no. 1 (2014): 57–87.
Rabe, S. *US Intervention in British Guiana: A Cold War Story*. Chapel Hill, NC: University of North Carolina Press, 2005.
Redfield, P. *Space in the Tropics: from Convicts to Rockets in French Guiana*. Berkeley, CA: University of California Press, 2000.
Renard, R. 'Labour Relations in Martinique and Guadeloupe, 1848–1870.' In *Caribbean Freedom: Society and Economy from Emancipation to the Present*, edited by H. Beckles and V. Shepherd. Kingston, Jamaica: Ian Randle Publishers, 1993.
Report from Select Committee on the Commercial State of the West India Colonies. London, 1832.
Report from the Select Committee on West India Colonies. London, 1842.
Report of the West India Royal Commission. London, 1884.
Report of the West India Royal Commission. London, 1897.
Report of the British Guiana and British Honduras Settlement Commission (Evans Commission). London, 1948.
Ritter, A.R M. *The Cuban Economy*. Pittsburgh, PA: University of Pittsburgh Press, 2004.
Roberts, G.W. 'A Life Table for a West Indian Slave Population.' *Population Studies* 5 (1952): 238–42.
Rodney, W. *A History of the Guyanese Working People, 1881–1905*. Baltimore, MD: The Johns Hopkins University Press, 1981.
Römer, R.A. *Curaçao*. San Juan, Puerto Rico: Association of Caribbean Universities and Research Institutes, UNICA, 1981.
Roopnarine, L. *Indian Indenture in the Danish West Indies, 1863–1873*. New York, NY: Palgrave Macmillan, 2016.
———. 'Maroon Resistance and Settlement in Danish St. Croix.' *Journal of Third World Studies* (September 2010): 1–21.
Ryan, S.D. *Eric Williams: The Myth and the Man*. Kingston, Jamaica: University of the West Indies Press, 2009.
Samaroo, B. 'The Immigrant Communities.' In *General History of the Caribbean. Vol. IV: The Long 19th Century*, edited by K.O. Laurence. Paris: UNESCO, 2011.

Sánchez, G. *Cuba and Venezuela: An Insight into Two Revolutions*. Melbourne, Victoria: Ocean, 2007.

Santamaría García, A. 'Economía, 1800–1898.' In *Historia de Puerto Rico*, edited by L. González Vales and M. Luque de Sánchez. Madrid: Consejo Superior de Investigaciones Científicas, 2010.

Schmidt, H. *The United States Occupation of Haiti, 1915–1934*. New Brunswick, NJ: Rutgers University Press, 1971.

Schmidt, N. 'Les migrations de main-d'oeuvre dans la politique colonial française aux Caraïbes pendant la seconde moitié du XIXe siècle.' *Le Mouvement Social* 151 (1990): 11–37.

Seecharan, C. *Sweetening Bitter Sugar: Jock Campbell – The Booker Reformer in British Guiana 1934–1966*. Kingston, Jamaica: Ian Randle Publishers, 2004.

Shoman, A. *13 Chapters of a History of Belize*. 2nd ed. Belize City, Belize: Angelus Press, 2011.

Simmons, D.C. *Confederate Settlements in British Honduras*. Jefferson, NC: McFarland, 2001.

Singh, K. *British-Controlled Trinidad and Venezuela: A History of Economic Interests and Subversion, 1830–1962*. Mona: University of the West Indies, 2010.

Smith, R.T. *British Guiana*. London: Oxford University Press, 1962.

Société d'Etudes pour la Colonisation de la Guyane. *Note sur la Fondation d'Une Nouvelle Colonie dans la Guyane Française*. Paris: Firmin Didot Frères, 1844.

van Soest, J. *Trustee of the Netherlands Antilles*. Zutphen: Walburg Pers, 1978.

Spieler, M.F. *Empire and Underworld: Captivity in French Guiana*. Cambridge, MA: Harvard University Press, 2012.

St. John, S. *Hayti: or, The Black Republic*. New York, NY: Scribner & Welford, 1889.

Suárez, D. 'Puerto Rico's Unlimited Generosity Towards Rum Companies.' *Centro de Periodismo Investigativo*. February 1, 2017.

Swan, M. *British Guiana: The Land of Six Peoples*. London: HMSO, 1957.

Sweig, J. *Inside the Cuban Revolution: Fidel Castro and the Urban Underground*. Cambridge, MA: Harvard University Press, 2002.

Szulc, T. *Fidel: A Critical Portrait*. New York, NY: Morrow, 1986.

Tejada, A.M. 'Estado, política y gobierno, 1795–2008.' In *Historia de la República Dominicana*, edited by F. Moya Pons, 396–405 Madrid: Consejo Superior de Investigaciones Científicas, 2010.

Thomas, C.Y. 'Guyana: The IMF-World Bank Group and the General Crisis.' *Social and Economic Studies* 31, no. 4 (1982): 16–70.

Thomas, M.E. *Jamaica and Voluntary Laborers from Africa, 1840–1865*. Gainesville, FL: University of Florida Press, 1974.

Togores, V., and A. García. 'Consumption, Markets and Monetary Duality.' In *The Cuban Economy at the Start of the Twenty-first Century*, edited by J.I. Domínguez, V.O.E. Pérez, and L. Barberia. Cambridge, MA: David Rockefeller Center for Latin American Studies, Harvard University, 2004.

Tomich, D.W. *Slavery in the Circuit of Sugar: Martinique and the World Economy, 1830–1848*. Baltimore, MD: Johns Hopkins University Press, 1990.

Tooke, C. 'The Danish Colonial Fiscal System in the West Indies.' *American Economic Association* 1, no. 3 (1900): 144–67.

Toth, S. *Beyond Papillon: The French Overseas Penal Colonies, 1854–1952*. Lincoln, NE: University of Nebraska Press, 2006.

van Traa, A. *Suriname, 1900–1940*. Deventer: W. van Hoeve, 1946.

Turnier, A. *Les États-Unis et le marché haïtien*. Washington, DC, 1955.

'Two Hundred Years of Coffee in Haiti.' *Tea and Coffee Trade Journal* 68 (1935): 103–05. New York, NY: F.H.Hobbs & Co.

US Department of Commerce. *Birth and Mortality Statistics of the Virgin Islands of the United States, 1901–19*. Washington, DC: United States Department of Commerce, 1920.

US Department of the Interior. *The Governor of the Virgin Islands to the Secretary of the Interior: Annual Report 1926*. Washington, DC: US Department of the Interior, 1926.

Valdés, A., and B. Schaeffer. *Surveillance of Agricultural Prices and Trade: A Handbook for the Dominican Republic*. Washington, DC: World Bank, 1995.

Vega, B. 'La Era de Trujillo, 1930–61.' In *Historia de la República Dominicana*, edited by F. Moya Pons. Madrid: Consejo Superior de Investigaciones Científicas, 2010.

Vidal, P., and A. Fundora. 'Trade-Growth Relationship in Cuba: Estimation Using the Kalman Filter.' *CEPAL Review* 94 (2008): 97–116.

Vincent, S. *Outline of Financial History of the Republic of Haiti.* Port-au-Prince: Imp. de l'etat, 1939.

Weisskoff, T. *Factories and Food Stamps: The Puerto Rican Model of Development.* Baltimore, MD: Johns Hopkins University Press, 1985.

Welch, R.E. *Response to Revolution: The United States and the Cuban Revolution, 1959–1961.* Chapel Hill, NC: University of North Carolina Press, 1985.

Westergaard, W. *The Danish West Indies under Company Rule (1671–1754): With a Supplementary Chapter, 1755–1917.* New York, NY: The Macmillan Company, 1917.

Williams, E.E. *History of the People of Trinidad and Tobago.* London: Andre Deutsch, 1964.

World Bank. 'World Development Indicators (WDI).' *World Bank,* n.d. http://data.worldbank.org.

Zimbalist, A.S., and C. Brundenius. *The Cuban Economy: Measurement and Analysis of Socialist Performance.* Baltimore, MD: Johns Hopkins University Press, 1989.

Index

Note: The term 'territories' has been used throughout the index as it is the most neutral word to describe the different constitutional status of the British, Dutch, French, Spanish, Scandinavian, and US countries in the Caribbean. The text provides differentiation between colonial, dependent, and independent status. Page numbers followed by *f*, *n*, and *t* indicate material in figures, notes, or tables.